Financial Accounting & Reporting

CPA Exam Review

2025
Edition

Permissions

The following items are utilized in this program, and are copyright property of the American Institute of Certified Public Accountants, Inc. (AICPA), all rights reserved:

- Uniform CPA Examination and Questions and Unofficial Answers, Copyright © 1991 – 2025
- Audit and Accounting Guides, Auditing Procedure Studies, Risk Alerts, Statements of Position, and Code of Professional Conduct
- Statements on Auditing Standards
- Statements on Standards for Accounting and Review Services
- Statements on Quality Control Standards
- Statements on Standards for Attestation Engagements
- Accounting Research Bulletins, APB Opinions
- Uniform CPA Examination Blueprints
- Independence Standards Board (ISB) Standards

Portions of various FASB and GASB documents, copyright property of the Financial Accounting Foundation, 401 Merritt 7, PO Box 5116, Norwalk, CT 06856-5116, are utilized with permission. Complete copies of these documents are available from the Financial Accounting Foundation. These selections include the following:

Financial Accounting Standards Board (FASB)

- The FASB Accounting Standards Codification™
- Statements of Financial Accounting Concepts
- FASB Statements, Interpretations, and Technical Bulletins

Governmental Accounting Standards Board (GASB)

- GASB Codification of Governmental Accounting and Financial Reporting Standards and GASB Statements
- GASB Concepts Statements
- GASB Interpretations and Technical Bulletins

Published by UWorld
9111 Cypress Waters Blvd.
Suite 300
Dallas, TX 75019
accounting.uworld.com/cpa-review

Printed in English, in the United States of America.

Acknowledgments

Keeping the course materials updated and accurate would not be possible without the contribution of our team of content experts. Our team includes academics and professionals who have expertise and experience in their respective fields; several have had experience at the Big Four or have PhDs in areas related to the exam. All are passionate about helping candidates pass the exam and about UWorld's dedication to creating the highest quality materials.

Financial Accounting & Reporting

Introduction

Introduction

Introduction

How to Best Use Your Course

Welcome to the UWorld CPA Review course! Our expert team is passionate about helping you succeed and has developed an award-winning program that is proven to yield results. Before you get started, please read through this guide on how to best use your course so that you can master all of the topics laid out for you in the AICPA Blueprints and ultimately pass the CPA Exam. At UWorld, our passion is to make the hard stuff easy to learn and understand.

Plan Your Studies

When preparing for the CPA Exam, half the battle is setting yourself up for success with a solid plan from the get go. This includes establishing short- and long-term goals to ensure you're staying on track.

To get started, use the Study Plan in your course. Start your plan by setting the beginning and ending dates for your schedule. Then select your pace (Fast Track vs Customize) and set the number of hours per day you will study. The system will create your plan based on your choices. It is important to follow your plan steadily so that you can ensure you hit your goals. If you miss a day, make it up!

Tip!

Download the app! This gives you access to everything your course offers while on the go.

Master the Concepts through Active Learning

With this program, you will build your foundational knowledge and mastery of core exam topics through **active learning**. This evidence-based learning methodology centers around the principle that students retain information best when they actively participate in answering questions.

- **Begin with the Representative Task.** Read through each representative task carefully. (The Representative Tasks are from the AICPA Blueprints and are presented in our books and videos to guide you through the materials.) Pay particular attention to the words at the beginning of the task; they provide guidance on level and focus
- **Scan the book chapter.** Do you feel confident with the material? If you do, you might want to move directly to the questions and begin to practice. If you find that you are hesitant about an area, read the book or watch the video to solidify your understanding before you practice on some questions
- **Watch the videos.** If you prefer to absorb material on video rather than by reading the book, you will notice that the videos are deliberately set up in small segments. Our team created these segments so you can review what you need, either as part of the whole topic or for specific review of a smaller area
- **Practice the questions.** In our question bank (our QBank) we have taken great care to provide you with very high-quality questions and explanations. Each explanation not only tells you why the concept tested is important to understand but also teaches you why the answer is correct and why the other answer choices are not correct. Images, tables, and links to definitions also help fill in gaps as you use the questions and explanations to learn by doing

Track Your Progress and Performance

As you complete each chapter, track your progress and performance using our signature **SmartPath Predictive Technology™**. SmartPath is a data-driven platform that provides recommended targets based on previous students who have passed the CPA Exam. This is an important tool to help you study efficiently and gauge whether you are *exam-ready*. Your goal is to hit both your progress target (Questions Attempted) and performance target (Score) for each chapter.

As you work through the material, don't worry about hitting your "Score" target right away and focus your efforts on hitting the "Questions Attempted" target first. This approach may feel uncomfortable, but trust that you are building your knowledge as you absorb the answer explanations.

Once you've completed all the topics in a chapter, you can go back and focus your efforts on hitting the "Score" target. If you are falling short, drill down in the Performance tab to see which topics need extra attention.

Tip!

Don't over-study. **SmartPath™** helps determine when you can move on to the next topic.

Solidify the Concepts

Need extra help mastering the concept? Take advantage of the additional learning tools that are integrated into your course. For example, you could be working through a difficult question and find you need further explanation. No problem! There's a link to the supporting lecture right there in the question. Want to remember something for later review? Easily transfer content directly from the question to a digital flashcard. These are just a few ways we make it easy to navigate to and access the right tools you need at the right time.

These additional tools are designed to enhance your studies—**you do not necessarily need to read or watch all of this material!** Rather, use these tools as a means to improve on weak areas:

- **Video Lectures** – From the Lectures tab or directly integrated in the link at the bottom of each practice question, you have access to the profession's most motivating and effective lecturers. Lectures break down difficult topics into simplified concepts and provide helpful memory aids. These are especially recommended for visual and auditory learners
- **Textbooks** – Digital eTextbooks are accessible side by side with the video lectures or in a printed format with some of our course packages. These can be used as a reference if you need further explanation of a concept. Many students also find it beneficial to follow along in the textbook while watching the lectures and either take notes directly in the physical books or by using the Notes feature and highlighting tool in the platform
- **Digital Flashcards** – Create custom flashcards directly from your practice questions by clicking on the lightning bolt symbol. Depending on your program package, your course may also be pre-loaded with an "Expert Deck" of flashcards covering the most heavily tested topics. You can review all your cards in Study Mode or using our **Spaced-Repetition Technology**. This is an evidence-based learning method that presents cards you've marked as *difficult* more frequently and cards you've marked as *easy* less frequently. The spacing of how and when the flashcards are introduced has been proven to increase retention and strengthen memory recall

Get Exam-Ready

The final days leading up to the exam are a critical time in which you're going to want to review your SmartPath data and ask, "Am I *exam-ready*?" If you have hit all the targets, you are in a really good spot. However, if any areas are still marked "Needs Improvement," now is the time to focus your efforts on meeting those targets.

Finally, we recommend you **take at least one full practice exam before exam day** (click on the "Exam Sim" tab in the QBank). This allows you to hone your test-taking skills in an exam-like environment that follows the same 5-testlet, 4-hour structure as the exam.

AICPA Blueprints

The UWorld CPA Review course is based on the AICPA Blueprints, which show candidates what skills and content topics will be tested on the CPA Exam. You don't have to make tough decisions about what concepts to focus on. If you follow our methodology, you will be well on your way to passing the exam.

Let's take a look at what we mean by starting with the AICPA Blueprints. The Blueprints have four levels:

- Area
- Group
- Topic
- Representative Task

Each Representative Task also has a Skill level.

- Remembering & Understanding
- Application
- Analysis
- Evaluation (used only in AUD)

Here is a snapshot of a Blueprint with the levels and skills marked.

Area I – Business Analysis (40–50%)

Content group/topic	Skill: Remembering & Understanding	Skill: Application	Skill: Analysis	Skill: Evaluation	Representative Task
A. Current period/historical analysis, including the use of data					
1. Financial statement analysis		✓			Determine attribute structures, format, and sources of data needed to prepare financial statement analysis.
			✓		Compare current period financial statement accounts to prior periods or budget and explain variances.
			✓		Interpret financial statement fluctuations and ratios (eg, profitability, liquidity, solvency, performance).
			✓		Use outputs (eg, reports, visualizations) from data analytic techniques to identify patterns, trends, and correlations to explain an entity's results.
			✓		Derive the impact of transactions on the financial statements and notes to the financial statements.

BAR
Area I: Business Analysis
Group A: Current Period/Historical Analysis
Topic 1: Financial Statement Analysis

The Table of Contents of the BAR book shows how each UWorld textbook is set up to follow the order of the AICPA Blueprints, with

- Area
- Group
- Topic

Business Analysis & Reporting

In the pages of each book, we provide the Representative Tasks from the AICPA Blueprints. We did that to make a direct connection between the exam and our content. Our team deliberately focused on what the Tasks say and wrote study materials that match with the Task. There is no closer connection between what will be tested and what you are studying.

1.01 Financial Statement Analysis

Overview

A company appraises the past, present, and future execution of goals and economic fitness by performing **financial statement analysis** on its results from operations in a given period. Refer to the financial ratios used in the FAR exam for this section.

The results are viewed in relation to prior periods, budgets, and key performance indicators (ie, benchmarks). Companies **make informed decisions** using this analysis. The analysis is often presented using summaries and visualizations that present the financial data in an easy-to-understand, meaningful report.

Attribute Structures, Format, and Sources of Data

Representative Task (Application): Determine attribute structures, format, and sources of data needed to prepare financial statement analysis.

Beyond connecting to the topics of the AICPA Blueprints, our team also differentiated the textbook content to match the skill levels of the Tasks.

- **Remembering & Understanding** tasks require you to understand the definitions and fundamentals of the topic. We have presented the information in these areas with an eye to creating clear explanations of the topics
- **Application** tasks are more about using your knowledge in scenarios to indicate that you understand the concepts. Our authors have therefore provided examples that show you how to apply your knowledge in specific situations. Many of these examples are similar to questions that you will find on the exam
- **Analysis** tasks require a higher level of thinking, many times leading you to choose one outcome over another or to make a decision. On the exam, these tasks will always be addressed in Task-Based Simulations, or TBSs. The AICPA intentionally makes these more challenging to determine if you really know the material and can work with it as a professional. In our materials, our authors often guide you through the critical thinking required to work with TBSs
- **Evaluation** tasks are only in the AUD section of the exam and are at the highest level of thinking. They go a step further than the Analysis level and require you to evaluate or judge different approaches or outcomes

The CPA Exam

Within the AICPA Blueprints, there is information about how much time candidates have for each section and how many questions by question type each section contains. Question types include Multiple-Choice Questions (MCQs) and Task-Based Simulations (TBSs).

Section	Section Time	Multiple-Choice Questions (MCQs)	Task-Based Simulations (TBSs)
AUD – Core	4 hours	78	7
FAR – Core	4 hours	50	7
REG – Core	4 hours	72	8
BAR – Discipline	4 hours	50	7
ISC – Discipline	4 hours	82	6
TCP – Discipline	4 hours	68	7

Scoring Weight by Exam Section

The AICPA also shows candidates how the question types for each section are weighted and account for their overall score.

	Score Weighting	
Section	**Multiple-Choice Questions (MCQs)**	**Task-Based Simulations (TBSs)**
AUD – Core	50%	50%
FAR – Core	50%	50%
REG – Core	50%	50%
BAR – Discipline	50%	50%
ISC – Discipline	60%	40%
TCP – Discipline	50%	50%

Skill Allocations

As mentioned earlier, each Representative Task is tested at a specific Skill Level, and each part of the exam has its own weighting of the Skill Levels, as seen here.

Section	Remembering & Understanding	Application	Analysis	Evaluation
AUD – Core	30–40%	30–40%	15–25%	5–15%
FAR – Core	5–15%	45–55%	35–45%	–
REG – Core	25–35%	35–45%	25–35%	–
BAR – Discipline	10–20%	45–55%	30–40%	–
ISC – Discipline	55–65%	20–30%	10–20%	–
TCP – Discipline	5–15%	55–65%	25–35%	–

Content Allocations

The AICPA Blueprints address how coverage of the various content areas is allocated in each exam. Using the UWorld system that ties directly to the Blueprint structure, it is easy to see which topics are covered to what extent.

AUD

Content Area		Allocation
Area I	Ethics, Professional Responsibilities, and General Principles	15–25%
Area II	Assessing Risk and Developing a Planned Response	25–35%
Area III	Performing Further Procedures and Obtaining Evidence	30–40%
Area IV	Forming Conclusions and Reporting	10–20%

FAR

Content Area		Allocation
Area I	Financial Reporting	30–40%
Area II	Select Balance Sheet Accounts	30–40%
Area III	Select Transactions	25–35%

REG

Content Area		Allocation
Area I	Ethics, Professional Responsibilities, and Federal Tax Procedures	10–20%
Area II	Business Law	15–25%
Area III	Federal Taxation of Property Transactions	5–15%
Area IV	Federal Taxation of Individuals	22–32%
Area V	Federal Taxation of Entities (including tax preparation)	23–33%

BAR

Content Area		Allocation
Area I	Business Analysis	40–50%
Area II	Technical Accounting and Reporting	35–45%
Area III	State and Local Governments	10–20%

ISC

Content Area		Allocation
Area I	Information Systems and Data Management	35–45%
Area II	Security, Confidentiality, and Privacy	35–45%
Area III	Considerations for System and Organization Controls (SOC) Engagements	15–25%

TCP

Content Area		Allocation
Area I	Tax Compliance and Planning for Individuals and Personal Financial Planning	30–40%
Area II	Entity Tax Compliance	30–40%
Area III	Entity Tax Planning	10–20%
Area IV	Property Transactions (disposition of assets)	10–20%

Exam Testlets

Each section of the exam is divided into five testlets. Two testlets cover MCQs, and three testlets cover TBSs. Not all sections have an equal number of MCQs and TBSs, as the following chart shows.

	Testlet					Total	
	1	2	3	4	5		
Section	MCQ	MCQ	TBS	TBS	TBS	MCQ	TBS
AUD - Core	39	39	2	3	2	78	7
FAR - Core	25	25	2	3	2	50	7
REG - Core	36	36	2	3	3	72	8
BAR - Discipline	25	25	2	3	2	50	7
ISC - Discipline	41	41	1	3	2	82	6
TCP - Discipline	34	34	2	3	2	68	7

Finally, to manage your time effectively in the exam, we recommend that you:

- Use 75 seconds per multiple-choice question as a benchmark,
- Allocate 15-20 minutes per task-based simulation, depending on complexity, and
- Take the standard 15-minute break after the third testlet; it doesn't count against your time.

To see the full AICPA Blueprints, visit
https://www.aicpa.org/becomeacpa/cpaexam/examinationcontent

Above all, start the study process with confidence! As Roger always says, "You do not have to be a genius to pass the CPA Exam. If you study, you will pass!" You've got this.

FAR

Area I: Financial Reporting

FAR 1
General-Purpose Financial Reporting: For-Profit Business Entities

FAR 1: General-Purpose Financial Reporting: For-Profit Business Entities

1.01 Balance Sheet/Statement of Financial Position

Reporting under GAAP

Publicly held companies are required to submit their financial statements (F/S) to the SEC prepared in accordance with a general purpose framework, either:

- Generally accepted accounting principles (GAAP), or
- International financial reporting standards (IFRS).

Nonpublic entities may choose to follow a general purpose framework or a special purpose framework. The FAR exam tests CPA candidates' knowledge of how transactions, events, and circumstances are accounted for and how they are reported on. Most FAR questions are based on GAAP.

For additional coverage on special purpose frameworks, see the FAR Special Purpose Frameworks chapter.

GAAP is developed by the Financial Accounting Standards Board (FASB), which is authorized to establish accounting standards by the Securities and Exchange Commission (SEC). The FASB Accounting Standards Codification (ASC) is the single source of authoritative GAAP for nongovernmental entities.

GAAP employs the **accrual basis** of accounting. Under accrual accounting, revenues are recognized in the period earned (regardless of when they are collected), and expenses are recognized in the period incurred (regardless of when they are paid). A recognized item is depicted in both words and numbers, with the amount included in F/S totals. An item must meet three criteria to be recognized in the F/S. The criteria are:

- **Definitions:** The item meets the definition of an element of F/S
- **Measurability:** The item is measurable and has a relevant measurement attribute
- **Faithful representation:** The item can be depicted and measured with faithful representation

Derecognition removes an item from the F/S when it no longer meets any one of the recognition criteria. Expenses may be recognized based on the following:

- Cause and effect: Expenses that produce revenue at identifiable points in time can be directly matched to revenues (eg, cost of goods sold)
- Systematic and rational allocation: Expenses that produce revenue over long periods of time are matched to those periods using a reasonable means of allocation (eg, depreciation)
- Immediate recognition: Some expenses cannot be directly related to specific benefits and are expensed as incurred (eg, monthly salaries of selling, general and administrative employees)

For further discussion of revenue recognition, see the FAR Revenue Recognition chapter.

Overview

Representative Task (Application): Prepare a classified balance sheet from a trial balance and supporting documentation.

The balance sheet, also called the statement of financial position, reports the resources of a company at a point in time. It is dated as of a specific date (eg, December 31, Year 1). On the balance sheet, a company discloses its economic resources (ie, assets) and the manner of financing the acquisition of those resources (ie, liabilities to creditors and equity from owners' contributions/prior year's earning).

Three Basic Elements of Financial Statements

Assets	=	Liabilities	+	Equity
• Economic resources • Include probable future benefits • Controlled by an entity • Derived from past events		• Unavoidable obligations • Settled with assets • Derived from past events		• Calculated as assets minus liabilities • Represents ownership interest

Assets are presented in order of decreasing liquidity (ie, ease of conversion to cash). The most liquid assets are shown first (eg, cash), and less liquid assets are shown last (eg, property, plant, and equipment). Liabilities are presented in order of maturity. Current liabilities are presented first, then long-term liabilities are presented. Owners' equity (also called shareholders' equity) items are shown in order of permanence.

Assets and liabilities are categorized into *current* and *noncurrent:*

- **Current assets** will be consumed or converted into cash within one year or the operating cycle, whichever is longer. Examples include cash, temporary trading securities, accounts receivable, notes receivable, inventories, and prepaid expenses
- **Current liabilities** will be settled within one year or the operating cycle, whichever is longer. Examples include accounts payable, accrued expenses, dividends payable, income taxes payable, and the current portion of long-term debt
- **Noncurrent assets and liabilities** are defined by exclusion. All assets and liabilities that do not meet the criteria necessary to be classified as current (ie, items that are generally longer than one year) are classified as noncurrent

The valuations of major balance sheet accounts are summarized below and will be further explained in the chapter that pertains to each account:

Account Type	Measurement Basis
Receivables	Net realizable value
Inventory	Lower of cost or market, or lower of cost or net realizable value

Account Type	Measurement Basis
Investments in marketable securities	Market value
Property, plant, and equipment and intangibles	Historical cost and depreciated/ amortized historical cost
Liabilities	Present value
Equity	Historical value of cash inflows and residual valuation

The balance sheet provides information useful in assessing the entity's financial strengths and weaknesses, especially risk (eg, relative proportion of debt to equity), and the allocation of assets.

The following is an example of a GAAP balance sheet:

Company Name
Balance Sheet/Statement of Financial Position
As of December 31, Year XX

Assets	**Liabilities and shareholders' equity**
Current assets:	Current liabilities:
Cash and cash equivalents	Short-term notes payable
Temporary term investments (eg, trading securities)	Accounts payable (eg, to vendors, accrued salaries and wages)
Receivables, net of allowance	Estimated current liabilities (eg, warranty expense)
Inventories	Unearned revenue
Prepaid expenses (eg, insurance, rent)	Current portion of long-term debt
Total current assets	*Total current liabilities*
Investments:	Noncurrent liabilities:
Nonmarketable securities (eg, equity method securities)	Notes payable (net of current portion)
	Bonds payable
Long-term investments in marketable debt securities (eg, AFS or HTM)	Deferred tax liability
	Total noncurrent liabilities
Property, plant, and equipment:	**Total liabilities**
Land, buildings, and improvements	
Machinery and equipment	Shareholders' equity:
	Preferred stock
Intangibles:	Common stock
Goodwill	Additional paid-in capital
Other identifiable intangibles (eg, trademarks, patents)	Retained earnings
	Accumulated other comprehensive income
Total noncurrent assets	*Total shareholders' equity*
Total assets	**Total liabilities and shareholders' equity**

1.02 Income Statement/Statement of Profit or Loss

Overview

Representative Task (Application): Prepare a single-step or multi-step income statement (eg, operating, nonoperating, discontinued operations) from a trial balance and supporting documentation.

The income statement, also called the statement of profit or loss, measures performance of a firm for a period of time (eg, monthly, quarterly, annually). The income statement is prepared using the all-inclusive approach. That is, most revenues, expenses, gains, and losses are shown on the income statement and are included in the calculation of net income.

There are other items that would appear to be income items but are reflected in comprehensive income rather than net income. These items include unrealized gains and losses on investments in securities available-for-sale, certain pension cost adjustments, and foreign currency translation adjustments. Similarly, prior-period adjustments are reflected in retained earnings rather than in net income.

An income statement generally contains two sections: **Income from Continuing Operations** and **Discontinued Operations**. Income from Continuing Operations may be prepared using the multi-step approach or single-step approach.

Revenues and expenses relate to the company's primary business operations, while gains and losses relate to peripheral or incidental transactions. The multi-step approach separates items related to the company's primary business (ie, operating items) from peripheral or incidental items (ie, nonoperating items). The single-step approach does not.

Single-Step Approach

The single-step format involves a presentation of income from continuing operations that is largely based on a single comparison of total revenues and gains to total expenses and losses. Here, revenues/gains and expenses/losses are grouped together.

Single-Step Income Statement

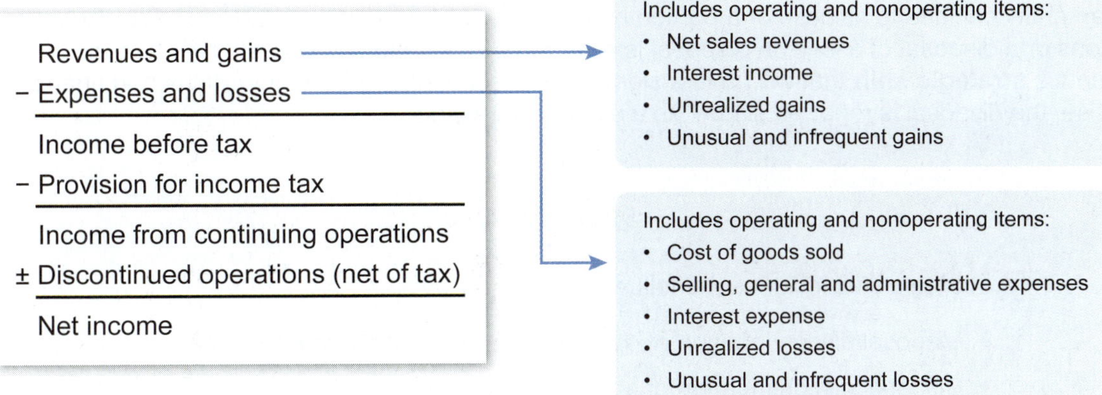

Multi-Step Approach

The multi-step format involves a presentation of income from continuing operations that includes multiple comparisons of revenues, expenses, gains, and losses. The statement begins with revenues, then subtracts expenses to arrive at operating income (ie, income directly tied to the company's primary business operations). Following operating income, incidental or peripheral gains and losses (ie, nonoperating items) are listed to arrive at income from continuing operations.

Multi-Step Income Statement

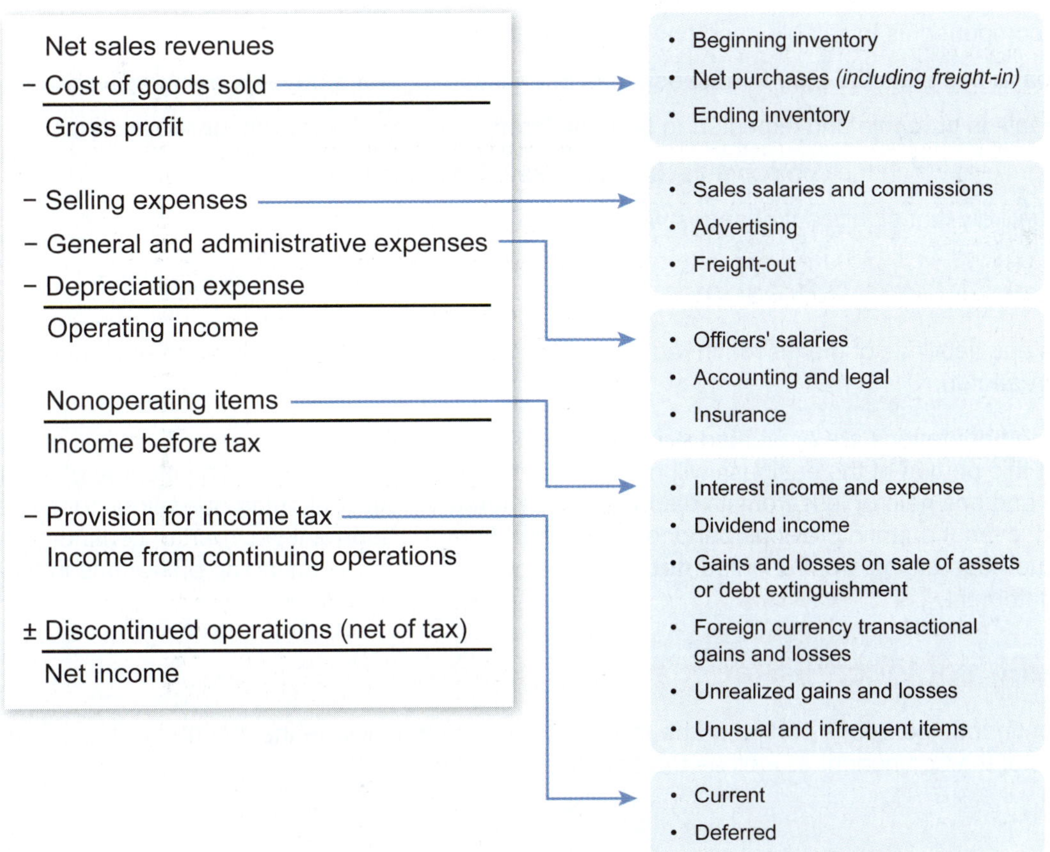

Note: credit loss expense could be either selling expense or general and administrative expense

Discontinued Operations

When an entity decides to dispose of a portion of its business, it may be accounted for as discontinued operations or a disposal of assets. A disposal is reported as discontinued operations when the disposal represents a **strategic shift** that will have a significant effect on the entity's operations and financial results. Otherwise, the disposal is reported simply as a disposal of assets.

Strategic Shift

A strategic shift includes the following:

- Disposal/discontinuation of operations in a major geographic area
- Disposal/discontinuation of a major line of business
- Disposal of a significant investment accounted for under the equity method
- Disposal/discontinuation of other major "parts" of an entity

Held for Sale

A component or group of components that qualifies as a strategic shift will be reported in discontinued operations if it is disposed of by sale or by some other means during the period or if it qualifies to be classified as "held for sale." A component qualifies as held for sale if all the following criteria are met:

- A plan to sell the component has been committed to by those who have the authority to do so
- The component is in salable condition and available for immediate sale
- Action to complete the plan for disposal has been initiated, and a buyer is being actively sought
- The sale is probable and expected to be completed and to qualify for recognition within one year
- The price at which the component is being marketed is reasonable
- It is unlikely that significant changes will be made to the plan or that it will be withdrawn

Financial Statement Presentation

All assets and liabilities of the discontinued operation are presented separately on the balance sheet for all periods presented.

Discontinued operations are presented separately on the income statement to alert financial statement users that this portion of the business will not be a part of ongoing operations. The income of a discontinued operation and any gain or loss from its disposal are separated from continuing operations for all periods presented, even though in previous periods the income from the segment was part of continuing operations. Discontinued operations are presented **net of tax** below income from continuing operations in the income statement.

Calculation of Income Statement Discontinued Operations

The discontinued operations portion of the income statement will include the income (or loss) from operations of the component as well as the gain (or loss) from the actual sale:

Sale of Discontinued Operation Financial Reporting

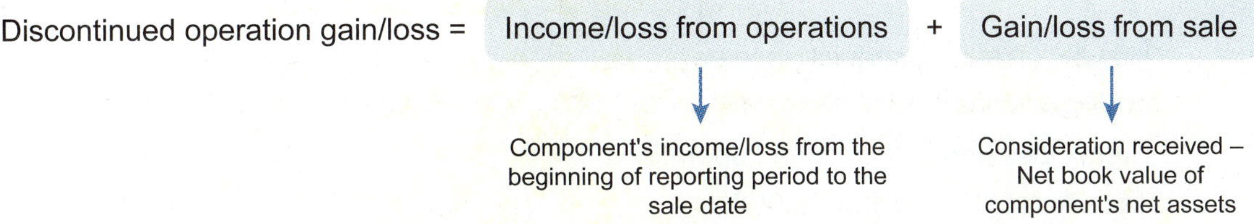

The following rules apply in the calculation of the discontinued operations for income statement purposes:

Recognizing Elements of a Discontinued Operation		
Element	**Accounting treatment**	**Calculation**
Operating income/loss	Recognized (net of tax) in period incurred	
Gain on sale	Recognized (net of tax) in year of disposal	Sales price – book value
Loss on sale (actual)	Recognized (net of tax) in year of disposal	Sales price – book value
Impairment loss (anticipated)	Recognized immediately upon "held for sale" classification • Occurs when an asset's book value exceeds its net realizable value (NRV, ie, fair value less cost of disposal)	NRV – book value

On the income statement, the gain or loss on disposal and the operating income of the discontinued component can be netted or presented separately. If they are netted, footnote disclosure must be included to show both amounts separately.

On June 1, Year 5, management of Hudson Co. committed to a plan to dispose of Howard Co., a major subsidiary. The sale meets the requirements for classification as discontinued operations and is anticipated to occur during Year 6.

Howard earns an operating income of $500,000 in Year 5, and management anticipates that Howard will incur an operating loss of $1,600,000 in Year 6. In Year 5, management determines that the book value of the business unit is $10,000,000 and the fair value less cost of disposal is $8,000,000.

Assume that the tax rate is 30%. Determine what Hudson should report for discontinued operations in its Year 5 income statement.

Operating income/loss is included as part of discontinued operations in the period it is incurred, not anticipated. Impairment losses are recognized immediately, even if the disposal has not occurred yet.

Hudson will report a $1,050,000 loss from discontinued operations in its Year 5 income statement:

Howard's Year 5 operating income	$ 500,000
Impairment loss ($8,000,000 NRV − $10,000,000 book value)	(2,000,000)
Pretax loss from discontinued operations	(1,500,000)
Tax effect [30% × ($1,500,000)]	450,000*
Income statement loss from discontinued operations	$(1,050,000)

**The discontinued operations loss decreases Hudson's net income and, therefore, Hudson's taxes owed. Since discontinued operations caused Hudson's net income to decrease by $1,500,000, the company will save $450,000 (30% × $1,500,000) in taxes.*

Foreign Currency Transactions

Representative Task (Application): Calculate transaction gains or losses recognized from monetary transactions denominated in a foreign currency.

Foreign currency transactions are transactions of a domestic entity denominated in (to be settled in) a foreign currency but to be recorded on the domestic entity's books in the domestic currency.

For example, a U.S. company buys goods from a Japanese company and agrees to pay for the goods with yen rather than dollars. In this case, the transaction is denominated in yen, but the amount recorded on the books of the U.S. entity is measured in U.S. dollars; therefore, the transaction amount must be converted from yen to dollars for reporting purposes.

When an entity enters into a transaction that will be settled in a foreign currency, a payable or receivable in a foreign currency is created. The payable or receivable is initially recorded in the entity's functional currency using the **transaction date exchange rate** (ie, spot rate).

These payables or receivables present a risk because of the changes in the exchange rates before settlement. As the exchange rate fluctuates between the time of purchase or sale and the time of payment, the company will record foreign currency transaction gains or losses (also called exchange gains or losses). These gains or losses are recorded in net income. The company will also revalue the receivable or payable (ie, adjust its value on the balance sheet) to accurately present it at each reporting period.

Foreign Currency Gains and Losses

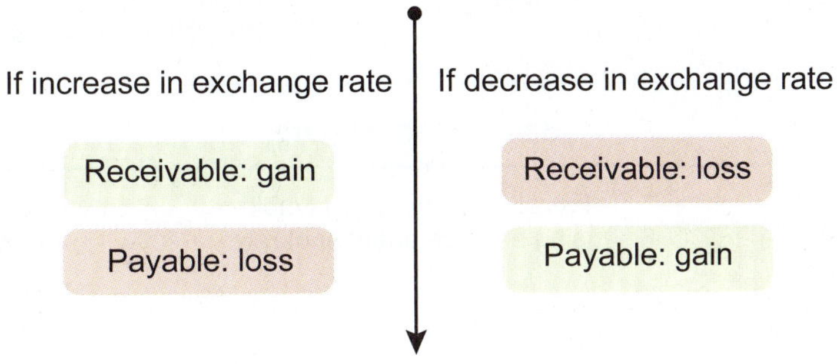

Over time, currencies can strengthen or weaken. A strengthening or weakening dollar means that the dollar buys more or less of the foreign currency. It also means that a company will receive more or less of the foreign currency owed to it.

For example, assume that a U.S. company has a €100,000 payable denominated in euros. If the dollar strengthens, fewer dollars will be required to purchase the same amount of euros. The payable is still €100,000; however, fewer dollars are now required to fulfill the obligation. The company will record a gain on the liability.

Strengthening or Weakening Currency and Transaction Gains and Losses

Domestic currency behavior	Impact	Transaction	
		Receivable denominated in foreign currency	Payable denominated in foreign currency
Domestic currency (dollar) weakens	More dollars are required to buy one unit of foreign currency	Transaction gain	Transaction loss
Domestic currency (dollar) strengthens	Fewer dollars are required to buy one unit of foreign currency	Transaction loss	Transaction gain

Foreign currency transactions are initially recorded at the transaction date. At the balance sheet date and settlement date, the associated receivables/payables are revalued, and a gain or loss is recorded through net income.

Foreign Currency Transactions

At **balance sheet date,** record foreign currency transaction gain/loss in income for difference in rate

At **settlement date,** record foreign currency transaction gain/loss in income for difference in rate

Transaction date

Record receivable/payable using transaction spot rate

Balance sheet date

Revalue receivable/payable using balance sheet spot rate

Settlement date

- Revalue receivable/payable using settlement spot rate
- Settle transaction in foreign currency

Stan Inc., a U.S. company, acquired machinery from a European manufacturer on October 1, Year 2 for €300,000. Payment was due in euros on January 31, Year 3. The spot rates to purchase one euro were as follows:

October 1, Year 2	$2.00
December 31, Year 2	$1.00
January 31, Year 3	$1.45

Determine the initial journal entry that Stan will record and calculate the foreign currency transaction gain or loss that Stan will recognize in Year 2 and Year 3.

October 1, Year 2: Stan will record the machinery purchase in U.S. dollars, using the spot rate.

Purchase Machinery: €300,000 × $2.00 (10/1 Year 2 Spot Rate)		
Machinery (historical exchange rate)	600,000	
Accounts payable		600,000

December 31, Year 2: The spot rate decreased from October 1 to December 31. A corresponding foreign currency transaction gain is recorded through net income in Year 2, reflecting the decreased dollars required to satisfy the payable.

Revalue Accounts Payable: ($2.00 – $1.00) × €300,000		
Accounts payable	300,000	
Foreign currency gain		300,000

January 31, Year 3: The spot rate increased from December 31 to January 31. A corresponding foreign currency transaction loss is recorded through net income in Year 3, reflecting the increased dollars required to satisfy the payable.

Revalue Accounts Payable: ($1.00 – $1.45) × €300,000		
Foreign currency loss	135,000	
Accounts payable		135,000

The account payable is now valued on Stan's books at $435,000 ($600,000 – $300,000 + $135,000).

Since the transaction was denominated in euros, Stan needs to purchase euros to settle the transaction on the date of settlement.

Purchase of Foreign Currency: €300,000 × $1.45 (1/31 Year 3 Spot Rate)		
Investment in euros	435,000	
Cash		435,000

Stan will then settle the accounts payable by paying the euros to the European manufacturer.

Accounts payable	435,000	
Investment in euros		435,000

Foreign currency transaction gains and losses are a **nonoperating item** and are recorded through net income. In a multi-step income statement, these gains and losses are part of nonoperating income (as shown in the multi-step income statement image above).

Foreign currency items are tested in both the FAR and BAR exams. Additional coverage on foreign currency topics is provided in the BAR text.

1.03 Statement of Comprehensive Income

Overview

Representative Task (Remembering & Understanding): Recall the purpose, objectives and structure of the statement of comprehensive income.

Representative Task (Remembering & Understanding): Identify items classified as other comprehensive income.

The purpose of reporting **comprehensive income** is to report a measure of overall enterprise performance. Comprehensive income includes all changes in equity during a period except those resulting from investments by owners/shareholders and distributions to owners/shareholders.

Net income is not replaced by comprehensive income. The purpose of requiring the reporting of comprehensive income is to report the net change in equity (other than from transactions with shareholders) in a single amount and to provide a more complete picture of the total earnings of the firm for a period.

The two components of comprehensive income are shown in the following equation:

Comprehensive income = Net income + Other comprehensive income (OCI)

Other Comprehensive Income (OCI)

OCI items are not recognized in net income. They are recorded directly as increases or decreases in shareholders' equity. The following items are included in OCI:

Net income + **Other comprehensive income** = Comprehensive income

- **D**erivative cash flow hedges
- **E**xcess adjustment on defined benefit pension plans
- **N**et unrealized holding gains and losses on available-for-sale debt securities
- **T**ranslation adjustments from foreign currency

Accumulated other comprehensive income (AOCI) is a running total of OCI items through the balance sheet date. AOCI includes cumulative OCI for all periods (ie, current and prior periods). Just as net income is closed to retained earnings, OCI is closed to AOCI at the end of each reporting period.

Other Comprehensive Income (OCI) and Accumulated Other Comprehensive Income (AOCI)

ABC Inc.
Income Statement
For the year ended December 31, Year 1

Sales revenue	$20,000
Cost of goods sold	12,000
Gross profit	8,000
Net income	$12,000
Other comprehensive income	
Deferred gain on an effective cash-flow hedge	8,000
Foreign currency translation gain	2,000
Prior service cost not recognized in net periodic pension cost	(5,000)
Total other comprehensive income	5,000
Comprehensive income	$17,000

ABC Inc.
Balance Sheet
As of December 31, Year 1

Assets	
Total assets	$29,000
Liabilities and shareholders' equity	
Total liabilities	2,000
Shareholders' equity	
Common stock	10,000
Retained earnings	12,000
Accumulated other comprehensive income	
Deferred gain on an effective cash-flow hedge	8,000
Foreign currency translation gain	2,000
Prior service cost not recognized in net periodic pension cost	(5,000)
Total shareholders' equity	27,000
Total liabilities and shareholders' equity	$29,000

**OCI and AOCI will be equal after a business's first year of operations*

Financial Statement Presentation

GAAP requires presentation of comprehensive income in one of two ways:

- **Combined statement of comprehensive income:** Presents the components of net income and leads to net income as a subtotal. Other comprehensive income (OCI) items lead to total comprehensive income
- **Separate statement of comprehensive income:** Separate income statement is presented immediately before the statement of comprehensive income. The net income amount resulting from the first statement is used as the beginning amount for the second statement, which then reports OCI leading to comprehensive income

The following is an example of a separate statement of comprehensive income:

Statement of Comprehensive Income
For the year ending December 31, 202X

Net income		$XXX,XXX
Other comprehensive income (net of tax)		
Derivative, cash flow hedges	$XXX	
Excess adjustment of pension PBO and FV of plan assets at year end	XXX	
Net unrealized holding gains/losses on available-for-sale debt securities	XXX	
Translations gains and losses (foreign currency)	XXX	
Total other comprehensive income		$X,XXX
Comprehensive income		$XXX,XXX

PBO = projected benefit obligation; FV = fair value

1.04 Statement of Changes in Equity

Overview

Representative Task (Application): Prepare a statement of changes in equity from a trial balance and supporting documentation.

Items related to equity are presented in the shareholders' equity section of the balance sheet and in the statement of changes in equity. Shareholders' equity includes the following:

Component of Shareholders' Equity	
Capital contributed by owners (common stock)	• Shares *authorized* under articles of incorporation • Shares *issued* (ie, sold) to investors • Shares *outstanding:* issued shares less treasury shares
Preferred shares	• Preferential rights to dividends and assets vs. common stock
Treasury shares	• Shares repurchased by the company
Retained earnings	• Cumulative earnings not paid as dividends
Accumulated other comprehensive income	• Cumulative amount of *other* unrealized gains or losses
Noncontrolling (minority) interest	• Equity portion of a consolidated subsidiary owned by others

These items are presented in the equity section of the balance sheet as such:

Stockholders' Equity

Contributed (paid-in) capital	$XXX
Preferred stock	XXX
Common stock	XXX
Additional paid-in capital (from various sources)	XXX
Total paid-in capital	XXX
Noncontrolling interest in consolidated subsidiaries (if consolidated financial statements)	XXX
Retained earnings (appropriated and unappropriated)	XXX
Accumulated other comprehensive income (loss)	XXX
Less: Treasury stock (cost method)	(XXX)
Total stockholders' equity	$XXX

The statement of changes in equity effectively expands the shareholders' equity section of the balance sheet. It presents the changes in these equity items over the reporting period. This statement covers the same time period as the income statement but presents the changes in contributed capital, additional paid-in capital, and retained earnings. These changes arise from the purchase and sale of shares of the entity's stock, changes in comprehensive income, and the payment of dividends.

The following is an example of a statement of changes in equity:

Company Name
Statement of Changes in Equity
For the year ended December 31, Year XX

	Common stock	Additional paid-in capital	Accumulated other comprehensive income	Retained earnings	Treasury stock	Total equity
Balance 1/1/Year 2	$40,000	$180,000	$20,000	$230,000	($30,000)	**$440,000**
Issued stock	5,000	30,000				**35,000**
Issued stock dividend	2,000	11,000		(13,000)		
Purchased treasury stock					(20,000)	**(20,000)**
Declared cash dividend				(25,000)		**(25,000)**
Net income				90,000		**90,000**
Other comprehensive income			(6,000)			**(6,000)**
Balance 12/31/Year 2	$47,000	$221,000	$14,000	$282,000	($50,000)	**$514,000**

Each column reconciles the beginning and ending account balance for one account by disclosing all the changes in the account during the period. Some events causing a change in equity require at least two entries per row (ie, more than one column is affected). Therefore, the total equity column is not always affected. Later lessons will cover the underlying accounting of the line items in this statement.

Other columns found on the statement of changes in equity may include the following:

- Preferred stock
- Additional paid-in capital, preferred stock
- Additional paid-in capital, treasury stock
- Equity attributable to noncontrolling interest

1.05 Detecting, Investigating, and Correcting Discrepancies

Overview

Representative Task (Application): Adjust the balance sheet to correct identified errors.

Representative Task (Application): Adjust the income statement to correct identified errors.

Representative Task (Application): Adjust the statement of changes in equity to correct identified errors.

Representative Task (Analysis): Detect, investigate and correct discrepancies while agreeing balance sheet amounts to supporting documentation, including the source data.

Representative Task (Analysis): Detect, investigate and correct discrepancies while agreeing income statement amounts to supporting documentation, including the source data.

Representative Task (Analysis): Detect, investigate and correct discrepancies while agreeing statement of changes in equity amounts to supporting documentation, including the source data.

Entities should have procedures in place to detect potential discrepancies and resolve any confirmed errors. Initially flagged irregularities may require additional investigation prior to any corrective action being taken.

Example

Assume that Encore Company manufactures and sells bicycles. The company is compiling its Year 3 financial statements and begins by preparing the trial balance.

Encore Company
Trial Balance
As of December 31, Year 3

Accounts	***Debit (Dr)***	***Credit (Cr)***
Accounts receivable	5,265	
Cash and cash equivalents	7,905	
COGS	5,694	
Depreciation expense	1,210	
Interest expense	750	
Inventory	1,934	
Payroll expense	6,450	
PP&E, net	9,230	
SG&A expense	2,030	
Accounts payable to suppliers		5,555
APIC		1,240
Common stock		8,000
Gain from sale of investments		900
Notes payable		4,775
Revenue		15,375
Totals	**40,468**	**35,845**

Encore discovers that there is a $4,623 discrepancy in the trial balance.

Debits per trial balance	$40,468
Credits per trial balance	(35,845)
Difference	$ 4,623

Using the trial balance and the exhibits provided, identify the cause of discrepancy. Then, adjust the balance sheet, income statement, and statement of changes in equity to reflect the correct amounts.

Exhibits

Exhibit 1

From: Lauren, Accounting Manager
To: Brandon, General Ledger
Sent: December 29, Year 3
Subject: Year-end Payroll Accrual

Hello Brandon,

I met with the payroll department this afternoon. They confirmed that all employees are still paid monthly, on the first of the month. All employees were last paid on December 1st and, on January 1st, employees will be paid $880 total.

Please confirm that we have accrued the wages that employees earned during the month of December.

Please let me know if you have any questions.

Lauren

Exhibit 2

Encore Company
General Ledger
For the month ended December 31, Year 3

Account: Inventory				**Account Number: 300**
DATE	**DESCRIPTION**	**DEBIT**	**CREDIT**	**BALANCE**
1-Dec	Beginning balance			2,900
5-Dec	Sale to Stage Co.		905	1,995
9-Dec	Purchase of inventory	3,000		4,995
16-Dec	Shipped goods to Headline Co., on consignment		1,950	3,045
19-Dec	Sale to Record Inc.		2,011	1,034
28-Dec	Purchase of inventory	900		1,934
31-Dec	**Totals and ending balance**	3,900	4,866	**1,934**

Exhibit 3

Encore Company
General Ledger
For the year ended December 31, Year 3

Account: Common Stock				Account Number: 800
DATE	DESCRIPTION	DEBIT	CREDIT	BALANCE
1-Jan	Beginning balance			6,000
5-May	Issuance of stock		2,000	8,000
31-Dec	**Totals and ending balance**	-	2,000	**8,000**

Account: Additional Paid in Capital				Account Number: 900
DATE	DESCRIPTION	DEBIT	CREDIT	BALANCE
1-Jan	Beginning balance			1,000
5-May	Issuance of stock		240	1,240
31-Dec	**Totals and ending balance**	-	240	**1,240**

Account: Retained Earnings				Account Number: 1000
DATE	DESCRIPTION	DEBIT	CREDIT	BALANCE
1-Jan	Beginning balance			4,623
31-Dec	Net income		141	4,764
31-Dec	**Totals and ending balance**	-	141	**4,764**

Task 1: In the table below, prepare the journal entries that Encore should record to correct the discrepancy in its financial statements:

	A	*B*	*C*
	Account	**Debit**	**Credit**
1	Payroll expense	880	
	Accrued payroll		880

JE #1: In accrual accounting, payroll expense is incurred as employees perform services, regardless of when they are paid. At the end of each reporting period, a liability (ie, accrued payroll) and corresponding expense (ie, payroll expense) are recorded for salaries earned by employees but not yet paid to them.

The email from the accounting manager reports Year 3 accrued payroll as $880. However, this accrued payroll is missing from the trial balance. Encore must record an adjusting entry to report payroll expense and accrued payroll for the $880 of salaries owed to employees at year-end.

2	Inventory	1,950	
	Cost of goods sold		1,950

JE #2: Encore incorrectly recorded $1,950 of goods on consignment as goods sold. In a consignment arrangement, a buyer, or consignee, receives the goods (ie, has physical possession of them) but does not purchase them from the consignor (seller). The consignor retains legal ownership and reports the goods on its balance sheet until sold.

Encore's goods are being held on consignment by Headline Company. Encore retains ownership of these goods and, as such, should report them on its balance sheet. Encore must record an adjustment to inventory and cost of goods sold for $1,950 for its goods on consignment.

Task 2: Adjust Encore's Year 3 trial balance to reflect the correct amounts. The "Per original trial balance" amounts are prepopulated as a starting point. Record the necessary adjustments in the "Adjustments needed" section.

Note: Adjustments required in Task 1 are not exhaustive. Additional, non-journal-entry, adjustments to the statements may be required beyond the adjustments listed in Task 1 above.

Encore Company
Adjusted Trial Balance
As of December 31, Year 3

Accounts	Per original trial balance			Adjustments needed			Adjusted trial balance	
	Debit (Dr)	Credit (Cr)		Debit (Dr)	Credit (Cr)		Debit (Dr)	Credit (Cr)
Accounts receivable	5,265						5,265	
Cash and cash equivalents	7,905						7,905	
COGS	5,694				1,950	JE #2	3,744	
Depreciation expense	1,210						1,210	
Interest expense	750						750	
Inventory	1,934		JE #2	1,950			3,884	
Payroll expense	6,450		JE #1	880			7,330	
PP&E, net	9,230						9,230	
SG&A expense	2,030						2,030	
Accounts payable to suppliers		5,555						5,555
Accrued payroll		–			880	JE #1		880
APIC		1,240						1,240
Common stock		8,000						8,000
Gain from sale of investments		900						900
Retained earnings, beginning					4,623	ADJ		4,623
Notes payable		4,775						4,775
Revenue		15,375						15,375
Totals	**40,468**	**35,845**		**2,830**	**7,453**		**41,348**	**41,348**
Net total	**4,623**				**4,623**			

Encore should increase payroll expense and increase accrued payroll by $880, as shown in JE #1 above. The company should also increase inventory and decrease cost of goods sold by $1,950, as shown in JE #2 above. An additional adjustment (tagged ADJ) is required to beginning retained earnings. Beginning retained earnings is missing from the original trial balance. However, per the equity general ledger exhibit, the beginning retained earnings balance is $4,623.

Task 3: Adjust Encore's Year 3 income statement, balance sheet, and statement of changes in equity to reflect the correct amounts. The "Per original trial balance" amounts are prepopulated as a starting point. Record the adjusted amounts in the "Per adjusted trial balance" section.

Encore Company
Income Statement
For the year ended December 31, Year 3

	Per original trial balance	Per adjusted trial balance	
Revenue	15,375	15,375	
Cost of sales	(5,694)	(3,744)	JE #2
Gross profit	9,681	11,631	
Operating expenses:			
Selling, general and administrative expense	2,030	2,030	
Depreciation expense	1,210	1,210	
Payroll expense	6,450	7,330	JE #1
Total operating expenses	9,690	10,570	
Operating income (loss)	(9)	1,061	
Non-operating items:			
Interest expense	(750)	(750)	
Gain from sale of investment	900	900	
Total non-operating income/(loss)	150	150	
Net income/(loss)	141	1,211	NI

Encore Company
Statement of Changes in Equity
For the year ended December 31, Year 3

	Common stock	APIC	Retained earnings		Total equity
Per original trial balance:					
Balance 1/1 Year 3	6,000	1,000			7,000
Issued stock	2,000	240			2,240
Net income			141		141
Balance 12/31 Year 3	8,000	1,240	141		9,381
Per adjusted trial balance:					
Balance 1/1 Year 3	6,000	1,000	4,623	ADJ	11,623
Issued stock	2,000	240			2,240
Net income			1,211	NI	1,211
Balance 12/31 Year 3	8,000	1,240	5,834	ADJ + NI	15,074

Encore Company
Balance Sheet
As of December 31, Year 3

	Per original trial balance	Per adjusted trial balance	
Assets			
Current assets:			
Cash and cash equivalents	7,905	7,905	
Accounts receivable	5,265	5,265	
Inventory	1,934	3,884	JE #2
Total current assets	15,104	17,054	
Noncurrent assets:			
PP&E, net	9,230	9,230	
Total assets	24,334	26,284	
Liabilities			
Current liabilities:			
Accounts payable to suppliers	5,555	5,555	
Accrued payroll	–	880	JE #1
Total current liabilities	5,555	6,435	
Noncurrent liabilities:			
Notes payable	4,775	4,775	
Total liabilities	10,330	11,210	
Shareholders' equity			
Common stock	8,000	8,000	
APIC	1,240	1,240	
Retained earnings	141	5,834	ADJ + NI
Total shareholders' equity	9,381	15,074	
Total liabilities and shareholders' equity	19,711	26,284	

1.06 Statement of Cash Flows

Overview

Representative Task (Application): Prepare a statement of cash flow using the indirect method and required disclosures from supporting documentation.

Representative Task (Analysis): Derive impact of transactions on the statement of cash flows.

A statement of cash flows (SCF) is required for all companies that present both financial position (balance sheet) and results of operations (income statement) for a period. The SCF is one of the basic financial statements.

The purpose of the SCF is to provide detailed information about an entity's cash inflows (ie, receipts or sources) and outflows (ie, disbursements or uses) from operating, investing, and financing activities. It provides information to aid investors, creditors, and other stakeholders in decision-making. The SCF also provides information about investing and financing activities that do not involve cash inflows or outflows (eg, acquiring a major long-term asset by incurring a liability).

The SCF explains all of the changes in cash, cash equivalents, and restricted cash between the beginning and end of the reporting period on the balance sheet:

- Cash equivalents are short-term, highly liquid investments that are readily convertible into cash. The original maturity of these investments must be three months or less from the date of purchase (eg, treasury bills, commercial paper, money market funds)
- Restricted cash is identified by the entity as cash that is held for a specific purpose and is not available for the company to use freely (eg, cash that is part of a collateral agreement with a third party)

The entity must disclose how the change in cash presented on the SCF reconciles to the components of cash presented on the balance sheet. This reconciliation can be on the face of the SCF or in the notes to the financial statements. The net change in cash must be exactly explained by the cash flows associated with operating, investing, and financing activities.

The SCF must report information in the following categories:

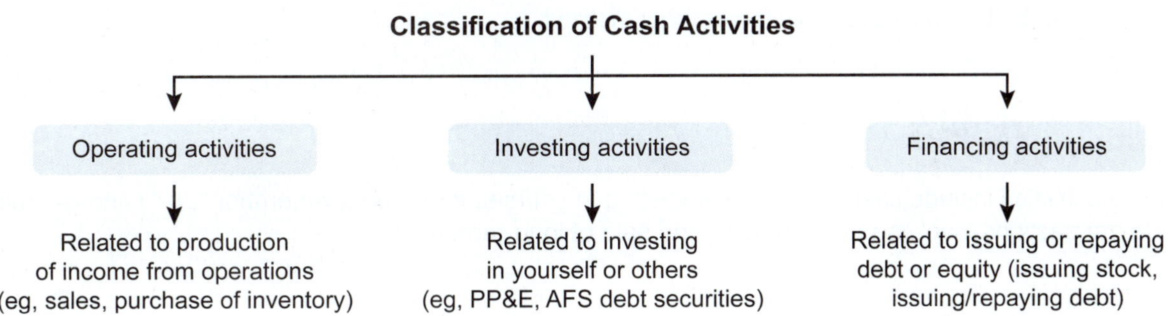

Noncash investing and financing activities are those that do not use cash to complete the transaction (eg, the conversion of bonds to equity). Though these transactions do not involve cash, significant noncash investing and financing activities must be disclosed on the face of the SCF, in a supplemental schedule, or in the notes to the F/S.

The statement of cash flows is consistently tested on the CPA exam, usually either as several multiple-choice questions or as part of a simulation. Remember to use only the cash component (ie, inflow or outflow) from the activity. Reconstructing the journal entries can help determine the amount of cash involved and the impact on the cash account.

Operating Activities

Operating activities include the inflows and outflows of cash related to the production of income from continuing operations (ie, normal business activities). Examples of cash flows from operating activities include the following:

Inflows (Cash Received)	Outflows (Cash Paid)
• From customers	• To suppliers (for goods/services and SG&A expenses) or to employees (payroll)
• Dividends (from investments)	• Interest paid
• Interest received	• Income taxes
• From disposal of trading securities	• For acquisition of trading securities

In general, an item is classified as an operating cash flow activity if it is associated with net income. Notice that interest paid and received and dividends received are all operating cash flows, as they are associated with income statement items (ie, interest expense and revenue, dividend revenue). However, dividends paid is a financing cash flow, as it is not associated with an income statement item but instead with a direct reduction to retained earnings.

Any cash inflow or cash outflow not properly classified as an investing or financing activity would be included as cash flow from operating activities (eg, collection of a lawsuit settlement). The net cash flow from operating activities can be positive or negative.

The operating section of the SCF can be presented using the direct or indirect method. Both are acceptable under GAAP; however, the direct method is outside the scope of the CPA exam. As such, the text will cover only the indirect method.

Investing Activities

Investing activities include cash flows from investing in yourself for others (remember "LIP") and typically include transactions involving the purchase and sale of long-term assets.

Examples of cash flows from investing activities include the following:

Loans made to others or principal collections

Interest and dividends received are operating

Acquisition or disposal of available-for-sale or held-to-maturity **i**nvestments

Trading securities are operating

Acquisition or disposal of **p**roperty, plant, and equipment and intangibles

Including cash paid for capitalized repairs

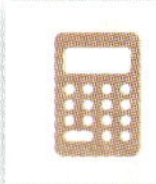

Arlington Company engaged in the following transactions January 1, Year 1:

- Purchase of a copier costing $40,000 with a $23,000 down payment and a note payable for the balance
- Purchase of available-for-sale debt securities for $100,000
- Issuance of a long-term loan to Orchard Company for $5,000

During the year, Arlington sold the same copier that it purchased earlier in the year for $36,000 after it had incurred $8,000 worth of depreciation. Arlington also sold the available-for-sale debt securities purchased earlier in the year for $80,000. Finally, Arlington received a payment of $2,100 on its long-term loan to Orchard. The $2,100 payment consisted of $100 earned interest and $2,000 principal repayment.

Determine the net cash flows provided (used) by the investing activities.

We can first use journal entries to understand the impact of the transactions on the cash account.

Property, plant, and equipment transaction:

Purchase of Copier		
PP&E	40,000	
Cash		23,000
Note payable*		17,000

**The $17,000 note payable will be disclosed as a noncash financing activity.*

Sale of Copier		
Cash	36,000	
Accumulated depreciation	8,000	
PP&E		40,000
Gain on sale (plug)		4,000

Investment transaction:

Purchase of AFS Debt Securities		
AFS debt securities	100,000	
Cash		100,000

Sale of AFS Debt Securities		
Cash	80,000	
Loss on sale (plug)	20,000	
AFS debt securities		100,000

Long-term loan to Orchard:

Issuance of loan		
Note receivable	5,000	
Cash		5,000

Partial Repayment of Loan		
Cash*	2,100	
Note receivable		2,000
Interest revenue		100

Total cash received contains both principal repayment and interest revenue. The $2,000 of principal collection is an* ***investing* *cash flow. The $100 of interest revenue is an* ***operating*** *cash flow.*

Based on the above entries, these transactions would appear in the "Cash flows from investing activities" section of the SCF as such:

Cash Flows from Investing Activities	
Cash payment for purchase of PP&E	$(23,000)
Cash proceeds from sale of PP&E	36,000
Cash paid for AFS debt securities	(100,000)
Cash proceeds from sale of AFS debt securities	80,000
Cash paid for issuance of long-term loan	(5,000)
Cash received for principal repayment	2,000
Net cash flows **used by** investing activities	$(10,000)

Financing Activities

Financing activities are cash flows from issuing debt or equity and typically include transactions involving long-term liabilities and stockholders' equity. Examples of cash flows from financing activities include the following:

Related to Debt	• Proceeds from issuance of bonds or retiring bonds • Proceeds from other borrowings (eg, a loan) • Principal repayment on borrowings • Note: related interest is *operating*
Related to Equity	• Issuance of stock or reacquisition/reissuance of treasury stock • Cash dividends (not property or stock) paid (not declared) • Note: dividends received is *operating*

Wrightwood Company engaged in the following transactions January 1, Year 1:

- Issuance of 80,000 shares of common stock for $800,000 (par value of $2.50 per share)
- Issuance of bond for $1,000,000

During the year, Wrightwood paid $100,000 for the repurchase of common stock. Wrightwood paid $220,000 on the bond ($200,000 for repayment of principal and $20,000 for payment of interest).

Determine the net cash flows provided (used) by the financing activities.

We can first use journal entries to understand the impact of the transactions on the cash account.

Stock transaction:

Issuance of Stock		
Cash	800,000	
Common stock		200,000
APIC		600,000

Repurchase of Stock		
Treasury stock	100,000	
Cash		100,000

Debt transaction:

Issuance of Bond		
Cash	1,000,000	
Bond payable		1,000,000

Partial Repayment of Bond		
Bond payable	200,000	
Interest expense	20,000	
Cash*		220,000

Total cash paid contains both principal repayment and interest expense. The $200,000 of principal paid is a* ***financing* *cash flow. The $20,000 of interest expense is an operating cash flow.*

Based on the above entries, these transactions would appear in the "Cash flows from financing activities" section of the SCF as such:

Cash Flows from Financing Activities	
Cash proceeds from issuance of stock	$ 800,000
Cash paid for treasury stock	(100,000)
Cash proceeds from issuance of bonds	1,000,000
Cash paid for bond principal repayment	(200,000)
Net cash flows **provided by** financing activities	$1,500,000

Some questions may require you to solve for cash dividends paid (ie, beginning and ending dividends payable and dividends declared are provided). In these scenarios, creating a T-account may be helpful:

Dividends Payable

Debit		Credit	
Dividends paid	?	100,000	Beginning balance
		1,000,000	Dividends declared
		600,000	Ending balance

The T-account requires a debit of $500,000 to balance.
Dividends paid are $500,000 ($100,000 + $1,000,000 − $600,000).

Indirect Method

Presentation

The indirect method can be used to calculate net cash provided (or used) by **operating activities**. Under the **indirect method**, income from continuing operations is reconciled to net cash flows from operating activities by adjusting for noncash items and nonoperating activities and changes in current assets (other than cash and cash equivalents) and current liabilities.

Cash Flow from Operating Activities (Indirect Method)

	Net income
Noncash expenses and nonoperating items that **decreased** net income	+ Depreciation + Amortization expense (eg, bond discount, patents) + Losses from sales of assets
Noncash revenue and nonoperating items that **increased** net income	− Equity in earnings from investee − Amortization of bond premium − Gains from sales of assets
Changes in current assets and current liabilities	+ Decreases in current assets (source of cash) − Increases in current assets (use of cash) + Increases in current liabilities (source of cash) − Decreases in current liabilities (use of cash)
	Net cash provided (or used) by operating activities

The indirect method begins with accrual-based net income. Then adjustments are made, including the following:

- Elimination of the effect on net income of **noncash items** (eg, depreciation, amortization, depletion, and equity in earnings) and items classified as **investing or financing activities** (eg, gains and losses on sale of equipment)
- Adjustment of net income for **changes in balances** of **current assets** (other than cash and cash equivalents) and **current liabilities** (eg, A/R, inventory, and A/P)

Presentation of cash flows from investing activities and financing activities does not change, regardless of whether the direct or indirect approach is used to present cash flows from operating activities.

On December 31, Year 2, Fullerton Inc. reported net income of $140,000. Fullerton's income statement is reported as follows:

Revenue	$605,000
Cost of goods sold	400,000
Gross profit	$205,000
Operating expenses:	
Depreciation expense	$ 50,000
Credit loss expense (change in allowance)	20,000
Total operating expenses	$ 70,000
Operating income/(loss)	$135,000
Nonoperating items:	
Gain on AFS debt security	$ 10,000
Amortization of bond discount	(5,000)
Total nonoperating income/(loss)	$ 5,000
Net income/(loss)	$140,000

From December 31, Year 1, to December 31, Year 2:

- Accounts receivable increased by $80,000
- Inventory increased by $30,000
- Accounts payable decreased by $20,000
- Taxes payable increased by $40,000

Prepare the "Cash flows from operating activities" section of the SCF using the indirect method.

Step 1: Eliminate the effect of noncash, nonoperating items on net income:

First, consider whether items that impacted net income involve cash. If the items do not involve cash, their effect on net income should be reversed to arrive at cash flows from operating activities.

If the items involve cash, consider if the items should be classified as investing or financing activities, rather than operating activities. If the items should be classified as investing or financing activities, their effect on net income should be reversed to arrive at cash flows from operating activities.

Depreciation expense **does not result in the use of any cash** but was deducted from net income. Therefore, the $50,000 depreciation expense is added back to net income to arrive at cash flows from operating activities.

Bond discount amortization expense **does not result in the use of any cash** but was deducted from net income. Therefore, the $5,000 amortization expense is added back to net income to arrive at cash flows from operating activities. Note: Amortization of a bond premium increases net income. If the amortization here was from a bond premium, it would be deducted from net income to arrive at cash flow from operating activities.

An increase in the allowance for credit losses through credit loss expense **does not result in the use of any cash** but was deducted from net income. Therefore, the $20,000 credit loss expense is added back to net income to arrive at cash flows from operating activities.

The sale of the AFS debt security resulted in a $10,000 gain reflected in net income. Although the sale involves cash, the cash proceeds from the sale are an investing activity, not operating. Additionally, the gain itself has **no impact on cash**. Since the gain increased net income but did not impact cash, it must be removed (here, deducted from) net income.

Step 2: Adjust net income for changes in balances of current assets and liabilities:

Cash Flow Statement Treatment for Changes in Current Assets and Liabilities (Indirect Method)

The impact of changes in current assets and current liabilities can be determined with the use of the DIAL mnemonic.

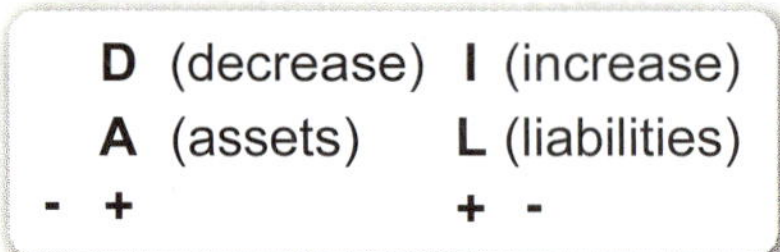

A decrease in assets is an increase to cash flow.

- decreasing assets (eg, selling inventory) creates sources of cash

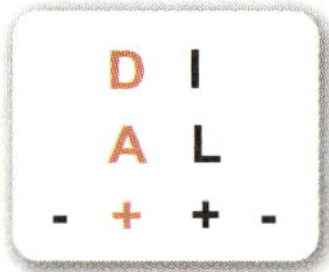

An increase in liabilities is an increase to cash flow.

- increasing liabilities (eg, issuing debt) creates sources of cash

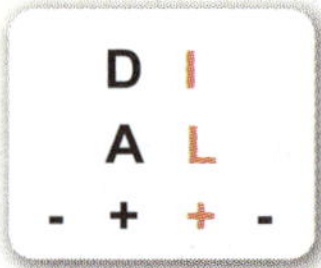

A decrease in liabilities is a decrease to cash flow.

- decreasing liabilities (eg, paying off accounts payable) is a use of cash

An increase in assets is a decrease to cash flow.

- increasing assets (eg, purchasing inventory) is a use of cash

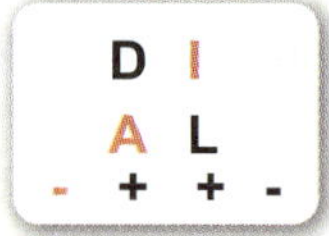

Accounts receivable increased by $80,000:

Accounts receivable	80,000	
Revenue		80,000

Revenue (and, therefore, net income) increased by $80,000. However, this journal entry did not involve cash. As such, its impact must be reversed out of net income to arrive at cash flow from operating activities. **The $80,000 increase in accounts receivable must be subtracted from net income.**

Inventory increased by $30,000:

Inventory	30,000	
Cash		30,000

The impact of this journal entry was not reflected in net income, but the entry involved a $30,000 decrease to cash. As such, its impact must be added to (or, here, subtracted from) net income to arrive at cash flow from operating activities. **The $30,000 increase in inventory must be subtracted from net income.**

Note: If it was instead assumed that the inventory was paid for on account (ie, debit inventory and credit accounts payable), the impact on net income would still be the same. Increases in current liabilities result in subtraction from net income.

Accounts payable decreased by $20,000:

Accounts payable	20,000	
Cash		20,000

The impact of this journal entry was not reflected in net income, but the entry involved a $20,000 decrease to cash. As such, its impact must be added to (or, here, subtracted from) net income to arrive at cash flow from operating activities. **The $20,000 decrease in accounts payable must be subtracted from net income.**

Taxes payable increased by $40,000:

Income tax expense	40,000	
Taxes payable		40,000

Income tax expense increased by $40,000. Therefore, net income decreased by $40,000. However, this journal entry did not involve cash. As such, its impact must be reversed out of net income to arrive at cash flow from operating activities. T**he $40,000 increase in taxes payable must be added back to net income.**

Fullerton's "Cash flows from operating activities" section of the SCF (under the indirect method) is as follows:

Net income	$140,000
Depreciation expense	50,000
Bond discount amortization expense	5,000
Credit loss expense	20,000
Gain on AFS debt security	(10,000)
Increase in accounts receivable	(80,000)
Increase in inventory	(30,000)
Decrease in accounts payable	(20,000)
Increase in taxes payable	40,000
Net cash **provided by** operating activities	$115,000

Changes in certain other balance sheet accounts are considered if they involve an operating account (eg, accumulated depreciation, discount or premium bonds payable). If the income statement impact of these items is not provided, the balance sheet accounts can be used to derive the income statement impact (ie, an increase in accumulated depreciation typically signifies an increase in depreciation expense).

Some questions may require you to solve for net income (ie, beginning and ending retained earnings and dividends declared may be provided). In these scenarios, creating a T-account may be helpful:

Retained Earnings

Dividends declared	2,000	5,000	Beginning balance
		?	Net income
		10,000	Ending balance

The T-account requires a credit of $7,000 to balance. Net income is $7,000 ($10,000 − $5,000 + $2,000).

The following is an example of a statement of cash flows:

Statement of Cash Flows	
Cash flows from **operating** activities	
Cash flows related to the production of income from continuing operations	
Net cash provided (used) by operating activities	$XXX
Cash flows from **investing** activities	
Cash flows from purchase and sale of long-term assets	
Net cash provided (used) by investing activities	XXX
Cash flows from **financing** activities	
Cash flows from issuance and repayment of debt and from transactions with owners	
Net cash provided (used) by financing activities	XXX
Net increase or decrease in cash	$XXX
Beginning cash balance	XXX
Ending cash balance	$XXX

Note: Beginning and ending cash balances include cash equivalents.

The net increase or decrease in cash calculated on the SCF must explain the difference between the beginning cash balance and ending cash balance. That is,

Net increase (or decrease) in cash during the year
± Beginning cash per balance sheet
Ending cash per balance sheet

Required Disclosures

Under the indirect method, the following must be disclosed:

- Cash payments for interest and income taxes
- Noncash investing and financing activities, such as converting debt to equity, exchanging one long-term asset for another long-term asset, noncash portion of an investing or financing activity
- Reconciliation of the change in cash presented on the SCF to the components of cash presented on the balance sheet
- Cash equivalents policy
- Restrictions on cash and cash equivalents

Companies are **not permitted** to disclose the cash flow per share, as it could be misinterpreted by financial statement users as an amount that could be paid out in dividends.

Detecting, Investigating, and Correcting Discrepancies

Representative Task (Application): Adjust a statement of cash flows to correct identified errors.

Representative Task (Analysis): Detect, investigate and correct discrepancies while agreeing the statement of cash flows amounts to supporting documentation, including the source data.

Example

The controller of Ruiz Co. has reviewed the draft SCF and believes it has several errors. The draft SCF, along with additional information, is provided in the exhibits below. While the draft SCF contains errors, the additional information and other exhibits are correct.

In the table below, input the correct amount for cash flows from operating, investing, and financing activities. For net cash inflow, use a positive whole number. For net cash outflow, use a negative whole number.

Exhibit 1

Ruiz Company
Draft Statement of Cash Flows
For the year ended December 31, Year 2

Cash flows from operating activities:	
Net income	790,000
Depreciation expense	–
Gain on sale of AFS debt securities	(35,000)
Increase in inventory	80,000
Decrease in accounts payable	(5,000)
Net cash provided (used) by operating activities	830,000
Cash flows from investing activities:	
Proceeds from sale of building	350,000
Payment for plant asset purchased	(700,000)
Net cash provided (used) by investing activities	(350,000)
Cash flows from financing activities:	
Proceeds from stock issuance	220,000
Proceeds from sale of AFS debt securities	135,000
Cash dividends paid	(340,000)
Proceeds from short-term bank loan	325,000
Net cash provided (used) by financing activities	340,000
Net increase (decrease) in cash	**820,000**
Cash balance at January 1, Year 2	530,000
Cash balance at December 31, Year 2	1,350,000*

** The ending cash balance calculated on the draft SCF does not tie to the ending cash balance per the balance sheet. When errors are corrected, ending cash balances will tie.*

Exhibit 2

Ruiz Company
Comparative Balance Sheet
December 31, Year 1 and Year 2

	Year 2	Year 1	Increase (Decrease)
Assets			
Cash	840,000	530,000	310,000
Accounts receivable, net	100,000	100,000	–
Inventory	540,000	460,000	80,000
Long-term investments	1,500,000	1,600,000	(100,000)
PP&E	4,100,000	3,400,000	700,000
Accumulated depreciation	(1,200,000)	(1,200,000)	–
Total assets	5,880,000	4,890,000	990,000
Liabilities			
Accounts payable	170,000	175,000	(5,000)
Dividends payable	400,000	240,000	160,000
Short-term bank debt	325,000	–	325,000
Long-term debt	400,000	400,000	–
Total liabilities	1,295,000	815,000	480,000
Shareholders' equity			
Common stock, $10 par	700,000	600,000	100,000
APIC	820,000	700,000	120,000
Retained earnings	3,065,000	2,775,000	290,000
Total shareholders' equity	4,585,000	4,075,000	510,000
Total liabilities & shareholders' equity	5,880,000	4,890,000	990,000

Additional information, during Year 2, is as follows:

- Net income was $790,000
- Long-term investments in AFS debt securities were sold for $135,000. There were no other transactions affecting long-term investments
- Cash dividends of $500,000 were declared
- 10,000 shares of common stock were issued for $22 per share
- Two property, plant, and equipment transactions occurred:
  - A building with an original cost of $600,000 and a carrying amount of $350,000 was sold for $350,000
  - A plant asset was purchased

	Section	Amount
1	Net cash flow provided (used) by operating activities	
2	Net cash flow provided (used) by investing activities	
3	Net cash flow provided (used) by financing activities	

Solution

	Section	Amount
1	Net cash flow provided (used) by operating activities	920,000
2	Net cash flow provided (used) by investing activities	(815,000)
3	Net cash flow provided (used) by financing activities	205,000

We will use the approach of correcting the draft statement of cash flows line by line.

Operating activities

Net income of $790,000 provided in the additional information reconciles to the draft SCF. No adjustment is needed.

Depreciation expense adjustment is listed as zero. According to the balance sheet, accumulated depreciation did not change. However, we cannot assume that this means no depreciation expense was incurred. According to the additional information, a building costing $600,000 with a carrying amount of $350,000 (ie, accumulated depreciation of $250,000) was sold. When the asset was removed from the company's books, accumulated depreciation decreased by $250,000. Therefore, depreciation expense must have also been $250,000 ($1,200,000 − $1,200,000 + $250,000).

Items on the income statement that relate to accrual concepts (eg, gains, losses, depreciation expense) often do not have an impact on cash. Depreciation expense does not result in the use of any cash but was deducted to arrive at net income. Therefore, depreciation expense is added back to net income to arrive at operating cash flows.

Accumulated Depreciation

Sale of building	250,000	1,200,000	Beginning balance
		?	Depreciation expense
		1,200,000	Ending balance

This $250,000 should be added back to net income.

Gain on sale of AFS debt securities is listed as a subtraction for $35,000. According to the additional information, the AFS debt security was sold for $135,000, and no other transactions affecting long-term investments occurred. The long-term investment account on the balance sheet decreased by $100,000. Therefore, the following journal entry must have been recorded:

Account	Debit	Credit
Cash	135,000	
Gain on sale of investment		**35,000**
Long-term investments		100,000

The gain of $35,000 is correct. Although the sale involves cash, the cash proceeds from the sale are an investing activity, not operating. Additionally, the gain itself has no impact on cash. Since the gain increased net income but did not impact cash, it must be reversed out of (ie, subtracted from) net income. No adjustment is needed.

Increase in inventory is listed as an addition of $80,000. According to the balance sheet, inventory increased by $80,000. However, increases in current assets should be subtracted from net income. Consider the idea of sources and uses of cash. Increasing (ie, buying) inventory *uses* cash, so it requires a negative adjustment to net income. **The $80,000 should be *subtracted* from net income, rather than added.**

Decrease in accounts payable is listed as a subtraction of $5,000. According to the balance sheet, accounts payable decreased by $5,000. Decreases in current liabilities should be subtracted from net income. Decreasing (ie, paying off) accounts payable *uses* cash, so it requires a negative adjustment to net income. No adjustment is needed.

Investing activities

Proceeds from the sale of the building are listed as $350,000. According to the additional information, a building costing $600,000 with a carrying amount of $350,000 was sold for $350,000. The sale of a building is a source of cash, so it should be added on the SCF. The sale of a building is an investing activity and is reported in the correct amount. No adjustment is needed.

Payment for the plant asset purchased is listed as $700,000. According to the balance sheet, during the year, plant assets increased by $700,000. However, plant assets were reduced when the building was sold in the previous entry by $600,000. The sale of the building and purchase of plant asset were the only purchases/disposals of PP&E during the year. This means that the plant asset purchase must have totaled $1,300,000 ($4,100,000 − $3,400,000 + $600,000). Acquisition of a building uses cash, so it should be subtracted on the SCF.

PP&E

Beginning balance	3,400,000		
Purchase of plant asset	?	600,000	Sale of building
Ending balance	4,100,000		

Payment for the plant asset purchased should be listed as $1,300,000.

Financing activities

Proceeds from stock issuance are listed as $220,000. According to the additional information, 10,000 shares of common stock were issued for $22 per share. The issuance of stock is a *source* of cash, so it should be added on the SCF. The issuance of common stock is a financing activity and is reported in the correct amount. No adjustment is needed.

Proceeds from sale of AFS debt securities are listed as $135,000. This line relates to the "gain on sale of AFS securities" item in the operating activities section. As calculated above, the proceeds are listed in the correct amount. The sale of a long-term investment is a *source* of cash, so it should be added on the SCF. However, sale of an investment is an *investing* activity, not a financing activity. **This item should be moved from the financing section to the investing section.**

Cash dividends paid is listed as $340,000. According to the additional information, $500,000 of dividends were declared during the year. According to the balance sheet, dividends payable only increased by $160,000. This means that $340,000 of the dividends declared must have been paid. Dividends paid are a use of cash, so they should be subtracted on the SCF. No adjustment is needed.

Dividends Payable

		240,000	Beginning balance
Dividends payable	?	500,000	Dividends declared
		400,000	Ending balance

$340,000 of dividends were paid ($500,000 + $240,000 − $400,000).

Proceeds from short-term bank loan are listed as $325,000. This means that the company borrowed $325,000 from the bank. Borrowing from a bank is a *source* of cash, so it should be added on the SCF. This is correctly reflected in the draft SCF. No adjustment is needed.

Corrected statement of cash flows

A blank SCF is provided first. Fill in the blank statement below for extra practice. The completed corrected SCF then follows. Lines that required adjustment are reflected in orange text.

Ruiz Company
Corrected Statement of Cash Flows
For the year ended December 31, Year 2

Cash flows from operating activities:	
Net income	
Depreciation expense	
Gain on sale of AFS debt securities	
Increase in inventory	
Decrease in accounts payable	
Net cash provided (used) by operating activities	
Cash flows from investing activities:	
Proceeds from sale of building	
Proceeds from sale of AFS debt securities	
Payment for plant asset purchased	
Net cash provided (used) by investing activities	
Cash flows from financing activities:	
Proceeds from stock issuance	
Cash dividends paid	
Proceeds from short-term bank loan	
Net cash provided (used) by financing activities	
Net increase (decrease) in cash	
Cash balance at January 1, Year 2	
Cash balance at December 31, Year 2	

Ruiz Company
Corrected Statement of Cash Flows
For the year ended December 31, Year 2

Cash flows from operating activities:	
Net income	790,000
Depreciation expense	250,000
Gain on sale of AFS debt securities	(35,000)
Increase in inventory	(80,000)
Decrease in accounts payable	(5,000)
Net cash provided (used) by operating activities	920,000
Cash flows from investing activities:	
Proceeds from sale of building	350,000
Proceeds from sale of AFS debt securities	135,000
Payment for plant asset purchased	(1,300,000)
Net cash provided (used) by investing activities	(815,000)
Cash flows from financing activities:	
Proceeds from stock issuance	220,000
Cash dividends paid	(340,000)
Proceeds from short-term bank loan	325,000
Net cash provided (used) by financing activities	205,000
Net increase (decrease) in cash	310,000
Cash balance at January 1, Year 2	530,000
Cash balance at December 31, Year 2	840,000*

** The adjusted ending cash balance calculated ties to the ending cash balance per the balance sheet.*

1.07 Consolidated Financial Statements

Overview

Representative Task (Application): Prepare consolidated financial statements (adjustments and/or eliminations) from supporting documentation.

Consolidated financial statements (F/S) are required when one entity has effective control over another entity. **Effective control** is usually present when one of the following conditions applies:

- One entity has a *controlling interest* over another. Here, an entity (investor/parent/acquirer) has a greater than 50% ownership (directly or indirectly) of another entity (investee/subsidiary/acquiree) and, therefore, can direct the activities of the investee/subsidiary/acquiree
- An entity (variable-interest holder) is the principal beneficiary of a variable-interest entity

According to the AICPA exam blueprint, variable-interest entities are now tested in the BAR exam. As such, information on variable-interest entities can be found in the BAR text.

In either of the above cases, the entities are separate legal entities but are under **common economic control**. The shareholders of the parent entity control that entity, which, in turn, has control of the subsidiary (sub) entity. Because the entities are under common economic control, GAAP requires **consolidated F/S**.

Consolidated F/S present the financial information of two or more separate legal entities, usually a parent company and one or more of its subs, as though they were a single economic entity. The consolidating process is the sequence of steps or activities carried out in order to combine the financial information of two or more entities. The consolidating process results in consolidated F/S.

Consolidated Financial Statements

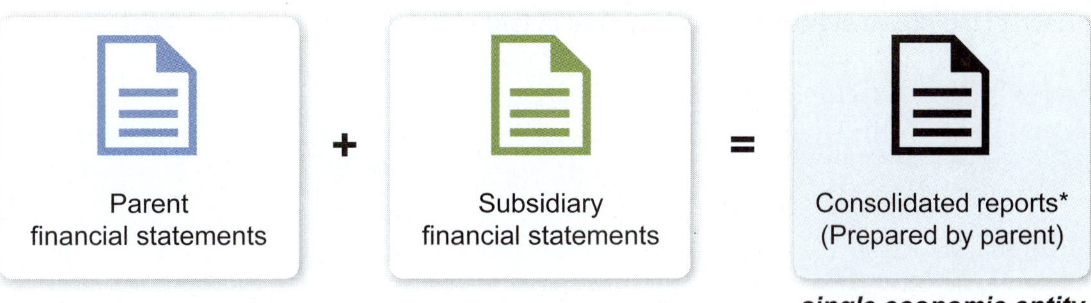

**Adjusted for consolidation eliminations*

If an investor has majority ownership of an investee (ie, greater than 50% of the voting stock of the investee) but is prevented from exercising that majority ownership to control the financial and operating policies or activities of the sub, it will not consolidate the sub. Effective control may be lacking (even for a majority-owned sub) if one of the following conditions applies:

- A foreign sub is largely controlled by the foreign government through prohibition on paying dividends, control of day-to-day operations, or other impediments to control
- A domestic sub is in bankruptcy and under the control of the courts

A parent records a sub on its books as an investment. A parent may carry its investment in a sub that will be consolidated on its books using the cost method, equity method, or any other method it chooses. Because the investment in sub accounts will be eliminated in consolidation, it does not matter which method the parent uses for internal recording.

The consolidating process is carried out on a **consolidating worksheet**, not on the books of any entity. The basic information for the worksheet comes from the account balances of the separate entities. The consolidating process is primarily concerned with adjusting and eliminating those balances to develop information that would report the separate entities as though they were a single entity.

The basic sequence of steps in carrying out the consolidating process are as follows:

Although the general process is the same for carrying out all consolidating processes, the specific adjustments, eliminations, and related amounts depend on the specific circumstances. The following alternatives will affect the specific adjustments and eliminations made during the consolidating process:

- Whether the consolidating process is being carried out at the date of the business combination or at a subsequent date
- Whether the parent owns 100% (all) of the voting stock of a sub or less than 100% of the voting stock
- Whether the parent carries its investment in a sub on its books using the cost or equity method of accounting
- Whether transactions between the affiliated entities (parent and its subs) originate with the parent or with a sub

Each of the above alternatives is discussed in further detail in the following pages.

Consolidation Concepts

Preparing consolidated F/S involves a process in which the following occur:

- The investment account is eliminated, as are the sub's equity accounts
- Those assets and liabilities that were part of the original acquisition and are still on the books will be adjusted for differences between their CV and FV on the acquisition date
- The income statement effects of differences between CV and FV will be recognized in income to the extent that they apply to the current period and to retained earnings to the extent that they apply to prior periods
- The noncontrolling interest (discussed below) will be recorded in equity based on the FV on the date of acquisition adjusted for changes due to income or distribution since that date
- The effects of intercompany transactions are eliminated

Business Combination

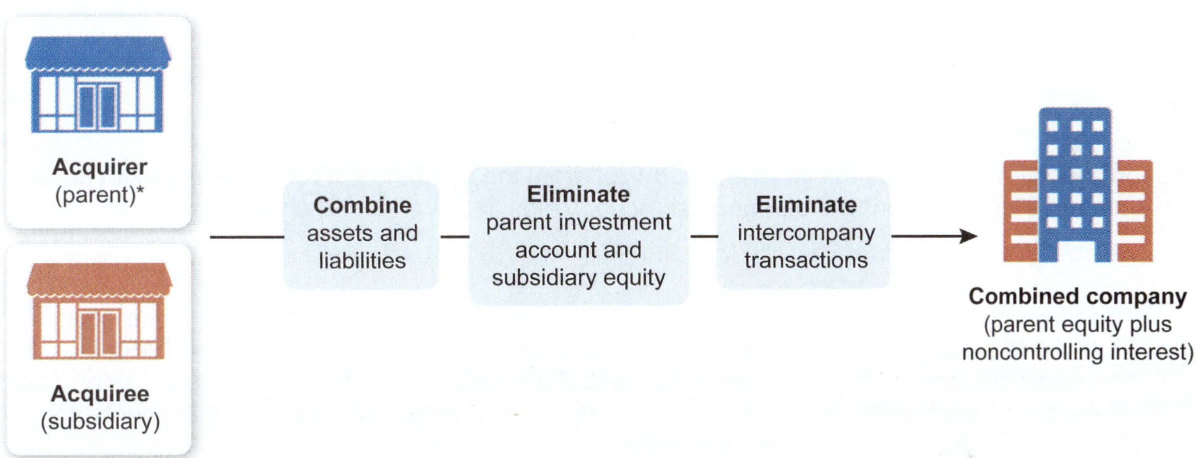

Includes equity issued to purchase acquiree

Immediately following an acquisition, the consolidated balance sheet will be different from the parent's (acquiring entity's) F/S. At the date of the combination, a consolidated balance sheet will "combine" the assets, liabilities, and shareholder claims (majority and noncontrolling, if any) of the parent and its newly acquired sub (or subs).

However, at the date of combination, a consolidated income statement, statement of retained earnings, or statement of cash flow would be the same as the statements of the parent entity. This is because there will not yet have been any activity including the sub.

At the date of combination, the method the parent will use to account for the investment in the sub (cost, equity, or other) is not a consideration—that is, there is no "carrying" period yet.

After the date of acquisition, activity involving the sub has probably occurred. As such, the parent company will account for its investment in the sub using either the *equity method* or the *cost method*. Remember that the parent's stand-alone F/S are not GAAP compliant because the parent must consolidate all subs under its control. In order to consolidate a parent and sub, we must first understand how the parent accounted for the investment in the sub (ie, the sub's activity), because upon consolidation, the investment in the sub account is *eliminated*.

Parent Uses the Equity Method

If the equity method is used to carry the investment in the sub, the parent will **adjust on its books the carrying value (CV) of its investment in the sub** to reflect the following:

- The parent's share of the sub's income or loss:

Investment in sub (B/S)	XXX	
Equity in earnings (I/S)		XXX

- The parent's share of dividends declared by the sub:

Dividends receivable/cash (B/S)	XXX	
Investment in sub (B/S)		XXX

- The amortization (ie, depreciation) of any difference between the fair value (FV) of identifiable assets and the CV of those assets. Assuming that FV is greater than CV:

Equity in earnings (I/S)	XXX	
Investment in sub (B/S)		XXX

The amortization entry reduces the income recognized from the sub (and the related investment increase) by the amount of "depreciation" the parent must recognize on its FV greater than CV.

Consolidations involve adjusting and eliminating accounts initially recorded using the equity method of accounting. The equity method of accounting is covered further in the FAR Investments chapter. If you are unfamiliar with the equity method of accounting, consider reading the relevant sections of the Investments chapter first to understand how these accounts are initially recorded before they are eliminated in consolidation.

Passing Company (P) purchased 100% of Score Company (S) for $200,000 on January 1, Year 2. On that date, the $150,000 CV of S equaled the FV of all of S's assets and liabilities except for equipment, which had an FV of $100,000 and CV of $80,000. Any additional excess purchase price is attributed to goodwill. The equipment has a remaining life of four years. S earned $50,000 in net income during the year.

A decomposition of the purchase price is as follows:

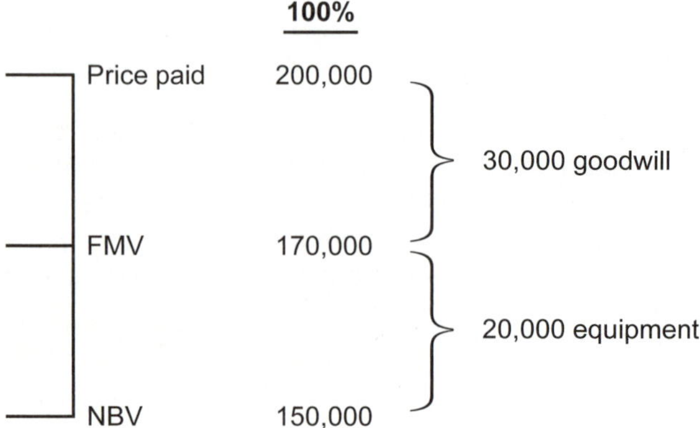

Under the equity method, an investment in a sub is reported in a single line (initially at cost) on the parent's balance sheet. At acquisition, the parent will *not* record any impact from the identified basis differences or equity method goodwill on its balance sheet.

The parent will track goodwill, basis differences, and the impact on equity earnings in future periods. Then, when the parent and sub are consolidated, these items will be recorded in the consolidated F/S.

The T-accounts for the equity method accounting recorded by P are as follows:

Investment in S

Cost 200,000	0 Dividends
P's share of S's net income 50,000	5,000 Depreciation of equipment ($20,000 / 4 yr)
Ending balance 245,000	

Equity in earnings from S

Depreciation of equipment 5,000	
	50,000 P's share of S's net income
	45,000 Ending balance

These T-accounts reflect the balances actually recorded at acquisition and subsequent to acquisition on the parent's books.

Remember that, although goodwill and excess FV over CV of net assets is noted at the acquisition date, it is only *recorded* in the consolidated F/S (not on the parent's books).

Parent Uses the Cost Method

If the cost method is used to carry the investment in the sub, the parent will **not adjust** on its books the CV of its investment in the sub to reflect the following:

- The parent's share of the sub's income or loss
- The parent's share of dividends declared by the sub
- The amortization (ie, depreciation) of any difference between the FV of identifiable assets and the CV of those assets

However, the parent will **recognize** its share of dividends declared by the sub as **dividend income**:

Dividends receivable/cash (B/S)	XXX	
Dividend income (I/S)		XXX

The cost method of accounting is covered further in the FAR Investments chapter. If you are unfamiliar with the cost method of accounting, consider reading the relevant sections of the Investments chapter first to understand how these accounts are initially recorded before they are eliminated in consolidation.

Investment Elimination

Once the assets and liabilities of both entities are combined, investment accounts and intercompany transactions must be eliminated. Additionally, if the parent does not own 100% of the sub, noncontrolling interest (NCI) must be recorded. This section covers elimination of investment accounts; elimination of intercompany transactions and the addition of NCI are covered below.

Unless explicitly stated otherwise, the remainder of this chapter assumes that the parent uses the equity method to account for its investment in the sub.

The investment elimination entry is made to eliminate the adjusted investment in the sub account and the sub shareholders' equity. The following is a sample elimination entry assuming that the parent owns 100% of the sub:

Common stock (C/S) of sub	XXX	
Additional paid-in capital (APIC) of sub	XXX	
Retained earnings (RE) of sub	XXX	
Identifiable assets of sub (FV at acquisition)	XXX	
Goodwill (if purchase price > FV of net assets at acquisition)	XXX	
Identifiable liabilities of sub (FV at acquisition)		XXX
Investment in sub		XXX

The effects of this entry on the worksheet are the following:

- To eliminate the investment account of the parent and the shareholder equity accounts of the sub
- To adjust identifiable assets and liabilities of the sub to FV as of the date of the business combination
- To recognize goodwill, if any, as of the date of the business combination; goodwill would be recognized at the original amount by which the purchase price > FV of identifiable net assets acquired

Example: Consolidation at Acquisition

Pear Co. (P) acquired 100% of the stock of Strawberry Co. (S) in an acquisition on 12/31/Year 1 for a payment of $900 cash. At the time, the CV of S was $600, and all of the assets and liabilities had FV equal to their CV, with the exception of equipment with a remaining life of five years and a FV $100 higher than CV. P used the equity method to account for its investment in S. At 12/31/Year 1, S had the following equity balances:

- Common stock: $100
- APIC: $100
- Retained earnings: $400

Determine the entry that P would record to acquire the investment and to consolidate at 12/31/Year 1.

Purchase price		$900
FV	FV increment	$700
CV		$600

FV appreciation equipment $100

Accounts	P Co.	S Co.	Debits	Credits	Consolidated
Cash	100	100			200
Equipment	8,000	500	100[1]		8,600
Inv in S	900			900[3]	–
Goodwill			200[2]		200
$1 C/S	1,000	100	100[3]		1,000
APIC	3,000	100	100[3]		3,000
RE	5,000	400	400[3]		5,000

1 *For excess equipment FV over CV*

2 *To record goodwill ($900 purchase price – $700 FV)*

3 *Investment in sub accounts and sub's common stock, APIC, and retained earnings are eliminated*

To acquire investment (on parent's books):

Investment in sub	900	
Cash		900

To consolidate (on consolidating worksheet):

Common stock	100	
APIC	100	
Retained earnings	400	
Equipment	100	
Goodwill	200	
Investment in sub		900

Goodwill is the balancing entry in the above. It represents the excess of the $900 investment over the $700 FV of the net identifiable assets.

Notice that there is no amortization of the excess of FV over CV because the consolidation is occurring at acquisition. If the consolidation happened in a later period, amortization would be recorded on the excess of FV over CV. This is the case in the next example.

Example: Consolidation after Acquisition

Assume the same facts as the previous example. P acquired 100% of S on 12/31/Year 1 for $900 cash. Equipment with a five-year life had a FV exceeding CV by $100 on 12/31/Year 1. Goodwill was $200 on 12/31/Year 1.

However, now assume that the goodwill is believed to be impaired as of 12/31/Year 2 and, as a result, only worth $195. Income during Year 2 for P was $3,000 and for S was $150. P accounts for the investment under the equity method. Determine the entries on the consolidating worksheet at 12/31/Year 2.

Summary: Acquire 100% for $900 on 12/31/Year 1 and consolidate on 12/31/Year 2.

- Income during the year:
  - P: $3,000
  - S: $150
- Equipment useful life = five years
- Goodwill impaired by $5

First, P will adjust its investment in sub account on its books to reflect activity during the year:

To account for S's income under the equity method:

Investment in sub	150	
Equity in earnings (I/S)		150

To depreciate the equipment ($100 excess FV over CV / 5 years = $20/year):

Equity in earnings (I/S)	20	
Investment in sub		20

To record impairment of goodwill:

Equity in earnings	5	
Investment in sub		5

Investment

900	
150	20
	5
1,025	

The consolidating entry is as follows:

Common stock	100	
APIC	100	
Retained earnings (400 + 150 income)	550	
Equipment (100 − 20 depreciation)	80	
Goodwill (200 − 5 impairment)	195	
Investment in sub		1,025

Accounts	P Co.	S Co.	Debits	Credits	Consolidated
Cash	3,100	250			3,350
Equipment	8,000	500	80[1]		8,580
Inv in S	1,025			1,025[3]	–
Goodwill			195[2]		195
$1 C/S	1,000	100	100[3]		1,000
APIC	3,000	100	100[3]		3,000
RE	8,125	550	550[3]		8,125

1 *For excess equipment FV over CV, less depreciation on excess ($100 excess − $20 depreciation)*

2 *To record goodwill, less impairment on goodwill ($200 goodwill − $5 impairment)*

3 *Investment in sub accounts and sub's common stock, APIC, and retained earnings are eliminated*

In the earlier example, the retained earnings of P and S were $5,000 and $400, respectively. The retained earnings of both companies have changed, of course: P earned $3,000 from its separate operations, and S earned $150. P uses the equity method of accounting and has reported $125 equity in earnings of S (see journal entries above).

P's RE = $5,000 beginning + $3,000 income in Year 2 + $125 equity in earnings in Year 2 = $8,125

S's RE = $400 beginning + $150 income in Year 2 = $550

Consolidation When Parent Has Less than 100% Ownership

If the parent does not own 100% of the sub, **the noncontrolling interest** (NCI) must be determined and recognized in the consolidated F/S.

NCI is originally recognized at its **FV on the date of acquisition**. If the shares are traded in an active market, the per-share market value will be multiplied by the number of shares owned by others. If the shares are not traded in an active market, an alternative method will be applied in determining FV.

On the CPA exam, rather than providing the FV of the sub's shares, questions may require candidates to derive the initial NCI FV using the parent's purchase price. For example, if the parent paid $500,000 to acquire 80% of the sub, the initial NCI value may be calculated as follows:

Total value × 80% = $500,000

Total value = $625,000

NCI = $625,000 × 20% = **$125,000**

However, if the FV of the sub's shares is provided, it should be used to calculate NCI.

On the **consolidated balance sheet**, NCI will be recognized as a separate line item in the equity section. The NCI on the balance sheet is calculated as follows:

	Initial FV of NCI
±	NCI % share of sub's net income
−	NCI % share of sub's dividends
	Ending NCI recognized on balance sheet

The consolidated balance sheet **will still include 100% of the sub's assets and liabilities** (regardless of the parent's ownership percentage). NCI is presented separately on the balance sheet as a component in equity. In the consolidation entry, NCI is credited (to add it onto the consolidated balance sheet).

On the **consolidated income statement**, the *NCI percentage claim* to consolidated net income will be shown as a separate line item. The NCI on the income statement is calculated as follows:

	Sub's net income
×	NCI % share
	Net income attributable to NCI recognized on income statement

The consolidated income statement **will still include 100% of the sub's revenues and expenses**. The statement will then report net income attributable to NCI in a separate line to calculate net income attributable to the acquirer.

Pancake Co. (P) acquired 90% (10% noncontrolling interest) of the stock of Syrup Co. (S) in an acquisition on 12/31/Year 1 for a payment of $900 cash. At the date of acquisition, S Co. had 100 shares of stock outstanding with an FV of $8 per share. The CV of S was $600, and all of the assets and liabilities had FV equal to their CV, with the exception of equipment with a remaining life of five years and a FV $100 higher than CV. P uses the equity method to account for the investment. At 12/31/Year 1, S had the following equity balances:

- Common stock: $100
- APIC: $100
- Retained earnings: $400

Determine the entry that P would record to acquire the investment and to consolidate at 12/31/Year 1.

Purchase price	$900	
FV	$700	FV increment
CV	$600	

The FV of the noncontrolling interest at the date of acquisition is $80 (100 × $8 = $800 × 10%).

The calculation of goodwill is as follows:

	FV of consideration transferred (cost to the acquirer)	$ 900
+	FV of NCI	$ 80
(–)	FV of net identifiable assets of acquiree	$(700)
	Goodwill	$ 280

Accounts	P Co.	S Co.	Debits	Credits	Consolidated
Cash	100	100			200
Equipment	8,000	500	100[1]		8,600
Inv in S	900			900[3]	–
Goodwill			280[2]		280
$1 C/S	1,000	100	100[3]		1,000
APIC	3,000	100	100[3]		3,000
NCI				80[4]	80
RE	5,000	400	400[3]		5,000

1 For excess equipment FV over CV

2 To record goodwill

3 Investment in sub accounts and sub's common stock, APIC, and retained earnings are eliminated

4 NCI is recorded at its FV on the consolidated F/S

Keep in mind that the income reported for Year 1 will be the acquirer's income only, since purchases are accounted for prospectively, not retroactively. The acquiree's income (or 90% of it, in the case of a 90% purchase) is included from the date of purchase onward.

To acquire investment (on parent's books):

Investment in sub	900	
Cash		900

To consolidate (on consolidating worksheet):

Common stock	100	
APIC	100	
Retained earnings	400	
Equipment	100	
Goodwill	280	
Investment in sub		900
NCI		80

Notice that, even though P does not own 100% of S, 100% of S's common stock, APIC, and retained earnings are eliminated in consolidation.

The consolidation entry also records 100% of goodwill and 100% of excess FV over CV. In this, P's ownership percentage impacts the investment in sub and NCI accounts only.

When it comes to NCI, remember the following:

Consolidated Balance Sheet	Consolidated Income Statement
NCI = Initial % of FV + % of net income (or – % of net loss) – % of dividends	NCI = % of sub's net income
100% of sub's assets and liabilities are reported, NCI is reported in equity	100% of sub's revenues and expenses are reported, then NCI is subtracted to arrive at portion allocated to parent

Intercompany Transactions

The process of consolidation results in the presentation of a single set of F/S, which treats the acquirer and acquiree as a single entity. Since an entity cannot engage in business transactions with itself, adjustments will have to be made on the consolidating worksheet in order to **eliminate the effects of intercompany transactions**. Transactions between affiliated subs must be eliminated as well.

Consolidations

Intercompany transactions
(Eliminated)

Subsidiary company

Parent company

External company

Unrelated transactions
(Not eliminated)

In principle, an eliminating entry has a simple objective: to remove any evidence from the consolidated F/S that the event occurred. If a transaction produced a receivable and payable, the elimination would involve debiting the payable and crediting the receivable. If a transaction produced a revenue and expense account, the elimination would involve debiting the revenue and crediting the expense.

During the period, Company P, the parent company, provided services to its sub, Company S. Company S owed Company P $10,000 for those services at the end of the period. Determine the eliminating entry that would be recorded on the consolidating worksheet related to this transaction.

On Company P's books, a debit for receivable from S would be recorded for $10,000. On Company S's books, a credit for payable to P would be recorded for $10,000.

On the consolidating worksheet, the following eliminating entry would be required so that no intercompany receivable or payable will show on the consolidated F/S:

Payable to P	10,000	
Receivable from S		10,000

The entry is the opposite of what P and S have on their individual books.

There are, however, special complications associated with certain transactions, since some transactions often involve income on one side of the journal entry but not on the other (ie, sales of inventory). These can be exceptionally complicated when the income is being reported by the acquiree in cases where the acquirer owns less than 100% of the acquiree.

Questions about intercompany transactions on the CPA exam have consistently directed the candidate to ignore the noncontrolling interest (minority interest).

Intercompany Dividends

Dividends paid by the **sub to the parent** must be eliminated in a consolidation, since an entity cannot pay dividends to itself. If the parent is using the equity method, nothing must be removed on the balance sheet since the equity accounts of the sub and the investment in sub account are eliminated in the combining of equity. The only exception is if a dividend has been *declared but not yet paid*, in which case an elimination of the receivable and payable may be needed.

During the period, S, the sub, declared $15,000 in dividends to its parent, P. At the end of the period, these dividends have not yet been paid. Determine the eliminating entry that would be recorded on the consolidating worksheet related to the dividends.

When the receivable was declared:

P Would Have Recorded		
Dividend receivable from S	15,000	
Investment in S		15,000

S Would Have Recorded		
Retained earnings	15,000	
Dividend payable to P		15,000

Therefore, on the consolidating worksheet, the following eliminating entry would be required so that no intercompany receivable or payable will show on the consolidated F/S:

Dividend payable to P	15,000	
Dividend receivable from S		15,000

Retained earnings on S's books and investment in S on P's books will both be eliminated in consolidation. As such, these accounts do not require additional adjustment in the consolidating worksheet.

When the parent does not own 100% of the sub (ie, there is NCI), dividends payable to the noncontrolling shareholders are not eliminated, since they are actual amounts owed to outside entities.

If the acquirer uses the cost method for internal purposes, dividends will have an impact on the income statement as well (as dividends are considered to be income). The initial entries to record the dividends would be as follows:

On Parent's Books		
Cash	XX	
Dividend income		XX

On Sub's Books		
Retained earnings	XX	
Cash		XX

Here, the eliminating entry would be as follows:

Dividend income	XX	
Retained earnings		XX

These entries would only be reflected on a consolidated income statement and consolidated statement of retained earnings (not a consolidated balance sheet). Dividend income closes to retained earnings; therefore, if only a balance sheet is presented, the above entries are not needed, as they cancel each other out on the balance sheet anyway.

Dividends **paid by the acquirer** are not eliminated (except in the rare cases that the acquiree owns some stock in the acquirer, in which case that part is eliminated). As a result, once an acquisition has taken place, the consolidated statement of retained earnings will only report dividends paid by the *acquirer*. This is consistent with the fact that the equity accounts of the acquiree are eliminated in a consolidation.

Intercompany Sales of Inventory

Intercompany sales of inventory are the most common intercompany transactions. These sales have up to three effects on the F/S that may need to be eliminated:

- Sale vs. purchase
- Receivable vs. payable
- Profit in ending inventory

The following example illustrates elimination of intercompany sales of inventory.

On 1/1/Year 1, Panther Company purchases inventory from an outside supplier for $8,000. Panther then sells this inventory to Shark Company (one of Panther's subs) later in the year for $12,000. Shark has not yet paid Panther for the goods. Determine the elimination entries that should be recorded related to the intercompany sale in each of the following scenarios: (1) Shark does not sell any of the inventory; (2) Shark sells half of the inventory.

When Panther sold the goods to Shark:

Panther Would Have Recorded			**Shark Would Have Recorded**		
Accounts receivable	12,000		Inventory	12,000	
Sales		12,000	Accounts payable		12,000
Cost of goods sold	8,000				
Inventory		8,000			

Because Panther sold the goods to Shark at more than Panther's initial cost, the CV of the inventory to Shark includes an intercompany profit that must be eliminated for consolidated purposes.

In scenario 1, 100% of the inventory is still in Shark's ending inventory. The elimination of the intercompany sale/cost of goods sold (COGS) and profit in ending inventory is as follows:

Sales	12,000	
Cost of goods sold		8,000
Inventory		4,000

The sales line eliminates (reverses) the revenue on the transaction recorded by Panther. These goods were sold to a sub of Panther, so no revenue should be recorded in consolidation.

The COGS line eliminates the COGS that Panther initially recorded related to this inventory.

The inventory line eliminates the intercompany profit in inventory:

Selling price to Shark	$12,000
COGS to Panther	8,000
Intercompany profit initially in Shark's inventory	4,000

The $4,000 intercompany profit is baked into Shark's reported inventory (as Shark paid $4,000 more for the inventory than what it cost to Panther). Because none of the inventory has been sold, the intercompany profit is still all in Shark's ending inventory and must be reversed out.

In scenario 2, 50% of the inventory is still in Shark's ending inventory, and 50% has been sold. The elimination of the intercompany sale/COGS and profit in ending inventory is as follows:

Sales	12,000	
Cost of goods sold		10,000
Inventory		2,000

The sales line eliminates (reverses) the revenue on the transaction recorded by Panther. These goods were sold to a sub of Panther, so no revenue should be recorded in consolidation.

Using the same logic from the previous scenario, the single $10,000 COGS line can be broken out into as a credit to COGS for $8,000 (to remove Panther's initial COGS when the company sold the goods to Shark) and a credit to COGS for $2,000 (to remove the portion of intercompany profit that was included in Shark's COGS when the goods were sold to customers):

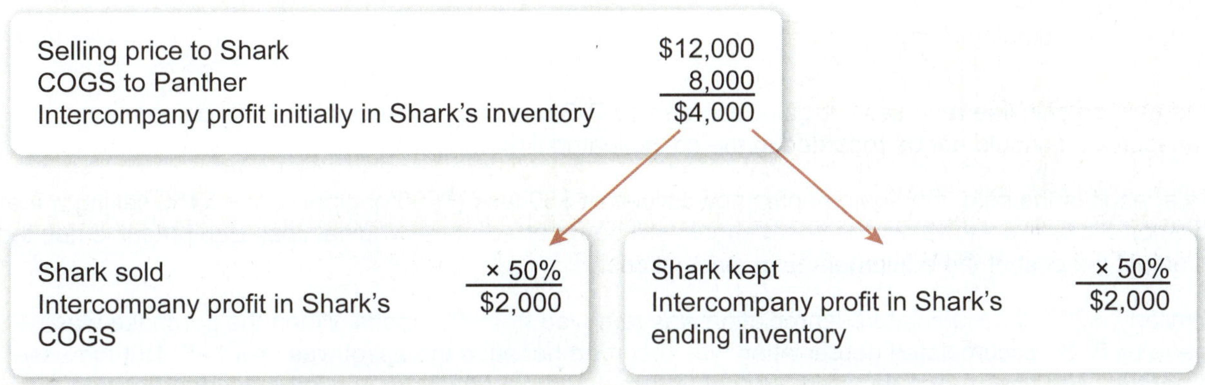

The inventory line eliminates the $2,000 intercompany profit in inventory (calculated above).

In both scenarios, since Shark has not yet paid Panther for the goods, the companies have a payable and a receivable recorded on their separate books, respectively. The elimination of the intercompany receivable-payable is as follows:

Accounts payable to Panther	12,000	
Accounts receivable from Shark		12,000

Intercompany Sales of PP&E

When one of the companies in a consolidated group sells a depreciable or amortizable asset to the other, two eliminations are probably needed:

1. Elimination of the gain on sale
2. Elimination on the additional depreciation or amortization resulting from the markup of the asset

The following example illustrates elimination of intercompany sales of PP&E.

On 1/2/Year 1, Parent (P) sells equipment with a $500 cost and $200 accumulated depreciation to one of its subs, S, for $450. On the date of sale, the asset has an estimated remaining life of five years. Determine the elimination entries that should be recorded related to the equipment sale.

When P sold the equipment to S:

P Would Have Recorded		
Cash	450	
Accumulated depreciation	200	
Equipment		500
Gain on sale		150

S Would Have Recorded		
Equipment	450	
Cash		450

To eliminate the changes that resulted from the sale itself, the following entry is made:

Gain on sale of equipment	150	
Equipment	50	
Accumulated depreciation		200

The gain on sale line reverses the gain recorded by P. Since this gain was on an intercompany transaction, it should not be recorded in the consolidated F/S.

As a result of the sale, the equipment is now valued at $50 less ($500 original cost − $450 selling price to S) on S's books. However, the asset should still be reported at the original cost. Equipment is debited to adjust the cost of the equipment to its original cost.

Similarly, $200 of accumulated depreciation was removed from P's books. When the purchase was made by S, $0 accumulated depreciation was recorded because the asset was new to S. But the asset is not new and has, in fact, incurred $200 of accumulated depreciation. Accumulated depreciation is credited for $200 to reflect this.

At year-end, S will have recorded $90 of depreciation expense on the equipment ($450 / 5 years). However, the depreciation expense is overstated by the intercompany profit (ie, gain) on the sale. S has calculated depreciation expense based on $450 equipment cost, but this $450 contains $150 of gain (excess that P charged S over the equipment's CV). The $150 gain will be reversed out of depreciation expense ratably over the remaining life of the asset at $30 per year. The entry to reverse depreciation in Year 2 is as follows:

Accumulated depreciation	30	
Depreciation expense		30

Intercompany Sale of Bonds

Bonds issued by one of the companies may be purchased by the other. These sales have up to three eliminations that may be needed:

- Investment in bonds vs. bonds payable
- Interest revenue vs. interest expense
- Accrued interest receivable vs. accrued interest payable

The following example illustrates elimination of intercompany sales of bonds.

South Dakota Co. issued 8% bonds to external parties at their $1,000 face value several years ago. On 12/31/Year 5, Pennsylvania Co. (South Dakota's acquirer) purchased all of the outstanding bonds on the open market for $900 plus accrued interest. The bonds pay interest annually on January 1. Determine the elimination entries that should be recorded related to the intercompany sale.

To eliminate the bond, the following entry is made:

Bond payable	1,000	
Investment in South Dakota's bonds		900
Gain on retirement		100

Notice that the purchase of the bond of one company by the other is treated as an early retirement, as it would have been had a single entity bought its own bond on the open market.

Since annual interest of $1,000 × 8% = $80 is due tomorrow, the acquirer must have paid $80 accrued interest on the purchase date, and this must be eliminated as well:

Accrued interest payable	80	
Accrued interest receivable		80

Summary

At a high level, if a worksheet is provided, the following is recorded:

- Eliminate investment in sub account (always zero at the end)
- Eliminate 100% of sub's equity (common stock, APIC, retained earnings)
- Set up NCI (adjust for percentage of income and dividends)
- Set up net assets excess FV over CV and record depreciation on excess FV over CV
- Record goodwill and impairment of goodwill
- Eliminate intercompany transactions
  - Receivables/payables
  - Dividends
  - Sales of inventory
  - Sales of PP&E
  - Sales of bonds

Pushdown Accounting Alternative

One of the more cumbersome aspects of preparing consolidated F/S is keeping track of the differences between the FV and CV of the acquiree's assets and liabilities at the acquisition date. Each period, until all of those items have been disposed of or settled, an adjustment will be required to recognize that difference as well as any depreciation, amortization, impairment, or other adjustment that would have been made to it since the date of acquisition.

GAAP provides an alternative in the form of pushdown accounting. When an acquiree decides to adopt pushdown accounting, it adjusts its assets and liabilities to the same amounts at which they will be reported by the acquirer and accounts for those assets and liabilities going forward on a basis similar to that which would be applied by the acquirer. As a result, the consolidation process is simplified, and the acquirer will only be required to eliminate inter-entity transactions, recognize the noncontrolling interest, and eliminate the investment account.

An acquiree is not required to adopt the pushdown basis of accounting but may decide to do so in any period in which there is a change in control event. If, for example, an investor with the ability to exercise significant influence over an investee acquires additional equity resulting in a controlling financial interest, the acquiree could adopt pushdown accounting in that period.

- An election to adopt pushdown accounting is irrevocable.
- If an entity does not elect to adopt pushdown accounting in the period of a change of control event, it may do so in a subsequent period and will account for the change as a change in accounting principle.

Measurement Period and Measurement Period Adjustments

In some circumstances, the acquirer may believe that the measurement of the FV of an acquiree, which is used to determine an appropriate acquisition price, is reliable, while the FV of some of the individual identifiable assets acquired and liabilities assumed could not be reliably determined on a timely basis.

If the acquirer is required to prepare consolidated F/S *prior* to being able to obtain a more accurate measurement, the following procedures will be applied:

- The asset or liability for which a reliable FV has not been determined will be recorded at management's *best estimate* based on information that is available, with that amount referred to as a "*provisional*" value
- As a result of using the provisional values, the amount reported as goodwill may be overstated or understated, depending on the overstatement or understatement of the assets and liabilities recorded at their provisional amounts
- Depreciation, amortization, interest income or expense, and other revenue and expense items that are affected by those values are recognized as if the provisional amounts are the actual FV, and the consolidated F/S are prepared accordingly

The entity then has one year from the date of acquisition, referred to as the *measurement period*, to obtain a more reliable measurement. If management is unable to do so, the provisional amounts are accepted as the actual amounts, and the items are accounted for as comparable items would be.

If, on the other hand, management can obtain a more reliable measurement, the following procedures will be followed:

- The assets or liabilities will be adjusted to the amounts that would have been their CV as of the balance sheet date if they had originally been recorded at their more reliable amounts
- The income statement effects that would have been affected by the change in CV will be recalculated as if the appropriate amount had been used on the date of acquisition

Detecting, Investigating, and Correcting Discrepancies

Representative Task (Application): Adjust consolidated financial statements to correct identified errors.

Representative Task (Analysis): Detect, investigate and correct discrepancies identified while agreeing the consolidated financial statement amounts to supporting documentation, including the source data.

The following task-based simulation (TBS) provides an example of detecting, investigating, and correcting discrepancies between a consolidation worksheet and supporting documentation.

Example

Poppy Company acquired 85% of Sunflower Company on December 31, Year 1. Poppy is preparing consolidated F/S for the year ended December 31, Year 1. Before creating the F/S, Poppy prepares a consolidating worksheet. Examine the consolidation worksheet and identify discrepancies between the worksheet and the information in the other exhibits provided.

Task

Using the consolidation worksheet and additional exhibits below, complete the following table.

- In column B, determine whether the corresponding adjustment reported in the "Adjustments" section of the consolidation worksheet is correct. If the adjustment on the worksheet is correct, select "Yes"; if the adjustment on the worksheet is incorrect, select "No"
- If the adjustment on the worksheet is *incorrect*:
  - In column C, enter the updated amount that the worksheet should report. Enter all amounts as positive whole numbers
  - In column D, select whether the updated adjustment should be in the debit or credit column on the worksheet
- If the adjustment on the worksheet is *correct*, leave the corresponding cells in columns C and D blank

	A	B	C	D
	Item	**Is the adjustment on the worksheet correct?**	**What is the amount that the worksheet should report in the "Adjustments" section?**	**Should the adjustment be in the debit or credit column?**
1	Inventory			
2	Machinery (net)			
3	NCI			
4	Goodwill			
5	Common stock			
6	Retained earnings			

Exhibits

Exhibit 1

Poppy Co. and Subsidiary
Consolidation Worksheet
As of December 31, Year 1

Accounts	Poppy Co.		Sunflower Co.		Adjustments		Consolidated	
	Debit (Dr)	Credit (Cr)	Debit (Dr)	Credit (Cr)	Debit (Dr)	Credit (Cr)	Debit (Dr)	Credit (Cr)
Cash	80,000		30,000				110,000	
Inventory	150,000		350,000				500,000	
Machinery (net)	430,000		80,000		70,000		580,000	
Investment in Sunflower	325,000					325,000		
Goodwill					55,000		55,000	
Current liabilities		150,000		110,000				260,000
Long-term debt		255,000		150,000				405,000
Common stock		280,000		140,000	140,000			280,000
Retained earnings		300,000		60,000	60,000			300,000
	985,000	**985,000**	**460,000**	**460,000**	**325,000**	**325,000**	**1,245,000**	**1,245,000**

Exhibit 2

MINUTES OF MEETING
BOARD OF DIRECTORS
POPPY COMPANY

January 10, Year 2

ITEM 3. ACQUISITION OF SUNFLOWER CO.

On December 31, Year 1, Poppy acquired 85% of Sunflower Company for $325,000. On the date of acquisition, Sunflower had 100,000 shares of stock outstanding at a price of $3.50 per share. The board believes that this acquisition will create synergies through more efficient operations. The acquisition aligns with the company's growth strategy going into Year 2.

Exhibit 3

Sunflower Company **Balance Sheet** *For the period ended December 31, Year 1*	
Cash	30,000
Inventory	350,000
Machinery	80,000
Total assets	460,000
Current liabilities	110,000
Long-term debt	150,000
Total liabilities	260,000
Common stock and APIC	140,000
Retained earnings	60,000
Total stockholders' equity	200,000
Total liabilities and stockholders' equity	460,000

Exhibit 4

From: Kimberly, Controller
To: Timothy, Accounting Manager
Sent: January 12, Year 2
Subject: Acquisition of Sunflower Company

Hello Timothy,

I received updates regarding the 12/31 acquisition of Sunflower Company. On the date of acquisition, the fair value of Sunflower's machinery was determined to be $150,000. All other assets and liabilities had fair values equal to their carrying values.

Additionally, on the date of acquisition, Poppy sold inventory to Sunflower for $14,000 at a profit margin of 40%. Sunflower has not sold any of this inventory yet. This transaction was recorded on Poppy's and Sunflower's books at December 31.

Please ensure that the above information is accounted for in consolidation. Let me know if you have any questions.

Kimberly

Solution

	A	B	C	D
	Item	**Is the adjustment on the worksheet correct?**	**What is the amount that the worksheet should report in the "Adjustments" section?**	**Should the adjustment be in the debit or credit column?**
1	Inventory	No	$5,600	Credit

The inventory intercompany transaction must be eliminated in consolidation. According to the email from the controller, on the date of acquisition, Poppy sold inventory to Sunflower for $14,000. The profit margin on the inventory was 40%. If 40% of the selling price is profit margin, the remaining 60% of the selling price is COGS. This means that the goods cost Poppy $8,400 ($14,000 × 60%).

In the consolidation worksheet, Poppy's $14,000 of revenue received from Sunflower and Poppy's $8,400 of COGS should be eliminated. By selling the inventory to Sunflower, $5,600 of intercompany profit was earned (the inventory was sold for $14,000 to Sunflower when it only cost $8,400 to Poppy). The intercompany profit on the sale must be eliminated as well.

Since Sunflower has not sold the related goods yet, all of the intercompany profit is still in Sunflower's inventory. Therefore, $5,600 must be reversed out of Sunflower's inventory. If Sunflower has not paid Poppy for the goods yet, an intercompany receivable and payable would need to be eliminated as well. The journal entry to record the inventory side of the elimination is as follows:

Sales	14,000	
Cost of goods sold		8,400
Inventory		5,600

2	Machinery (net)	Yes		

In consolidation, a sub's assets should be recorded at their FV on the date of acquisition. According to the email from the controller, on the date of acquisition, all assets and liabilities had FV equal to their CV, except for machinery. The FV of machinery was $150,000. According to Sunflower's balance sheet, the CV of machinery was $80,000. Therefore, machinery should be written up (debited) for $70,000 on the consolidation worksheet ($150,000 − $80,000). This is accurately recorded on the consolidation worksheet. No change is needed.

3	NCI	No	52,500	Credit

NCI is missing on the consolidation worksheet. Because Poppy did not acquire 100% of Sunflower, NCI should be recorded.

NCI is initially recorded at its FV. According to the excerpt from the board meeting minutes, on the date of acquisition, Sunflower had 100,000 shares of stock outstanding at $3.50 per share. Therefore, the total FV of Sunflower on the acquisition date was $350,000 (100,000 shares × $3.50 per share). Poppy only acquired 85%. As such, 15% of the FV must be allocated to NCI. NCI is $52,500 ($350,000 × 15%). NCI is an equity account; therefore, it is recorded with a credit.

4	Goodwill	No	107,500	Debit

In consolidation, goodwill should be recorded for the excess of the acquirer's purchase price and the FV of NCI over the FV of net assets.

The FV of Sunflower's net assets is as follows:

CV of assets (per balance sheet)	$460,000
FV adjustment for machinery (see line 2 explanation)	70,000
FV of assets	530,000
FV of liabilities (per balance sheet, equal to CV)	(260,000)
FV of net assets	$270,000

Therefore, goodwill is calculated as follows:

	Poppy's purchase price (per board meeting minutes)	$325,000
+	FV of NCI (see line 3 explanation)	52,500
(–)	FV of net assets of acquiree	(270,000)
	Goodwill	$107,500

Goodwill is an asset, so this $107,500 should be recorded in the debit column on the consolidation worksheet.

5	Common stock	Yes		

In consolidation, the investment in the sub and the sub's equity accounts are eliminated. Here, Sunflower's common stock is debited for $140,000 to eliminate it in consolidation. This is correct. No change is needed.

6	Retained earnings	No	65,600	Debit

The inventory intercompany transaction will have an impact on retained earnings. Per the journal entry in the line 1 explanation, as a result of the transaction, sales is debited for $14,000, and COGS is credited for $8,400. The net impact is a $5,600 credit to net income. As net income closes to retained earnings, retained earnings should be credited for $65,600 total ($60,000 initial value + $5,600 adjustment for intercompany transaction).

Poppy's adjusted consolidation worksheet is as follows. Necessary changes from above are displayed in orange text:

Poppy Co. and Subsidiary
Updated Consolidation Worksheet
As of December 31, Year 1

Accounts	Poppy Co.		Sunflower Co.		Adjustments		Consolidated	
	Debit (Dr)	Credit (Cr)	Debit (Dr)	Credit (Cr)	Debit (Dr)	Credit (Cr)	Debit (Dr)	Credit (Cr)
Cash	80,000		30,000				110,000	
Inventory	150,000		350,000			5,600	494,400	
Machinery (net)	430,000		80,000		70,000		580,000	
Investment in Sunflower	325,000					325,000		
Goodwill					107,500		107,500	
Current liabilities		150,000		110,000				260,000
Long-term debt		255,000		150,000				405,000
Common stock		280,000		140,000	140,000			280,000
Retained earnings		300,000		60,000	65,600			294,400
NCI						52,500		52,500
	985,000	**985,000**	**460,000**	**460,000**	**383,100**	**383,100**	**1,291,900**	**1,291,900**

1.08 Notes to the Financial Statements

Overview

The purpose of **financial statements** (F/S) is to give users information for making decisions. However, not all relevant information can be presented directly in the statements. Therefore, GAAP requires that F/S be **accompanied by informative disclosures** (ie, F/S notes) that provide more detail about the amounts presented and help users interpret and understand the F/S.

These disclosures are an **integral part** of the **F/S** and provide additional information; they do *not* duplicate material already included in the statements. Summaries of the major required financial report disclosures follow.

Financial Statement Note Disclosures	
Characteristics	• Required by GAAP • Integral part of the financial statements (F/S) ○ Assists users in understanding and interpreting the F/S
Examples	• Summary of significant accounting policies • Long-term obligations • Related party transactions • Contingencies • Subsequent events

Summary of Significant Accounting Policies

The first footnote is typically a **summary of significant accounting policies** (ie, the principles and methods chosen by management where GAAP allows a choice). This disclosure is required because users' understanding of F/S amounts is greatly facilitated by knowing the methods used in preparing the statements.

This footnote typically includes information about the following:

Summary of Significant Accounting Policies	
Purpose	**Examples**
Identify accounting principles used (where GAAP allows alternatives) and the methods of applying those principles	• Revenue recognition policies • Inventory costing system (eg, FIFO, LIFO) • Depreciation method (eg, straight-line, sum-of-the-years' digits) • Long-term contract accounting (eg, over time, at a point in time) • Criteria for classification of investments (eg, cash equivalents, trading securities) • Basis of consolidation

This summary must include information about all significant accounting policies but is not required in interim statements if the policies have not changed.

In addition to the summary of significant accounting policies, the other footnotes must contain all the other relevant information that investors and creditors may find useful. Examples of this information include disclosures related to the following:

- Related party transactions (related parties include a parent and its subsidiaries, subsidiaries of a common parent, a firm and its principal owners and management and members of their immediate families, a firm and its equity-method investees, and others)
- Noncurrent liabilities
- Capital structure
- Contingent liabilities and gains
- Contractual obligations
- Material changes in account balances
- Errors and irregularities
- Illegal acts
- Governmental assistance

Management's Discussion and Analysis

Management's discussion and analysis (MD&A) is a narrative written by management. Although it is *not considered part of the footnotes*, it is nonetheless an important disclosure supplementing the F/S. Publicly held firms are required to include the MD&A in the annual report.

The MD&A provides management's discussion about the operations of the firm, its liquidity, and capital resources. It also includes additional discussion on management's view of the firm's financial condition, changes in financial condition, and results of operations through analysis of the F/S. The MD&A explains details on the effects of significant and unusual events as well.

The MD&A also provides forward-looking information not reflected in the F/S. This information includes management's general prognosis about future sales, effects of competition, and expected effects of general macroeconomic conditions. For example, the MD&A may discuss the possible effects of uncertainties on the firm's F/S.

Risks and Uncertainties

Information about the **risks and uncertainties** that a firm faces enhances F/S users' ability to predict the future cash flows and operations of the firm. GAAP requires certain information about risks and uncertainties to be disclosed. The applicable accounting standard provides for selectivity whereby specified criteria are used to screen all the possible risks, so that the required disclosures are limited to matters that materially affect a particular entity.

The disclosures are primarily concerned with risks and uncertainties that could **materially affect F/S amounts within one year** of the date the F/S are issued (ie, in the near term). The required disclosures involve the following sources of risk and uncertainty:

- Nature of the entity's operations
- Use of estimates in financial statements
- Certain significant estimates

- Current vulnerability due to significant concentrations in certain aspects of operations
- The entity's ability to exist as a going concern

Each source is discussed in more detail below. The five areas are not mutually exclusive; rather, there may be some overlap.

Nature of Operations

Different types of businesses have different risks. Knowledge of the firm's **products and services**, **geographical locations, and principal markets** will assist users in assessing risks concerning the firm's operations. For example, this knowledge aids in identifying competition and understanding vulnerability to technological change.

The F/S and notes are required to include a description of the major products or services of the firm and its principal markets and their locations. If the firm operates in more than one type of business, the relative importance of the operations in each business is disclosed, along with the basis of this determination (eg, based on assets, revenues, or earnings). These disclosures are not required to be on a quantified basis; relative importance can be described in such terms as "major," "intermediate," "minor," and other similar ways.

Use of Estimates

A company must communicate the following:

- That the use of estimates is inescapable in preparing F/S that conform with GAAP
- That the use of estimates results in approximate amounts, not certainty
- That estimates involve assumptions about future events

The degree to which estimates can be relied on is affected by many factors including whether the business and economic environment is stable or unstable at the time. This area of disclosure reminds users that they should not place an unwarranted degree of reliability on the reported amounts in F/S.

Certain Significant Estimates

When estimates used to value assets, liabilities, or contingencies are **subject to a reasonable possibility of material change**, disclosures may be required. Disclosure about an estimate is required when information available before the F/S are issued or are available to be issued indicates that the following two criteria are met:

- It is at least reasonably possible that an estimate will change in the near term
- The effect of the change would be material
  - Materiality is based on the effect of using the new estimate on the F/S

The disclosures must include the following:

- The **nature** of the uncertainty that may cause an estimate to change and a statement that it is at least reasonably possible that a change in an estimate will occur in the near term. If the estimate concerns a *loss contingency*, the disclosure must also include an estimate of the possible loss or range of loss or state that such an estimate cannot be made
- The **estimated effect** of the change as of the date of the F/S

If the criteria above are not met because the firm uses a risk-reduction technique, the disclosures are encouraged but not required. The following are examples of assets and liabilities, related revenues and expenses, and disclosures of gain or loss contingencies that may be particularly sensitive to change in the near term:

- Inventory subject to obsolescence
- Equipment subject to technological obsolescence
- Deferred tax asset valuation allowances

- Capitalized software costs
- Environmental remediation obligations
- Litigation obligations

Significant Concentrations of Risk or Uncertainty

Susceptibility to risk and uncertainty increases when diversification is lacking (ie, when the firm has concentrations in various aspects of its business). Examples of concentrations include excessive reliance on one customer, having one product or service account for most of the firm's revenues, and reliance on one or a small number of suppliers.

The standard is concerned with "**severe impacts**" caused by **concentrations**. A severe impact is a significant financially disruptive effect on the normal functioning of the firm, where "severe" is greater than material but less than catastrophic. Bankruptcy, for example, would be considered catastrophic.

The standard applies only to the following defined set of four concentrations, rather than all possible concentrations:

- Concentrations in the volume of business with a particular customer, supplier, lender, grantor, or contributor. The loss of the relationship is an example of an event that could cause a severe impact. It is always at least reasonably possible to lose such a customer, grantor, or contributor, although the impact may not be severe
- Concentrations in revenue from specific products, services, or fund-raising sources. A price or demand change could cause a severe impact
- Concentrations in specific sources (suppliers) of services, materials, labor, licenses, or other rights used in operations. Losses of a key supplier or a patent are examples of events that could cause a severe impact
- Concentrations in the market or geographic area of operations. It is always at least reasonably possible that operations located outside the firm's home country will be disrupted in the near term

Disclosure of a concentration is required if all the following criteria are met. These concentrations are called **disclosable concentrations**:

- The concentration exists at the balance sheet date
- The entity is vulnerable to the risk of a near-term severe impact because of a concentration
- It is at least reasonably possible that events capable of causing a severe impact will occur in the near term (note: reasonably possible is less than probable)

For disclosable concentrations (those meeting the above criteria), the following is to be disclosed:

- The firm must disclose information adequate to inform users about the nature of the risk associated with the concentration
- For concentrations of labor subject to collective bargaining agreements, the firm must disclose the following:
  - The percentage of the labor force covered by the agreement
  - The percentage of the labor force covered by the agreement that will expire within one year
- For concentrations of operations located outside the entity's home country, the firm must disclose the carrying amounts of net assets and the geographic areas in which they are located

A public entity sells steel for use in construction. One of its customers accounts for 43% of sales, and another customer accounts for 40% of sales. Determine what the entity should disclose in its annual financial statements related to these two customers.

- The payment terms of accounts receivable due from each of the two customers
- The amount of the entity's revenue from each of the two customers
- The names of the two customers
- The financial condition of the two customers

Risks and Uncertainties Disclosures

- Nature of operations
- Use of estimates
- Certain significant estimates
- Current vulnerability associated with certain concentrations

GAAP requires notes disclosure of risks and uncertainties to help users understand limitations of the amounts (and additional information) shown in the F/S and ensure fair presentation.

In this scenario, the entity is vulnerable due to customer concentration, since 83% (43% and 40%) of revenues are from two customers. If either customer were to cease doing business with the entity, operations could be significantly impacted. Therefore, **amounts of revenue** from each customer are disclosed.

Customer payment terms affect cash flow but not sales revenues or the entity's overall risk. Customer names do not impact accounting information. The financial condition of significant customers may be disclosed, but only if there is a going concern risk to the reporting entity.

Management's Going Concern Assessment

Management must assess the entity's ability to continue as a **going concern**. Management's assessment should be based on facts and circumstances that are "known or reasonably knowable" as of the date the F/S are issued. Note that this assessment is not as of the balance sheet date but rather should include information up to the date that the financial statements are issued.

There is uncertainty regarding the entity's ability to meet maturing obligations if there is **substantial doubt** that the entity can meet its obligations as they become due. "Substantial doubt" means that it is probable that the entity will be unable to meet its obligations. "Probable" is the threshold associated with contingencies and is broadly interpreted to mean greater than 70% or 80% probability that the event will occur. The look-forward period for this assessment is **one year from the issuance of the F/S**.

Both quantitative and qualitative information should be considered when assessing the entity's ability to meet its obligations. The following information should be taken into consideration:

- The company's current financial condition, including its current liquid resources (eg, available cash or available access to credit)
- Conditional and unconditional obligations due or anticipated in the next year (whether or not they are recognized in the F/S)
- Funds necessary to maintain operations considering the company's current financial condition, obligations, and other expected cash flows in the next year

- Other conditions that could adversely affect the company's ability to meet its obligations in the next year (when considered in conjunction with the above), such as the following:
    - Negative financial trends (eg, recurring operating losses, working capital deficiencies, or negative operating cash flows)
    - Other indications of financial difficulties (eg, default on loans, denial of supplier credit, a need to restructure debt or seek new debt, noncompliance with statutory capital requirements, or a need to dispose of substantial assets)
    - Internal matters (eg, labor difficulties, substantial dependence on the success of a project, uneconomic long-term commitments, or a need to significantly revise operations)
    - External matters (eg, significant litigation; loss of a key customer, franchise, license, patent, or supplier; or an uninsured natural disaster)

Disclosures are required only when conditions give rise to substantial doubt about the entity's going concern. No disclosures are required if there are no going concern *uncertainties*. If the substantial doubt is alleviated because management developed a plan to mitigate the effects of the uncertainties, the disclosures are still needed, and the disclosures would include a description of management's plans to alleviate the substantial doubt. These disclosures include the following:

- The principal conditions that give rise to the uncertainties
- Management's evaluation of these conditions
- Management's plans to alleviate the substantial doubt

Disclosures for the Effect of Changing Prices

Accounting for the **effects of changing prices is optional**. When the client elects to present such data as supplementary information accompanying the basic F/S, it may present two different types of information:

- Current cost information
- Price-level adjusted data

To understand the effects of changing prices, it is important to distinguish monetary assets and liabilities from nonmonetary items.

- A **monetary** item is an asset or liability whose value is fixed in money terms. Examples include the following:
    - Cash
    - Accounts and notes receivable
    - Bond investments that will be held to maturity
    - Prepaid expenses
    - Accounts, notes, and bonds payable
- A **nonmonetary** item is one that does not guarantee a fixed amount of money being received or paid. Examples include the following:
    - Inventories
    - Plant and equipment
    - Intangibles
    - Marketable securities (including bonds that may be sold prior to maturity)

Current cost accounting reports assets on the balance sheet at **replacement cost**. In determining the replacement cost of fixed assets, the estimated cost of a used asset must be utilized. If this isn't available, the cost of a new asset may be adjusted for estimated depreciation.

A firm acquired a machine with a 10-year useful life and no expected salvage value on 1/1/Year 1 for $100,000, and it was being depreciated on a straight-line basis. At 12/31/Year 3, accumulated depreciation was $30,000, and book value was $70,000.

In determining the current cost of the machine, the client is unable to identify a price for a three-year-old machine, but the replacement cost for an identical new machine on 12/31/Year 3 was $120,000.

By applying the same depreciation approach, accumulated depreciation is estimated at $36,000 ($120,000 × [3 / 10]), and the current cost of the machine is reported at $84,000 ($120,000 − $36,000).

On the income statement, cost of sales is reported at the **average current cost of goods sold**.

Assume that the following historical information is available for FIFO calculation of cost of sales in Year 1:

	Units	Dollars
Beginning inventory	10	100
Purchases	40	440
Ending inventory	(20)	(280)
Cost of sales	30	260

The current cost of the inventory was $10 per unit at 1/1/Year 1 ($100 / 10 units) and $14 per unit at 12/31/Year 1 ($280 / 20 units), so the average current cost per unit was $12 ([$10 + $14] / 2). The average current cost of goods sold was $360 (30 units sold × $12 per unit).

Price-level adjusted numbers continue to carry assets at **historical cost**, but nonmonetary items are adjusted to reflect changes in the consumer price index.

Land was acquired in Year 1 at $500,000 when the price index was 1.00, and the price index at 12/31/Year 3 is 1.10. The land is carried on a price-level adjusted 12/31/Year 3 balance sheet at $550,000 (500,000 × [1.10 / 1.00]).

Monetary assets and liabilities are not adjusted for inflation, since they do not increase in value from it. Because these items' value does not increase, a purchasing power loss occurs when monetary assets are held, and a purchasing power gain occurs when monetary liabilities are held (since the failure of assets to increase in value is unfavorable but the failure of liabilities to increase is favorable).

To measure **purchasing power gains and losses**, the change in value that would have occurred on net monetary items if they had been *nonmonetary* is compared to the items' actual value. The calculation is being made of the gain or loss over the course of the year, so all amounts are adjusted to reflect the average price level for the year.

Price-Level Adjusted Inflation Impacts:	
Monetary **asset**	Purchasing power **loss**
Monetary **liability**	Purchasing power **gain**

A firm began the year with net monetary assets of $400,000 and ended the year with net monetary assets of $600,000. The price index at the beginning of the year was 1.00 and at the end of the year was 1.20, with an average of 1.10. Expressed in nominal dollars (ie, not adjusted for inflation), the change during the year can be summarized as follows:

Beginning	$400,000
Increase	200,000
Ending	$600,000

If all figures are adjusted to a common price level of 1.10 (the average for the year), then:

- Beginning net monetary assets are $440,000 ($400,000 × [1.10 / 1.00]).
- The increase (which occurred over the course of the year) is $200,000 ($200,000 × [1.10 / 1.10]). If the assets were nonmonetary and, therefore, their value changed from inflation, they would have been valued at $640,000 ($440,000 + $200,000).

However, ending net monetary assets are only valued at $550,000 ($600,000 × [1.10 / 1.20]). The amount needed to reconcile the balances is the **purchasing power loss**:

Beginning	$440,000
Increase	200,000
Subtotal	$640,000
Ending	(550,000)
Purchasing power loss	**$90,000**

The purchasing power loss to the company represents the difference between what the assets would have been worth if they had benefited from inflation ($640,000) and what they were actually worth ($550,000).

Detecting, Investigating, and Correcting Discrepancies

Representative Task (Application): Adjust the notes to the financial statements to correct identified errors and omissions.

Representative Task (Analysis): Compare the notes to the financial statements to the financial statements and supporting documentation, including the source data, to identify inconsistencies and investigate those inconsistencies.

Example

Doodle Co. is a public company in the U.S. that has prepared its F/S for the year ended December 31, Year 2. Doodle is reconciling the F/S to the notes to the F/S to identify and correct discrepancies, as appropriate.

Task

For each item listed in column A, use the exhibits to identify the appropriate course of action in column B. Options are listed in the menu below. These options can be used once, more than once, or not at all.

Select an Option Below:
Correct the financial statements only.
Correct the footnote disclosure only.
Correct both the financial statements and footnote disclosure.
Both the financial statements and the footnote disclosure are correct as is.

1	*A*	*B*
2	**Item**	**Required correction**
3	Inventory	
4	Land and buildings	
5	Summary of significant accounting policies	

Exhibits

Exhibit 1

Doodle Co.
Balance Sheet

	Year 2	Year 1
Current assets:		
Cash and cash equivalents	400,310	175,700
Accounts receivable	780,900	865,500
Inventory	199,700	252,100
Prepaid expenses	26,750	46,600
Total current assets	1,407,660	1,339,900
Fixed assets:		
Land and buildings, net	873,210	911,855
Plant and machinery, net	504,700	504,700
Total fixed assets	1,377,910	1,416,555
Total assets	**2,785,570**	**2,756,455**
Current liabilities:		
Accounts payable	615,290	848,000
Accrued and other liabilities	290,280	619,155
Total current liabilities	905,570	1,467,155
Long-term liabilities:		
Notes payable	1,173,000	1,049,000
Total liabilities	2,078,570	2,516,155
Stockholders' equity:		
Common stock (10,000 shares at $1 par)	10,000	10,000
Additional paid-in capital	40,000	40,000
Retained earnings	657,000	190,300
Total liabilities and equity	**2,785,570**	**2,756,455**

Exhibit 2

Excerpt from Notes on Inventory

Our inventories are stated on the FIFO method. The inventory balance at Year 1 and Year 2 consists of the following components:

December 31	Year 2	Year 1
Raw materials	56,900	50,650
Work in process	(10,340)	(15,220)
Finished goods	132,460	186,230
Inventories	179,020	221,660

Exhibit 3

Excerpt from Notes on Land and Buildings

The land and buildings balance at Year 1 and Year 2 consists of the following components:

December 31	**Year 2**			**Year 1**		
	Gross	Accumulated depreciation	Net	Gross	Accumulated depreciation	Net
Land	200,000		200,000	200,000		200,000
Buildings	750,500	75,050	675,450	750,500	37,525	712,975
	950,500	75,050	875,450	950,500	37,525	912,975

Exhibit 4

Fixed Assets Report

Account: 500 Land and Buildings Retrieval date: 12/31/Year 2

Asset	Description	In Service	Historical Cost/Basis	Method of Depr.	YTD Depr.	Total Depr.
A	Building - 15 YR DEPR	1/1/Year 1	250,200	SL	16,680	33,360
B	Building - 20 YR DEPR	1/1/Year 1	195,300	SL	9,765	19,530
C	Building - 25 YR DEPR	1/1/Year 1	305,000	SL	12,200	24,400
	Land	1/1/Year 1	200,000	N/A		
			950,500		**38,645**	**77,290**

Exhibit 5

Excerpt from Notes on Summary of Significant Accounting Policies (Accounts Receivable)

Customer accounts receivables are recorded at the invoiced amounts and do not bear interest. Uncollectible receivables are accounted for in accordance with the direct write-off method. Credit loss expense is recognized when specific accounts are determined to be uncollectible. We review customer accounts regularly to determine which accounts should be written off.

Solution

1	A	B
2	**Item**	**Required correction**
3	Inventory	Correct the footnote disclosure only.

Explanation: In both years, the amounts in the inventory footnote do not tie to the amounts in the financial statements.

The discrepancy is caused by the work in process account. In the notes, the work in process account is *incorrectly subtracted* to arrive at the inventory balance, rather than added. Work in process items are partially finished goods waiting for completion. These items should be included in (ie, added to) the inventory balance.

The adjusted footnote is below. The total inventory amounts now tie to the balance sheet in both years.

Adjusted **Excerpt from Notes on Inventory**

Our inventories are stated on the FIFO method. The inventory balance at Year 1 and Year 2 consists of the following components:

December 31	Year 2	Year 1
Raw materials	56,900	50,650
Work in process	10,340	15,220
Finished goods	132,460	186,230
Inventories	199,700	252,100

4	Land and buildings	Correct the footnote disclosure only.

Explanation: In both years, the net amounts in the land and buildings footnote do not tie to the amounts in the financial statements.

Total historical cost of $950,500 ($750,500 for buildings and $200,000 for land) agrees between the land and buildings footnote and the fixed assets report. Therefore, the discrepancy must be caused by accumulated depreciation on the buildings (as land is not depreciated).

Per the fixed assets report, depreciation during Year 2 was $38,645, and accumulated depreciation at the end of Year 2 was $77,290. Depreciation is accounted for using the straight-line (SL) method; therefore, depreciation during Year 2 is the same as depreciation in Year 1. Since the buildings were acquired on 1/1/Year 1, both YTD and total accumulated depreciation in Year 1 would be $38,645.

The adjusted footnote is below. The net land and buildings balance now ties to the balance sheet in both years.

***Adjusted* Excerpt from Notes on Land and Buildings**

The land and buildings balance at Year 1 and Year 2 consists of the following components:

December 31	**Year 2**			**Year 1**		
	Gross	Accumulated depreciation	Net	Gross	Accumulated depreciation	Net
Land	200,000		200,000	200,000		200,000
Buildings	750,500	77,290	673,210	750,500	38,645	711,855
	950,500	77,290	873,210	950,500	38,645	911,855

5	Summary of significant accounting policies	Correct both the financial statements and footnote disclosure.

Explanation: Doodle is a U.S. public company; therefore, all accounting policies employed by the company must be in accordance with GAAP. However, the company is using the direct write-off method to record credit loss expense, which is not in accordance with GAAP. To conform to GAAP, the company should be using the allowance method, in which credit loss is estimated each period on the basis of the amount of receivables that probably will not be collected.

Doodle will need to update its accounting policies surrounding accounts receivable. An adjustment to the financial statements will need to be made as well to reflect the appropriate credit loss expense and allowance for credit losses. One example of an adjusted footnote is as follows:

***Adjusted* Excerpt from Notes on Summary of Significant Accounting Policies (Accounts Receivable)**

Customer accounts receivables are recorded at the invoiced amounts and do not bear interest. Uncollectible receivables are accounted for in accordance with the allowance method. Each period, the allowance for credit losses is adjusted (and credit loss expense is recorded) based on the amount of receivables that likely will not be collected. We review the allowance quarterly and balances that are 100 days past due or more are reviewed for uncollectibility.

FAR 2
General-Purpose Financial Reporting: Nongovernmental Not-for-Profit Entities

FAR 2: General-Purpose Financial Reporting: Nongovernmental Not-for-Profit Entities

2.01 Not-for-Profit Overview

Overview

Not-for-profit organizations (NPOs) consist of a wide variety of institutions, including some governmentally affiliated entities such as state universities and city and county hospitals.

Types of Not-for-Profit Organizations	
Type	**Description**
Hospitals and other health care entities*	Includes hospitals (both for-profit and not-for-profit), nursing homes, home health agencies, continuing care retirement communities, and health maintenance organizations
Colleges, universities, and other educational organizations*	Includes private four-year colleges and universities and other types of schools
Voluntary health and welfare organizations (VHWOs)	Includes organizations that promote research and education in social- and health-related areas and that receive the majority of their funding from grants and voluntary contributions from the general public; examples include United Way, Red Cross, Greenpeace, American Cancer Society, and Salvation Army
Other not-for-profit organizations	Includes social clubs, political parties, fraternities, labor unions, museums, and libraries

**Exceptions:* *Government-run health care entities and public (ie, state-run) colleges and universities follow GASB standards.*

Not-for-profit organizations follow FASB standards, and governmental entities follow GASB standards.

NPOs provide services funded with public or private resources that generally come from contributions or fees that are not taxable. Not-for-profit reporting focuses on presenting **basic information for the entity as a whole** and emphasizes disclosure of the sources of resources and how they were expended.

Full accrual accounting is used for NPOs, and the required financial statements (F/S) parallel the three basic F/S (balance sheet, income statement, statement of cash flows) used by private businesses. The three basic statements for NPOs include the following:

- Statement of financial position
- Statement of activities
- Statement of cash flows

In addition, all NPOs must report expenses by nature (eg, salaries, rent, supplies, etc.) and function (ie, major program services and supporting activities) in one location, either on the face of the statement of activities, as a schedule in the notes to the F/S, or as a separate financial statement.

Comparison of Types of Financial Statements Issued	
For-Profit Entities	**Not-for-Profit Entities**
Balance sheet	Statement of financial position
Income statement	Statement of activities
Statement of cash flows	Statement of cash flows
N/A	Statement of functional expenses*

**May be presented as a separate statement, on the statement of activities, or within the notes to the F/S*

There are two different types of support that NPOs receive: contributions and pledges. The recognition of contributions and pledges determines how they are reported, on which statement, and when.

Contributions

Representative Task (Application): Calculate the amount to be recognized for contributions (financial assets and nonfinancial assets) to a nongovernmental, not-for-profit entity.

Representative Task (Application): Determine the amount and timing of revenue to be recognized by a nongovernmental, not-for-profit entity for contributed services received and prepare journal entries.

Contributions are **nonreciprocal** receipts of assets or services. They are *not* exchange transactions, in which each party in the transaction gives up something of value. They are asymmetrical transactions in which one party relinquishes something of value to another party, but the other party provides nothing in return. The item of value may be cash, marketable securities, inventory, property, or even services (subject to limitations noted later).

Classification of Resources Provided to Not-for-Profit Organizations

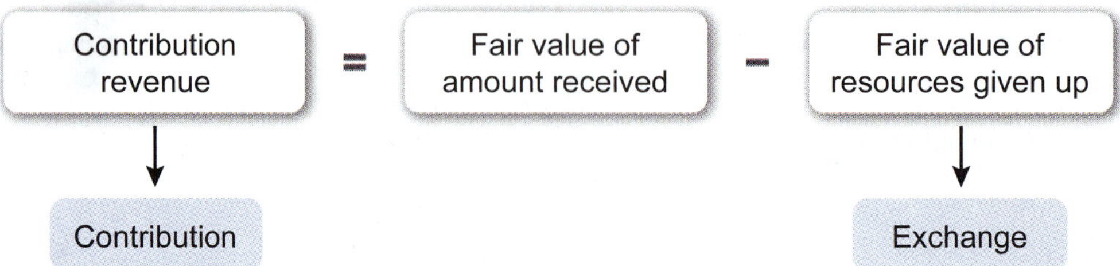

Many not-for-profit organizations rely on contributions from donors to fulfill their mission. Therefore, revenue recognition rules for contributions are a major issue for these organizations, and the topic is consistently tested on the CPA Exam.

Contribution Revenue with and without Donor Restrictions

Unconditional contribution revenue must be reported in one of two categories based on whether the donor stipulates any restrictions on the use of the revenue. The two categories are the following:

- **Contributions without donor restrictions**, which provide resources that are available for expenditure in the current period for any purpose
- **Contributions with donor restrictions**, which fall into four main types:
  - Resources restricted for **specified operating purposes**, known as "program" or "purpose" restrictions
  - Resources available after a **specified time has elapsed**, known as "time restrictions"
  - Resources restricted for **acquisition or construction of capital assets**, known as "capital restrictions"
  - Resources **not available for expenditure at any time** (although the earnings on the resources may be expended), known as "endowments"

Contribution revenue is reported as net assets with or without donor restrictions on the statement of activities.

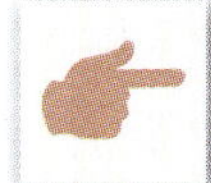

For a contribution to be classified as a contribution *with* donor restriction, the restriction on the contribution must be made by an external party (the donor). Revenue subject to internal restrictions, such as might be made by the Board of Directors, and revenue from exchange transactions (ie, dues, sales of goods, charges for services, etc.) are classified as contributions *without* donor restrictions.

Not-for-Profit Organization Revenues (eg, Donations)

Without restrictions

Not subject to donor-imposed limitations and available for general use

With restrictions

Subject to limitations (eg, for a specific purpose) from the donor

Contributions of Cash

Cash donations to the NPO are reported as contribution revenue with or without donor restrictions (depending on donor-imposed specifications).

Animal Action recently received $100,000 in contributions. $30,000 of this amount was restricted by donors to cover the costs of a spay/neuter clinic. The director set aside an additional $50,000 of this amount to be used to build an addition to the animal shelter.

Animal Action reports $30,000 as contribution *with* restrictions (because it is restricted by donors) and $70,000 as contribution *without* restrictions. The director setting aside money for a specific purpose is only an internal designation, not a donor restriction.

Cash	100,000	
Contribution revenue *with* restrictions		30,000
Contribution revenue *without* restrictions		70,000

Contributions of Property

Contributions of property are normally reported as revenues in the same manner as contributions of cash. They are **recorded at fair value (FV)** and may be reported as contribution revenue with or without donor restrictions.

If the not-for-profit receives **donated materials**, it records both an asset and contribution revenue.

A special rule may be applied to certain donations of **art**, **artifacts**, **or antiques**. The NPO is permitted to exclude the donation from the face of its F/S and only disclose it in the notes if:

- The NPO intends to use the donated item for display or research purposes only;
- The organization cares for it themselves; **AND**
- If sold, the proceeds are either:
  - Reinvested in other collectible items; **OR**
  - Used for the direct care of existing collections.

Including these high-value items in the F/S might cause the organization to appear to possess great wealth (and potentially not need public support), when in reality it is holding assets that cannot be used to finance the operations of the NPO. If the above requirements are *not* met, then the entity recognizes both an **asset** and a **revenue**.

Gifts in kind are **noncash** contributions to a not-for-profit organization. They are recorded at FV.

Pedro Picasso donates a work of art with a FV of $5,000 to the Modern Art Museum. The donation specifies that the museum will sell the art work at an auction and use the funds for its general operating activities.

The museum intends to sell the artwork, and the proceeds are not going to be reinvested in collectible items or used for the care of existing collections. As such, the museum cannot exclude the donation from its F/S. The museum must report the art at its FV ($5,000) as both an asset *and* contribution revenue without restrictions.

Asset—art for resale	5,000	
Contribution revenue *without* restrictions		5,000

Contributions of Services

Donations of services are normally not recorded. However, contribution revenue is recognized if:

- Non-financial assets (eg, inventory, land, building) are created or enhanced; **OR**
- The donated services require a person with **specialized skills** providing those specialized skills to an organization that **normally would have paid** for those specialized skills.

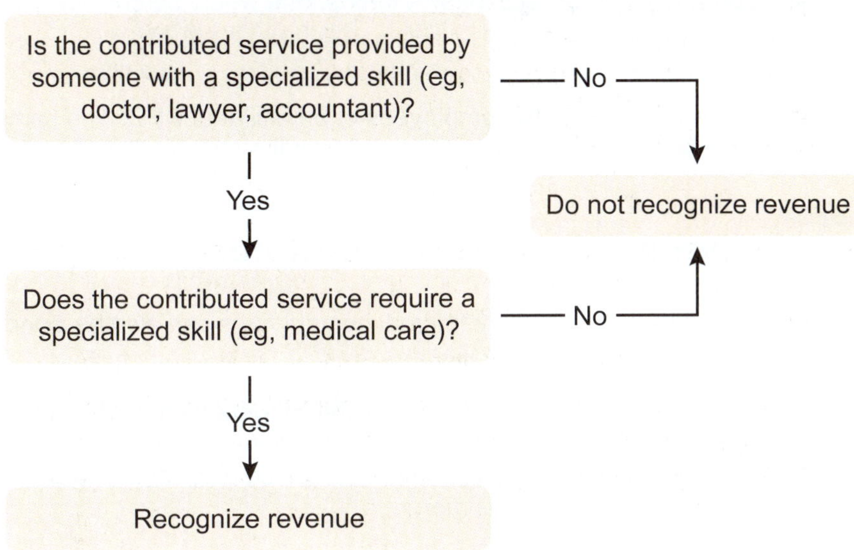

If donated services are recorded, they are **recognized at FV**. Frequently, there are differences between rates charged and standard (ie, FV) rates. The services should be recorded at the FV rate.

A hospital receives *donated time* from retired nurses that enables it to avoid hiring and paying additional workers, and the estimated amount that time would have cost the hospital is $30,000. The following entry is made:

Expenses	30,000	
Contribution revenue *without* restrictions		30,000

The nurses possess the specialized skill of caring for patients, and they are performing that specialized skill here. The hospital ordinarily would have paid for this skill. Therefore, the donation is recognized as contribution revenue. Notice that the donation increases the nursing expense as well as contribution revenue without donor restrictions, since services that have been provided cannot be withdrawn later.

NPOs also frequently receive donations of services from volunteers providing **unskilled services** that it would **not** have contracted to obtain had they not been donated. These are excluded from the financial reporting since they do not assist the organization in reducing its expenses.

The Turtle Society, a nongovernmental not-for-profit organization, receives numerous contributed hours from volunteers during its busy season. A clerk at the local tax collector's office volunteered 10 hours per week for 24 weeks transferring turtle food from the port to the turtle shelter. The clerk's rate of pay at the tax office is $10 per hour, and the prevailing wage rate for laborers is $6.50 per hour. Determine the amount of contribution revenue that Turtle Society should record for this service.

In this scenario, transferring turtle food from the port to the shelter is **not** contribution revenue for the Turtle Society because the task requires **unskilled** labor and could be performed by any volunteer. Note that if a veterinarian donated time to care for sick turtles, that would be considered revenue.

In some cases, services may be provided by the employees of an affiliated NPO. The same basic recognition rules apply, and the services are generally recorded at the affiliated NPO's cost.

Conditional and Unconditional Contributions

In addition to being donor restricted or not donor restricted, contributions can also be **conditional or unconditional**.

Conditional contributions depend on the occurrence of some future, uncertain event. In this case, revenue recognition occurs when the condition is met or the chance of not meeting the condition becomes remote. The not-for-profit should account for conditional contributions received (eg, cash is deposited) as a **refundable advance** (liability) until the condition is met.

A contribution is considered **conditional** only if both of the following are true (ie, otherwise, the contribution is considered unconditional):

- There is a barrier that must be overcome (eg, measurable performance-related requirements, such as a specified level of service, a specific output/outcome, matching, or other events outside the control of the recipient, etc.)
- The donor has a right to the return of assets transferred or a right to be released from their obligation to transfer assets

If a contribution is determined to be **unconditional**, one must then determine if it is donor restricted or unrestricted. (Note that a donor-imposed condition is not the same as a donor-imposed restriction.) *Conditions* must be met *before contribution revenue can be recognized*. Restrictions specify what the contribution must be used for and indicate where contribution revenue is recognized in the NPO's statement of activities.

A donor-imposed restriction limits the time or use of the contribution; it does not affect whether the recipient is entitled to the contribution. Examples of a donor-imposed restriction might be that a contribution can only be used the following year or to buy shoes for needy children.

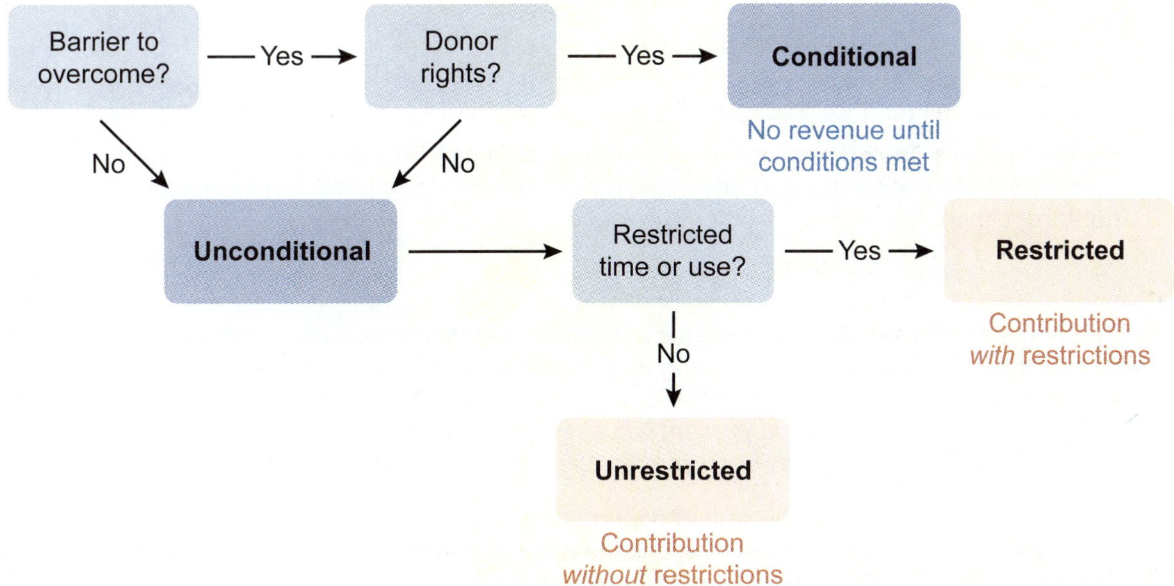

Boyd University is a private university. A successful alumnus has recently donated $1,000,000 to Boyd for the purpose of funding a "center for the study of sports ethics." This donation is conditional on the university raising matching funds within the next 12 months. The university administrators estimate that they have a 50% chance of raising the additional money.

The donation is **conditional** on the university raising matching funds within 12 months. In order to use the money, this barrier must be overcome, and the alumnus has a right to the return of the $1,000,000 if not. The donation is also restricted to a specific purpose (the money must be used for funding the center for the study of sports ethics).

As the condition has not yet been met, contribution revenue cannot be recognized. Boyd will recognize the cash received and a refundable advance liability:

Cash	1,000,000	
Refundable advance		1,000,000

Once Boyd satisfies the condition, it will remove the refundable advance and recognize contribution revenue (here with donor restrictions because the money is to be used for a specific purpose).

Pledges

Representative Task (Remembering & Understanding): Recall the recognition requirements associated with conditional and unconditional promises to give (pledges) for a nongovernmental, not-for-profit entity.

Promises to give (pledges) may be accrued as a receivable and recognized as contribution revenue (net assets with or without donor restrictions) as long as they are **unconditional**. An *allowance for uncollectible pledges* should be recorded in a manner similar to a for-profit organization's accounting for accounts receivable. The pledges are recorded at *present value (PV)* for annuities or *amounts not expected to be collected for over a year.* Cash contributions, conversely, are a revenue or gain when received.

Conditional pledges to give are promises that *depend on a specific event occurring in the future*. They cannot be recognized as contributions until the uncertain future event has occurred. Conditional pledges are recognized when the conditions are **substantially met** or when the likelihood that the conditions will not be met is remote.

Pledges to a Not-for-Profit Organization (NPO)	
Unconditional	**Conditional**
• No action required by the NPO to get the promised resources • Recorded as revenue and pledge receivable when promise is made	• NPO must overcome donor-imposed barriers before getting the promised resources • Not recognized until pledge conditions are satisfied

Simmons promises to give $1,000,000 to World Crisis Services to purchase food supplies for a drought-ridden country. Simmons also promises to give an additional $500,000 if the drought is not broken in six months.

The $1,000,000 is an unconditional pledge. No action is required by the NPO to get the promised resources. However, the money must be used for a specific purpose (ie, it is donor restricted). World Crisis Services should recognize the $1,000,000 as a contribution revenue *with* restrictions (as it must be used to purchase food supplies for a drought-ridden country).

The $500,000 is a conditional pledge. There is a donor-imposed barrier that must be overcome before getting the promised resources (ie, the drought must not be broken). Therefore, the $500,000 cannot be recognized since it is conditioned on an uncertain future event.

Assume that an Independence Day pledge drive by the NPO in Year 1 has netted promises with a PV of $20,000, with half of the pledges due by the end of the current year and the remainder due by the end of Year 2. Based on experience, the organization expects 10% of pledges not to be honored. The entry to be recorded when pledges are received is as follows:

Pledges receivable (at PV)	20,000	
Allowance for uncollectible pledges		2,000
Revenues *without* donor restrictions		9,000
Revenues *with* donor restrictions		9,000

The pledges are recorded at their PV ($20,000). An allowance for uncollectible pledges is recorded at $2,000 (10% expected not to be honored × $20,000). $18,000 pledges are expected to be honored.

Half of these ($9,000) are due by the end of the current year, and the other half ($9,000) are due by the end of Year 2. The pledges due at the end of Year 2 are subject to a time restriction (because they will not be paid or be accessible until the following year). The pledges due by the end of the current year are recognized as revenue without donor restrictions, and the pledges due at the end of Year 2 are recognized as revenue with donor restrictions.

At the end of Year 1, the revenue with donor restrictions account is closed to net assets with donor restrictions (similar to a for-profit entity closing net income to equity). Assuming collection is as expected, the pledges collected in Year 2 effectively eliminate the **time restriction**. The pledges will be reclassified from with donor restrictions to without donor restrictions:

Net assets *with* donor restrictions	9,000	
Net assets *without* donor restrictions		9,000

The timing of the receipt of cash related to pledges is a frequent distractor on the CPA Exam. Revenue recognition is not tied to the receipt of cash, and the cash payment information should often be ignored. An unconditional pledge in the current period is recognized as revenue when the promise is made, not when the cash is received.

Investments in Debt and Equity Securities

NPOs are required to use **fair value accounting** for most equity and debt investments. FV is used because it is the most likely amount the NPO will receive if it sells the investment for cash.

Whether the investments are donated to or purchased by the NPO, they are **initially recorded at FV** (as assets on the statement of financial position) and revalued each reporting period. **Realized and unrealized** gains and losses are reported directly in the statement of activities, and the FV of the investments is reported on the statement of financial position.

Valuation of Noncash Contributions to Not-for-Profit Organizations

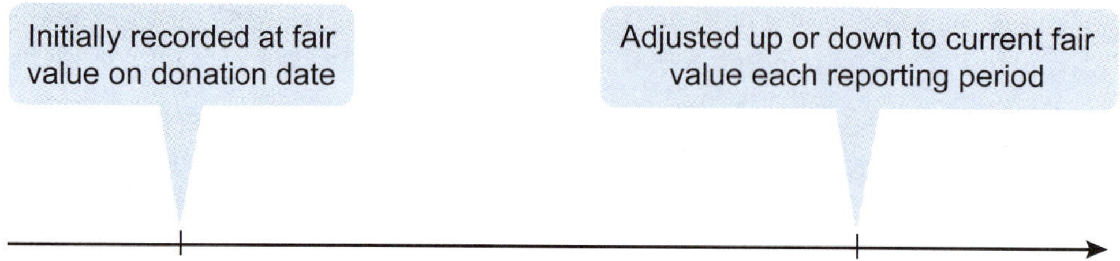

A nongovernmental, not-for-profit organization has the following investments:

Investment	Cost	Estimated Sales Proceeds	FV (End of Year)
Bonds	$8,200	$9,500	$9,000
Stock UWD (200 shares)	$30 per share	$28 per share	$25 per share
Stock AIC (100 shares)	$45 per share	$49 per share	$52 per share

To determine the total value of investments reported in the year-end **statement of financial position**, the NPO calculates the total **FV** at the end of the reporting period.

Investment	FV
Bonds	$9,000
Stock UWD (200 shares × $25)	5,000
Stock AIC (100 shares × $52)	5,200
Total	$19,200

Endowments

An endowment is an established fund of cash, securities, or other assets. **Permanent endowments** come with the restriction to *invest the principal* (corpus) and maintain it in perpetuity, whereas any *investment income can be used for the organization's general operations*. Here, the gains (losses) realized from the investments of the endowment are reported as increases (decreases) in net assets *without* donor restrictions.

However, in some circumstances, the donor may stipulate that any earnings from the endowment are also restricted for a specific purpose. In that case, an expenditure of the restricted resources must first be released from net assets *with* restrictions to net assets *without* restrictions prior to recording an expense.

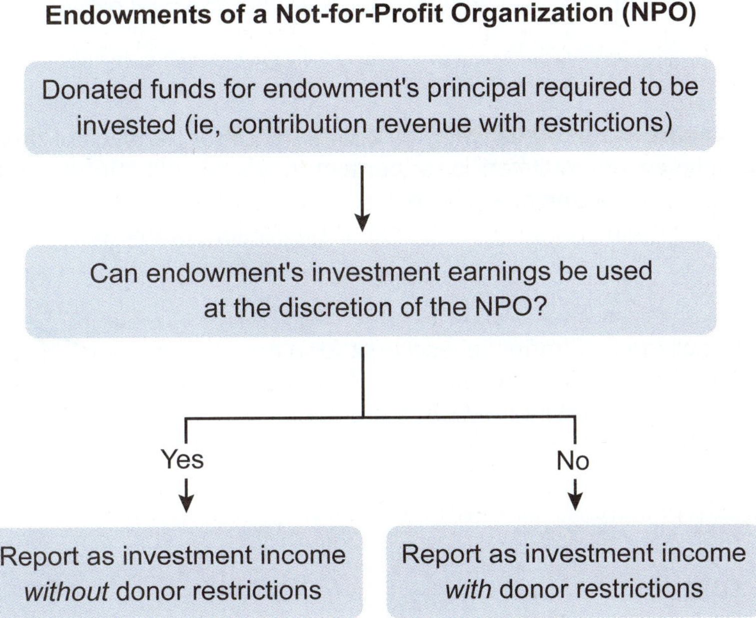

A not-for-profit voluntary health and welfare organization received a $50,000 permanent endowment during the year. The donor stipulated that the income must be used for a mental health program. The endowment fund reported $3,000 in investment income. The organization spent $7,000 on the mental health program during the year. Determine the increase in net assets *with* donor restrictions that the organization should report.

- The endowment is permanent, which means the principal cannot be spent. Net assets with restrictions will increase by $50,000
- Because the donor stipulated that the endowment's income must be used for a mental health program (ie, restricted purpose), the $3,000 in investment earnings will increase net assets with restrictions as well
- Net assets with restrictions will decrease by the $3,000 used for the mental health program. The restriction was satisfied on this $3,000; therefore, it is reclassified from *with* donor restrictions to *without* donor restrictions. A total of $7,000 was expended for the program; therefore, the remaining $4,000 must come from other, unrestricted sources

Net assets with donor restrictions will increase by $50,000 ($50,000 + 3,000 − 3,000).

Quasi-endowments are amounts *set aside by the governing board* of the organization, rather than outside sources, of which the principal must be retained and invested. Although these resources act like an endowment, they cannot be considered regular endowments as the *restrictions on endowment resources must come from an external party*. Quasi-endowments are included in net assets without donor restriction.

Term endowments are gifts and bequests from third parties that are to be *retained and invested for a period of time or until a specific event occurs*. However, after the criterion has been met, the full amount can be spent. The earnings on the invested amount are paid to a separate beneficiary (usually a spouse or a child) until the criterion is met. Because they can ultimately be spent, they are classified as net assets with donor restriction until the criterion is met (eg, the spouse dies), after which the amount remaining in the endowment is reclassified as without donor restriction.

Board-designated funds are amounts *set aside by the governing board* of the organization to be spent for specific purposes. These funds are not endowments because the *principal can be spent*.

Split-Interest Arrangements

Split-interest arrangements are agreements whereby both a donor (or beneficiary) and an NPO receive benefits, often at different times in a multiyear arrangement. A typical split-interest arrangement has two components: a lead interest and a remainder interest. A lead interest provides disbursements throughout the term of the arrangement. A remainder interest is a final disbursement at the termination of the arrangement.

Roger Smith established a charitable lead trust for a donation to Globe Health, an NPO. Roger put $1,000,000 in the trust to be invested for 10 years. Globe Health receives the trust income for the 10-year period (a lead interest). At the end of the 10-year period, the principal of the trust goes to Roger's children (the remainder interest).

Hospitals

Nongovernmental, not-for-profit health care entities have standard rates for services offered; however, the amount of patient revenue recorded at the time of service is based on the amount that the entity expects to collect.

Charity care is *not* considered gross revenue because these are services with no expectation of collection (ie, no contract with a customer exists). Conversely, to arrive at **net patient service revenue**, gross revenue is *reduced for discounts, contractual adjustments, and implicit price concessions* (ie, contract exists but customers will pay less than the standard rates):

Net Patient Service Revenue
Gross patient service revenue*
– Discounts
– Contractual adjustments
– Implicit price concessions
Net patient service revenue**

**Excludes charity care (ie, no expectation of payment) from gross patient revenue*

***Provision for credit losses reported separately as an operating expense*

Donated supplies are recognized as revenue (and a corresponding asset or expense) at FV in the period received.

Colleges and Universities

Tuition revenues are shown at net of scholarship allowances and uncollectible amounts. Scholarships, assistantships, fellowships, and tuition waivers that are given in return for services provided to the institutions are reported as *expenses* for the department and function where the services are provided.

Scholarship allowances and scholarships are not the same thing. Scholarship allowances are the difference between the stated tuition rate and the amount that is actually paid by the student and/or third parties making payments on behalf of the student. Scholarships are actual amounts paid to students by the college rather than a reduction of charges. Tuition waivers may be given as a result of employment by the university, such as those given to graduate assistants.

Tuition refunds (ie, money returned to students because they did not take classes) are deducted from assessed student tuition and fees to derive gross tuition revenues.

Students at Maplewood College register for classes for which the gross tuition is $1,000,000. The college:

- Grants $250,000 to 50 students for student assistantships in return for a service requirement,
- Grants scholarships without a work requirement totaling $100,000 to 10 students, and
- Waives tuition of $30,000 for college employees who are also taking classes

Refunds of $50,000 are given to students who drop classes before classes start. Determine Maplewood's gross tuition revenue, net tuition and fees and scholarship and fellowship expense.

Maplewood will report:

- Gross tuition revenue of $950,000 ($1,000,000 tuition − $50,000 refunds). Tuition refunds are deducted to derive gross tuition revenues
- Net tuition and fees of $850,000 ($950,000 gross tuition − $100,000 scholarship allowances). The $100,000 is a scholarship allowance as it is a reduction of charges, rather than an actual amount paid to students. Scholarship allowances are deducted to derive net tuition
- Scholarship and fellowship expense of $280,000 ($250,000 scholarships + $30,000 tuition waivers). The $250,000 represents scholarships since this amount is actually paid to students. Scholarships and tuition waivers are classified as expenses

Agent or Trustee

Representative Task (Remembering & Understanding): Identify transfers to a nongovernmental, not-for-profit entity acting as an agent or intermediary that are not recognized as contributions.

An agent or trustee (eg, United Way) acts as an intermediary. These organizations collect contributions (ie, transfers) from donors and then give these contributions to beneficiaries selected by the donors.

If the agent or trustee collects money for others, it can be considered either contribution revenue or a liability at FV. It is considered a **revenue** if the agent or trustee either:

- Has variance power over the donation; **OR**
- Is financially related to or has an ongoing economic interest in the net assets of the beneficiary of the donation.

Variance power is the unilateral power to redirect the transferred assets to another beneficiary (other than the beneficiary initially intended by the donor). Unilateral power means that the recipient entity can override the donor's instructions without seeking approval.

The donor decides who the intended beneficiary is. However, if the donor decides to grant variance power, the agent is ultimately responsible for who eventually receives the donation.

If a donation is made to a disaster relief NPO (eg, the Red Cross) specifically for hurricane relief victims, the NPO cannot redirect the funds to build a new administrative facility in the state of New York. Variance power is not granted.

If one of the two above conditions applies and the transfer is considered revenue, the journal entry is as follows:

Cash/asset at FV	XX	
Contribution revenue		XX

If neither of the two above conditions applies, the donation is a **liability**.

Cash/asset at FV	XX	
Liability		XX

The Jones family lost their home in a fire. On December 25, Year 3, a philanthropist sent $10,000 to the Amer Benevolent Society, a nongovernmental not-for-profit organization, to purchase furniture for the Jones family. During January, Year 4, Amer purchased the furniture for the family. Determine how Amer should report the receipt of the money in its Year 3 F/S.

In this scenario, the Amer Benevolent Society received funds that were specifically pledged to the Jones family. Since Amer **has no variance power** to redirect the funds, it has a future obligation (ie, **liability**) to purchase furniture for the family.

Cash	10,000	
Liability		10,000

2.02 Statement of Financial Position

Representative Task (Remembering & Understanding): Recall the purpose and objectives of the statement of financial position for a nongovernmental, not-for-profit entity.

The **statement of financial position** is similar to a balance sheet and reports assets, liabilities, and net assets of the NPO as a whole. The purpose of the statement of financial position is to *provide the financial status of the organization at a specific point in time*. This enables users (eg, donors) to see the short- and long-term financial position of the NPO.

Assets and liabilities may be classified or reported in order of liquidity and payment date. Net assets **with donor restrictions** must be reported separately from those that are **not restricted**.

The bottom of the statement of financial position reports the residual interest (assets – liabilities) of the NPO. For-profit entities call this residual interest owners' or shareholders' equity, while not-for-profit entities call this residual interest net assets. The net assets section of the statement includes two accounts: net assets *without* donor restrictions and net assets *with* donor restrictions.

Net assets *without* donor restrictions

Net assets *with* donor restrictions
- Temporary
  - Purpose
  - Time
- Permanent

Net assets *without* donor restrictions

Net assets *without* donor restrictions are those resources of the NPO that are **available for the general use of the entity** and can include assets set aside by the board of trustees, including a board-designated endowment fund, since a true restriction must come from an outside donor. Net assets without donor restrictions are the *remainder of the net assets of an NPO after considering those that are subject to donor-imposed restrictions*.

Net assets *with* donor restrictions

Net assets *with* donor restrictions are those resources of the NPO that are subject to **donor-imposed** restrictions. For example, a donor may stipulate that a sum be earmarked for cancer research or for the improvement of a building or may only be used after a prescribed period of time or upon the occurrence of an event.

Temporary

When a **temporary** restriction is met, the amount of the restriction met is *reclassified* from net assets with donor restrictions to net assets without donor restrictions. The following are the two types of temporary restrictions:

Purpose

Purpose restriction occurs when the donor stipulates that the resources from the donation must be spent on something specific (eg, drug-free youth education programs at the YMCA).

Time

Time restriction occurs when the donor stipulates that the resources from the donation must be spent in a certain time period (eg, a $50,000 donation to be spent $10,000 yearly for five years) or cannot be spent until after a specified time has elapsed.

Permanent

Permanent restriction includes endowments. Typically, the donor restriction is to protect the original donated amount (aka, the principal or corpus) from being depleted. The earnings from the endowment, however, may be either with or without restriction. That is, a portion of the fund's income/gains may be required to be reinvested and added to the principal, or the fund's income or gains may be available for operational expenditures by the NPO.

The following is an example of an NPO's statement of financial position:

Not-for-Profit Organization
Statements of Financial Position

June 30, Year 2 and Year 1 (in thousands)

	Year 2	Year 1
Assets		
Cash and cash equivalents	$ 75	$ 460
Accounts and interest receivable	2,130	1,670
Inventories and prepaid expenses	610	1,000
Contributions receivable	3,025	2,700
Short-term investments	1,400	1,000
Assets restricted to investment in land, buildings, and equipment	5,210	4,560
Land, buildings, and equipment	61,700	63,590
Long-term investments	218,070	203,500
Total assets	$ 292,220	$ 278,480
Liabilities and net assets		
Accounts payable	$ 2,570	$ 1,900
Refundable advance		650
Grants payable	875	1,300
Notes payable		1,140
Annuity obligations	1,685	1,700
Long-term debt	5,500	6,500
Total liabilities	10,630	13,190
Net assets		
Net assets without donor restrictions	115,228	103,648
Net assets with donor restrictions	166,362	161,642
Total net assets	281,590	265,290
Total liabilities and net assets	$ 292,220	$ 278,480

2.03 Statement of Activities

Statement of Activities

Representative Task (Remembering & Understanding): Recall the purpose and objectives of the statement of activities for a nongovernmental, not-for-profit entity.

The **statement of activities** is similar to an income statement and reports revenues, net assets released from restriction, and expenses. The principal requirement of the statement is to *provide the change in net assets for the organization as a whole*. The changes in net assets are separated into two columns on the statement: one for amounts *without* donor restrictions and one for those *with* donor restrictions.

The four sections of the statement of activities are revenues, gains, and other support; net assets released from restrictions; expenses and losses; and change in net assets, which includes a reconciliation of beginning and ending net assets.

Key areas of emphasis for purposes of the CPA exam are classification of revenues, classification of expenses, timing of release of assets from restrictions, and evaluation of the effect on net assets with donor restrictions and net assets without donor restrictions when donor-restricted monies are spent for their intended purpose.

Revenues, Gains, and Other Support

Revenues, **gains**, **and other support** typically include contributions from donors and investment income. They are reported in the appropriate column depending on whether the revenues have donor restrictions. Recall the following from the earlier section on contributions:

- Property is included at FV at the date of the gift
- Services are included only if they are professional services and the NPO would have otherwise paid for them
- Debt and equity investments are included at FV, and both realized and unrealized gains are recognized on the statement of activities

Within the statement of activities, contributions are disclosed in two categories: (1) contributions of cash and other financial assets, and (2) contributions of nonfinancial assets (sometimes referred to as "in-kind contributions").

Net Assets Released from Restrictions

Net assets released from restrictions report only *formerly donor-restricted net assets* that became free of donor restrictions during the year, generally due to the expiration of time restrictions or the performance of purpose restrictions. Such amounts are reclassified from the "with donor restrictions" column to the "without donor restrictions" column.

Expenses and Losses

Expenses are reported only in the "*without* donor restrictions" column. The expenditure of net assets with donor restrictions has the effect of releasing the assets from restriction and is reported as both a release, as discussed in the preceding paragraph, and an expense from the "without donor restrictions" category.

Expenses can be reported by **nature** (eg, salaries, rent), by **function** (ie, program costs, support services), or both. If they are not reported by both nature and function on the face of the statement of activities, this information should be presented in the notes or in a separate financial statement.

All NPOs are required to recognize depreciation using the same criteria as commercial enterprises in allocating the depreciable cost of fixed assets over their estimated useful lives.

Change in Net Assets

Change in net assets is similar to net income for for-profit entities and is the bottom line of the statement of activities. The change in net assets line item is followed by the reconciliation:

Change in net assets (per statement of activities)
± Beginning net assets (per statement of financial position)
Ending net assets (per statement of financial position)

The ending net assets balance on the statement of activities must tie to the net assets total on the statement of financial position.

Just as net income closes to retained earnings, the change in net assets on the statement of activities closes to the net asset balances on the statement of financial position.

At the beginning of the year, a nongovernmental not-for-profit corporation received a $150,000 contribution restricted to recreational activity programs. During the year, recreational activities generated revenues of $90,000 and had program expenses of $105,000.

Because the **donor** restricted the purpose of the money (to be used for recreational activity programs), the journal entry to record the receipt of the donation is as follows:

Cash (net assets *with* donor restrictions)	150,000	
Revenues *with* donor restrictions		150,000

When the restriction is **satisfied**, that amount is released from net assets *with* restrictions to net assets *without* restrictions. In this scenario, spending the money on recreational activity programs satisfies the restriction. The restriction satisfaction is recorded first. Then expenditure of the money is recorded. The journal entry to record the expenditure is as follows:

Reclassification from net assets *with* donor restrictions	105,000	
Reclassification to net assets *without* donor restrictions		105,000
Program expenses	105,000	
Cash (net assets *without* donor restrictions)		105,000

The statement of activities reports revenues and expenses from ongoing major operations separately at their gross amounts. For example, an annual fundraising campaign is critical in obtaining resources to operate and is an integral part of an NPO's ongoing activities. The fundraising revenues and expenses must be reported at their gross amounts so that donors can properly understand the nature of the campaign and its success. On the other hand, secondary activities and peripheral information may be reported at net amounts since a high-level knowledge of the NPO's secondary operations is generally adequate for understanding them. For example, the sale of equipment or buildings may be reported net of selling expenses.

Summary of Changes in Net Assets on Statement of Activities

	***Without* donor restrictions**	***With* donor restrictions**
Revenues	Increase	Increase
Released assets	Increase	Decrease
Expenses	Decrease	N/A

The following is an example of an NPO's statement of activities:

Not-for-Profit Organization
Statement of Activities

Year ended June 30, Year 1 (in thousands)

	Without donor restrictions	**With donor restrictions**	**Total**
Revenues, gains, and other support:			
Contributions	$ 8,640	$ 8,390	$ 17,030
Fees	5,400		5,400
Net assets released from restrictions:			
Satisfaction of program restrictions	11,990	(11,990)	
Satisfaction of equipment acquisition restrictions	1,500	(1,500)	
Total revenues, gains, and other support	27,530	(5,100)	22,430
Expenses and losses:			
Program A	13,100		13,100
Program C	5,760		5,760
Fundraising	2,150		2,150
Fire loss	80		80
Total expenses and losses	21,090		21,090
Change in net assets	6,440	(5,100)	1,340
Net assets at beginning of year	103,648	161,642	265,290
Net assets at end of year	$110,088	$156,542	$266,630

Statement of Functional Expenses

Representative Task (Application): Report expenses by nature and function in either the statement of activities, the notes to the financial statements or a statement of functional expenses for a nongovernmental, not-for-profit entity.

In addition to the three F/S required of all NPOs, an **analysis of functional expenses** is required. The analysis is not an additional financial statement. Instead, it is a detailed schedule of expenses by function (such as program expenses and support services) broken down into "natural expense" categories (like rent, utilities, salaries, depreciation, etc.). It may be presented on the face of the statement of activities, as a separate statement, or as a note to the NPO's F/S.

There are two categories of functional expenses:

- **Program activities** further the mission of the organization and are directly related to the program. For example, a relief organization might report categories for emergency relief, community education, training, research, hospice services, etc.
- **Supporting activities** are secondary to the mission. Supporting activities include the following:
  - Management and general: Includes marketing, tax preparation, printing annual report, business management, and budgeting
  - Fundraising: Includes printing and mailing pledge cards, maintaining donor list, preparing and distributing fundraising materials, sending merchandise to potential contributors, paying salaries of fundraisers, and conducting other activities designed to solicit contributions

The following is an example of an NPO's statement of functional expenses:

ABC Health Center
Statement of Functional Expenses

	Program A	Program B	Mgmt and General	Fundraising	Total expenses
Salaries and benefits	$6,000	$3,500	$1,000	$800	$11,300
Travel and supplies	800	900	190	400	$2,290
Depreciation	1,100	700	200	120	$2,120
Total expenses	**$7,900**	**$5,100**	**$1,390**	**$1,320**	$15,710

Natural classification   Functional classification

A nongovernmental, not-for-profit museum had the following balances in its statement of functional expenses:

Education	$300,000
Fundraising	250,000
Management and general	200,000
Research	50,000

Determine the amount that the museum should report as expenses for **support services**.

Program services are primary to the NPO's mission, while support services are secondary to the NPO's mission. A museum's primary purpose is to display objects of importance and educate the public. As such, education costs ($300,000) and research costs ($50,000) are both program-related activities for the museum.

Fundraising ($250,000) and management and general costs ($200,000) are support services, as they indirectly support the museum's efforts to educate the public. Total support services = $250,000 fundraising + $200,000 management and general = **$450,000**.

2.04 Statement of Cash Flows

Representative Task (Remembering & Understanding): Recall the purpose and objectives of the statement of cash flows for a nongovernmental, not-for-profit entity.

The not-for-profit statement of cash flows is comparable to the same statement for for-profit businesses, reporting cash flows from operating, investing, and financing activities. The principal difference is that contributions restricted for **long-term purposes** (eg, subject to capital restrictions) are reported in the **financing** activities section. **Unrestricted** contributions and contributions subject to **temporary** (purpose or time) restrictions are reported in the **operating** activities section.

The statement may be prepared using either the direct or indirect method. If using the direct method, an indirect reconciliation may be included but is not required.

Sections of the Statement of Cash Flows:
Not-for-Profit Organizations

Operating activities
Normal business operations

Investing activities
Investing in yourself or others

Financing activities
Issuing debt or equity

Operating activities represent most of the cash flow effects of the items reported in the **statement of activities**.

- Inflows include unrestricted contributions, revenue from exchange transactions, revenue restricted for operating purposes
- Outflows include expenses paid and grants to other organizations

Investing activities generally represent the cash flow effects of **asset** transactions.

- Inflows include proceeds from the sales of assets or works of art
- Outflows include payments for asset purchases

Financing activities generally represent the cash flow effects of **liability** transactions and include two subsections:

- Proceeds from contributions subject to long-term donor restrictions (eg, restrictions for acquisition of capital assets, endowments)
- Other financing activities, which includes proceeds from (inflows) and principal payments on (outflows) loans or other long-term debt

The Maroon Foundation, a private not-for-profit organization, had the following cash contributions and expenditures in Year 5:

Unrestricted cash contributions	$500,000
Cash contributions restricted by the donor to the acquisition of property	300,000
Cash expenditures to acquire property with the donation from above	200,000

Unrestricted cash contributions can be used for any purpose, so they are reported as a **$500,000 inflow for operating activities**.

Contributions restricted for long-term purchases fall under the financing section, so in this scenario, there is a **$300,000 inflow for financing activities**.

Cash spent to acquire an asset is an investing activity, so Maroon Foundation has a **$200,000 outflow for investing activities**.

The following is an example of an NPO's statement of cash flows:

Not-for-Profit Organization
Statement of Cash Flows

Year ended June 30, Year 1 (in thousands)

Cash flows from operating activities:	
Cash received from unrestricted contributions	5,000
Cash received from time-restricted contributions	3,000
Cash paid to employees	(3,200)
Cash paid for supplies	(1,100)
Net cash provided by operating activities	3,700
Cash flows from investing activities:	
Purchase of equipment	(1,500)
Proceeds from sale of investments	2,600
Net cash provided by investing activities	1,100
Cash flows from financing activities:	
Proceeds from contributions restricted for investment in PP&E	1,200
Payment on long-term debt	(1,500)
Net cash used by financing activities	(300)
Net increase (decrease) in cash and cash equivalents	4,500
Cash and cash equivalents at beginning of year	15,900
Cash and cash equivalents at end of year	20,400

2.05 Notes to the Financial Statements

Not-for-profit organizations are required to make several disclosures if the relevant information is not presented on the face of the F/S. Two have already been mentioned in this chapter:

- Statement of functional expenses
- Donated works of art not recognized on the F/S

Additionally, the following information regarding **financial liquidity and flexibility** should be displayed either on the face of the statement of financial position or in the notes to the F/S:

- Relevant information about the nature and amount of limitations on the use of cash and cash equivalents (eg, cash held on deposit as a compensating balance)
- Contractual limitations on the use of particular assets, which include, for example, restricted cash or other assets set aside under debt agreements, assets set aside under self-insurance funding arrangements, assets set aside under collateral arrangements, or assets set aside to satisfy reserve requirements that states may impose under charitable gift annuity agreements
- Quantitative information about the availability of an NPO's financial assets to meet cash needs for general expenditures within one year of the date of the statement of financial position

Certain information about **endowment funds** should be disclosed in the notes to the F/S, including the net asset classification, composition, and changes, as well as the related investment policies. The notes also should provide the NPO's spending policies regarding endowment funds, including **underwater endowment funds**. Endowment funds are considered underwater when the FV at the reporting date is less than either the original gift value or the amount required (either by law or the donor) to be maintained in the fund.

Claudia Monay donates a work of art with a FV of $50,000 to become part of the permanent collection at the Modern Art Museum. Because the museum intends to use the donated item for display only, the museum does not recognize the contribution as revenue or record an asset. Instead, it reports the donation in the **notes to the F/S**.

2.06 Preparing the Financial Statements

Overview

Representative Task (Application): Prepare a statement of financial position for a nongovernmental, not-for-profit entity from a trial balance and supporting documentation.

Representative Task (Application): Prepare a statement of activities for a nongovernmental, not-for-profit entity, including donor restrictions and releases from donor restrictions, from a trial balance and supporting documentation.

Representative Task (Application): Prepare a statement of cash flows and required disclosures using the direct method or indirect method for a nongovernmental, not-for-profit entity.

Analysis level tasks are typically tested in a task-based simulation (TBS). Below is an example TBS that covers the primary knowledge needed to build F/S based on transactions and scenarios. This TBS focuses on which statements are impacted in various situations.

Example

For each of the independent transactions listed, determine the following:

1. If the transaction requires an entry on the **statement of financial position**. If so, determine which account(s) must be debited or credited.
2. If the transaction requires an entry on the **statement of activities**. If so, determine which account(s) must be debited or credited.
3. If the transaction requires an entry on the **statement of cash flows**. If so, determine the appropriate section and whether the transaction represents an inflow or an outflow.

Note that some transactions may not require an entry. If no entry is required, leave the cell blank.

	Statement of Financial Position		Statement of Activities		Statement of Cash Flows		
	Debit	Credit	Debit	Credit	Operating	Investing	Financing
1. A local CPA firm donated its services to perform the regular annual financial statement audit and preparation of IRS Form 990 for a not-for-profit museum.							
2. Several local Rotary Club members used their personal vehicles to deliver meals to senior citizens for Meals on Wheels.							
3. A donor contributed $2 million to a not-for-profit hospital.							
4. A donor contributed $4 million to a not-for-profit university to be permanently invested.							
5. A not-for-profit university purchased long-term investments for $4 million.							
6. $100,000 in earnings from a permanent scholarship endowment are released to fund scholarships (the scholarships have not been awarded yet).							
7. A donor offers to donate $500,000 to a local mental health clinic if the clinic can raise a matching amount in the next 60 days.							
8. A psychiatrist volunteers ten hours each week at a not-for-profit counseling center to assist persons with drug and alcohol addiction.							

	Statement of Financial Position		Statement of Activities		Statement of Cash Flows		
	Debit	**Credit**	**Debit**	**Credit**	**Operating**	**Investing**	**Financing**
9. A museum receives a Picasso painting to add to its modern art collection. The modern art collection is held for public exhibition, is protected and cared for, and is subject to a policy that requires the proceeds of items that are sold to be used to acquire other items for the collection.							
10. A local chapter of United Way receives $25,000 in cash from a donor who stipulates that the donation must go to a local drug rehabilitation program.							
11. A religious organization receives a donation of land valued at $750,000. The donor does not indicate how the donated land should be used.							
12. A museum receives $150,000 in Year 1 from a donor who stipulates that the donated funds are to be used in Years 2 and 3.							
13. A not-for-profit aquarium gift shop sells posters of Zeida, a popular sloth in its Caribbean exhibit.							
14. A local art museum paid for television and radio announcements to request contributions.							
15. A local art museum paid for brochures with general information about the museum's programs. The brochures were not printed as part of a fund drive.							

Answers and Explanations

	Statement of Financial Position		Statement of Activities		Statement of Cash Flows		
	Debit	Credit	Debit	Credit	Operating	Investing	Financing
1. A local CPA firm donated its services to perform the regular annual financial statement audit and preparation of IRS Form 990 for a not-for-profit museum.			Management and general expense	Contribution without donor restriction			

The donated services meet the three requirements for recognition as contribution revenue: services require specialized skills, the individual possesses those skills, and the NPO would have purchased the services if they had not been donated. There is no restriction on donated services, so it is recognized as without donor restrictions.

	Statement of Financial Position		Statement of Activities		Statement of Cash Flows		
	Debit	Credit	Debit	Credit	Operating	Investing	Financing
2. Several local Rotary Club members used their personal vehicles to deliver meals to senior citizens for Meals on Wheels.							

The donated services do not meet the three requirements for recognition as contribution revenue because they do not require specialized skills. No entry is required.

	Statement of Financial Position		Statement of Activities		Statement of Cash Flows		
	Debit	Credit	Debit	Credit	Operating	Investing	Financing
3. A donor contributed $2 million to a not-for-profit hospital.	Cash (asset)			Contribution without donor restriction	Inflow		

The donor did not place a restriction on the use of the contribution; therefore, it is reported as a contribution without donor restriction. Unrestricted cash donations are categorized as operating inflows on the statement of cash flows.

	Statement of Financial Position		Statement of Activities		Statement of Cash Flows		
	Debit	**Credit**	**Debit**	**Credit**	**Operating**	**Investing**	**Financing**
4. A donor contributed $4 million to a not-for-profit university to be permanently invested.	Cash (asset)			Contribution with donor restriction			Inflow

The donor placed a restriction on the use of the contribution; therefore, it is reported as a contribution with donor restrictions. Proceeds from contributions subject to long-term donor restrictions are categorized as financing inflows on the statement of cash flows.

	Statement of Financial Position		Statement of Activities		Statement of Cash Flows		
	Debit	**Credit**	**Debit**	**Credit**	**Operating**	**Investing**	**Financing**
5. A not-for-profit university purchased long-term investments for $4 million.	Investments (asset)	Cash (asset)				Outflow	

Purchases of long-term investments are reported on the statement of financial position and categorized as investing activities on the statement of cash flows.

	Statement of Financial Position		Statement of Activities		Statement of Cash Flows		
	Debit	**Credit**	**Debit**	**Credit**	**Operating**	**Investing**	**Financing**
6. $100,000 in earnings from a permanent scholarship endowment are released to fund scholarships (the scholarships have not been awarded yet).			Net assets released from donor restrictions out	Net assets released from donor restrictions in			

The donor restriction was satisfied, and, therefore, the amount is reclassified from net assets *with* donor restriction to net assets *without* donor restriction. The scholarships have not yet been awarded; therefore, the expense and cash given are not yet recognized.

	Statement of Financial Position		Statement of Activities		Statement of Cash Flows		
	Debit	Credit	Debit	Credit	Operating	Investing	Financing
7. A donor offers to donate $500,000 to a local mental health clinic if the clinic can raise a matching amount in the next 60 days.							

This pledge contains a condition that must be met before contribution revenue can be recognized. No entry is required.

	Statement of Financial Position		Statement of Activities		Statement of Cash Flows		
	Debit	Credit	Debit	Credit	Operating	Investing	Financing
8. A psychiatrist volunteers ten hours each week at a not-for-profit counseling center to assist persons with drug and alcohol addiction.			Program expense	Contribution without donor restriction			

The donated services meet the three requirements for recognition as revenue: services require specialized skills, the individual possesses those skills, and the NPO would have purchased the services if they had not been donated. There is no restriction on donated services, so they are recognized as without donor restriction.

	Statement of Financial Position		Statement of Activities		Statement of Cash Flows		
	Debit	Credit	Debit	Credit	Operating	Investing	Financing
9. A museum receives a Picasso painting to add to its modern art collection. The modern art collection is held for public exhibition, is protected and cared for, and is subject to a policy that requires the proceeds of items that are sold to be used to acquire other items for the collection.							

Gifts to a collection are not recognized as contribution revenue if the NPO maintains the collection for public exhibition or education, preserves the collection, and uses the proceeds from the sale of items in the collection to acquire other items for the collection. No entry is required.

	Statement of Financial Position		Statement of Activities		Statement of Cash Flows		
	Debit	**Credit**	**Debit**	**Credit**	**Operating**	**Investing**	**Financing**
10. A local chapter of United Way receives $25,000 in cash from a donor who stipulates that the donation must go to a local drug rehabilitation program.	Cash (asset)	Liability			Inflow		

Since the intermediary does not have variance power, the donation is a liability rather than revenue. Collecting donations to be sent to specified beneficiaries is a major part of United Way's operations. As such, the donation is categorized as an operating activity on the statement of cash flows.

	Statement of Financial Position		Statement of Activities		Statement of Cash Flows		
	Debit	**Credit**	**Debit**	**Credit**	**Operating**	**Investing**	**Financing**
11. A religious organization receives a donation of land valued at $750,000. The donor does not indicate how the donated land should be used.	Land (asset)			Contribution without donor restriction			

The donor did not restrict the use of the land; therefore, it is reported as a contribution without donor restriction.

	Statement of Financial Position		Statement of Activities		Statement of Cash Flows		
	Debit	**Credit**	**Debit**	**Credit**	**Operating**	**Investing**	**Financing**
12. A museum receives $150,000 in Year 1 from a donor who stipulates that the donated funds are to be used in Years 2 and 3.	Cash (asset)			Contribution with donor restriction	Inflow		

Because the donor specified when the donation can be used (ie, imposed a time restriction), it is reported as a contribution *with* donor restriction. The donation is only subject to temporary restriction, so it is categorized as an operating activity on the statement of cash flows.

	Statement of Financial Position		Statement of Activities		Statement of Cash Flows		
	Debit	Credit	Debit	Credit	Operating	Investing	Financing
13. A not-for-profit aquarium gift shop sells posters of Zeida, a popular sloth in its Caribbean exhibit.	Cash (asset)			Revenue	Inflow		

Auxiliary sales are revenues generated from activities other than the primary mission of the organization. They are categorized as operating activities on the statement of cash flows.

	Statement of Financial Position		Statement of Activities		Statement of Cash Flows		
	Debit	Credit	Debit	Credit	Operating	Investing	Financing
14. A local art museum paid for television and radio announcements to request contributions.		Cash (asset)	Fundraising expense		Outflow		

The advertisements specifically solicited contributions, so the costs are categorized as fundraising expenses. Fundraising is an operating expense, so the outflow is categorized as an operating activity on the statement of cash flows.

	Statement of Financial Position		Statement of Activities		Statement of Cash Flows		
	Debit	Credit	Debit	Credit	Operating	Investing	Financing
15. A local art museum paid for brochures with general information about the museum's programs. The brochures were not printed as part of a fund drive.		Cash (asset)	Management and general expense		Outflow		

Since the brochures are not specifically related to a fundraising event, they are a management and general expense. This is also categorized as an operating activity on the statement of cash flows.

2.07 Adjusting the Financial Statements

Overview

Representative Task (Application): Adjust the statement of financial position for a nongovernmental, not-for-profit entity to correct identified errors.

Representative Task (Application): Adjust the statement of activities for a nongovernmental, not-for-profit entity to correct identified errors.

Representative Task (Application): Adjust the statement of cash flows for a nongovernmental, not-for-profit entity to correct identified errors.

Representative Task (Application): Adjust the notes to the financial statements to correct identified errors and omissions.

Below is an example of a TBS that might be encountered on the CPA exam for adjusting the F/S of not-for-profit entities.

Example

Review the following draft F/S and partial draft of the notes to the F/S. First, identify any errors within the draft statements. Next, determine how to correct them.

Exhibits

Exhibit 1

Excel Animal Shelter Foundation
Statement of Activities (Draft)
Year Ended December 31, 20X2

	Without donor restrictions	With donor restrictions	Total
Revenues and other support			
Contributions	$100,000	$80,000	$180,000
Total revenues and other support	100,000	80,000	180,000
Expenses			
Rescue program	15,000	10,000	25,000
Adoption program	16,000	7,000	23,000
Management and general	3,000	2,000	5,000
Fundraising	1,000	1,000	2,000
Total expenses	35,000	20,000	55,000
Change in net assets	65,000	60,000	125,000
Net assets, January 1, 20X2	175,000	190,000	365,000
Net assets, December 31, 20X2	$240,000	$250,000	$490,000

Exhibit 2

Excel Animal Shelter Foundation
Statement of Financial Position (Draft)
December 31, 20X2 and 20X1

	20X2	20X1
Assets		
Cash and cash equivalents	$255,000	$275,000
Contributions receivable	80,000	70,000
Inventory	105,000	105,000
Long-term investments	330,000	300,000
Total assets	770,000	750,000
Liabilities and net assets		
Accounts payable	33,000	78,000
Long-term debt	247,000	307,000
Total liabilities	280,000	385,000
Net assets		
Without donor restrictions	240,000	175,000
With donor restrictions	250,000	109,000
Total net assets	490,000	284,000
Total liabilities and net assets	$770,000	$669,000

Exhibit 3

Excel Animal Shelter Foundation
Statement of Cash Flows (Draft)
Year Ended December 31, 20X2

Cash flows from operating activities	
Cash received from contributions	$170,000
Cash paid to employees and vendors	(100,000)
Net cash provided by operating activities	70,000
Cash flows from investing activities	
Purchases of investments	(70,000)
Proceeds from sale of investments	40,000
Net cash used by investing activities	(30,000)
Cash flows from financing activities	
Payments on long-term debt	60,000
Net cash provided by financing activities	60,000
Net increase in cash and cash equivalents	100,000
Cash and cash equivalents, beginning of year	275,000
Cash and cash equivalents, end of year	$375,000

Exhibit 4

Excel Animal Shelter Foundation
Notes to the Financial Statements (Partial Draft)

Note F – Functional Expenses

The table below presents expenses by both their nature and their function for fiscal year 20X2. The financial statements report certain categories of expenses that are attributable to more than one program or supporting function.Therefore, these expenses require allocation on a reasonable basis that is consistently applied. The expenses that are allocated include salaries and benefits, office supplies, and rent and utilities. They are allocated on the basis of estimates of time and effort.

	Program activities			**Supporting activities**			
	Rescue program	**Adoption program**	**Programs subtotal**	**Management and general**	**Fundraising**	**Supporting subtotal**	**Total expenses**
Salaries and benefits	$20,000	$20,000	$40,000	$4,400		$4,400	$44,400
Office supplies				300		300	300
Travel	200	200	400	100	200	300	700
Professional fees	3,000	1,000	4,000		1,800	1,800	5,800
Rent and utilities	800	800	1,600	200		200	1,800
Total expenses	$24,000	$22,000	$46,000	$5,000	$2,000	$7,000	$53,000

Exhibit 5

Date: Tuesday, February 14, 20X3
From: Excel Animal Shelter Controller
To: G/L Accounting
Subject: Office supplies expense

Team,

When reviewing the draft financial statements and notes, I noticed that $2,000 of office supplies were accurately reported on the statement of activities but were missing from the program activities section of the statement of functional expenses. Will you please correct this omission? The total should be allocated evenly between both programs.

Thank you,
Terry

Answers and Explanations

Similar to for-profit F/S, F/S for NPOs are interconnected. It is important to prepare the statements such that one flows to the next and the appropriate balances are tied to each other.

- The **statement of activities** is similar to an income statement in for-profit entities. The beginning and ending net assets, both *without* and *with* donor restrictions, should tie to the **statement of financial position**
- The statement of financial position is similar to a balance sheet. It starts with cash and cash equivalents, which should tie to the cash at the bottom of the **statement of cash flows**. Assets should equal liabilities plus net assets on the statement of financial position
- The **statement of functional expenses**, whether presented as part of the statement of activities, part of the notes, or in its own separate statement, should tie to the expenses on the statement of activities, both in total and by program and function

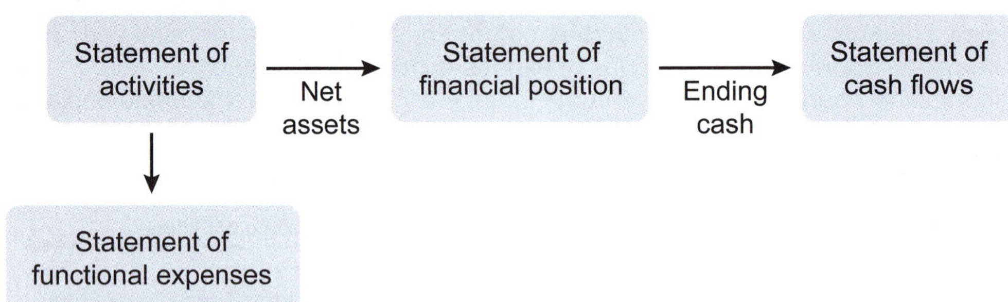

Statement of Activities

In the statement of activities for a not-for-profit organization, all expenses are categorized as *without* donor restrictions. The draft statement of activities reported expenses in both columns. The adjusted statement of activities correctly reports all expenses as *without* donor restrictions.

Total net assets without donor restrictions at December 31, 20X2, is now $220,000. Total net assets with donor restrictions at December 31, 20X2, is now $270,000.

Exhibit 1 – Adjusted

Excel Animal Shelter Foundation
Statement of Activities (Draft)
Year Ended December 31, 20X2

	Without donor restrictions	With donor restrictions	Total
Revenues and other support			
Contributions	$100,000	$80,000	$180,000
Total revenues and other support	100,000	80,000	180,000
Expenses			
Rescue program	25,000		25,000
Adoption program	23,000		23,000
Management and general	5,000		5,000
Fundraising	2,000		2,000
Total expenses	55,000		55,000
Change in net assets	45,000	80,000	125,000
Net assets, January 1, 20X2	175,000	190,000	365,000
Net assets, December 31, 20X2	$220,000	$270,000	$490,000

Statement of Financial Position

A transposition error occurred from the draft statement of activities to the draft statement of financial position. 20X1 net assets with donor restrictions on the draft statement of financial position should have been reported at $190,000 (as it is on the statement of activities), but it was incorrectly reported at $109,000.

An $81,000 adjustment ($190,000 − 109,000) is required to 20X1 net assets with donor restrictions on the statement of financial position. 20X1 net assets with donor restrictions are now $190,000, and 20X1 total net assets are now $365,000. Both of these figures tie to the statement of activities, and 20X1 total assets equal total liabilities plus net assets ($750,000).

20X2 net assets with and without donor restrictions ($270,000 and 220,000, respectively) are also updated to reflect the correct amounts per the adjusted statement of activities.

Exhibit 2 – Adjusted

Excel Animal Shelter Foundation
Statement of Financial Position (Draft)
December 31, 20X2 and 20X1

	20X2	20X1
Assets		
Cash and cash equivalents	$255,000	$275,000
Contributions receivable	80,000	70,000
Inventory	105,000	105,000
Long-term investments	330,000	300,000
Total assets	770,000	750,000
Liabilities and net assets		
Accounts payable	33,000	78,000
Long-term debt	247,000	307,000
Total liabilities	280,000	385,000
Net assets		
Without donor restrictions	220,000	175,000
With donor restrictions	270,000	190,000
Total net assets	490,000	365,000
Total liabilities and net assets	$770,000	$750,000

Statement of Cash Flows

The 20X2 cash and cash equivalents balance per the draft statement of cash flows ($375,000) does not equal the balance per the statement of financial position ($255,000).

On the statement of cash flows, cash **inflows** (eg, cash received, sale proceeds) are reported as increases to cash and have **positive** values. Cash **outflows** (eg, cash paid, purchases, payments on debt) are reported as decreases to cash and have **negative** values.

On the draft statement of cash flows, the payments on long-term debt were incorrectly reported as a positive $60,000 inflow. The adjusted statement of cash flows corrects this to a cash outflow of ($60,000). The adjusted ending cash balance is now $255,000, which ties to the statement of financial position.

Exhibit 3 – Adjusted

Excel Animal Shelter Foundation
Statement of Cash Flows (Draft)
Year Ended December 31, 20X2

Cash flows from operating activities	
Cash received from contributions	$170,000
Cash paid to employees and vendors	(100,000)
Net cash provided by operating activities	70,000
Cash flows from investing activities	
Purchases of investments	(70,000)
Proceeds from sale of investments	40,000
Net cash used by investing activities	(30,000)
Cash flows from financing activities	
Payments on long-term debt	(60,000)
Net cash used by financing activities	(60,000)
Net increase in cash and cash equivalents	(20,000)
Cash and cash equivalents, beginning of year	275,000
Cash and cash equivalents, end of year	$255,000

Notes to the Financial Statements

Per the email from the controller, $2,000 of office supplies expense was missing from the program activities on the draft statement of functional expenses. This $2,000 should be split evenly over both the Rescue and Adoption Programs. These expenses were correctly reported on the adjusted statement of activities.

The adjusted statement of functional expenses reflects an additional $1,000 of office supplies expense to both programs. Now the expenses tie back to the statement of activities, both in total ($55,000) and individually.

Exhibit 4 – Adjusted

Excel Animal Shelter Foundation
Notes to the Financial Statements (Partial Draft)

Note F – Functional Expenses

The table below presents expenses by both their nature and their function for fiscal year 20X2. The financial statements report certain categories of expenses that are attributable to more than one program or supporting function.Therefore, these expenses require allocation on a reasonable basis that is consistently applied. The expenses that are allocated include salaries and benefits, office supplies, and rent and utilities. They are allocated on the basis of estimates of time and effort.

	Program activities			Supporting activities			
	Rescue program	**Adoption program**	**Programs subtotal**	**Management and general**	**Fundraising**	**Supporting subtotal**	**Total expenses**
Salaries and benefits	$20,000	$20,000	$40,000	$4,400		$4,400	$44,400
Office supplies	1,000	1,000	2,000	300		300	300
Travel	200	200	400	100	200	300	700
Professional fees	3,000	1,000	4,000		1,800	1,800	5,800
Rent and utilities	800	800	1,600	200		200	1,800
Total expenses	$25,000	$23,000	$48,000	$5,000	$2,000	$7,000	$55,000

FAR 3
State and Local Government Concepts

FAR 3: State and Local Government Concepts

3.01 State and Local Government Concepts

FAR versus BAR Coverage

The AICPA Blueprint splits coverage of state and local government concepts between Financial Accounting and Reporting (FAR) and Business Analysis and Reporting (BAR). FAR primarily addresses the following:

- Measurement focus and basis of accounting
- Purpose of funds

BAR addresses the remaining governmental topics, including the following:

- Format and content of the financial section of the annual comprehensive financial report (ACFR)
- Derivation of government-wide financial statements (GWFS) and reconciliation requirements
- Typical items and specific types of transactions and events (measurement, valuation, calculation, and presentation in government entity financial statements [F/S])

Overview

Governments are large, complex organizations with many semiautonomous entities. A financial reporting entity consists of the primary government and its component units, if any, that present the results of the government's operations and financial position. Each entity must be **accountable** for the **public resources** it receives and can expend those resources only in compliance with specific legal restrictions.

Example of a Government Financial Reporting Entity

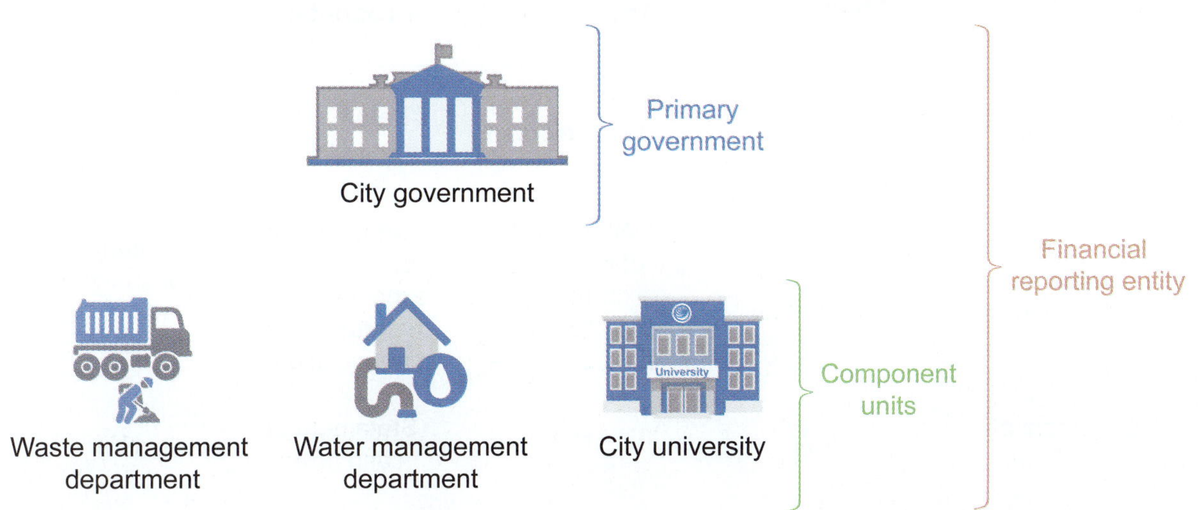

Government-wide F/S present an entire government entity's results. These F/S provide information about the government's overall operating results and how effectively it used its resources to fulfill its obligations.

Additionally, self-balancing sets of accounts called **funds** are established to categorize and report operating results in the government F/S. Funds help ensure fiscal compliance by segregating each unit's resources for tracking and reporting purposes.

Required Financial Statements

Basic financial statements for a government entity include the following:

- Government-wide financial statements
  - Statement of net position
  - Statement of activities
- Governmental funds financial statements
  - Balance sheet
  - Statement of revenues, expenditures, and changes in fund balances
- Proprietary funds financial statements
  - Statement of net position
  - Statement of revenues, expenses, and changes in fund net position
  - Statement of cash flows (direct method)
- Fiduciary funds financial statements
  - Statement of fiduciary net position
  - Statement of changes in fiduciary net position

Comparison of Types of Financial Statements Issued

For-Profit Entities (GAAP)	**Government Entities (GASB)**			
	Government-wide Statements	**Fund Statements**		
		Governmental Funds	**Proprietary Funds**	**Fiduciary Funds**
Balance sheet	Statement of net position	Balance sheet	Statement of net position	Statement of fiduciary net position
Income statement	Statement of activities	Statement of revenues, expenditures, and changes in fund balances	Statement of revenues, expenses, and changes in fund net position	Statement of changes in fiduciary net position
Statement of cash flows	N/A	N/A	Statement of cash flows	N/A
Full accrual	**Full accrual**	**Modified accrual**	**Full accrual**	**Full accrual**

Measurement Focus and Basis of Accounting

Representative Task (Remembering & Understanding): Recall the measurement focus and basis of accounting used by state and local governments for fund and government-wide financial reporting.

State and local (eg, city) government F/S are characterized by their **measurement focus** (ie, which items are reported) and **basis of accounting** (ie, when and how to report items).

There are two types of measurement focus:

- The **economic resources measurement focus** requires reporting all resources obtained and obligations (current and long term) incurred. This focus is always associated with full accrual accounting
- The **current financial resources measurement focus** is a single-period focus that measures the extent to which financial resources obtained during a period are sufficient to cover costs incurred (ie, budgets) during that same period. This focus is always associated with modified accrual accounting

There are also two bases of accounting:

- **Full accrual accounting** is the method typically required by GAAP
- **Modified accrual accounting** has a **budgetary focus**, highlighting the extent to which financial resources obtained during a period are **sufficient to cover costs** incurred during that same period

State and Local Government Fund Characteristics		
Entity	**Accounting System**	**Measurement Focus**
Governmental funds	Modified accrual	Current financial resources
Proprietary funds	Full accrual	Economic resources
Fiduciary funds	Full accrual	Economic resources
Government-wide	Full accrual	Economic resources

Modified Accrual Accounting

Governmental funds use **modified accrual accounting** rather than full accrual accounting. The modified accrual method combines cash accounting with full accrual accounting. The **interperiod equity concept** is a central principle of modified accrual accounting.

The interperiod equity concept keeps the focus on a *single period*, with that period's revenues intended to cover its spending. This is consistent with the idea of trying to maintain a **balanced budget** so that costs in the current period aren't paid by future taxpayers. At the same time, evaluating government activity one period at a time means that future periods are essentially ignored.

In measuring the transactions under modified accrual accounting, the following **measurement principles** are used:

- **Revenues:** These are recognized in the period they are **available to spend**, which means they are collectible in the current period to pay liabilities, or **within 60 days** after year-end. Revenues billed or collected in advance are deferred until the appropriate future period. Revenues that are not measurable are treated as available to spend once they are collected
- **Costs:** These are recognized using the expenditure principle. Costs are recorded in the period during which the obligation to pay them arises, whether this occurs before or after the period in which the government is actually using the assets or services. Costs are generally recorded when the related fund liability is incurred, except as it relates to unmatured interest on L/T debt, as this is only recorded when it becomes legally due
- **Long-term assets and liabilities:** These are generally *not accounted* for since they represent future period activity. The purchase of an asset is simply treated as a current outflow of financial resources, and the proceeds from long-term borrowing are treated as a current inflow. No depreciation is recorded on assets, and interest and principal owed on long-term debt are not recorded until the periods in which they must be paid
- **Reporting:** The F/S prepared include a balance sheet to present the financial position and a statement of revenues, expenditures, and changes in fund balance to present the flow of financial resources during the year. There is no equivalent to a statement of cash flows in modified accrual reporting
- **Accountability:** Budgets are typically developed at the beginning of each year, and governmental financial reporting focuses on determining compliance with budgets and accountability for resources. Any fund utilizing annual budgets must prepare a reconciliation

At the beginning of Year 2, Boulder City had a $650,000 outstanding judgment. Boulder City paid $350,000 of the judgment during Year 2. The remaining balance of the judgment includes $125,000 payable early in Year 3 and $175,000 payable at the end of Year 4. Determine the amount that Boulder should report as a liability for the judgment in its Year 2 governmental fund financial statements.

Governmental funds are budgetary in nature and use modified accrual accounting. Under modified accrual, governmental fund liabilities are recognized to the extent they will be paid with available resources. This generally means that current liabilities are accrued because they are due within the next year and will be paid with currently available resources. Conversely, long-term liabilities are likely to be paid with future (ie, currently unavailable) resources and are therefore not accrued.

In Boulder's case, $300,000 of the outstanding judgment remains unpaid. Boulder will accrue a $125,000 liability in the governmental funds' Year 2 F/S because the amount due in Year 3 will be paid primarily with resources already available to the government. The remaining amount is not accrued.

Purpose of Funds

Representative Task (Application): Determine the appropriate fund(s) that a state or local government should use to record its activities.

Government activities are not all accounted for using the modified accrual method. Some activities closely resemble those of private businesses and use accrual accounting. A **self-balancing set of accounts**, known as a **fund**, is established for each category of activity.

There are three broad categories of funds:

- **Governmental funds:** These funds generally have a budgetary focus and the main emphasis of reporting is the sources, uses, and balances of *current financial resources*. Governmental funds are for activities that are primarily funded by taxation or other mandatory payments and are virtually unique to government. **Modified accrual** accounting is used
- **Proprietary funds:** These funds generally have an operations orientation, and the main emphasis of reporting is determining income, financial position, changes in financial position, and cash flows using the economic resources approach. Proprietary funds are for business-like activities that are primarily funded by users' voluntary payments for goods and services. **Accrual accounting** is used, in a virtually identical fashion to private businesses
- **Fiduciary funds:** These funds are generally oriented toward the accounting for assets, and the main emphasis of reporting is net position and changes to net position using the economic resources approach. Fiduciary funds are for activities that most closely resemble not-for-profit organizations, including trusts and agency activities. The trust and custodial funds use **accrual accounting**

Government Entities: Funds and Basis of Accounting

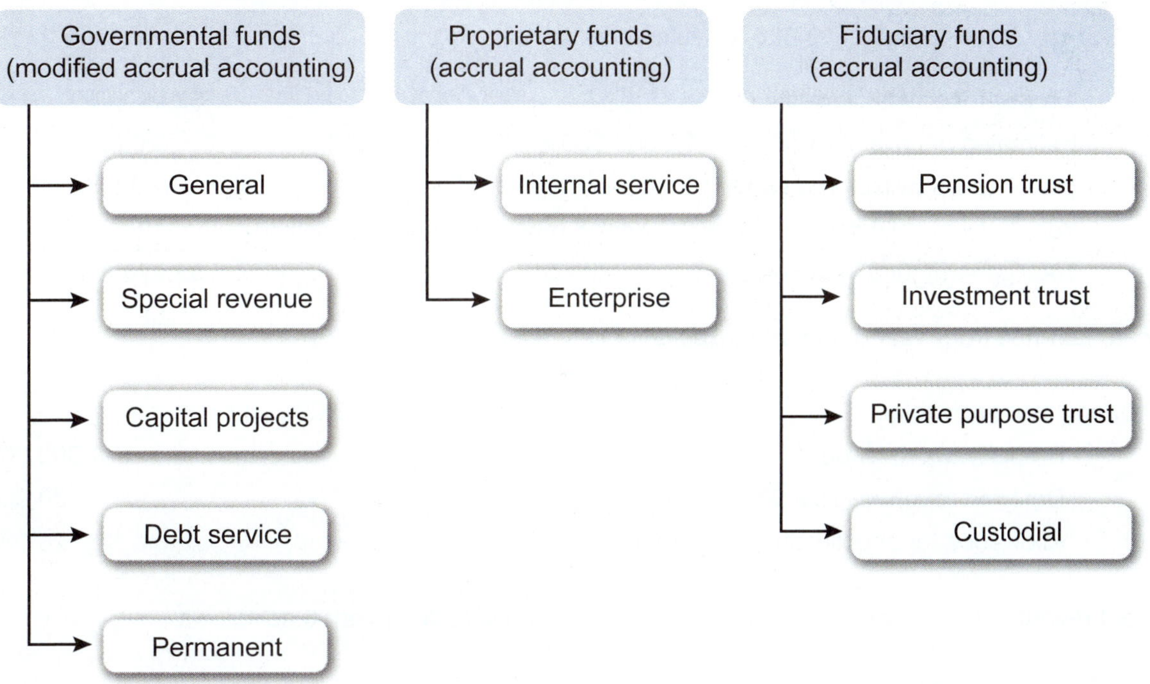

Governmental Funds

General Fund

A government unit must have one **general fund** but can establish as many special revenue, capital projects, and permanent funds as needed to account for the various activities that fit these categories. A debt service fund is only needed if the entity issues general obligation debts.

This general fund accounts for and reports any activity or function by the government unit that is not being accounted for in another fund, such as general operations, public safety, public works, culture, and recreation. Revenue sources include income, sales and property taxes, fees, fines, licenses, permits, and grants.

Jesber County levied property taxes of $2,000,000 in Year 6, of which 1% is expected to be uncollectible. The county has a calendar year end and provides the following additional information with regard to collections:

- $50,000 of taxes levied in Year 6 will be collected on January 31, Year 7
- $80,000 of taxes levied in Year 6 will be collected on March 31, Year 7
- $120,000 of taxes levied in Year 5 will be collected on March 31, Year 6

Calculate the amount of property tax revenue that Jesber County should report in its Year 6 **general fund,** and prepare the journal entry to record revenue from Year 6 levied taxes.

Under the modified accrual approach, property tax revenues are recognized in the **year the tax levy takes place** (ie, in advance of collection). Revenue recognized is directly reduced from the levied amount due to the following:

- Amounts expected to be collected more than 60 days after year-end (ie, deferred revenue)
- Amounts estimated to be uncollectible

Property tax revenue is $2,020,000, calculated as follows:

Gross property tax levied	$2,000,000
Estimated uncollectible amount ($2,000,000 × 1% uncollectible)	(20,000)
Year 6 taxes collected on March 31, Year 7 (deferred revenue)	(80,000)
Year 5 taxes collected on March 31, Year 6 (not previously recognized)	120,000
Total general fund Year 6 property tax revenue	**$2,020,000**

Record revenue from Year 6 property taxes levied as follows:

Property tax receivable	2,000,000	
Property tax revenue		1,900,000
Deferred revenue (Year 6)		80,000
Allowance for uncollectible property taxes		20,000

Record revenue from property taxes levied in Year 5 but available in Year 6 as follows:

Deferred revenue (Year 5)	120,000	
Property tax revenue		120,000

Special Revenue Fund

Special revenue funds are used to account for and report specific revenues from earmarked sources that are restricted or committed to be used to finance designated activities other than capital projects and debt service. An example is a gas tax that finances repairs and maintenance of roads. Revenue sources include fees, grants, specific taxes, and other earmarked revenue sources.

Riverview County received the following proceeds that are legally restricted to expenditure for specified purposes:

Special assessments on affected property owners to install sidewalks	$500,000
Gasoline taxes to finance road repairs	$900,000

Determine the amount that should be accounted for in Riverview's special revenue funds.

Special revenue funds are governmental funds used to account for revenues that are **restricted or committed to finance specific activities** other than capital projects or debt service. When a revenue source is restricted, the government should create a special revenue fund to designate that all money from that source be used for one specified activity.

A **special assessment** is a charge issued by a government against property owners (or landowners) to finance a public project that will specifically benefit those owners. The special assessment's proceeds are generally accounted for as either a custodial fund (if the government acts as a facilitator by collecting and disbursing the funds) or a debt service fund (if the levies are used to repay a bond the government issued to finance the project).

In this scenario, the type of revenue source (ie, tax versus assessment) and beneficiaries (ie, general public versus specific homeowners/taxpayers) determines how each transaction is accounted for. The gasoline taxes are restricted to finance road repairs (for the general public), and, therefore, Riverview would report the **$900,000** collected in a special revenue fund. However, the $500,000 from the special assessment to install sidewalks for specific homeowners is accounted for as either a custodial fund or debt service fund, not a special revenue fund.

Capital Projects Fund

Capital projects funds account for major acquisition or construction activities of capital assets, other than those financed by proprietary or trust funds. These funds account for and report the financial resources that are restricted, committed, or assigned for these types of capital outlays. An example is the construction of a city hall, a convention center, or a county courthouse. Revenue sources include special tax revenues, proceeds from bonds, transfers, or capital grants.

A capital projects fund for a new city convention center recorded a receivable of $550,000 from a state grant and a $275,000 transfer from the general fund. Determine the amount that should be reported as revenue by the capital projects fund.

Governmental Funds: Classifications of Financial Inflows	
Revenues	• All financial inflows not classified as other financing sources • Examples include taxes, fines, licenses, permits, charges for services, grants, voluntary donations
Other Financing Sources	• Certain financial inflows, excluding revenues • Examples include transfers in from other funds and proceeds from long-term borrowings

Governmental funds (eg, capital projects fund) receive resources from a variety of sources. How each inflow is classified depends on the **source generating the inflow** and whether it relates to the fund's general operations. **Other financing sources** include transfers in from other funds as well as the proceeds from long-term borrowings.

Revenues include all other financial inflows besides interfund transfers and long-term borrowing proceeds, including government-mandated nonexchange revenue, which results from one governmental unit's provision of resources to another governmental unit for a specific purpose.

In this scenario, the state grant provided to the city is government-mandated **nonexchange revenue**. Accordingly, the city will report **$550,000 of revenue** in the capital projects fund.

Operating transfers are one-way movements of resources from one fund to finance current-period activities in another fund. In this case, the city has an operating transfer when **$275,000** is moved from the general fund to the capital projects fund. Such transfers are classified as **other financing sources**, not revenue.

Debt Service Fund

Debt service funds are responsible for accumulating and making interest and principal payments on the tax-supported debts of the governmental funds. The debt service fund accounts for and reports the resources that are restricted, committed, or assigned for this long-term debt purpose. The expenditures may also include premiums on issuance of bonds. Revenue sources include portions of property taxes and transfers.

In the current year, Poplar City paid $5,000 interest and $20,000 principal on its outstanding general obligation bonds. The payment was made from a debt service fund using cash transferred earlier that same year from the general fund. Determine how the city should report the expenditures:

	General Fund	Debt Service Fund	Permanent Fund
A)	$25,000	$25,000	$0
B)	$0	$25,000	$20,000
C)	$25,000	$5,000	$0
D)	$0	$25,000	$0

The **debt service fund** is a governmental fund type used to account for resources designated for **interest** and **principal expenditures** on the entity's debt. Cash transfers between governmental funds are reported under **other financing sources** (transferee) and **other financing uses** (transferor) to distinguish them from ordinary revenues and expenditures. When the cash is used, the expenditure is recognized in the fund that makes the payment.

Here, the correct answer is **Choice D**. The city should report $0 in expenditures under the general fund since the payment was made from the debt service fund. Interest of $5,000 and principal of $20,000 should both be reported in the debt service fund for a total of $25,000. An amount of $0 should be reported under permanent fund (like an endowment) since there is no restriction on the principal.

Permanent Fund

Permanent funds account for and report assets whose principal is restricted and may not be spent (nonexpendable fund) but must be invested permanently (the income is, however, spendable/expendable—endowment fund). Investments are reported at their fair values, with a few minor exceptions, following GASB 72. Revenue sources are usually from the investment earnings of the trust.

The city of Denton has two trust funds for the benefit of the city's parking garage: Trust Fund 1 and Trust Fund 2. Only the earnings from Trust Fund 1 can be expended, but both the principal and interest from Trust Fund 2 can be expended. Determine how the city should report each trust fund.

Assets provided by a government entity from which only the earnings (not the principal) are spendable are accounted for as **permanent funds**. Revenues from earmarked sources used to finance designated activities are reported in the **special revenue fund**.

Since Denton is holding funds for the benefit of another government entity (the city's parking garage), the funds from the two trusts are considered governmental funds. Denton should report Trust Fund 1 as a permanent fund since only the earnings can be expended. Trust Fund 2 should be reported as a special revenue fund because both the interest and principal revenues are from an earmarked source and are spendable.

Remember the types of funds and their bases of accounting using the acronym "Grandma G's cooking deserves praise":

Governmental funds

Modified, Accrual

General

Special revenue

Capital projects

Debt service

Permanent

Proprietary Funds

Proprietary funds use accrual accounting and have an operations orientation. These funds resemble **private businesses** because they are funded primarily by **payments from users** for goods and services.

If the users are internal (eg, other funds of the government), the proprietary fund is classified as an *internal service fund*. If the users are external (eg, taxpayers), the fund is classified as an *enterprise fund*. Governments establish as many enterprise and internal service funds as needed to account for activities that fit these descriptions:

- **Internal service** funds render services or provide goods to other funds within the government entity, charging the other funds directly for those services. Examples include a maintenance department, IT department, janitorial department, or motor pool. Revenue sources include billings for services, grants, and interest earnings. Capital assets are depreciated
- **Enterprise** funds account for activities financed by voluntary payments for goods and services rendered to the payers. Often a user fee is paid. Examples include city-operated water utilities, airports, transit systems, public hospitals, public universities, public housing, lotteries, or post offices. Revenue sources include charges for services, interest and investment income, shared revenues (property or gas tax), and transfers in

Required F/S for proprietary funds include the following:

- The **statement of net position** (balance sheet equivalent) presents the fund's assets, deferred outflows, liabilities, deferred inflows, and net position
- The **statement of revenues**, **expenses**, **and changes in fund net position** (income statement equivalent) is the fund's operating statement. It tracks the flow of resources into and out of the fund
- The **statement of cash flows** tracks the cash receipts and disbursements during a period. This statement has four categories of cash flow activities: operating, investing, capital and related financing, and noncapital financing. It must be prepared using the direct method

A city government reported a $7,400 increase in net position in the motor pool internal service fund, a $25,000 increase in net position in the water enterprise fund, and a $7,000 increase in the employee pension fund.

Determine the amount the city should report as the change in net position for business-type activities in its statement of activities.

The primary government's net position is presented in two columns on this statement:

- Governmental activities aggregate the financial position of the governmental funds and internal service funds
- Business-type activities aggregate the financial position of the enterprise funds

Here, the city's funds would be accounted for on the statement of net position as follows:

- The water **enterprise fund** is a business-type activity (ie, transacts with external parties); therefore, the city will report the fund's **$25,000 increase in net position** in the business-type activities column
- The motor pool is a governmental activity because **internal service funds** account for goods and services provided to other government departments (eg, police department). The city will report the pool's **$7,400** increase in net position in the governmental activities column
- The pension trust fund is a fiduciary fund. Fiduciary funds are not included on the statement of net position because they have no net position, so their inclusion would be misleading

Fiduciary Funds

Fiduciary funds account for resources held by a government in a trustee or custodial capacity for other entities. All **trust funds** make use of the **economic resources measurement focus** and the **accrual** basis of accounting in the same way as proprietary funds. **Custodial funds**, however, are atypical in that they only report assets and liabilities. Accordingly, custodial funds do not report equity and do not utilize measurement focus but do employ the **accrual** basis of accounting to recognize assets and liabilities.

- **Pension trust** (and other employee benefits): These account for government employee pensions and other post-retirement benefits for which the government is a trustee. Two required supplementary information schedules are required: funding progress and employer contributions
- **Investment trust:** These account for pooled resources that are being invested on behalf of multiple government entities for which this specific government entity is a trustee
- **Private purpose trust:** These account for resources that are being held for the benefit of private persons or organizations or other governments. Examples include a fund to hold cash for unclaimed tax refunds or escheat property as well as a scholarship fund. These could be expendable or nonexpendable
- **Custodial:** These account for collected amounts that must be transferred to other funds or outsiders. An odd characteristic of custodial funds (formerly referred to as agency funds) is that all of the assets held belong to others (held in a custodial capacity), so assets always equal liabilities and the custodial fund has no equity section at all

Deland County received a $3,500,000 capital grant to be equally distributed among its five municipalities. The grant is to finance the construction of capital assets. Deland had no administrative or direct financial involvement in the construction. In which fiduciary fund should Deland record the receipt of cash?

The fiduciary fund category accounts for resources held for others. The **custodial fund** under the fiduciary fund category accounts for collected amounts that must be transferred to other funds or to outsider entities. Because the **amount** held in a custodial fund **belongs to others**, it is recorded as both an asset and a liability. Since Deland acts as an intermediary in the distribution of funds among its five municipalities, the $3,500,000 capital grant should be recorded in the custodial fund.

Select the appropriate measurement focus and basis of accounting to be used by a local government's private-purpose trust fund:

	Measurement Focus	Basis Of Accounting
A)	Current financial resources	Modified accrual
B)	Economic resources	Modified accrual
C)	Current financial resources	Accrual
D)	Economic resources	Accrual

Fiduciary funds (eg, **private-purpose trust funds**) account for resources held on behalf of other entities (ie, assets managed by a trustee). The resources managed in these funds are typically held for several years. Therefore, **fiduciary funds** use full **accrual accounting** and the **economic resources approach** to determine the net position and changes in net position of those resources.

Government-Wide Financial Statements

In addition to fund statements, another category of F/S is required: government-wide financial statements (GWFS). Like GAAP F/S, GWFS provide information about how effectively and **efficiently** the entity has used its current resources and the resources available to meet its **future obligations**.

GWFS consist of a statement of net position (ie, balance sheet) and a statement of activities (ie, income statement). Aggregate information is reported under the following columns:

- **Governmental activities**, which include transactions involving taxes and other nonexchange transactions. Governmental activities aggregate the financial position of the governmental and internal service funds
- **Business-type activities**, which include transactions involving user charges and fees to external entities for goods and services provided. Business-type activities aggregate the financial position of the enterprise funds

Statement of Net Position: Primary Government Categories	
Governmental Activities	**Business-type Activities**
• General administration and public services provided by the government • Financed primarily through taxes, nonexchange transactions, and intragovernmental transfers • Include governmental funds and internal service funds	• Quasi-business organizations of the government • Financed by charges and fees charged to external users for providing goods and services • Include enterprise funds

- A **total column** summing the governmental and business-type activities (ie, primary government total)
- **Component units** (if any), which are legally separate semiautonomous organizations of the primary government

Sample City
Statement of Net Position
December 31, Year 1

	Primary government			
Assets	**Governmental activities**	**Business-type activities**	**Total**	**Component units**
Cash and cash equivalents	$13,597,899	$10,279,143	$23,877,042	$ 303,935
Investments	27,365,221	-	27,365,221	7,428,952
Receivables (net)	12,833,132	3,609,615	16,442,747	4,042,290

Determine which of the following is recognized for governmental activities in the government-wide F/S but **not** in the governmental fund F/S:

A) Transfers between governmental funds
B) Deferred property tax revenue
C) State grant awarded for road repairs completed this fiscal year
D) Salaries payable at the end of the current year

Remember, governmental funds use modified accrual (MA) accounting, while government-wide F/S use full accrual (FA) accounting. Because there are two systems, some items will appear on the governmental fund F/S but not on the government-wide F/S, and vice versa.

The correct answer is **Choice B**. Property tax revenue is generally considered earned and available to spend in the year assessed. However, amounts not expected to be collected within 60 days of year-end are considered unavailable (ie, not revenue under MA) because incoming cash flow is less certain.

Earned but unavailable property tax revenue would be reported on the government-wide statement of activities, not on the statement of revenues, expenditures, and changes in fund balance for governmental funds.

Transfers between governmental funds would be presented on both FA and MA F/S. Because the state grant was both awarded and received during the year (ie, earned and available), it would be recognized under both FA and MA accounting. Salaries payable is a short-term operating account; salaries would be expensed when incurred, and the accrual would appear on both FA and MA F/S.

FAR 4
Public Company Reporting Topics

FAR 4: Public Company Reporting Topics

4.01 Public Company Reporting Topics

Overview

Representative Task (Remembering & Understanding): Recall the purpose of forms 10-Q, 10-K and 8-K that a U.S. registrant is required to file with the U.S. Securities and Exchange Commission under the Securities Exchange Act of 1934.

Representative Task (Remembering & Understanding): Identify the items of Form 10-Q (Part I Items 1 through 3) and Form 10-K (Part II Items 7, 7A and 8) filed with the U.S. Securities and Exchange Commission.

The Securities and Exchange Commission (SEC) is a federal agency whose mission is to protect investors, maintain fair, orderly, and efficient markets, and facilitate capital formation (https://www.sec.gov/about/what-we-do). The SEC administers the U.S. securities laws and requires publicly held companies to adhere to U.S. GAAP when reporting financial statements.

The SEC regulates the **issuance of securities** by publicly traded companies and the **trading of those securities** on secondary markets. The SEC's intent is to ensure that there is adequate information in the public domain before firms issue securities and before those securities are subsequently traded. Financial information provided by firms influences many stakeholders' decisions. As such, the SEC is very involved with **financial reporting** and **accounting standards**.

Although the SEC can prescribe accounting standards, it has delegated this task to the **Financial Accounting Standards Board** (FASB). However, the SEC maintains the **enforcement power** for all publicly traded companies to assure compliance with U.S. GAAP. When the SEC determines that a firm has reported in violation of GAAP, it sends a deficiency letter to the firm. If the violation is not resolved, the SEC can then stop the trading of the firm's securities. If warranted, the Department of Justice becomes involved, and criminal charges for violations of the securities laws are filed.

Filing Requirements

The **Securities Exchange Act of 1934** established the SEC. The act regulates the trading of securities after the securities are issued and provides requirements for periodic reporting and disclosures. These requirements were created to promote full disclosure of relevant information by publicly traded firms.

Unless exempt by regulation, companies with **$10+ million** of assets, **2,000+** shareholders (500+ if nonaccredited investor shareholders), and **securities that trade on a national securities exchange** or an over-the-counter market must have their securities registered.

Filing requirements are as follows:

<table>
<tr><th>Type of Filer</th><th>Market Value of Outstanding Securities</th><th>Annual Revenues</th><th>10-K</th><th>10-Q</th></tr>
<tr><td>Large, accelerated filer</td><td>$700M and up</td><td>N/A</td><td>60 days</td><td>40 days</td></tr>
<tr><td>Accelerated filer</td><td>$250M–$700M</td><td rowspan="2">$100M and up</td><td rowspan="2">75 days</td><td rowspan="2">40 days</td></tr>
<tr><td>Accelerated filer and SRC</td><td>$75M–$250M</td></tr>
<tr><td rowspan="2">Nonaccelerated filer and SRC</td><td>$75M–$700M</td><td>Under $100M</td><td rowspan="2">90 days</td><td rowspan="2">45 days</td></tr>
<tr><td>Under $75M</td><td>Unlimited</td></tr>
</table>

Note that the SEC requires fewer disclosures from smaller reporting companies (SRCs). A company qualifies as an SRC if it has:

- Less than $250 million in public float (ie, equity held by nonaffiliated investors), or
- Less than $700 million in public float and less than $100 million in annual revenues.

SEC Reports

Common SEC Reports

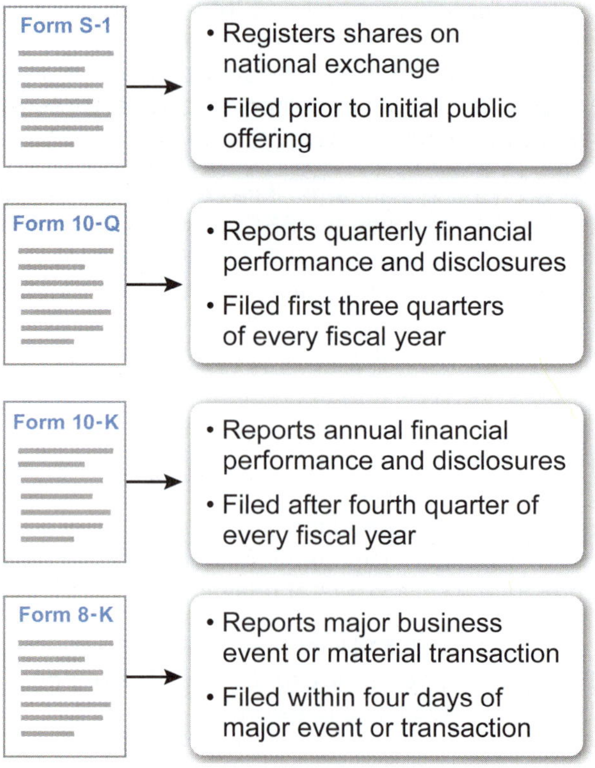

Form S-1 →
- Registers shares on national exchange
- Filed prior to initial public offering

Form 10-Q →
- Reports quarterly financial performance and disclosures
- Filed first three quarters of every fiscal year

Form 10-K →
- Reports annual financial performance and disclosures
- Filed after fourth quarter of every fiscal year

Form 8-K →
- Reports major business event or material transaction
- Filed within four days of major event or transaction

Registration Statement (Form S-1)

Form S-1 is filed prior to a company's initial public offering. It registers the company's shares on the national exchange.

Quarterly Report (Form 10-Q)

The 10-Q is intended to provide investors with an update since the last annual report. Form 10-Q, Part I, requires the following sections:

- **Financial statements** (F/S) (Item 1) are **reviewed** (as opposed to audited) and include the following:
  - Balance sheet for the quarter and prior fiscal year end
  - Quarterly and year-to-date income statements for this quarter and the same period in the previous year
  - Cumulative year-to-date statements of cash flow for the current and prior fiscal years
- **Management's discussion and analysis** (MD&A) (Item 2) provides the company's perspective on the business results for the period. MD&A presents information about the company's financial condition (and changes in financial condition), results of operations, liquidity, capital resources and any significant trends or uncertainties. This area also provides critical accounting judgments (eg, estimates and assumptions).
- **Quantitative and qualitative disclosures about market risk** (Item 3) requires information about the company's exposure to market risk (eg, interest rate risk, foreign currency exchange risk, commodity price risk, equity price risk). This item also provides information about risk factors, unresolved SEC comments on reporting, legal proceedings, etc.

Form 10-Q is required within:

- **40 days** of the end of each of the first three quarters for accelerated and large, accelerated filers, or
- **45 days** for nonaccelerated filers.

The 10-Q must be filed for the first three quarters of the fiscal year (the fourth quarter requires the 10-K [ie, annual report], rather than another 10-Q). While management provides its evaluation as to the effectiveness of internal controls on an annual basis, Form 10-Q requires information about changes in controls over financial reporting that are likely to have a material effect since the previous report. Information about controls and procedures is covered in Part I, Item 4, of Form 10-Q.

Annual Report (Form 10-K)

Form 10-K provides a comprehensive picture of a company's business, its risks, and its performance, including **audited** F/S. Form 10-K, Part II, requires the same sections as the 10-Q but presented in a different order:

- **Management's discussion and analysis** (MD&A) (Item 7)
- **Quantitative and qualitative disclosures about market risk** (Item 7A)
- **Financial statements and supplementary data** (Item 8): Two years of balance sheets, three years of income statements, statement of cash flows, and statement of comprehensive income

The **deadline** for filing the Form 10-K is within:

- **60 days** after the close of the company's fiscal year for large, accelerated filers,
- **75 days** for accelerated filers, or
- **90 days** for nonaccelerated filers.

Information Statements (Form 8-K)

Form 8-K reports **significant events** affecting the company and is required to be filed within **four business** days of such an event. Examples of significant events include the following:

- Entering into or terminating a material agreement
- Bankruptcy
- Acquisition or disposal of assets
- Change in directors, CEO, or auditor

Earnings Per Share (EPS)

Representative Task (Application): Calculate basic earnings per share and diluted earnings per share considering the impact of stock options, preferred stock, convertible preferred stock and/or convertible debt.

Earnings per share (EPS) represents the amount of earnings attributable to one share of **common stock**. Companies with publicly traded stock are required to provide two different EPS figures: basic and diluted. Basic EPS is the EPS based only on actual transactions for the year. Diluted EPS is a "worst-case" figure reflecting the potential dilution of stock options and convertible securities. Both allow comparisons of performance and profitability for firms of any size and indicate the amount of dividends that could have been paid, regardless of actual dividends paid.

If EPS were $4, this means that $4 of dividends could have been paid, on average, to each share of common stock outstanding during the year, from earnings in that year. It does not mean the firm is obligated to pay that much or that it will pay that much. Also, actual common stock dividends paid do not reduce EPS.

If a company only has common stock, nonconvertible preferred stock, and other instruments that cannot be converted into common stock, it has a **simple** capital structure and reports basic EPS. Diluted EPS is only applicable for companies with **complex** capital structures (ie, companies with outstanding stock options or convertible securities).

Both basic and diluted EPS are reported **separately** for income from **continuing operations** and, if applicable, for income from **discontinued operations**. The EPS for income from continuing operations is reported on the face of the income statement, while the EPS for income from discontinued operations may be reported either on the face of the statement or in the notes.

Disclosure of Earnings per Share Information

	Basic Earnings per Share	**Diluted Earnings per Share** *(if company has complex capital structure)*
Income from Continuing Operations *(and net income, if different)*	Always reported on income statement	Reported on income statement
Income from Discontinued Operations	May be reported on income statement or in notes	May be reported on income statement or in notes

Basic EPS

Companies with simple capital structures (ie, only common stock and nonconvertible preferred stock/other instruments) report **basic EPS** only. Basic EPS includes only actual common shares outstanding. In the basic EPS formula shown below, the **numerator** is net income available to common shareholders. This is calculated as net income less preferred stock dividends (as these dividends are never available for common shareholders).

For *cumulative* preferred stock, the current-year dividend (declared or undeclared) is always subtracted from net income. This is because cumulative preferred stock pays a fixed dividend on a predetermined schedule, so the company is responsible for paying any unpaid, missed dividends to cumulative preferred shareholders first.

On the CPA exam, questions may present information on dividends in arrears (ie, cumulative dividends that are unpaid). If dividends in arrears from a previous year are paid in addition to the current-year dividend, still only one year is subtracted from the current-year numerator. This is because basic EPS in the previous year has already been reduced by the skipped dividends.

For *noncumulative* preferred stock, only declared dividends are subtracted.

- **Noncumulative:** Only declared dividends
- **Cumulative:** Deduct annual dividend (regardless if declared or paid); ignore dividends in arrears

$$\textbf{Basic EPS} = \frac{\text{Net income} - \text{Preferred stock dividends}}{\text{Weighted average number of common shares outstanding}}$$

- **Issued and/or reacquired shares:** Prorated for portion of year outstanding
- **Stock splits and stock dividends:** Treated retroactively (as if occurred at the beginning of year or earliest period presented)

The **denominator** in the formula is the weighted average number of common shares outstanding throughout the year. Shares that are issued or reacquired during the year are **prorated** for the portion of the year they are outstanding (eg, shares issued on June 30 are outstanding for six of 12 months). Stock splits and stock dividends are treated as **retroactive** adjustments to the beginning of the period.

Based on the common stock transactions below, calculate the weighted average number of shares outstanding as of December 31, Year 1, that should be used in the calculation of basic earnings per share in the financial statements.

Date	Transaction
January 1, Year 1	Beginning balance 100,000
April 1, Year 1	Issued 30,000 shares for cash
June 1, Year 1	50% stock dividend
August 15, Year 1	2-for-1 stock split
October 31, Year 1	Repurchased 42,000 shares

The weighted average number of shares outstanding must reflect stock changes during the reporting period:

Date	Transaction	Treatment	Cumulative Weighted Shares
January 1	Beginning balance	Outstanding all year	100,000
April 1	Issued 30,000 shares	Weighted, outstanding for nine months	100,000 + (30,000 × 9/12) = 122,500
June 1	50% stock dividend	Treat as if occurred January 1	122,500 × 1.5 = 183,750
August 15	2-for-1 stock split	Treat as if occurred January 1	183,750 × 2 = 367,500
October 31	Repurchased 42,000 shares	Weighted for two months	367,500 − (42,000 × 2/12) = **360,500**

A company had the following outstanding shares as of January 1, Year 3:

Preferred stock, $75 par, 5%, cumulative	15,000 shares
Common stock, $5 par	60,000 shares

On September 1, Year 3, the company sold 30,000 shares of previously unissued common stock. No dividends were in arrears at the beginning of the period, and no dividends were declared or paid during Year 3. Net income for Year 3 totaled $305,000. Calculate the basic earnings per share for the year ended December 31, Year 3.

For the numerator, net income is $305,000 and the annual dividend on the *cumulative* preferred stock is 15,000 shares × $75 par × 5% = $56,250.

For the denominator, the company had 60,000 common shares outstanding from January through August (eight months). On September 1, the company sold an additional 30,000 common shares. The company had 90,000 (60,000 + 30,000) common shares outstanding from September through December (four months).*

$$\frac{\$305{,}000 - \$56{,}250}{(60{,}000 \times \frac{8}{12}) + (90{,}000 \times \frac{4}{12})} = \frac{\$248{,}750}{70{,}000} = \$3.55$$

*The denominator can also be calculated as (60,000 × 12/12 months) + (30,000 × 4/12 months). The previous approach uses a cumulative total outstanding, while this approach treats each issuance separately (it reflects that the initial 60,000 were outstanding for the entire year and the additional 30,000 were only outstanding for 4/12 months). Both approaches will arrive at the same result.

Diluted EPS

If a company has outstanding stock options or convertible securities, it has a **complex** capital structure and reports both **basic and diluted** EPS. Diluted EPS is an imaginary calculation based on events that have not happened as of the balance sheet date. It reflects the maximum dilution or lowest value of EPS that is possible given the firm's outstanding securities at the balance sheet date.

Only dilutive potential changes to common stock are included in the diluted EPS calculation. If a potential change to the common stock *increases* EPS, it is considered **antidilutive** and is ignored for the EPS calculation.

Treasury Stock Method

Diluted Earnings Per Share (EPS) with Stock Options

$$\textbf{Diluted EPS} = \frac{\text{Net income} - \text{Preferred stock dividends*}}{\text{Weighted-average number of shares} + \text{Incremental shares}}$$

Incremental shares:

$$\text{Options} - \left(\frac{\text{Options} \times \text{Exercise price}}{\text{Market price}} \right)$$

**Includes current-year cumulative preferred stock dividends (whether or not declared) and declared noncumulative dividends*

Employee stock options and warrants can be dilutive because their exercise *may increase the number of common shares outstanding*. Increasing the common shares outstanding increases the **denominator** in the EPS formula, which results in decreased (diluted) EPS.

To enter stock options and warrants into the calculation for diluted earnings per share, a three-step process called the **treasury stock method** is used. Under the treasury stock method, it is assumed that the potential proceeds from the exercising of options are used to repurchase shares in order to mitigate the dilutive impact of the options.

1. **Assume** all options are exercised.
2. **Purchase** treasury shares with the **proceeds** from the exercise.
3. **Add** the incremental shares to the denominator in the EPS calculation.

Options are dilutive (and, therefore, included in the diluted EPS calculation) when the exercise price (also called option price) is **lower** than the market price. When the exercise price is **greater** than the market price, the options are **antidilutive** and are not included in the calculation.

The easy way to remember the relationship between exercise price, market price, and dilution is that no one would exercise a stock option if it required paying more than market price. If exercise price is lower than market price, people will exercise the options, and the result will be dilutive.

A company had net income of $550,000 and 100,000 common shares outstanding, for a basic earnings per share of $5.50. It also had 20,000 stock options outstanding the entire year. The exercise price of the options is $30, and the average market price of common stock for the period was $40.

Step 1: assume all options are exercised

20,000 options × $30 option exercise price = **$600,000**

Step 2: purchase treasury shares with the proceeds from the exercise

$600,000 ÷ $40 share market price = **15,000 shares**

Step 3: add the incremental shares to the denominator

20,000 options − 15,000 shares = **5,000 incremental shares**

The diluted EPS calculation assumes that all 20,000 options were exercised to create 20,000 new shares of common stock and a cash inflow of $600,000. The company then took that $600,000 and repurchased 15,000 existing, outstanding shares of common stock in order to minimize the impact of the stock options being exercised. The total net impact was an increase of 5,000 shares of common stock outstanding (20,000 created − 15,000 repurchased).

Exercise price is lower than market price, so the options are dilutive. 5,000 shares are added to the denominator to calculate diluted EPS. Diluted EPS is $5.24.

$$\frac{\$550{,}000}{100{,}000 + 5{,}000} = \frac{\$550{,}000}{105{,}000} = \$5.24$$

If-Converted Method

Diluted Earnings Per Share (EPS) with Convertible Securities

Dividends not paid on preferred stock

After-tax interest expense on convertible debt

$$\textbf{Diluted EPS} = \frac{\left(\text{Net income} - \text{Preferred stock dividends*}\right) + \textit{Convertible}\text{ preferred stock dividends} + \textit{Convertible}\text{ debt interest}}{\text{Weighted-average number of shares} + \text{New shares issued from conversion}}$$

**Includes current-year cumulative preferred stock dividends (whether declared or not) and declared noncumulative dividends*

To include convertible securities (eg, convertible preferred stock, convertible bonds) into the calculation for diluted earnings per share, the **if-converted method** is used. Here, diluted EPS is calculated assuming that all convertible securities are converted. In the diluted EPS formula shown above, the **numerator** is net income less preferred stock dividends, just like the basic EPS numerator, **plus** both convertible preferred stock dividends and convertible debt interest.

If the **convertible preferred shares** are exchanged for common stock, the company will not have to pay the preferred stock dividends, so this amount is added back to the numerator. If **convertible bonds** are exchanged for common stock, the company will not have to pay the annual interest expense on the bond, so this amount is added (less the tax effect, or 1 − tax rate) back to the numerator.

Interest expense is not always just the face value of the bond multiplied by the stated rate. Amortization of a premium or discount should be considered when determining the interest expense. Amortization of a bond premium decreases interest expense (and the amortization of a bond discount increases interest expense).

The **denominator** in the formula is the weighted average number of common shares outstanding throughout the year **plus** the new shares that would be issued if the securities were converted. The conversion to common stock is considered to have occurred at the beginning of the earliest period reported. However, if the convertible securities are issued during the year, the date of issuance is used as the conversion date instead.

Conversion Date for Convertible Securities (If-Converted Method)

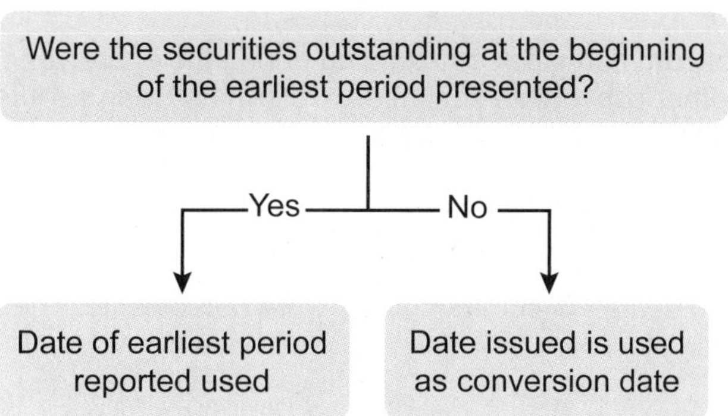

A company had 220,000 shares of common stock outstanding at January 1, Year 2. On July 1, Year 2, it issued 80,000 additional shares of common stock. 20,000 shares of convertible cumulative preferred stock ($55 par, 2%) were outstanding all year. Each share of the convertible preferred stock is convertible into one share of common stock. If the company's tax rate is 30% and Year 2 net income is $540,000, calculate its diluted earnings per share.

For the numerator, net income is $540,000, and the annual dividend on the cumulative preferred stock is 20,000 shares × $55 par × 2% = $22,000.

For the denominator, 220,000 common shares are outstanding from January through June (six months). 300,000 common shares (220,000 + 80,000) are outstanding from July through December (six months). Additionally, the convertible preferred stock adds 20,000 new shares (one share of preferred stock is convertible into one share of common stock) if converted.

$$\frac{\$540{,}000 - \$22{,}000 + \$22{,}000}{(220{,}000 \times \frac{6}{12}) + (300{,}000 \times \frac{6}{12}) + 20{,}000} = \frac{\$540{,}000}{280{,}000} = \$1.93$$

Basic EPS is $1.99. Because diluted EPS is less than basic EPS, the convertible preferred stock is dilutive. Diluted EPS is reported at $1.93.

During the current year, Chan Co. had net income of $120,000 and an income tax rate of 30%. Chan had convertible 10-year bonds with a face value of $1,000,000 outstanding since January 1. The stated rate of interest on the bonds is 9%. The bonds are convertible into 5,000 shares of Chan's common stock.

Chan had 12,000 shares of common stock outstanding during the entire year. Chan has no preferred stock outstanding and no other convertible securities. Determine Chan's diluted earnings per share for the year ended December 31.

For the numerator, net income is $120,000, and $63,000 interest expense ([$1,000,000 × 9%] × 1 − 30%) on the convertible bonds is added back to net income.

For the denominator, 12,000 shares of common stock were outstanding. The bonds can be converted into 5,000 shares of common stock.

$$\frac{\$120{,}000 + [(\$1{,}000{,}000 \times 9\%) \times (1 - 30\%)]}{12{,}000 + 5{,}000} = \frac{\$120{,}000 + 63{,}000}{17{,}000} = \frac{\$183{,}000}{17{,}000} = \$10.76$$

However, basic EPS is $10 ($120,000 / 12,000). Because diluted EPS is greater than basic EPS, the convertible bonds are antidilutive. Therefore, the convertible bonds will be ignored for purpose of calculating diluted EPS. Both basic and diluted EPS will be reported at $10.

FAR 5
Special Purpose Frameworks

FAR 5: Special Purpose Frameworks

5.01 Special Purpose Frameworks

Overview

Public business enterprises issue general-purpose financial statements that are based on general-purpose frameworks. **General-purpose frameworks** include generally accepted accounting principles (GAAP) for U.S. companies and international financial reporting standards (IFRS) for companies that file internationally. However, financial statements (F/S) not based on GAAP (or IFRS) may be issued by nonpublic business entities to avoid the time-consuming and costly application of GAAP (or IFRS). These financial statements are prepared in accordance with **special purpose frameworks**.

Special purpose frameworks (also called other comprehensive bases of accounting, or OCBOA) include cash basis, modified cash basis, income tax basis, contractual basis, and regulatory basis. Cash basis, modified cash basis, and income tax basis are the most common frameworks used.

Financial Statement Titles

Representative Task (Remembering & Understanding): Recall appropriate financial statement titles to be used for the financial statements prepared under a special purpose framework.

Financial statement titles in cash-, modified-cash-, and tax-basis F/S are not required to be modified. However, users of the F/S should be able to easily identify the basis of accounting used to prepare the F/S. The table below provides examples of financial statement titles that may be used in place of the GAAP titles "income statement" and "balance sheet."

Equivalents to GAAP Financial Statement Titles

GAAP (Accrual Basis)	Cash Basis	Modified Cash Basis	Income Tax Basis
Balance Sheet	Statement of assets and liabilities arising from cash transactions	Statement of assets and liabilities—modified cash basis	Statement of assets, liabilities, and capital—tax basis
Income Statement	Statement of cash receipts and disbursements	Statement of revenues collected and expenses paid—modified cash basis	Statement of revenues and expenses—tax basis

The preceding examples are not meant to be all-inclusive and are not the only acceptable titles.

Cash Basis and Modified Cash Basis

Representative Task (Application): Prepare financial statements using the cash basis or modified cash basis of accounting.

Representative Task (Application): Perform calculations to convert cash basis or modified cash basis financial statements to accrual basis financial statements.

Cash Basis

Under the **cash basis** of accounting:

- Revenues are recognized when they are received, regardless of when they are earned.
- Expenses are recognized when they are paid, regardless of when they are incurred.
- Fixed assets and inventory are expensed, not capitalized.
- Accruals are not made, and prepaid assets are not recorded.

CG, Inc. bought a $10,000 piece of equipment during the year. The equipment has a useful life of five years and no salvage value. The following journal entries express the purchase under the cash basis versus GAAP:

Cash Basis			**GAAP**		
Equipment expense	10,000		Equipment (asset)	10,000	
Cash		10,000	Cash		10,000

Under the cash basis, the equipment is expensed immediately, and no depreciation is recorded in the future. Under GAAP, depreciation will be recorded over the life of the equipment:

Cash Basis			**GAAP**		
			Depreciation expense	2,000	
			Accumulated depreciation		2,000

Modified Cash Basis

The **modified cash basis** results from using a combination of cash-basis accounting and accrual-basis (ie, GAAP) accounting. In general, a modification to the cash basis is acceptable if it is logical and consistent and the affected transactions involve cash.

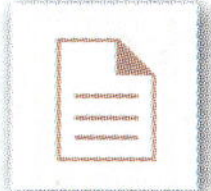

For example, if a company purchased equipment with cash, capitalization and depreciation of the equipment under a modified cash basis would be acceptable. This is because the **transaction involved cash**. However, accruing accounts receivable is probably not acceptable, because no cash has been exchanged.

Modifications to the cash basis of accounting generally result when cash receipts or disbursements provide a benefit or obligation that covers multiple reporting periods. The most common and acceptable modifications to cash basis accounting include the following:

Common Modifications to Cash Basis Accounting

- Capitalization and depreciation of PP&E acquired with cash
- Capitalization of inventory acquired with cash
- Recognition of deferred revenue from cash receipts
- Recognition of long-term notes and other debt arising from cash transactions

When modifications to the cash basis of accounting are made, all related accounts must be reported using the same basis of accounting. For example, if long-term assets are recognized, then the related depreciation expense and accumulated depreciation must be recognized. Similarly, if debt is recognized, then the related interest expense (accrued and paid) must be recognized.

Converting from Cash Basis or Modified Cash Basis to Accrual Basis

Nonpublic entities may use the cash basis or the modified cash basis of accounting. However, in certain circumstances (eg, applying for a bank loan, reporting to owners), these entities may need to report using the accrual basis of accounting. In such cases, conversion from cash basis or modified cash basis to accrual basis will be required.

Under the **accrual basis of accounting** (ie, GAAP), *revenues are recognized when earned, and expenses are recognized when incurred*. This means that revenue and expense recognition under the accrual basis does not relate to cash collection or disbursement. Conversely, recall that under the **cash basis**, *revenues are recognized upon cash collection, and expenses are recognized upon cash disbursement*.

The change in the account balances between periods on the accrual-basis balance sheet can be used to derive accrual-basis revenues and expenses.

The material in this section is very similar to that covered in the Statement of Cash Flows (SCF) section of FAR 1. While the SCF typically requires conversion from accrual basis to cash basis, the representative task here requires conversion from cash basis to accrual basis. The same methodology can be used in both scenarios; the process is simply reversed.

Converting Cash Receipts to Accrual-Basis Revenue

To convert cash receipts (ie, cash-basis revenue) to accrual-basis revenue, prepare journal entries for the increases or decreases in balance sheet accounts related to revenue. The two key accounts related to revenue are accounts receivable (A/R) and unearned revenue.

Scenario 1: Accounts receivable increases by $100,000 during the year

The corresponding journal entry is as follows:

Accounts receivable	100,000	
Revenue		100,000

The company earned revenue of $100,000 but has not received the corresponding cash yet. Under the cash basis, this would not be included as revenue (as no cash has been collected). However, the $100,000 of earned revenue should be recognized for accrual purposes, so $100,000 should be added to cash collected to arrive at accrual-basis revenue.

Scenario 2: Accounts receivable decreases by $110,000 during the year

The corresponding journal entry is as follows:

Cash	110,000	
Accounts receivable		110,000

The company received cash of $110,000 from a customer paying off a receivable. Under the cash basis, this $110,000 would be recognized as revenue (because cash was collected). However, under the accrual basis, this revenue was recognized previously, when the receivable was initially recorded, so $110,000 should be subtracted from cash collected to arrive at accrual-basis revenue.

Scenario 3: Unearned revenue increases by $80,000 during the year

The corresponding journal entry is as follows:

Cash	80,000	
Unearned revenue		80,000

The company received $80,000 cash in advance of providing goods or performing services. Under the cash basis, this $80,000 would be recognized as revenue immediately (because cash was collected). However, this revenue has not yet been earned, so $80,000 should be subtracted from cash collected to arrive at accrual-basis revenue.

Scenario 4: Unearned revenue decreases by $85,000 during the year

The corresponding journal entry is as follows:

Unearned revenue	85,000	
Revenue		85,000

The company provided goods or performed services to earn $85,000 of revenue. The corresponding cash was previously received, so under the cash basis, this $85,000 would not be included in revenue (as no cash has been collected as a result of this entry). However, $85,000 of revenue has now been earned and can be recognized for accrual purposes, so $85,000 should be added to cash collected to arrive at accrual-basis revenue.

If a company collected cash of $250,000 during the year, accrual-basis revenue would be calculated as follows:

Converting Cash Receipts to Accrual-Basis Revenue

Cash collected during the year (cash-basis revenue)		$250,000
Add:	Increase in A/R (scenario 1)	100,000
	Decrease in unearned revenue (scenario 4)	85,000
Deduct:	Decrease in A/R (scenario 2)	(110,000)
	Increase in unearned revenue (scenario 3)	(80,000)
Accrual-basis revenue during the year		$245,000

Converting Cash Paid for Operating Expenses to Accrual-Basis Operating Expenses

To convert cash paid for operating expenses (ie, cash-basis operating expenses) to accrual-basis operating expenses, prepare journal entries for the increases or decreases in balance sheet accounts related to expenses. The two key accounts related to operating expenses are accrued liabilities and prepaid expenses.

Scenario 5: Accrued liabilities increases by $50,000 during the year

The corresponding journal entry is as follows:

Expense	50,000	
Accrued liabilities		50,000

Under the accrual method, when an expense is incurred without cash paid, the company records a corresponding accrued liability (eg, wages expense and wages payable). Here, the company recognized an expense of $50,000. Under the cash basis, this would not be included as an expense (as no cash has been paid). However, the $50,000 incurred expense should be recognized for accrual purposes, so $50,000 should be added to cash paid for operating expenses to arrive at accrual-basis operating expenses.

Scenario 6: Accrued liabilities decreases by $35,000 during the year

The corresponding journal entry is as follows:

Accrued liabilities	35,000	
Cash		35,000

The company disbursed cash of $35,000 to pay off a liability. Under the cash basis, this $35,000 would be recognized as an expense (because cash was paid). However, under the accrual basis, this expense was recognized previously, when it was initially incurred, so $35,000 should be subtracted from cash paid for operating expenses to arrive at accrual-basis operating expenses.

Scenario 7: Prepaid expenses increases by $70,000 during the year

The corresponding journal entry is as follows:

Prepaid expense (asset)	70,000	
Cash		70,000

The company paid $70,000 cash for something that will not benefit it until a future period (eg, prepaid rent, prepaid insurance). Under the cash basis, this $70,000 would be recognized as an expense immediately (because cash was paid). However, under the accrual basis, this expense has not been incurred, as the benefit of the asset has not yet been realized, so $70,000 should be subtracted from cash paid for operating expenses to arrive at accrual-basis operating expenses.

Scenario 8: Prepaid expenses decreases by $60,000 during the year

The corresponding journal entry is as follows:

Expense	60,000	
Prepaid expense (asset)		60,000

Over time, as the prepaid asset's future benefit is realized (eg, coverage begins after prepaying for insurance), the expense is incurred. The corresponding cash was previously paid, so under the cash basis, this would not be included in operating expenses (as no cash has been collected as a result of this entry). However, $60,000 of expense has now been incurred and can be recognized for accrual purposes, so $60,000 should be added to cash paid for operating expenses to arrive at accrual-basis operating expenses.

If a company paid cash of $210,000 for operating expenses during the year, accrual-basis operating expenses would be calculated as follows:

Converting Cash Paid for Operating Expenses to Accrual-Basis Expenses		
Cash paid for operating expenses (cash-basis expenses)		$210,000
Add:	Increase in accrued liabilities (scenario 5)	50,000
	Decrease in prepaid expenses (scenario 8)	60,000
Deduct:	Decrease in accrued liabilities (scenario 6)	(35,000)
	Increase in prepaid expenses (scenario 7)	(70,000)
Accrual-basis operating expenses during the year		$215,000

Converting Cash Paid to Suppliers to Accrual-Basis Cost of Goods Sold

To convert cash paid to suppliers (ie, cash-basis expenses) to accrual-basis cost of goods sold (COGS), prepare journal entries for the increases or decreases in balance sheet accounts related to COGS. The two key accounts related to COGS are accounts payable (A/P) and inventory.

Scenario 9: Accounts payable increases by $60,000 during the year

The corresponding journal entry is as follows:

Inventory	60,000	
Accounts payable		60,000

The company purchased inventory on account for $60,000. Under the cash basis, there would be no journal entry recorded (as no cash has been paid). However, the $60,000 represents goods available for sale (ie, an asset) that the company has not yet paid for. The goods purchased on account should be recognized for accrual purposes, so $60,000 should be added to cash paid for purchases to arrive at accrual-basis COGS.

Note: If the company accounts for inventory on a periodic system, the purchases account rather than the inventory account would be debited at the time of purchase.

Scenario 10: Accounts payable decreases by $40,000 during the year

The corresponding journal entry is as follows:

Accounts payable	40,000	
Cash		40,000

The company disbursed cash of $40,000 to pay off its payable. Under the cash basis, this $40,000 would be recognized as an expense (because cash was paid). However, under the accrual basis, no expense is actually incurred, so $40,000 should be subtracted from cash paid for purchases to arrive at accrual-basis COGS.

Scenario 11: Inventory increases by $30,000 during the year

The corresponding journal entry is as follows:

Inventory	30,000	
Cash		30,000

The company paid $30,000 cash for inventory. Under the cash basis, this $30,000 would be recognized as an expense immediately (because cash was paid and inventory is not capitalized). However, under the accrual basis, no COGS has been incurred, as the inventory has not yet been sold, so $30,000 should be subtracted from cash paid for purchases to arrive at accrual-basis COGS.

Scenario 12: Inventory decreases by $25,000 during the year

The corresponding journal entry is as follows:

COGS	25,000	
Inventory		25,000

As the inventory is sold, COGS is recognized. The corresponding cash was previously paid, so under the cash basis, this would not be included in operating expenses (as no cash has been paid as a result of this entry). However, $25,000 of COGS has now been incurred and will be recognized for accrual purposes, so $25,000 should be added to cash paid for purchases to arrive at accrual-basis COGS.

If a company paid cash of $195,000 during the year for purchases, accrual-basis COGS would be calculated as follows:

Converting Cash Paid to Suppliers to Arrive at Accrual-Basis COGS		
Cash paid for purchases (cash-basis expenses)		$195,000
Add:	Increase in A/P (scenario 9)	60,000
	Decrease in inventory (scenario 12)	25,000
Deduct:	Decrease in A/P (scenario 10)	(40,000)
	Increase in inventory (scenario 11)	(30,000)
Accrual-basis COGS during the year		$210,000

Questions on the CPA exam may provide beginning and ending account balances rather than increases and decreases in the account balance. The beginning and ending balances can be used to derive the increase or decrease in the account during the year.

Converting Balance Sheet Amounts from Cash Basis to Accrual Basis

In addition to expenses and revenues, balance sheet amounts must also be converted from cash basis to accrual basis. Recall that, under the cash basis, many balance sheet amounts are not recognized:

- Fixed assets are not capitalized, as they are expensed when purchased.
- Inventory is not capitalized, as it is expensed when purchased.
- Accounts receivable and unearned revenue are not recognized, as revenue is recorded when cash is received.
- Accounts payable and accrued liabilities are not recognized, as expense is recorded when cash is paid.
- Prepaid expenses are not recognized, as expense is recorded when cash is paid.

These amounts will need to be added onto the balance sheet. Corresponding expenses (eg, depreciation expense) should be reflected in the income statement. If companies employ the modified basis of accrual, some of these items may already be recognized on the balance sheet.

Income Tax Basis

Representative Task (Application): Prepare financial statements using the income tax basis of accounting.

Income-tax-basis financial statements result from using the federal income tax rules and regulations that a firm uses, or expects to use, in filing its income tax return. In income-tax-basis accounting, the effects of events on a business are recognized when taxable income or a deductible expense would be recognized on the tax return. **Income** is recognized on the financial statements **in the period it is taxable**, and **expenses** are recognized on the financial statements **in the period they are deductible**.

The specific requirements of federal income tax accounting specify different income and expense recognition rules depending on the nature of the item and the type of taxpayer. Therefore, financial statements based on the income tax basis of accounting will include items based on various recognition principles, from pure cash to full accrual accounting, depending on that tax code's treatment of these items.

Some items of economic and accounting consequence to an entity are never recognized for tax purposes. These are commonly called permanent differences.

For example, proceeds from company officer life insurance policies or portions of intercompany dividends are not taxable income to an entity but provide cash to the entity. Similarly, the premium on life insurance policies on officers and certain fines are not deductible for income tax purposes but require the payment of cash.

Under the income tax basis of accounting, **nontaxable receipts** (revenue) and **nondeductible payments** (expenses) related to these permanent differences **would generally still be recognized** in a statement of revenues and expenses.

Because items and amounts reported for tax purposes are subject to adjustment by the IRS, the corresponding amounts reported in tax-basis financial statements are subject to change as the tax code is changed by the U.S. Congress. Therefore, the notes to the financial statements should clearly indicate not only the basis on which the statements were prepared, but also that they are subject to change as a result of IRS determinations.

F/S that reflect the tax basis of accounting are prepared according to federal tax laws. For brevity, the above section provides a more general overview of these F/S. Any tax knowledge required for the FAR exam is covered in FAR 19: Accounting for Income Taxes. For more comprehensive material related to federal tax laws, refer to the REG and TCP texts.

FAR 6
Financial Statement Ratios and Performance Metrics

FAR 6: Financial Statement Ratios and Performance Metrics

6.01 Financial Statement Ratios and Performance Metrics

Overview

Representative Task (Remembering & Understanding): Identify the appropriate financial statement ratio or performance metric to perform a specified type of analysis.

Financial statement ratios and **performance metrics** are used to evaluate companies on a host of factors including profitability, liquidity, and solvency. A company can compare its financial ratios internally over different time periods, with competitor ratios, or in relation to industry averages to benchmark performance. This comparison provides insight that management can use to determine the company's strategy going forward. The ratios are also used by investors and lenders in assessing the company's health.

These ratios typically fall in one of the following categories:

Ratio type	Purpose
Profitability ratios	To assess a company's ability to generate profit from its sales, operations, assets, or equity
Liquidity ratios	To assess a company's ability to pay off short-term liabilities
Solvency ratios	To assess a company's ability to pay off long-term liabilities

Companies also calculate **performance metrics** to analyze the company's abilities, efficiency, operations, growth, and more. Performance metrics include items expressed as ratios (eg, price-to-earnings ratio) and items that are not expressed as ratios (eg, EBITDA).

Effects of Changes on Ratios

It's important to understand how changes to financial statement accounts can impact ratios.

- The **numerator** has a **direct relationship** with the ratio; increases to the numerator result in an increased ratio.
- The **denominator** has an **inverse relationship** with the ratio; increases to the denominator result in a decreased ratio.
- If the numerator and the denominator are *both* impacted by a change, the impact to the ratio may not be easy to determine; substitute numbers into the ratio to see the impact of the change in this instance.

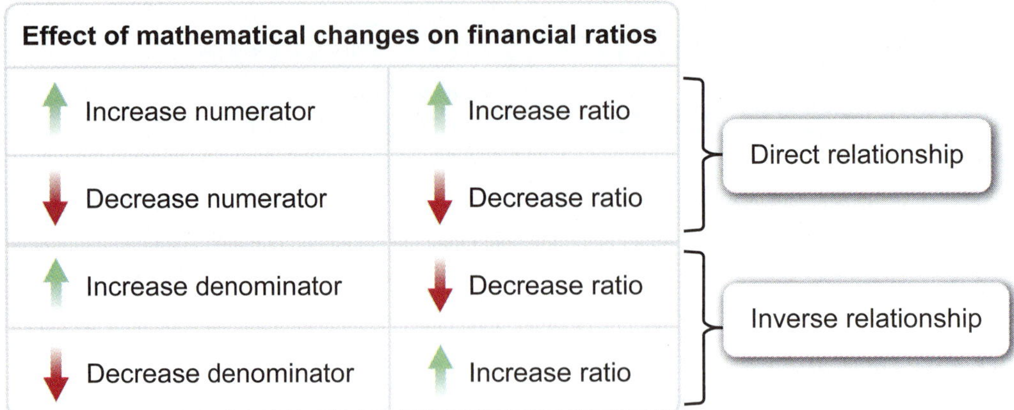

Calculating Financial Statement Ratios and Performance Metrics

Let's look at the financial results of a company to understand and calculate financial statement ratios and performance metrics. GreenWood Furniture produces custom-made furniture for its customers. Additional information about Greenwood is as follows:

- GreenWood has 10,000 shares of stock, trading at $32.50 per share in Year 2.
- GreenWood has no preferred stock.
- In Year 2 of operations, GreenWood declared and paid $20,000 in dividends.
- All sales and purchases are on credit.
- GreenWood uses the LIFO inventory method.
- GreenWood is a small company that has elected to amortize goodwill over 10 years.
- Year 2 beginning account balances include the following:
    - Total assets: $531,900
    - Total equity: $193,300
    - Accounts receivable: $75,000
    - Accounts payable: $60,000
    - Inventory: $40,000

Calculate financial statement ratios and performance metrics using GreenWood's Year 2 balance sheet and income statement.

GreenWood Furniture
Balance Sheet
As of December 31, Year 2

ASSETS	
Current assets	
Cash and cash equivalents	$ 8,500
Accounts receivable - net	104,800
Other receivables	2,300
Inventory	45,000
Prepaid expenses	2,800
Total current assets	163,400
Property, plant & equipment - net	
Land	35,000
Buildings	115,000
Equipment	210,000
(Less: Accumulated depreciation)	(34,600)
Property, plant & equipment - net	325,400
Intangible assets	
Goodwill	80,000
(Less: Accumulated amortization)	(16,000)
Total intangible assets	64,000
Total assets	$552,800
LIABILITIES	
Current liabilities	
Short-term loans payable	$ 10,000
Current portion of long-term debt	20,000
Accounts payable	64,000
Accrued compensation	3,500
Income taxes payable	1,800
Other accrued liabilities	6,500
Total current liabilities	105,800
Long-term liabilities	
Notes payable	20,000
Bonds payable	200,000
Total long-term liabilities	220,000
Total liabilities	325,800
STOCKHOLDERS' EQUITY	
Common stock (10,000 shares at $3 par value)	30,000
Additional paid-in capital in excess of par	70,000
Retained earnings	127,000
Total stockholders' equity	227,000
Total liabilities & stockholders' equity	$552,800

GreenWood Furniture
Income Statement
For the year ended December 31, Year 2

Net sales	$ 220,000
Cost of goods sold	122,900
Gross profit	97,100
Depreciation & amortization	19,600
Other operating expenses	13,600
Earnings before interest and taxes	63,900
Interest expense	12,800
Income before income taxes	51,100
Income tax expense	10,200
Net income	$ 40,900

Profitability Ratios

Representative Task (Application): Calculate profitability ratios (eg, gross profit margin, return on sales, return on assets, return on equity).

Profitability ratios are used to assess a company's ability to generate profit. Examples of profitability ratios include the following:

Ratio	Formula	Calculation	
Profit margin	Net income / Net sales	$40,900 / $220,000	= 18.59%
Return on sales*	EBIT / Net sales	$63,900 / $220,000	= 29.05%
Gross profit margin	Gross profit / Net sales	$97,100 / $220,000	= 44.14%
Return on assets	Net income / Average total assets	$40,900 / ($531,900 + $552,800) / 2	= 7.54%
Return on equity	Net income / Average total equity	$40,900 / ($193,300 + $227,000) / 2	= 19.46%

**Note: Interest expense and income tax expense are added back to net income for this ratio, because net income includes a reduction for interest expense and income tax expense.*

Profit margin measures how much profit a company makes for every dollar of revenue generated. GreenWood's profit margin indicates that the company generates $18.59 in profit for every $100 in sales.

Return on sales is similar to profit margin. However, in the numerator, rather than net income, the ratio uses earnings before interest and taxes (EBIT). As such, return on sales (here, $29.05 for every $100 in sales) is generally higher than profit margin because the numerator doesn't include the additional expenses of interest and taxes.

Gross profit margin uses gross profit (ie, sales − cost of goods sold) in the numerator. Gross profit margin (here, $44.14 for every $100 in sales) is generally higher than both profit margin and return on sales because cost of goods sold is the only expense included in the numerator.

GreenWood's **return on assets** (7.54%) and **return on equity** (19.46%) are measures of how effectively the company is generating profit with its assets and equity. Greenwood is generating $7.54 and $19.46 in net income for every $100 of assets and equity, respectively.

In general, managers and investors aim to have higher profitability ratios than industry averages and competitors. Higher profitability ratios show an increased ability to generate profits from products and services and earn returns on the company's investments.

Many ratios (eg, return on assets, return on equity) require an average balance in the denominator. For these ratios, we must average the Year 2 beginning balance (which is the same as the Year 1 ending balance) with the Year 2 ending balance:

$$\frac{\text{Year 2 beginning balance + Year 2 ending balance}}{2} = \text{Average balance}$$

Note: Questions on the CPA exam may instruct you to use the ending balance only in the calculation of a ratio that would typically require an average balance. Read the questions and instructions carefully.

Liquidity Ratios

Representative Task (Application): Calculate liquidity ratios (eg, current, quick, accounts receivable turnover, inventory turnover, accounts payable turnover).

Liquidity ratios are used to assess a company's ability to pay off short-term liabilities. Examples of liquidity ratios include the following:

Ratio	Formula	Calculation
Current ratio	$\frac{\text{Current assets}}{\text{Current liabilities}}$	$\frac{\$163{,}400}{\$105{,}800} = 1.54$
Quick ratio	$\frac{\text{(Cash + cash equivalents + marketable securities + net accounts receivable)}}{\text{Current liabilities}}$	$\frac{\$8{,}500+\$104{,}800}{\$105{,}800} = 1.07$

The **current ratio** measures a firm's ability to meet its short-term (ie, less than one year) obligations. A current ratio greater than 1.0 generally indicates that a company is able to do so.

The **quick ratio** is a similar measure of liquidity, but it excludes current assets that are difficult to convert into cash (such as inventory and prepaid expenses). Instead, only cash, cash equivalents, marketable securities, and net accounts receivable (ie, current assets that can be converted into cash more easily) are included in the numerator.

GreenWood's current ratio (1.54) and quick ratio (1.07) are both greater than 1.0. This indicates that Greenwood has enough liquidity to meet its short-term obligations. However, these ratios should be compared to industry averages to get a better sense of how GreenWood is performing in this regard.

Accounts receivable turnover	$\frac{\text{Net credit sales}}{\text{Average net accounts receivable}}$	$\frac{\$220,000}{(\$75,000 + \$104,800) / 2}$	= 2.45
Accounts payable turnover	$\frac{\text{Cost of goods sold}}{\text{Average accounts payable}}$	$\frac{\$122,900}{(\$60,000 + \$64,000) / 2}$	= 1.98
Inventory turnover	$\frac{\text{Cost of goods sold}}{\text{Average inventory}}$	$\frac{\$122,900}{(\$40,000 + \$45,000) / 2}$	= 2.89

The **accounts receivable turnover ratio** is a measure of how well a company is managing the credit it extends to its customers. A higher accounts receivable turnover generally indicates that it takes less time to collect cash from customers. GreenWood's accounts receivable turnover is 2.45.

The **accounts payable turnover ratio** indicates how quickly a company pays its vendors for inventory purchased on account. A lower accounts payable turnover ratio is generally preferred because companies can keep their cash invested for longer (ie, the cash can generate a larger return). However, companies should pay vendors on time and take advantage of purchase discounts for early payment as they are offered. GreenWood's accounts payable turnover is 1.98.

The **inventory turnover ratio** indicates how quickly finished inventory is sold to customers. A high inventory turnover ratio generally indicates that a company's products are in high demand. However, if the inventory ratio is too high, it may indicate that a company is charging too little (ie, inventory is flying off the shelves). GreenWood's inventory turnover ratio is 2.89.

Days sales in receivables	$\frac{\text{365 days}}{\text{Accounts receivable turnover}}$	$\frac{\text{365 days}}{2.45}$	= 148.98 days
Days payables outstanding	$\frac{\text{365 days}}{\text{Accounts payable turnover}}$	$\frac{\text{365 days}}{1.98}$	= 184.34 days
Days supply in inventory	$\frac{\text{365 days}}{\text{Inventory turnover}}$	$\frac{\text{365 days}}{2.89}$	= 126.30 days

Days sales in receivables, days payables outstanding, and days supply in inventory can be calculated by dividing 365 by the corresponding turnover ratio.

Days sales in receivables is, on average, how long it takes to receive payment from customers after a sale on account is made. Days payables outstanding measures, on average, how long it takes to pay invoices for goods and services received from suppliers. Days supply in inventory measures, on average, how long a company holds inventory before it is sold.

Cash conversion cycle	Days sales in receivables + Days supply in inventory − Days payables outstanding	148.98 + 126.30 − 184.34 = 90.94 days
Operating cycle	Days sales in receivables + Days supply in inventory	148.98 + 126.30 = 275.28 days

The **cash conversion** cycle measures the number of days it takes for a company to convert the cash it spends on inventory back into cash through its sales. The **operating cycle** measures the number of days between producing/purchasing inventory and collecting cash for selling that inventory. Companies typically aim to have lower cash conversion and operating cycles. The quicker the company can convert cash spent into cash earned, the better.

Solvency Ratios

Representative Task (Application): Calculate solvency ratios (eg, debt-to-equity, total debt, times interest earned).

Solvency ratios are used to assess a company's ability to pay off long-term liabilities. Examples of solvency ratios include the following:

Ratio	Formula	Calculation
Debt-to-equity	$\frac{\text{Total debt}}{\text{Total equity}}$	$\frac{\$325,800}{\$227,000} = 1.44$
Total debt	$\frac{\text{Total debt}}{\text{Total assets}}$	$\frac{\$325,800}{\$552,800} = 0.59$
Times interest earned*	$\frac{\text{EBIT}}{\text{Interest expense}}$	$\frac{\$63,900}{\$12,800} = 4.99$

**Note: Interest expense is added back to net income for this ratio, because net income includes a reduction for interest expense.*

The **debt-to-equity ratio** measures how much of the company is financed by creditors relative to that financed by stockholders. GreenWood has $1.44 in debt for every dollar in equity.

The **total debt ratio** is a similar measure that indicates the proportion of assets that is financed by creditors rather than stockholders. For GreenWood, 59% of assets are financed with debt, while 41% is financed through stockholder capital.

The **times interest earned ratio** is a measure of a company's ability to cover its interest expense with the income the company generates. GreenWood generates enough earnings to pay interest expense 4.99 times.

Other Ratios and Performance Metrics

Representative Task (Application): Calculate performance metrics (eg, EBITDA, price-to-earnings, dividend payout, asset turnover).

Financial statement users can calculate various performance metrics to evaluate and compare companies. Examples of performance ratios include the following:

Ratio	Formula	Calculation	
EBITDA	Net income + Tax expense + Interest expense + Depreciation + Amortization	\$40,900 + \$10,200 + \$12,800 + \$19,600	= \$83,500
Price-to-earnings ratio	Share price / Earnings per share	\$32.50 / (\$40,900/10,000 shares)	= 7.95
Dividend payout	Dividends / Net income	\$20,000 / \$40,900	= 48.90%
Asset turnover	Net sales / Average total assets	\$220,000 / ((\$531,900 + \$552,800) / 2)	= 0.41

EBITDA, or earnings before interest, taxes, depreciation, and amortization, is an alternative measure of profitability that focuses on cash profit rather than accounting profit. As such, in addition to adding back taxes and interest to net income, it also adds back the noncash expenses of amortization and depreciation. This provides a figure that is more equivalent to cash profits. EBITDA is sometimes expressed as a ratio by dividing the dollar value of EBITDA by net sales.

The **price-to-earnings** ratio measures the market price of a company's shares relative to the per-share income the company generates. This is calculated by dividing the share price (here, \$32.50) by the net income per share (\$40,900/10,000 shares outstanding). A high price-to-earnings ratio signifies that investors expect the company profitability to grow over time and, thus, are willing to purchase stock at a higher price.

The **dividend payout ratio** measures the amount of income that is paid out to owners of a company. For GreenWood, the ratio indicates that 48.90% of net income is paid out to shareholders in the form of dividends rather than being reinvested in the company.

The **asset turnover ratio** is indicative of how effectively companies use their assets to generate sales. GreenWood generates \$41 in sales for every \$100 the company has in assets.

Ratio Analysis Limitations

Companies use ratios to analyze and access financial performance or position. Although ratio analysis may provide useful insight, it also comes with limitations that may make comparison with other companies difficult or infeasible:

- **Heterogeneity in operation**: If the company's divisions individually operate in distinct industries, then combining performance may oversimplify data at an aggregate level and not provide insight into divisional performance.

- **Inconsistent interpretation of results**: Different ratios may provide conflicting interpretations of performance for the same company. For example, one ratio can suggest improving liquidity, whereas another ratio can suggest worsening liquidity.
- **The need for judgment**: Companies must determine whether ratios are reliable in the context of industry and company history. Ratios are statistical measures with no inherent value and alone are incomplete; it is the company's interpretation that creates insight.
- **Different accounting standards**: Differences in accounting methods or standards limit the comparability of ratios across companies. For example, one company may use FIFO inventory reporting, whereas another company may use LIFO inventory reporting.

Calculating Variances

Representative Task (Application): Calculate variances between budget and actual results.

Companies also evaluate performance by comparing financial statement accounts to prior-period or budgeted amounts. This provides helpful context for current-period performance. **Variances** are used to identify and investigate areas where the actual results were over or under the amounts being compared. Variances are either **favorable** (ie, positive) or **unfavorable** (ie, negative). A favorable variance is the result of **actual performance being better** than the amounts compared. This can mean that revenue is higher than expected or that costs are lower than expected.

Variance analysis can be performed monthly, quarterly, annually, or even for longer periods of time. Once the variance is determined, the reasons for the variance are investigated.

A service company compares budgeted expenses to actual expenses each period. Calculate the variances by comparing budgeted and actual amounts. Then indicate whether each variance is favorable or unfavorable.

Expenses:	**Budget**	**Actual**
Personnel		
Contract	17,843	17,402
In-house	67,435	71,094
Benefits	6,329	8,985
Sales & marketing		
Services	5,900	12,565
Marketing collateral	500	1,963
Other		
Technology	8,000	9,035
Legal & professional	12,000	6,587
Occupancy	3,000	2,490
Other office G&A	2,500	83
Interest expense	5,000	4,305
Amortization	1,600	1,609
Total expenses	130,107	136,118

Solution:

Variances are favorable if the actual expense is less than budget and unfavorable if the actual expense is greater than budget.

Expenses:	**Budget**	**Actual**	**Variance**	
Personnel				
Contract	17,843	17,402	441	Favorable
In-house	67,435	71,094	3,659	Unfavorable
Benefits	6,329	8,985	2,656	Unfavorable
Sales & marketing				
Services	5,900	12,565	6,665	Unfavorable
Marketing collateral	500	1,963	1,463	Unfavorable
Other				
Technology	8,000	9,035	1,035	Unfavorable
Legal & professional	12,000	6,587	5,413	Favorable
Occupancy	3,000	2,490	510	Favorable
Other office G&A	2,500	83	2,417	Favorable
Interest expense	5,000	4,305	695	Favorable
Amortization	1,600	1,609	9	Unfavorable
Total expenses	130,107	136,118	6,011	Unfavorable

In this example, overall expenses were $6,011 more than budgeted. However, that shows only part of the picture. A comparison of each expense line shows important details that can be investigated further, for example:

- Marketing and personnel costs were higher than expected.
- Legal and other general and administrative expenses were lower than expected.

Examining detailed variances can lead to insight and improved operations.

FAR

Area II: Select Balance Sheet Accounts

FAR 7
Cash & Cash Equivalents

FAR 7: Cash & Cash Equivalents

7.01 Cash & Cash Equivalents

Overview

Representative Task (Application): Calculate cash and cash equivalents balances to be reported in the financial statements.

Cash is the most liquid asset an entity can hold; thus, it is usually the first item presented in the current assets section of the balance sheet.

A **cash equivalent** is a financial instrument (investment) that meets the following criteria:

- It is easily convertible into a known amount of cash (highly liquid)
- It has an original maturity of three months or less from the date of purchase

For example, a five-year U.S. Treasury note will be considered a cash equivalent if the investor acquires the investment on the open market when its *remaining time to maturity* is under three months. An investment so close to maturity presents very little risk of change in value due to fluctuating interest rates.

An investment that has been excluded from cash equivalents because of a term exceeding three months will not be reclassified to cash equivalents as it approaches the maturity date. This is because no transaction or event occurs three months before maturity that would justify the preparation of a journal entry.

Other examples of cash and cash equivalents include the following:

- Coin and currency on hand (petty cash)
- Money market accounts
- Unmailed checks
- Savings accounts
- CDs with an original maturity of three months or less
- Negotiable paper (bank checks, traveler's checks, money orders)

Items **excluded** from unrestricted cash include the following:

- Compensating balances are minimum balances that must be maintained by the firm in relation to a borrowing or loan account. If the balance is related to a short-term liability, the compensating balance is shown as a current asset but is not considered part of the unrestricted cash balance. If it is related to a long-term liability, the compensating balance is a noncurrent asset
- Postdated or NSF (nonsufficient [or insufficient] funds) checks are receivables
- Restricted cash
  - Current: Cash that is restricted for use on a current asset/liability within one year is considered current. However, it is kept separate because it is not yet available for use in current operations
  - Noncurrent: Cash that is restricted for use on a noncurrent asset/liability (eg, bond sinking funds) is considered noncurrent. It is presented in either other assets or investments
- **Postage stamps** are considered supplies (prepaid expense)

Delta Co. had the following balances at December 31, Year 4:

Cash in checking account	$ 25,000
Cash in savings account restricted for paying long-term debt	125,000
Cash in money market account	55,000
U.S. Treasury bill purchased December 1, Year 4; maturing May 30, Year 5	150,000

Determine the amount Delta should report as cash and cash equivalents on its December 31, Year 4, balance sheet.

Delta will report cash and cash equivalents of **$80,000** ($25,000 from its checking account, plus $55,000 from its money market account) on its December 31, Year 4, balance sheet. The $125,000 cash in savings is restricted, and the $150,000 Treasury bill matures after more than three months; thus, neither is classified as a cash equivalent.

If more than one account exists at the same bank, the accounts are netted together. If the net balance is positive, it is listed as cash. If the net balance is **negative**, it is listed as a **current liability**. Cash accounts in different banks cannot be netted. In this case, the positive account is listed as an asset, and the negative account is listed as a current liability.

Cash Balances: Balance Sheet Presentation

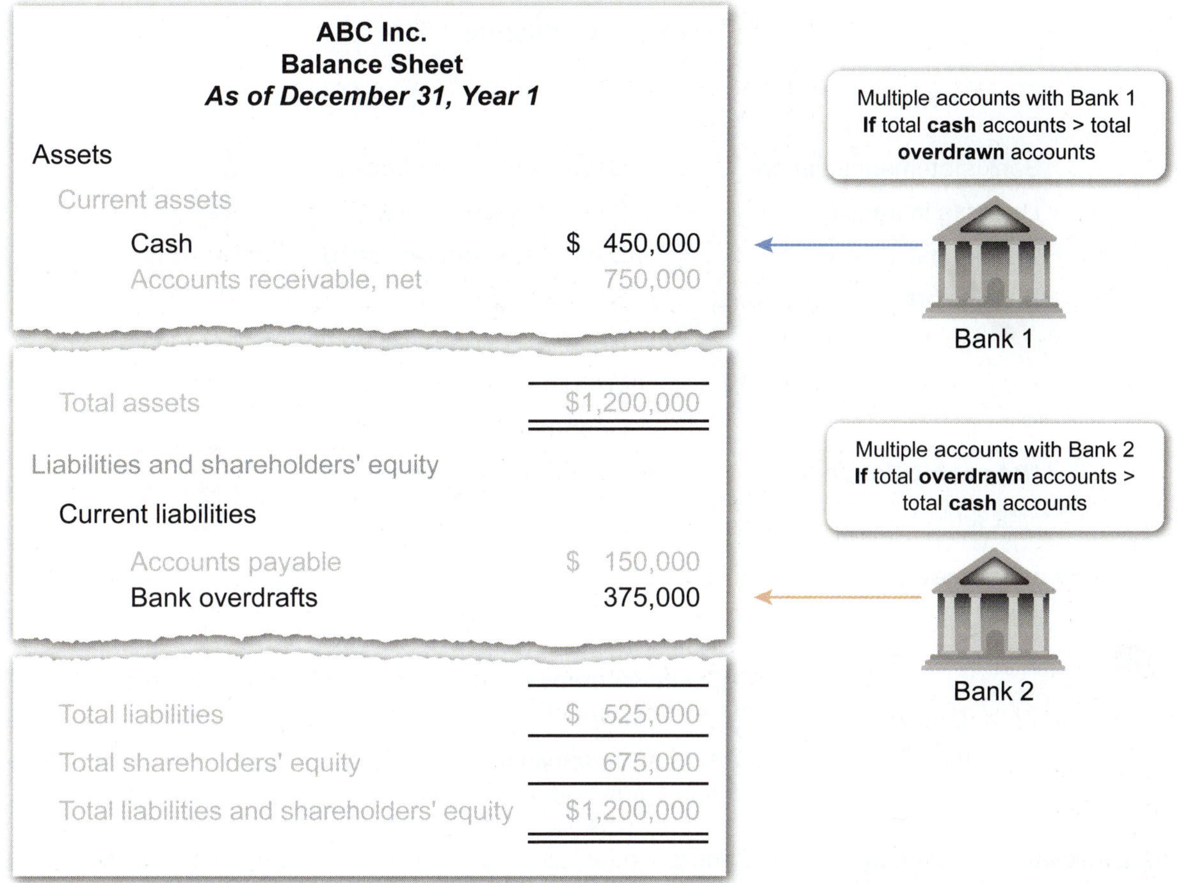

Bank Reconciliation

Representative Task (Analysis): Reconcile the cash balance per the bank statement to the general ledger.

Representative Task (Analysis): Investigate unreconciled cash balances to determine whether an adjustment to the general ledger is necessary.

Bank reconciliations are used to explain differences between cash balances per bank and per book to arrive at a corrected balance between the two. Several factors can cause a difference between bank and book cash balances, such as deposits in transit, outstanding checks, errors, bank service charges, or returned checks (ie, NSF).

The reconciliation can begin with the cash balance per the books or the bank, depending on the information provided. After adjustments are made, the book balance and bank balance should be equal, each representing the correct cash balance.

The following is an example of a simple bank reconciliation:

Bank Reconciliation

Bank	Book
Bank statement balance	Cash balance per books
+ Deposits in transit	+ Interest paid by bank
− Checks outstanding	+ Deposits not yet recorded in books
± Bank errors	− Bank charges
	− Returned checks (eg, for insufficient funds)
	− Withdrawals not yet recorded in books
	± Recording errors
Net cash balance ↔	**Net cash balance**

Bank balance adjustments include the following:

Bank Balance Adjustments	**Deposits in Transit**	• Deposits made by the company that have not cleared the bank by the end of the period • Occurs when banks have a policy that all deposits made after a certain cutoff time will be posted the next business day
	Checks Outstanding	• Checks written and mailed by the company that have not cleared the bank by the end of the period
	Bank Errors	• Transactions recorded by the bank for the wrong amount or in the wrong account • For example, checks written by the ABC Company may be erroneously subtracted from the balance of the ABZ Company

Book balance adjustments are often recorded by the company upon receipt of the bank statement. Book balance adjustments include the following:

Book Balance Adjustments	**Interest Paid by bank**	• Interest earned on the checking account
	Unrecorded Deposits	• Customer makes payment directly to the bank • Payment is cleared by the bank but not yet recorded by the company
	Bank Charges	• Service charges or fees
	Returned Checks	• Insufficient funds (NSF) checks received from customers • Originally increased the company's account balance when deposited, but bank reversed the deposit when the check was returned as unpaid from the customer. The net effect is $0
	Recording Errors	• Transactions recorded by the company for the wrong amount or in the wrong account • Adjusting entry is equal to the error amount

Today, many companies use electronic funds transfers (EFTs) rather than mailing paper checks. When an EFT is used, money moves digitally and almost instantaneously from one bank account to another. Consequently, adjustments resulting from checks in the mail (eg, checks outstanding, deposits in transit) would not be required.

Hilltop Co.'s monthly bank statement shows a balance of $54,200. Before adjusting for information on the bank statement, Hilltop's books show a balance of $53,737. Reconciliation of the bank statement with the company books reveals the following information:

Bank service charge	$ 10
Insufficient funds check	650
Checks outstanding	1,500
Deposits in transit	350
Check deposited by Hilltop and cleared by the bank for $125 but improperly recorded by Hilltop as $152	

Determine the net cash balance after the reconciliation.

Hilltop adjusts both the bank balance and book balance independently to arrive at a corrected balance between the two.

For the bank to adjusted balance calculation, Hilltop starts with the *bank balance* and adds or subtracts all items that have not yet been recorded by the bank. Because deposits in transit and checks outstanding are still on the way to the bank, they are not yet reflected in the bank statement. They must be added and subtracted, respectively.

For the book to adjusted balance calculation, Hilltop starts with the *book balance* and adds or subtracts items that have not yet been recorded on its books. Before Hilltop received its bank statement, the bank service charge and insufficient funds check were not yet recorded by the entity. Therefore, both items must be accounted for in (ie, subtracted from) the book balance. Hilltop should also subtract $27 ($152 − $125) to correct the recording error.

Bank statement balance	$54,200	Book balance	$53,737
+ Deposits in transit	350	− Bank service charge	(10)
− Checks outstanding	(1,500)	− Insufficient funds check	(650)
		− Recording error check	(27)
Adjusted cash balance	$53,050	Adjusted cash balance	$53,050

Example

Analysis-level tasks are tested with a task-based simulation (TBS) on the CPA exam. Some simulations, such as the one below, include exhibits that must be reviewed to extract information necessary to complete the TBS.

Zims Corporation manufactures small appliances and has a calendar year-end. At December 31, Year 6, Zims' bank statement shows a cash balance of $206,605, while Zims' books show a cash balance of $216,280.

Review the following documents and email correspondence. Then, complete the bank reconciliation to arrive at Zims' correct cash balance for the year ending December 31, Year 6. The bank balance and book balance will be independently reconciled to arrive at an adjusted cash balance.

- Enter the unadjusted balance for bank and book in the appropriate Amount cells
- For each cell in the Description column, select the appropriate item title. Then, in the Amount column, enter the necessary adjustment amount
- Enter adjustments to increase the cash balance as positive whole dollars and adjustments to decrease the cash balance as negative whole dollars

Exhibits

Information from bank statement

Balance per bank statement on December 31, Year 6	$206,605
Bank service charges	(2,675)
Nonsufficient funds checks from customers	(15,900)
Collection of account receivable in December; customer sent check directly to bank	4,500

Information from accounting records

Balance per company books on December 31, Year 6	$216,280
Deposits in transit, mailed to bank on December 30, Year 6	49,600
Outstanding checks, not cleared by bank as of December 31, Year 6	(52,200)

From: cashreceipts@zimscorp.com
Sent: December 31, Year 6
To: accounting@zimscorp.com
Subject: Deposit discrepancy

While reconciling the accounts receivable subsidiary ledger to the general ledger, a discrepancy was noted. A check from a customer in the amount of $5,300 was erroneously recorded as $3,500 in the cash general ledger account. No adjustment has been made. Let me know if you have any questions.

Solution:

	A	B
1	**Description**	**Amount**
2	Unadjusted bank balance, December 31, Year 6	$206,605
3	Deposits in transit	49,600
4	Outstanding checks	(52,200)
5	Adjusted cash balance, December 31, Year 6	**$204,005**
6	Unadjusted book balance, December 31, Year 6	$216,280
7	Bank service charge	(2,675)
8	Insufficient funds check	(15,900)
9	Collection of account receivable	4,500
10	Recording error	1,800
11	Adjusted cash balance, December 31, Year 6	**$204,005**

Bank Adjustments

Deposits in transit: Deposits were mailed to the bank on December 30. These deposits were recorded on the company's books but have not yet been received by the bank. $49,600 must be added to the bank balance.

Outstanding checks: Checks were not cleared by the bank as of December 31. These checks were recorded on the company's books but have not yet been reflected in the bank balance. $52,200 must be subtracted from the bank balance.

Book Adjustments

Bank service charge: The bank recorded a service charge to the company's account. This charge is not yet reflected in the company's books. $2,675 must be subtracted from the company's book balance.

Insufficient funds check: The bank returned checks for nonsufficient funds. When a check is returned for nonsufficient funds, the bank reverses the deposit and may charge fees and penalties. This deposit reversal has not yet been recorded in the company's books. $15,900 must be subtracted from the company's book balance.

Collection of account receivable: One of Zims' customers paid off an outstanding account receivable and sent the check directly to the bank. Because the cash was paid directly to the bank, the company has not yet recorded it. $4,500 must be added to the company's books.

Recording error: The email to accounting states that a check from a customer for $5,300 was erroneously recorded as $3,500 in the cash general ledger account. $1,800 must be added to the company's books to correct the error.

Generally, one combined journal entry is posted for adjustments to the book balance. Remember that any items on the *bank* to adjusted balance reconciliation would be posted by the bank, not the company. The combined adjusting entry for Zims at year-end is as follows:

Bank service charge	2,675	
Accounts receivable ($15,900 − $4,500 − $1,800)	9,600	
Cash ($4,500 + $1,800 − $2,675 − $15,900)		12,275

FAR 8
Trade Receivables

FAR 8: Trade Receivables

8.01 Trade Receivables

Trade Receivables

Representative Task (Application): Calculate trade receivables and allowances (eg, credit losses, sales returns) and prepare journal entries.

Overview

Trade accounts receivable (A/R) result from credit sales of goods or services in the ordinary course of business, covered in ASC 606, *Revenue from Contracts with Customers*. **Notes receivable (N/R)** often relate to noncustomer transactions and are a contractual agreement between a creditor and a debtor to pay a specific amount at a future date. Receivables that are not related to normal operations, such as amounts due from officers, employees, or stockholders, are reported separately from trade A/R (ASC 310).

When a company sells goods or performs services on account, it will recognize revenue and record a corresponding trade A/R. Receivables are valued on the balance sheet at **net realizable value (NRV)**, the amount of cash that the entity expects to collect at due date or at maturity. There are several factors (eg, trade discounts, cash discounts, reductions for returned goods) that cause the valuation of a receivable to be less than its face or nominal value.

A **trade discount** is a deduction (eg, a 15% discount on an order) that a seller offers a buyer. Generally, trade discounts are offered to incentivize purchases. Trade discounts may be given to buyers that purchase in bulk from the seller, buyers that have a good relationship with the seller, etc.

Variable Consideration

A sales contract contains **variable consideration** when it includes provisions that have the potential to reduce the amount of consideration given. Variable consideration reduces the revenue recognized upon sale and is estimated according to the guidelines in ASC 606. Variable consideration includes the following:

Variable Consideration
• Cash discounts for prompt payment • Reductions for returned goods • Reductions for defective or nonconforming goods

Cash discounts for prompt payment: These discounts are often expressed in terms of a formula, such as 2/10, net 30. This indicates that the customer may take a 2% discount if payment is made within 10 days. Otherwise, no discount is given and the total amount is due in 30 days. Those customers who are able will generally take advantage of these discounts because not doing so results in a very high effective interest rate.

With terms 2/10, net 30, the customer is receiving a 2% discount for paying 20 days earlier than the entire amount is due. With approximately 360 days in a year, there are roughly eighteen 20-day periods. The result is an effective rate of roughly 36% per year (18 periods × 2% discount per period = 36%).

Companies can use the **gross method**, which records receivables at gross invoice price (before cash discount) or the net method, which records receivables at net invoice price (after cash discount). Either method is acceptable under GAAP.

Assume that a company sells $2,000 (list price) of goods, terms 3/10, net 30. The sale is subject to a 5% trade discount. The initial entry to record the transaction would be:

	Gross		Net	
Accounts receivable	1,900		1,843	
Sales		1,900		1,843

Under the gross method, the company would record $1,900 ($2,000 × 95%). This is the amount after the 5% trade discount but before the 3% cash discount. Under the net method, the company would record $1,843 ($2,000 × 95% × 97%). This is the amount after the 5% trade discount and after the 3% cash discount. If payment is received within the 10-day discount period, the company would record the following:

	Gross		Net	
Cash	1,843		1,843	
Sales discounts	57			
Accounts receivable		1,900		1,843

The sales discounts account is a contra account to sales. It reduces gross sales to net sales. The gross method separately records cash discounts ($2,000 × 95% × 3%). The net method initially records sales net of cash discounts and does not require an adjustment for cash discounts taken by customers. If payment is received after the 10-day discount period, the company would record the following:

	Gross		Net	
Cash	1,900		1,900	
Sales discounts forfeited				57
Accounts receivable		1,900		1,843

The sales discounts forfeited account is a miscellaneous revenue account. The net method separately records cash discounts not taken by customers. Management can track these sales discounts forfeited to understand how many customers are forgoing the offered discounts. The company can then adjust its discounts offered going forward if needed.

Reductions for returned goods: Many times, customers are allowed to return goods within a reasonable period of time. Upon returning the goods, the customer will receive a reduction of the amount to be paid or a refund of amounts already paid. At that time, the company will record the return as a debit to sales returns and allowances and credit to accounts receivable. Sales returns and allowances is a contra account to sales.

At the end of the reporting period, companies must estimate and record future cash discounts expected to be taken (under the gross method) as well as future expected sales returns and allowances.

At the end of Year 2, Company ABC estimates that $30,000 of cash discounts will be taken by customers in Year 3 on Year 2 sales. The following adjusting journal entry is made at the end of Year 2:

Sales discounts	30,000	
Allowance for sales discounts		30,000

Sales discounts and the allowance for sales discounts are contra accounts to sales and accounts receivable, respectively. The entry reduces net sales and net accounts receivable.

If, in Year 3, only $25,000 of discounts are taken on Year 2 sales, the allowance for sales discounts will be debited. The remaining $5,000 is treated as an estimate change and reduces the amount of estimated sales discounts to be recognized in the Year 3 year end adjusting entry.

Allowance for sales discounts	5,000	
Sales discounts		5,000

Reductions for defective or nonconforming goods: When a seller sells damaged or nonconforming goods, the buyer may retain the goods and obtain a discount due to the defects or nonconformity. In this, the buyer does not bear the inconvenience of returning the goods. Rather, the buyer can then sell the goods at a cheaper price.

Transactions Affecting A/R and Allowance for Credit Losses

As mentioned previously, A/R is presented at net realizable value. Credit sales, collections, estimated credit losses, write-offs, and subsequent recoveries all impact the net realizable value of A/R.

Credit Losses

Credit losses are the portion of trade receivables that the seller does not expect to collect due to the customers' inability to pay. Credit losses are estimated considering the seller's experience, industry standards, economic conditions, and other factors.

Two methods exist for recording credit losses: the direct write-off method and the allowance method.

	Direct Write-Off	Allowance
Required for	Tax reporting	Financial reporting
Credit Loss Expense Recognized	When account deemed uncollectible	Estimated at end of each period
Uses Allowance for Credit Losses Account	No	Yes
Reported Value of Receivables	Gross amount	Net carrying value (Receivables, less allowance)

Only the allowance method is acceptable under GAAP. The **direct write-off method** is used for tax purposes. Under the direct write-off method, credit loss expense is only recognized when a specific account is determined to be uncollectible. No valuation account is used.

Under the direct write-off method, when an account is determined to be uncollectible, the following entry would be recorded:

Credit loss expense	XXX	
Accounts receivable		XXX

The direct write-off method is not allowed under GAAP because it violates GAAP in two ways:

- Not matching: Credit loss (ie, bad debt) expense is not recorded at the time of sale
- Not conservative: A/R is carried at its face amount, which will overstate the A/R balance on the balance sheet

The **allowance** method, or the **current expected credit loss** (CECL) model, must be used for GAAP purposes. Under the CECL, credit losses are estimated each period and are reported as an expense on the income statement, along with an increase to allowance for credit losses, a contra account to A/R.

At each reporting period, the allowance account is adjusted so that the net carrying value of A/R equals what is expected to be collected after considering credit risk.

Allowance for Credit Losses

Debit	Credit
	Beginning (unadjusted) balance
Accounts written off	Accounts recovered
	Credit loss expense
	Ending balance

Ending balance: Expected uncollectible portion of accounts receivable

Under the CECL model, the amount for the allowance account may be determined using various methods. **FASB does not** require the use of a **specific method** because economic and environmental conditions vary among companies. FASB *does require* companies to consider all relevant quantitative and qualitative factors that relate to the collectibility of receivables. Thus, the method selected should be consistently applied and realistically reflect expected credit losses. Methods of estimating credit losses include the following:

Methods of Estimating Credit Losses	
Aging	Based on account balances stratified by due date, with different percentages applied to each stratum
Discounted cash flow	Based on the present value of expected future cash flows
Loss rate	Based on a percentage of total exposure
Roll rate	Based on the time required for the conversion cycle (ie, period required to be realized)
Probability of default	Based on multiplying the likelihood that an instrument will be defaulted by the balance of that instrument

The aging and the loss rate methods for estimating credit losses under the CECL model are the most likely to be tested on the CPA exam.

In some cases, the amount that is unlikely to be collectible cannot be estimated. This could be for a variety of reasons, such as economic conditions or industry circumstances that are atypical. The inability to estimate credit losses precludes recognition of the receivable. When there is significant uncertainty as to collection, other methods of accounting may be used. These may include the cash basis, the cost recovery basis, or some other method.

Daniels Company uses the percentage-of-receivables (loss rate) method to estimate its allowance for credit losses. At December 31, Year 4, the balance in the allowance account was \$20,000. At December 31, Year 5, Daniels recorded a gross receivables balance of \$870,000. Daniels estimates that 3% of receivables are uncollectible. Daniels also recorded \$1,000 of write-offs during Year 5. Prepare the journal entry that Daniels should record for the recognition of credit loss expense at December 31, Year 5.

Daniels should record \$7,100 of credit loss expense at December 31, Year 5.

Allowance for Credit Losses

		20,000	Beg. bal.
Write-offs	1,000	0	Recoveries
		7,100	Credit loss expense
		26,100 (870,000 × 3%)	End. bal.

Daniels should record the following journal entry to recognize credit loss expense:

Credit loss expense	7,100	
Allowance for credit loss		7,100

Write-Offs

Credit sales, collections, write-offs, and subsequent recoveries all affect A/R:

Transactions Affecting Accounts Receivable

Accounts Receivable	
Beginning balance	Collections
Credit sales	Write-offs
Reinstatement of accounts written-off	Recoveries
Ending balance	

The above T-account is also used to prepare the A/R rollforward. The second representative task in this chapter covers preparation of the A/R rollforward.

The CECL model requires specific receivables to be written off in the period in which it is determined that they are uncollectible. Every reporting period, companies perform analyses to determine which specific accounts are uncollectible. They will then write off these accounts. Write-offs decrease A/R as well as the allowance for credit losses.

Assume that Zoo Company determines that two customer accounts, Lion Inc. for $5,700 and Tiger Inc. for $3,600, are uncollectible. As such, the company writes off both accounts.

The journal entry for Zoo Company to record the write-off is as follows:

Allowance for credit losses	9,300	
Accounts receivable		9,300

If accounts previously written off are subsequently collected, the company should first reinstate the previously written-off account. By reinstating the account, the company knows that the account was eventually paid instead of assuming that it was never paid. Then, the company will record the collection on the previously written-off account.

Assume that Tiger Inc. subsequently pays off its receivable outstanding to Zoo Company.

Zoo Company should first reinstate its previously written-off account:

Accounts receivable	3,600	
Allowance for credit losses		3,600

Zoo Company should then record the collection of the previously written-off account:

Cash	3,600	
Accounts receivable		3,600

A/R Rollforward

Representative Task (Analysis): Prepare a rollforward of the trade receivables account balance using various sources of data and information.

A **rollforward** is a high-level, summary method to review periodic activity in related accounts. For trade A/R, a rollforward starts with the beginning balance of A/R and lists all activity that increased or decreased the account during the period (ie, monthly, quarterly, or annually), resulting in the ending balance. The A/R rollforward includes credit sales, collections, write-offs/recoveries, and any additional adjustments needed to correctly present the A/R balance in the financial statements.

Analysis-level tasks are typically tested in a task-based simulation (TBS). Below is an example of a TBS that might be encountered on the CPA exam for accounts receivable.

Example

Oat Company sells dairy products. Oat prepares a rollforward of trade receivables at the end of each month. Assume that the balance in Oat's trade receivables account at the end of January, Year 2, was $45,010. Prepare Oat's rollforward for February, Year 2. Exhibits are given first, then the solution will follow.

Exhibit 1: Sales Report

Run date : March 3, Year 2, 12:05pm
Run by : Employee 123456
Run period : February, Year 2

Oat Company Sales Report

Date	Customer	Invoice	Method of Payment	Amount
1-Feb	Koffee korner	201	On account	$3,900
5-Feb	Giant grocers	202	Cash/Check/Credit card	$1,050
11-Feb	Tiara's tea	203	On account	$2,300
14-Feb	Ice cream inc.	204	On account	$6,700
20-Feb	Froyo world	205	On account	$4,000
25-Feb	Carlisle chocolate	206	Cash/Check/Credit card	$5,200
28-Feb	Delicious treats co.	207	On account	$3,600
				$26,750

Exhibit 2: Email from Controller

From : Jennifer, Controller
To : Michael, Accounting Manager
Sent : March 5, Year 2
Subject : February Year 2 Write-offs and Cash Collections

Hello Michael,
I met with the credit and collections department this morning to discuss write-offs. Two customer accounts have been outstanding for over 120 days. In light of this, I have approved the following write-offs for February, Year 2:

Customer	Write-Off Amount	Account	Reason
Croatian cafe co.	$570	Trade A/R	120+ days
Breakfast place	$900	Trade A/R	120+ days
	$1,470		

During February, total cash collections were $15,200. This includes collection of one account that was initially written off in January. See below for details:

Customer	Amount Collected	Account
Snow supermarket	$600	Trade A/R

Please include these items in the February rollforward as needed. Please let me know if you have any questions.

Jennifer

Solution

Beginning balance	$45,010
Credit sales	20,500
Collections	(15,200)
Write-offs	(1,470)
Other adjustments	600
Ending balance	$49,440

Credit sales: According to the sales report, Oat will record credit sales (an increase to A/R) of $20,500. The sales to Giant Grocers and Carlisle Chocolate are excluded, as they were paid for up-front, rather than on account.

Collections: Per the controller's email, Oat will record collections (a decrease to A/R) of $15,200. This $15,200 is inclusive of routine cash collections as well as the $600 recovery of an account previously written off.

Write-offs: Per the controller's email, Oat will record write-offs (a decrease to A/R) of $1,470 in February.

Other adjustments: Per the controller's email, $600 was collected on an account previously written off. Oat must first reinstate the account (an increase to A/R) in the other adjustments line. Oat will then record the recovery in the collections line (a decrease to A/R). These entries offset each other and result in a net zero impact to total A/R.

Note: All transactions in the rollforward are included in the A/R T-account, shown below:

Accounts Receivable

	Debit	Credit	
Beg. bal.	45,010		
Credit sales	20,500	15,200	Collections/recoveries
Reinstatement of accounts written-off	600	1,470	Write-offs
End. bal.	49,440		

Transfer of Receivables

Representative Task (Application): Prepare any required journal entries to record the transfer of trade receivables (secured borrowings, factoring, assignment, pledging).

Business entities may use receivables as immediate sources of cash. Firms can use the receivables as collateral for a loan or sell the receivables to a third party rather than wait for cash to be collected from customers. Companies may transfer receivables to eliminate the need for a credit department, to receive cash so that they can meet current operating expenses more readily, etc.

Control Criteria

When a company transfers receivables to a third party or uses the receivables as collateral for a loan, it must determine if the transaction is a **sale** or a **borrowing transaction**. If all the following conditions are met, **control** has effectively passed to the transferee, and the transaction is accounted for as a sale:

1. The transferred assets have been isolated from the transferor, even in bankruptcy
2. The transferee is free to pledge or exchange the assets
3. The transferor does not maintain effective control over the transferred assets through either one of the following:
   a. An agreement that requires the transferor to repurchase the assets
   b. An agreement that requires the transferor to return specific assets

If the above conditions are not met, the asset is considered to have been used as collateral for a loan (borrowing transaction).

In a transaction accounted for as a sale, the transferor will remove the receivable from its books and record a gain or loss on the sale of the receivable. In a transaction accounted for as a borrowing transaction, the transferor will not record any gain or loss but instead will record interest expense.

If a company is experiencing cash-flow issues, it can sell its receivables to a bank for a fee. This process is called factoring or discounting. **Factoring** is the sale of short-term A/R. **Discounting** is the sale of long-term notes receivable. Factoring and discounting transactions can be accounted for as a sale or a borrowing transaction.

Factoring and discounting can be performed with recourse or without recourse:

- In a sale **with recourse**, the company (seller) retains the risk of uncollectible accounts. The factor (ie, buyer) has the right to demand payment for any defaulted receivable
- In a sale **without recourse**, the factor assumes the risk for any uncollectible receivables

Even if the receivables are sold without recourse, there could be losses not related to collectibility (eg, future sales returns, disputed accounts). To protect the factor, an amount is often withheld from the sales proceeds, known as **factor's holdback** (or due from factor).

Factoring

Factoring is the sale of short-term receivables to a third party. When A/R is factored, the buyer applies a factoring fee, which is generally a straight percentage of the factored receivables.

When receivables are **factored without recourse**, it is accounted for as a sale because the factor has no recourse against the transferor if there is a default on the receivables. The factor bears the cost of uncollectible accounts. The seller bears the cost of sale adjustments, such as sales discounts and returns and allowances.

A firm has A/R of $100,000. The firm factors all of its receivables without recourse. The factor retains 5% of the A/R as an allowance for sales returns and charges a fee of 9% of the A/R.

The firm would record the following:

Cash ($100,000 × (100% − 5% − 9%))	86,000	
Due from factor ($100,000 × 5%)	5,000	
Loss on factoring ($100,000 × 9%)	9,000	
Accounts receivable		100,000

When receivables are **factored with recourse**, the three control criteria must be used to determine if the transaction is accounted for as a sale or borrowing transaction. If accounted for as a sale, the entries are similar to factoring without recourse, except that the transferor must estimate and record a recourse liability. This liability reflects additional amounts expected to be paid by the transferor (eg, for uncollectible accounts).

A firm has gross A/R of $100,000. The firm factors all of its receivables with recourse. The factor charges a fee of 3% of A/R. The firm estimates that its liability for bad debts (the recourse liability) is $5,000. The three control criteria are met in order for the transaction to be recorded as a sale.

The firm would record the following:

Cash ($100,000 × (100% − 3%))	97,000	
Loss on factoring ($100,000 × 3%) + 5,000	8,000	
Accounts receivable		100,000
Recourse liability		5,000

When accounts are deemed uncollectible, the transferor remits the necessary cash to the factor:

Recourse liability	5,000	
Cash		5,000

If the receivables factored with recourse are accounted for as a borrowing transaction, the transferor will maintain the receivables on its books and record a loan/interest expense over the term of the agreement.

Discounting

Discounting is the sale of long-term notes receivable to a third party. When a note is discounted, the buyer applies an annualized discount rate that is dependent on time until collection is due. Net cash proceeds from the bank are calculated as follows:

Proceeds on Discounted Notes Receivable
Face amount (Principal)
+ Interest (Principal × Interest rate × Term)
Maturity value
− Discount (Maturity value × Discount rate × Time remaining)
Net cash proceeds from bank

The discounting can be with recourse or without recourse:

- Notes receivable that have been **discounted with recourse** are reported on the balance sheet with a corresponding contra account (ie, notes receivable discounted)
  - Because default is reasonably possible, the company must disclose, in the footnotes to the financial statements, the amount that might have to be paid (ie, the maturity value) to the bank as a **contingent liability**
- Notes receivable **discounted without recourse** have essentially been sold and should be removed from the balance sheet

A firm sells inventory on 6/30/Year 1 for $150,000 and receives a one-year note for $150,000, bearing interest at 10%. The entry for the sale is the following (ignoring the cost of sales):

6/30/Year 1		
Note receivable	150,000	
Sales		150,000

Three months later, the client discounts the note at a bank at a 16% discount rate. The amount to be received is calculated as follows:

Face value	$150,000
+ Interest at maturity ($150,000 × 10% × 12/12)	15,000
Maturity value	165,000
− Discount ($165,000 × 16% × 9/12)	19,800
Net paid by bank	145,200

The entry for the discounting activity is as follows:

9/30/Year 1		
Cash	145,200	
Loss on discounting*	4,800	
Note receivable		150,000

**Loss on discounting may be reported as interest expense if the transaction is considered to be a borrowing.*

Notes receivable are discussed further in the last section of this chapter.

Assigning and Pledging

When A/R is **assigned**, a company borrows cash from a third party and agrees to use the proceeds from the receivable to repay the third party.

- The borrower retains the receivables on its books and reclassifies them as accounts receivable assigned, a subcategory of total accounts receivable. As cash is received, it is remitted to the lender in payment of the loan
- The lender has the right to seek payment from the receivables should the borrower default on the loan

Pledging of A/R is less formal and more common in practice than assignment. A company borrows cash and "pledges" (offers) the receivables to the lender as collateral to secure the loan.

- Receivables are not reclassified
- Requires only footnote disclosure, and A/R account is not adjusted

Reconciliation of Receivables Subledger and General Ledger

Representative Task (Analysis): Reconcile and investigate differences between the subledger and general ledger for trade receivables to determine whether an adjustment is necessary.

The **general ledger** is the central **recordkeeping** system for an entity's **accounting transactions**. Account balances in the general ledger are supported by **detailed account records** kept in separate subsidiary ledgers (ie, **subledgers**). General ledger balances are reported in the entity's financial statements (F/S).

The subledgers provide more **granular details** for specific types of transactions like customer accounts, vendor accounts, fixed assets, etc. The total of the subledger each period should match the total reported in the general ledger. Subledgers help organize and control transaction-level data that flows into F/S.

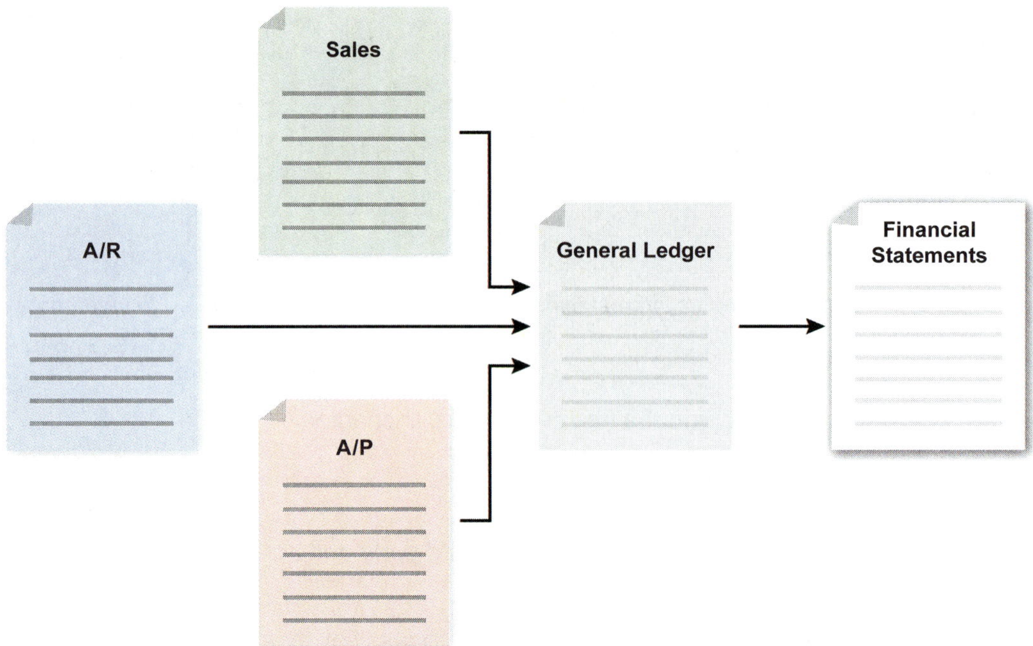

There are times when amounts are included in the subledger but not in the general ledger. In a computerized accounting system, this can happen when a transaction is entered in the receivables subledger but not posted due to a failed posting process or the data-entry clerk not having system permissions to post the transaction. Likewise, an accounting clerk may post a general journal transaction that impacts the receivables account but does not record it in the receivables subledger.

It is important to make sure that the total of the items in the subledger matches the corresponding account in the general ledger by performing a reconciliation that compares the subledger to the general ledger to identify any discrepancies. Generally, the reconciliation process follows these steps:

- Compare the ending balances of the general ledger to the subledger
- Identify any differences by confirming beginning balances (for balance sheet accounts), ensuring daily postings from the subledger to the general ledger match, and researching any nonrecurring or unusual transactions
- Investigate reasons for the differences. Typically, these are errors or items posted in the general ledger and not the subledger, or vice versa
- Adjust the appropriate ledger
- Compare adjusted balances

Example

Roy Company manufactures and sells sports equipment. Each month, the receivables subsidiary ledger is reconciled to the general ledger. For May, Year 3, Roy reviews the postings to the receivables subledger and general ledger and investigates any differences.

Roy Company
Accounts Receivable by Customer Subledger Detail (Unadjusted)
For the period May 1, Year 3 to May 31, Year 3

Date	Transaction #		Sale Amount	Payment	Return	Ending Balance
			Keeley's Outlets			
30-Apr	**Balance**					**2,400**
17-May	INV343	Shipment	1,090			1,090
31-May	**Balance**		1,090	–	–	**3,490**
			BGD Academy			
30-Apr	**Balance**					–
04-May	INV342	Shipment	4,500	4,500		–
31-May	**Balance**		4,500	4,500	–	–
			PM Youth Football League			
30-Apr	**Balance**					**5,900**
02-May	INV341	Shipment	5,200		5,200	–
30-May	INV345	Shipment	2,060			2,060
31-May	**Balance**		7,260	–	5,200	**7,960**
			Higgins Day Camp			
30-Apr	**Balance**					**150**
19-May	INV344	Shipment	1,200			1,200
31-May	**Balance**		1,200	–	–	**1,350**
			Welton Athletic Club			
30-Apr	**Balance**					–
08-May	INV202	Reinstatement of write-off	2,700			2,700
31-May	**Balance**		2,700	–	–	**2,700**
	Totals		16,750	4,500	5,200	**15,500**

Roy Company General Ledger

Account: Accounts Receivable				**Account Number: 300**
Date	**Description**	**Debit**	**Credit**	**Balance**
01-May	Beginning balance			8,450
02-May	INV341	5,200		13,650
04-May	INV342	4,500		18,150
08-May	INV202 reinstatement	2,700	2,700	18,150
17-May	INV343	1,090		19,240
19-May	INV344	1,200		20,440
29-May	Payment on INV342		4,500	15,940
30-May	INV345	2,060		18,000
31-May	**Totals and ending balance**	16,750	7,200	**18,000**

Difference between subledger and general ledger = $2,500 ($18,000 − $15,500)

The first step in the monthly reconciliation between the receivables subledger and general ledger is to compare the ending balances. For May, Year 3, Roy discovers a $2,500 discrepancy.

Next, Roy identifies the differences. Roy notes that the beginning balances agree between the receivables subledger and general ledger. However, there are the following discrepancies:

- The $5,200 return by PM Youth Football League (INV341) is missing from the general ledger
- The $2,700 payment of Welton Athletic Club's previously written-off account (INV202) is missing from the subledger

$5,200 return by PM Youth Football League: The return on INV341 was posted to the receivables subledger but not the general ledger. Roy confirmed that the order was returned on May 25. While researching the missing posting, Roy discovers that the entry in the receivables subledger was not approved because of an unexpected accounting system outage on that day. The A/R manager forgot to approve the day's activity when the accounting system restarted the next day. To correct this, the posting was processed, and the return was added to the general ledger. Roy makes the following entry to correct the general ledger balance:

Sales returns and allowances	5,200	
Accounts receivable		5,200

$2,700 payment by Welton Athletic Club: The general ledger shows a $2,700 debit and credit for the reinstatement of INV202. Welton Athletic Club's account was previously written off and subsequently paid on May 8. The receivables subledger shows that this account was reinstated for $2,700, but the payment was not recorded in the subledger. $2,700 needs to be subtracted from the receivables subledger to reflect the payment.

Once all adjustments and correcting journal entries are recorded, Roy compares the receivables subledger and the general ledger to ensure that the balances are reconciled.

Receivables subledger original balance	$15,500	General ledger original balance	$18,000
Subtract payment on Welton account	(2,700)	Subtract return on PM account	(5,200)
Receivables subledger adjusted balance	**$12,800**	**General ledger adjusted balance**	**$12,800**

The adjusted balance in the receivables subledger and general ledger is $12,800. The corrected receivables subledger and general ledger are below:

Roy Company
Accounts Receivable by Customer Subledger Detail (Adjusted)
For the period May 1, Year 3 to May 31, Year 3

Date	Transaction #		Sale Amount	Payment	Return	Ending Balance
			Keeley's Outlets			
30-Apr	**Balance**					**2,400**
17-May	INV343	Shipment	1,090			1,090
31-May	**Balance**		1,090	–	–	**3,490**
			BGD Academy			
30-Apr	**Balance**					–
04-May	INV342	Shipment	4,500	4,500		–
31-May	**Balance**		4,500	4,500	–	–
			PM Youth Football League			
30-Apr	**Balance**					**5,900**
02-May	INV341	Shipment	5,200		5,200	–
30-May	INV345	Shipment	2,060			2,060
31-May	**Balance**		7,260	–	5,200	**7,960**
			Higgins Day Camp			
30-Apr	**Balance**					**150**
19-May	INV344	Shipment	1,200			1,200
31-May	**Balance**		1,200	–	–	**1,350**
			Welton Athletic Club			
30-Apr	**Balance**					–
08-May	INV202	Reinstatement of write-off	2,700	2,700		–
31-May	**Balance**		2,700	2,700	–	–
	Totals		16,750	7,200	5,200	**12,800**

Roy Company General Ledger

Account: Accounts Receivable				**Account Number: 300**
Date	**Description**	**Debit**	**Credit**	**Balance**
01-May	Beginning balance			8,450
02-May	INV341	5,200		13,650
04-May	INV342	4,500		18,150
08-May	INV202 reinstatement	2,700	2,700	18,150
17-May	INV343	1,090		19,240
19-May	INV344	1,200		20,440
25-May	Return on INV341		5,200	15,240
29-May	Payment on INV342		4,500	10,740
30-May	INV345	2,060		12,800
31-May	**Totals and ending balance**	16,750	12,400	12,800

Notes Receivable

Notes receivable (N/R) are contractual agreements between a creditor and a debtor to pay a specific amount at a future date. N/R can be interest-bearing or noninterest-bearing. In an **interest-bearing note**, the interest element is explicitly stated. In a **noninterest-bearing note**, the interest element is not explicitly stated but, rather, is included in the face value of the note.

Notes receivable typically result from the sale of property, conversion of accounts receivable, and lending transactions. Accounts receivable occur in the ordinary course of business and are recorded at face value. Because N/R do not occur in the ordinary course of business, they are recorded in the following ways:

- N/R issued in exchange for goods and services are recorded at the FMV of the goods or services or the FMV of the N/R
    - If neither is known, the PV of future payments is used
- N/R collectible within one year and created under customary trade terms are reported at face value

Noninterest-Bearing Notes

The face value of noninterest-bearing notes represents the principal and implicit interest that will be collected at the maturity date. When the note is issued, implied interest must be recorded as a contra account called **discount on N/R**.

Implied interest is calculated as follows:

Discount on Noninterest-Bearing Note
Face value of note
− PV of note based on market rate of interest
Discount on note receivable

Consistent with the matching principle, the discount on N/R is amortized at year end using the effective interest method over the life of the note. The amortization reduces (debits) the discount and increases (credits) interest revenue.

Questions on the CPA exam will typically involve calculation of the discount based on the PV of future payments. However, if the FMV of goods/services or FMV of the note is provided, this should be used instead.

Hart Company sells a product on 1/1/Year 1 for $50,000, with payment not due for three years and no interest to be assessed. Since the period of collection exceeds one year, we must impute interest on the note.

Hart can carry the note receivable at either of the following:

- Cash selling price (FMV of the goods): This is the price Hart charges for sales to customers who pay in full on the date of sale
- Present value (PV of future payments): This is the future cash flows of the receivable discounted at a fair interest rate

The first approach is preferred, since a cash selling price is more verifiable and, therefore, a more reliable measurement. The latter approach requires the determination of a fair rate of interest, and there can be reasonable disagreement as to the appropriate rate to utilize.

Assume, however, that the cash selling price is not determinable and that a fair interest rate of 10% is determined. The present value of $1 for three years at 10% is 0.7513, so the present value of $50,000 payment due in three years is $37,565. The sale is recorded as follows:

1/1/Year 1		
Note receivable	50,000	
Discount on note		12,435
Sales ($50,000 × .7513)		37,565

The discount on note, which is simply the difference between the gross receivable and the present value of the receivable, is a form of **unearned interest income**.

Once the receivable is recorded, it will bear interest at the appropriate rate. Hart will use the effective interest method to amortize the discount over three years until the note comes due. As the discount is amortized, interest income is recorded. Amortization of the discount is as follows:

CV	×	Effective Interest Rate	=	Interest Income	–	(Face × Stated × Time) Cash Payment	=	Amortization
37,565	×	10%	=	3,757	–	0	=	3,757
+ 3,757								
41,322	×	10%	=	4,132	–	0	=	4,132
+ 4,132								
45,454	×	10%	=	4,545	–	0	=	4,545
+ 4,545								
50,000*								

**The above numbers add to 49,999 due to rounding. If decimals were carried through, the total would be $50,000. The total is expressed as $50,000 here to tie to the face value of the note.*

Hart will record an entry at the end of each period to amortize the discount on the note. At the end of Year 1, Hart will record the following entry:

12/31/Year 1		
Discount on note	3,757	
Interest income		3,757

Interest-Bearing Notes

If a note receivable is issued at the **market rate**, the PV of the note is the same as the face value. The initial entry will be recorded at face value (also equal to PV), and no discount or premium will be recorded.

For each accounting period, any interest that has been earned is accrued. The amount of accrued interest is calculated as follows:

Accrued Interest on Interest-Bearing Note

	Face value of note
×	Interest rate
×	Number of months elapsed
	Accrued interest

Unpaid interest is accrued as time passes and is recorded with a debit to interest receivable and a credit to interest revenue for each accounting period. When the note matures (ie, is due), the accrued interest receivable is removed from the books, any remaining interest that has been earned is accrued, and the note is settled.

Happy Company sold goods on 3/1/Year 1 and received an 11%, three-year note receivable for $75,000. The market rate of interest is 11% on 3/1/Year 1. Interest payments are due to Happy semiannually on 9/1 and 3/1. On 3/1/Year 1, Happy should record the following:

3/1/Year 1		
Note receivable	75,000	
Sales		75,000

When Happy receives interest on 9/1/Year 1, Happy should record the following:

9/1/Year 1		
Cash ($75,000 × 11% × 6/12)	4,125	
Interest revenue		4,125

Happy must accrue interest at year end. At 12/31/Year 1, Happy should record the following:

12/31/Year 1		
Interest receivable ($75,000 × 11% × 4/12)	2,750	
Interest revenue		2,750

When Happy receives interest on 3/1/Year 2, Happy should record the following:

3/1/Year 2		
Cash ($75,000 × 11% × 6/12)	4,125	
Interest receivable		2,750
Interest revenue ($75,000 ×11% × 2/12)		1,375

If the interest rate on the note is not equal to the market rate, the PV of the note will differ from the face value. The note will be initially recorded at the PV, and a discount or premium will be recorded for the difference between the PV and face value of the note. This discount is amortized over time as interest is earned.

FAR 9
Inventory

FAR 9: Inventory

9.01 Inventory

Overview

For a typical business entity, **inventory** includes resources held for resale, resources in the process of production, and resources consumed in the process of production. Inventories are current assets to the seller even though they may be noncurrent assets to the buyer.

Inventory by Firm Type			
Manufacturing	**Merchandising**	**Real-estate development**	**Construction**
Raw materials inventory, work in process inventory, finished goods inventory	Purchased goods (Property held for resale)	Land	Partially completed buildings, bridges, and roads

The FAR exam typically deals with merchandise inventory only. Inventory costs related to a manufacturing firm (ie, direct materials, direct labor and manufacturing overhead) are usually tested in the cost accounting topic, which is part of the BAR exam.

Costs Included in Inventory

The cost of inventory is capitalized to an inventory account (ie, initially accounted for as an asset, then expensed when sold). The cost of inventory includes all costs of acquisition and preparation for sale (ie, its **intended use**):

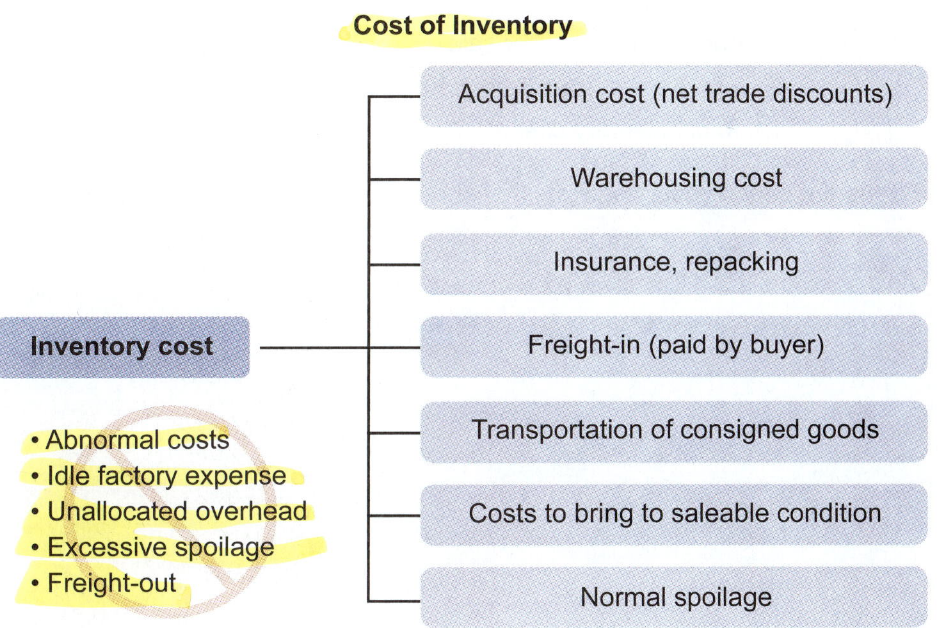

Costs that should **not** be capitalized in inventory include the following:

- **Abnormal costs**: Abnormal costs should be expensed immediately. This includes items such as idle factory expense, unallocated fixed overhead costs, excessive spoilage, double freight, and rehandling costs
- **Financing costs**: Financing costs should be reported as interest expense. This includes interest on loans obtained to purchase inventory, payments made to the seller for interest on unpaid balances, and early-payment discounts not taken
- **Selling costs**: Costs incurred at the time of sale (eg, freight-out paid by the seller and sales commission) are generally recognized as selling expenses at the time of sale

If goods that have been sold are **returned**, the seller should **reduce net sales** and **add the cost of the items back to inventory**. This should take place as soon as the seller has authorized the goods for return, meaning the goods can be added back to inventory prior to physical receipt of the returned goods as long as the actual return of the item is considered probable.

A firm incurred the following costs related to the acquisition and sale of inventory:

Direct purchase cost	$50,000
Purchases returns	4,000
Freight-in	9,000
Freight-out	2,000
Interest on purchase	1,000
Packaging costs (for sale)	4,000
Insurance in transit from supplier	500
Promotional expenses	2,500

The inventory should be recorded at the following amount:

Direct purchase cost	$50,000
Purchases returns	(4,000)
Freight-in	9,000
Packaging costs (for sale)	4,000
Insurance in transit from supplier	500
Total inventory cost	$59,500

The excluded costs are period costs (ie, costs that should be expensed immediately).

Goods in Transit

In order to determine what items are included in ending inventory, it is important to identify which party **owns** any **goods that are in transit**. This is especially critical at the end of the reporting period. If the merchandise is owned by a business enterprise on the last day of the period, regardless of location, the merchandise should be included in ending inventory.

FOB Shipping Terms

Seller — Title and risk of loss transfer ↓ — Buyer
FOB destination point
Seller owns goods and pays shipping

Seller — Title and risk of loss transfer ↓ — Buyer
FOB shipping point
Buyer owns goods and pays shipping

FOB = free on board

When inventory is **FOB shipping point**, once the goods are shipped, title transfers to the buyer, and the inventory is included on the buyer's books. Freight-in cost to the buyer will be capitalized in the buyer's inventory account.

When inventory is **FOB destination point**, title does not transfer to the buyer until the buyer receives the goods. Therefore, the inventory is not included on the buyer's books until received by the buyer. Freight-out cost is considered to be a selling expense for the seller.

Southern Inc. is located in Alabama and has a major supplier located in Texas. On December 31, Year 7, the supplier sent merchandise to Southern on a train.

If the goods were shipped *FOB shipping point*, title has transferred, and the purchased goods in transit should be included in Southern's ending inventory.

If the goods were shipped *FOB destination*, the purchased goods in transit should **not** yet be included in Southern's ending inventory. (The goods have not arrived to Southern yet; therefore, title has not transferred.) Rather, the goods would still be included in the supplier's ending inventory.

Consignment Inventory

Consignment Arrangement

Consignor (wholesaler)

Consignee (retailer/dealer)

Delivers merchandise

Remits payment when sold*

Sells on consignor's behalf to customers

**Less commission and reimbursable costs*

In a **consignment** agreement, a seller (consignor) arranges for the goods to be delivered to another firm (consignee) but retains legal ownership of the goods. If the merchandise is sold, the consignee will keep a portion of the sale as commission and remit the remainder to the consignor.

Importantly, the **merchandise is included in the consignor's ending inventory**, even though the inventory typically is not on the consignor's premises. It is *legal ownership rather than location* that determines who includes the goods in inventory, just as with goods in transit. The consignor usually pays the transportation costs, which are added to the consignor's inventory cost (note that these are not the same as freight-out costs since no sale has occurred yet).

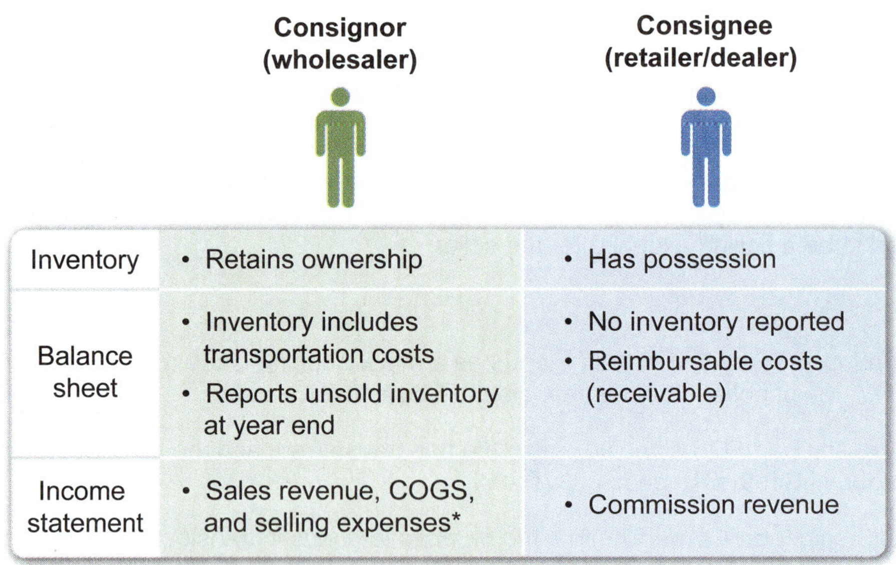

	Consignor (wholesaler)	Consignee (retailer/dealer)
Inventory	• Retains ownership	• Has possession
Balance sheet	• Inventory includes transportation costs • Reports unsold inventory at year end	• No inventory reported • Reimbursable costs (receivable)
Income statement	• Sales revenue, COGS, and selling expenses*	• Commission revenue

COGS = Cost of goods sold
**Advertising costs and commissions paid*

Periodic and Perpetual Inventory Systems

Two systems exist for measuring inventory quantities: the periodic system and the perpetual system.

Periodic Inventory System

Under a **periodic inventory system**, inventory quantity is determined by a **physical count**, usually done at the end of the reporting period. When inventory is purchased, the transaction is recorded as a debit to the purchases account. No adjustment is made to the inventory account until the end of the period, at which time a physical inventory count is made and ending inventory (EI) is calculated. Cost of goods sold (COGS) is a plug figure, and the exact amount of inventory shortages cannot be determined.

COGS for a company employing the periodic inventory system is calculated as follows:

COGS calculation
Beginning inventory
+ Net cost of purchases
Cost of goods available for sale
− Ending inventory
Cost of goods sold

GP Company reported the following data:

Beginning inventory	20,000	Ending inventory	32,000
Purchases	100,000	Purchase returns	4,000
Purchase discounts	8,000	Transportation in	9,000
Transportation out	6,000		

To determine COGS, the company must first determine **net purchases**:

Net purchases = Purchases + Transportation in − Purchase discounts − Purchase returns

$97,000 = $100,000 + 9,000 − 8,000 − 4,000

Then, the company will use net purchases in the **COGS calculation**:

COGS = Beginning inventory + Net purchases − Ending inventory

$85,000 = $20,000 + 97,000 − 32,000

Perpetual Inventory System

Under a **perpetual inventory system**, inventory purchases are recorded as a debit to the inventory account. Importantly, the inventory account is updated as an **ongoing, real-time** count of inventory purchased and sold. COGS is recorded at time of sale.

An advantage of a perpetual inventory system is that it enables an entity to determine how much inventory is on hand at any given point in time. Not only does this assist in the management of inventory, but it also helps more quickly identify potential theft and other shrinkage.

Even in a perpetual system, a physical count of ending inventory should be completed. This physical count will then be confirmed to inventory records (through an **inventory reconciliation**). If differences are identified, the company should determine the reasons for the differences (eg, recording errors or shrinkage due to loss, theft, or breakage). An appropriate adjusting entry would be prepared to properly reflect the inventory balance.

An inventory reconciliation is performed this way:

To reconcile from recorded amount to physical count:	To reconcile from physical count to recorded amounts:
Recorded amount	Physical count
+ Goods held on consignment	− Goods held on consignment
+ Goods sold FOB shipping point and set aside but included in the count	− Goods sold FOB shipping point and set aside but included in the count
− Goods in transit that were sold FOB destination	+ Goods in transit that were sold FOB destination
− Goods in transit that were purchased FOB shipping point	+ Goods in transit that were purchased FOB shipping point
Physical count*	Recorded amount*

**Remaining differences are caused by shrinkage, error, or fraud*

Notice that the process is simply reversed from one reconciliation to the other (ie, the reconciliations are inverses of each other).

Comparison of Periodic and Perpetual Inventory Systems

There are two main differences between the journal entries under a periodic system and those for a perpetual system:

- **Acquisition of inventory and adjustments such as returns and discounts**: In a perpetual system, this is recorded in the *inventory account*; in a periodic system, this is recorded in the *purchases account*
- **Recording of COGS**: In a perpetual system, this is recorded at the *time of sale*; in a periodic system, this is recorded at the *end of the period*

Perpetual vs. Periodic Inventory Systems

At time of purchase

Perpetual		
Inventory	XXX	
A/P or Cash		XXX

Periodic		
Purchases	XXX	
A/P or Cash		XXX

At time of sale

Perpetual:

Cash or A/R	XXX	
Sales revenue		XXX

Cost of goods sold	XXX	
Inventory		XXX

Periodic:

Cash or A/R	XXX	
Sales revenue		XXX

At year-end

Periodic:

Ending inventory	XXX	
Cost of goods sold (plug)	XXX	
Purchases		XXX

A/P = Accounts payable; A/R = Accounts receivable

Cost of Goods Sold (COGS)

Ultimately, inventory sold is expensed using the expense account COGS.

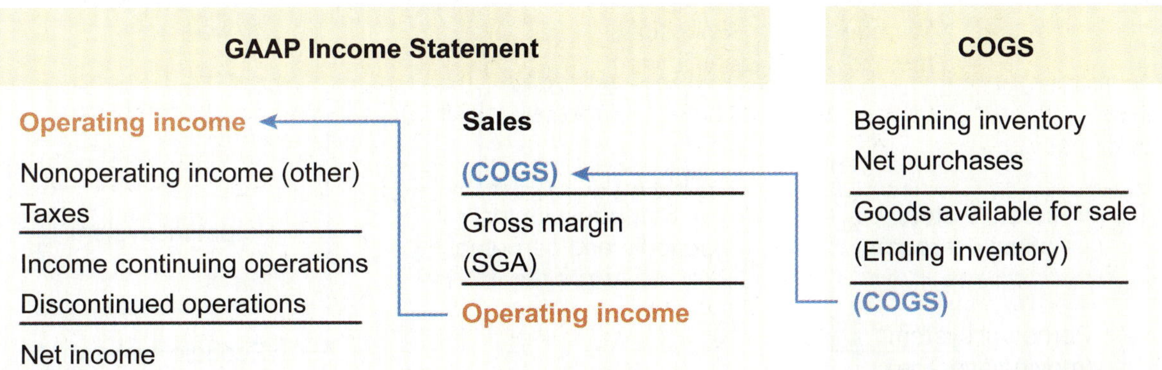

More details on calculating COGS using absorption costing are covered in the cost accounting topic, which is part of the BAR exam.

Inventory Costing Methods

Representative Task (Application): Calculate the carrying amount of inventory and prepare journal entries using various costing methods.

Specific Identification

If inventory includes **heterogeneous** items (ie, items that are unique or different), the **specific identification** method should be used. This method is also used for very expensive items, such as automobiles. Under this method, each inventory item must be identifiable when sold.

For example, an automobile dealer counted a total of 49 automobiles in inventory at year end. The dealer can identify each automobile by vehicle number and match the invoice cost by vehicle number. To value its ending inventory, the dealership is able to specifically identify the cost of each of the inventory items and then total the individual cost of all the inventory items. Likewise, the dealership can specifically identify the cost of each item sold and total these amounts to determine COGS for the period.

If inventory items are **homogeneous**, then an alternative cost-flow assumption must be made. The potential alternative cost-flow assumptions with homogeneous inventory include the following: FIFO (first in, first out), LIFO (last in, first out), and average methods. A less commonly used but sometimes tested alternative is dollar-value LIFO.

Some of the cost-flow assumptions have the same results, regardless of whether a periodic or perpetual system is used, while others have different results:

Inventory Cost Flow Methods

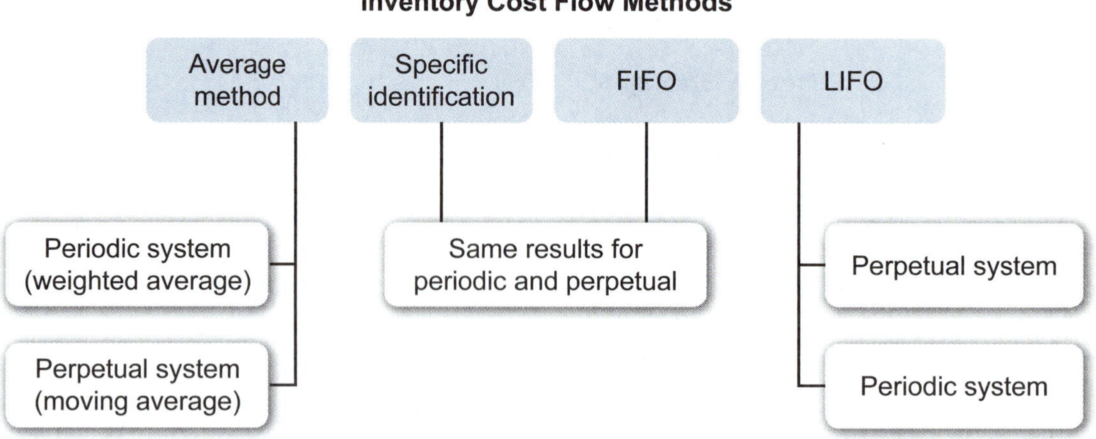

FIFO: First In, First Out

This cost-flow assumption is based on a **first in, first out (FIFO)** philosophy. At the end of the accounting period, it is assumed that the ending inventory is composed of units of inventory ***most recently acquired***. Conversely, the COGS is made up of the ***oldest*** (ie, "first in") merchandise. The FIFO cost-flow assumption reflects the way most firms actually move their inventory. However, GAAP does not require that firms choose the inventory cost-flow assumption that reflects the actual movement of goods.

Impact of Inventory Costing Methods in a Period of Rising Prices

	COGS valuation	Impact on COGS	Impact on net income
FIFO	Older, lower costs	Lower ↓	Higher ↑

During periods of **rising inventory prices, FIFO produces the highest net income** because COGS is costed with the lowest-cost (earliest) purchases in the period. Ending inventory reflects the highest (latest) costs. Importantly, when using a FIFO cost-flow assumption, perpetual and periodic inventory systems yield the same results.

If FIFO is chosen, the inventory value on the balance sheet is a current and relevant amount, because it reflects the most current costs. However, COGS and, therefore, gross margin and income are considered to be less current or relevant, because they reflect older costs. As such, revenues and expenses may not be matched well on the income statement. Revenues of the current year are often matched with the cost of merchandise acquired in a prior accounting period.

FIFO favors the balance sheet. These effects hold regardless of the direction of price-level changes (ie, increase or decrease) during the period.

Angelo's LLC made the following purchases and sales during the period:

	Units	Cost per unit
Beginning inventory	400 units	$10
Purchase #1	100 units	$11
Sale #1*	200 units	
Purchase #2	200 units	$12
Sale #2*	400 units	
Purchase #3	200 units	$13

**Note that, for each sale, no unit cost is given. The cost assigned to each sale depends on the cost-flow assumption chosen.*

The basic equation in units helps to identify one side of the equation for costing purposes:

Beginning inventory + Purchases	= Ending inventory + Sales
(400 units × $10) + (100 units × $11) + (200 units × $12) + (200 units × $13)	= 900 units, totaling $10,100

Because beginning inventory + purchases equals 900 units at $10,100, the sum of ending inventory and COGS for all inventory costing methods must also equal 900 units at $10,100.

Of the 900 units available for sale, sales totaled 600 units, so 300 units remain in ending inventory.

Under the **FIFO cost-flow assumption**, the results are the same for periodic and perpetual systems:

COGS = The cost of the 600 oldest units available
= (400 units × $10) + (100 units × $11) + (100 units × $12)
= $6,300

Ending inventory = The cost of the 300 most recently added units
= (100 units × $12) + (200 units × $13)
= $3,800

COGS + Ending inventory = $6,300 + 3,800 = $10,100

LIFO: Last In, First Out

This cost-flow assumption is based on a **last in, first out (LIFO)** philosophy. At the end of the accounting period, it is assumed the ending inventory is composed of the ***oldest*** inventory layers, while the COGS is composed of the units of inventory ***most recently acquired*** (ie, "last in").

Impact of Inventory Costing Methods in a Period of Rising Prices

	COGS valuation	Impact on COGS	Impact on net income
LIFO Dollar-value LIFO	Recent, higher costs	Higher ↑	Lower ↓

During periods of **rising inventory prices, LIFO produces the lowest net income** because COGS is costed with the highest-cost (latest) purchases in the period. This feature of LIFO is considered an advantage because reported gross margin matches current purchase costs to current revenues. Therefore, it is more indicative of future gross margin.

However, the ending inventory reflects the lowest (earliest) costs. Whenever the firm purchases (or produces) more units than it sells, a **layer** is added. This layer is costed with the earliest costs of the period in which the layer is added, under the periodic system. After several years of adding layers, ending inventory may reflect very old costs.

Importantly, when using a LIFO cost-flow assumption, perpetual and periodic inventory systems are *different*. Under a periodic LIFO cost-flow assumption, the last purchase for an entire period is the first inventory price applied to the sales. Conversely, a perpetual LIFO cost-flow assumption continuously updates and, therefore, uses the price of the most recent purchase preceding each sale.

If LIFO is chosen, the inventory value in the balance sheet is considered to be less current or relevant, because it reflects older costs. However, COGS and, therefore, gross margin and income are considered to be much more current and relevant, because they reflect the most current costs. Revenues and expenses are matched more appropriately on the income statement.

LIFO favors the income statement. These effects hold regardless of the direction of price-level changes (ie, increase or decrease) during the period.

Recall the fact pattern for Angelo's LLC above. Angelo's made the following purchases and sales during the period:

	Units	Cost per unit
Beginning inventory (BI)	400 units	$10
Purchase #1	100 units	$11
Sale #1*	200 units	
Purchase #2	200 units	$12
Sale #2*	400 units	
Purchase #3	200 units	$13

**Note that, for each sale, no unit cost is given. The cost assigned to each sale depends on the cost-flow assumption chosen.*

Under the **LIFO cost-flow assumption**, the results are different for periodic and perpetual systems:

In a periodic system:

COGS = The cost of the 600 most recently added units
= (200 units × $13) + (200 units × $12) + (100 units × $11) + (100 units × $10)
= $7,100

Ending inventory = The cost of the 300 oldest units available
= (300 units × $10)
= $3,000

COGS + Ending inventory = $7,100 + 3,000 = $10,100

In a perpetual system:

COGS

For Sale #1, 200 units sold:	
(100 units × $11) are sold from Purchase #1* + (100 units × $10) are sold from BI*	= $2,100
For Sale #2, 400 units sold:	
(200 units × $12) are sold from Purchase #2** + (200 units × $10) are sold from BI**	= $4,400
COGS	**$6,500**

**Following this, no units are left from Purchase #1, and BI has 300 units left.*

***Following this, no units are left from Purchase #2, and BI has 100 units left.*

Ending Inventory

From Purchase #3 (all units remain):	
(200 units × $13)	= $2,600
From Beginning inventory (100 units remaining):	
(100 units × $10)	= $1,000
Ending inventory	**$3,600**

COGS + Ending inventory = $6,500 + 3,600 = $10,100

LIFO Liquidation

When LIFO is used for tax purposes, the LIFO conformity rule requires that LIFO also be used for financial reporting purposes. The main advantage of choosing LIFO is **tax minimization**. Under LIFO, COGS is typically higher, and net income (and, therefore, taxable income) is typically lower. However, LIFO liquidations can cause negative tax effects and poor matching of revenues to expenses.

Liquidation occurs when the number of units purchased or produced is less than the number of units sold. Under LIFO, the computation of COGS for the current period first uses all the purchases for the period. Then, it works backward in time and liquidates layers that were added in previous periods (latest layer added first), until the total number of units sold for the period is costed. A LIFO liquidation is the part of current-period COGS represented by the cost of goods acquired in prior years. LIFO liquidations often occur from either poor planning or lack of supply.

Assume that a company reports the following figures in the current year. The company uses LIFO, and beginning inventory is composed of a single layer added in the previous year.

	Units	Cost per unit
Beginning inventory	400,000 units	$35
Purchases	500,000 units	$55

The company sold 505,000 units during the year. Under LIFO, COGS is $27,675,000 [(500,000 × $55) + (5,000 × $35)]. The current year purchases are "sold" first, then the earlier layers are "sold." Note: the older inventory items are not actually physically present. Rather, the cost of those items is used in ending inventory.

The amount of LIFO liquidation is $175,000 (5,000 × $35). 5,000 more goods were sold than acquired during the year. The $175,000 amount is the portion of COGS represented by goods acquired in earlier years.

The older units are cheaper than the newer units. Therefore, when the firm sells older units, their COGS is lower, and, therefore, net income (and taxable income) is higher. If the firm had been able to purchase 505,000 units in the period, COGS would have been $27,775,000 (505,000 × $55). COGS would have been $100,000 ($27,775,000 − 27,675,000) higher; thus, net income and taxable income would have been $100,000 lower.

Because the firm liquidated units, net income and taxable income are $100,000 higher. This extra tax liability could have been avoided if the firm purchased adequate units to cover sales during the period.

Additionally, an advantage of LIFO is matching current-period costs with current revenues. The liquidation distorts the relationship between current sales and current COGS. Here, current sales will be matched against 5,000 units costed at prior-period prices. The larger the liquidation, the worse the distortion.

Comparison of FIFO and LIFO

Significant differences between the FIFO and LIFO inventory cost-flow methods are as follows:

Inventory Cost-Flow Methods

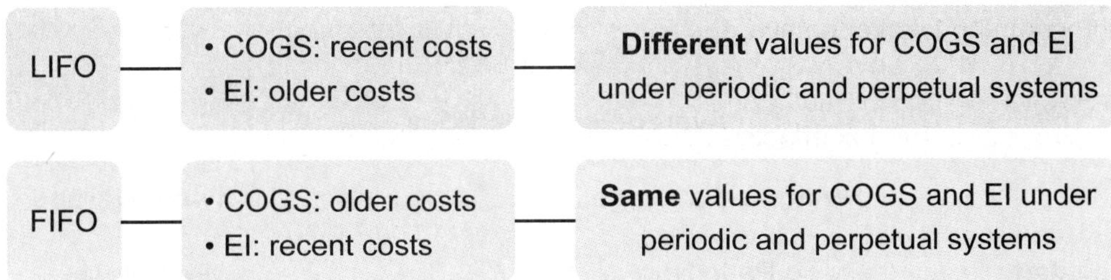

COGS = Cost of goods sold; EI = Ending inventory

The following example highlights differences between FIFO and LIFO under the perpetual and periodic inventory systems:

Assume that a company had the following activity in the month of January:

Date	Units purchased (sold)	
Beginning inventory, 1/1	2	A, B
Purchases, 1/5	2	C, D
Sale, 1/12	(1)	
Purchases, 1/19	2	E, F
Sale, 1/26	(1)	
Ending inventory, 1/31	4	

To make it easier to follow, let's name the first two units in inventory A and B, the two units purchased on 1/5 C and D, and the two units purchased on 1/19 E and F.

Assuming that the **perpetual** approach is used, each transaction is processed as it happens. Let's see which units are left in inventory after each transaction, using FIFO and LIFO:

Units after transaction	FIFO	LIFO
Start of month	A+B	A+B
January 5, plus 2	A+B+C+D	A+B+C+D
January 12, minus 1	B+C+D	A+B+C
January 19, plus 2	B+C+D+E+F	A+B+C+E+F
January 26, minus 1	C+D+E+F	A+B+C+E

If a **periodic** approach is used, all the purchases are recorded first, then the sales:

Units after transaction	FIFO	LIFO
Start of month	A+B	A+B
Purchases, plus 4	A+B+C+D+E+F	A+B+C+D+E+F
Sales, minus 2	C+D+E+F	A+B+C+D

Average Inventory Methods

Average inventory methods take the average value of goods over a period.

Average cost methods

	Weighted average	Moving average
Recording system	Periodic	Perpetual
Units included in calculation	Beginning inventory (at start of period) + Purchases (over entire period)	Beginning inventory (since last calculation) + Purchases (since last calculation)
Frequency of average cost calculation	End of period	Every purchase, return, and sale

With a **periodic inventory system**, this is referred to as a **weighted-average method**. A single weighted average cost per unit is used for an accounting period. With a **perpetual inventory system**, a **moving average method** is used. Rather than having a single weighted average cost per unit for the accounting period, the company computes a new weighted average cost per unit after each purchase of inventory. That moving average is used for costing all subsequent sales until another purchase takes place, at which time the moving average is modified by the new purchase.

Recall the fact pattern for Angelo's LLC above. Angelo's made the following purchases and sales during the period:

	Units	Cost per unit
Beginning inventory	400 units	$10
Purchase #1	100 units	$11
Sale #1*	200 units	
Purchase #2	200 units	$12
Sale #2*	400 units	
Purchase #3	200 units	$13

**Note that, for each sale, no unit cost is given. The cost assigned to each sale depends on the cost-flow assumption chosen.*

Under the **weighted average (periodic) cost-flow assumption**, the cost calculations are as follows:

Weighted Average Cost Calculations

Step 1

$$\text{Average cost per unit} = \frac{\text{Cost of beginning inventory + Cost of purchases}}{\text{Beginning inventory units + Units purchased}}$$

Step 2

Cost of goods sold = Number of units sold × Average cost per unit

Ending inventory = Number of units remaining at end of period × Average cost per unit

$$\text{Average cost per unit} = \frac{(400 \text{ units} \times \$10) + (100 \text{ units} \times \$11) + (200 \text{ units} \times \$12) + (200 \text{ units} \times \$13)}{400 \text{ units} + 100 \text{ units} + 200 \text{ units} + 200 \text{ units}} = \$11.22$$

COGS = 600 units sold × $11.22 = $6,732

EI = 300 units remaining × $11.22 = $3,366

COGS + EI = $6,732 + 3,366 = $10,098*

**There is a $2 difference due to rounding*

Under the **moving average (perpetual) cost-flow assumption**, the average cost per unit is not needed until there is a sale to cost.

For example, Sale #1 occurs after Purchase #1. The average cost per unit uses beginning inventory and the first purchase only. The following table illustrates the application of the moving averages:

Event	Units	Cost	Computation	Moving average cost per unit
Beginning inventory	400	400 × $10 = $4,000		
+ Purchase #1	100	100 × $11 = $1,100		
= Available for sale	500	$5,100	$5,100 / 500	$10.20
− Sale #1	(200)	(200) × $10.20 = ($2,040)		
= Available for sale	300	$3,060		
+ Purchase #2	200	200 × $12 = $2,400		
= Available for sale	500	$5,460	$5,460 / 500	$10.92
− Sale #2	(400)	(400) × $10.92 = ($4,368)		
= Available for sale	100	$1,092		
+ Purchase #3	200	200 × $13 = $2,600		
= Available for sale	300	$3,692	$3,692 / 300	$12.31

Sale #1 is costed at $10.20, the moving average of goods on hand just before the sale. Removing the units sold leaves 300 units in inventory and $3,060 in cost.

Purchase #2, at $12 per unit, is added into both the units and cost columns. $12 exceeds the previous moving average; therefore, the moving average after Purchase #2 increases. That average is applied to Sale #2 and so forth.

The final moving average of $12.31 reflects the higher purchase cost of Purchase #3 and will be used to cost sales the next period until the first purchase in that period is made.

Here,

COGS = Each sale's current weighted average cost per unit × # units sold
= For Sale 1, $10.20 × 200 units sold = $2,040
= For Sale 2, $10.92 × 400 units sold = $4,368
= $6,408

EI = Current weighted average cost per unit × units remaining available for sale
= $12.31 × 300 units available = $3,693

COGS + EI = $6,408 + 3,693 = $10,101*

**There is a $1 difference due to rounding.*

Impact of Inventory Costing Methods in a Period of Rising Prices

	COGS valuation	Impact on COGS	Impact on net income
Weighted average	Average cost of all units at end of period	Average cost	Between LIFO and FIFO
Moving average	Average cost of units at time of each sale	Average cost	Between LIFO and FIFO

In a period of steadily rising prices, the moving average method (perpetual) results in lower COGS than the weighted average method (periodic). The moving average method applies earlier (and, therefore, lower) costs to sales during the year relative to the overall higher weighted average cost for the entire period.

Dollar-Value LIFO

Two potential difficulties arise from the application of LIFO:

- When using the LIFO cost-flow assumption, a company needs to keep track of the different unit costs for items acquired on different dates, going all the way back to the date the company first adopted the method, which could be the date the company was founded. This need to keep cumulative accurate records will result in increasing record-keeping costs over time
- When inventory levels decline temporarily, older costs previously inventoried will become a part of COGS, causing a distortion of that account if there have been substantial price changes over time. This is because the unit costs in inventory that are several years old are likely to be radically different from the approximation of replacement cost represented by the most recent purchases

A possible alternative LIFO application is **dollar-value LIFO (DV LIFO)**. Under this approach, related inventory items are grouped in **pools**, and an overall price index is used to approximate changes in inventory costs. With this method, it is only necessary to **keep track of annual layers** of inventory cost and price indexes for each inventory pool, instead of retaining detailed records of each unit cost of each item purchased over the life of the company.

The advantages of DV LIFO over the quantity of goods LIFO approach include the following:

- Reduces the effect of the liquidation problem: The DV LIFO conversion technique takes a company's ending inventory in FIFO dollars (usually) and converts them to LIFO dollars. In doing so, the impact of the liquidation problem is reduced
- Allows companies to use FIFO internally: Most companies prefer to use FIFO for internal management reports and internal operating decisions. Through the use of DV LIFO, a company can maintain a FIFO system for internal purposes and then convert those results to LIFO for external purposes
- Reduces clerical costs: It is only necessary to keep track of annual layers of inventory cost and price indexes for each inventory pool, instead of retaining detailed records of each unit cost of each item purchased over the life of the company

Steps in Implementing Dollar-Value LIFO

First, a company establishes **inventory pools**. This means that the company groups similar products into inventory groups. For example, a department store might have one inventory pool that includes appliances.

Second, the **conversion index** (also called *price level index*) can be calculated internally or obtained from an external source. The conversion index is calculated as follows:

$$\text{Conversion index} = \frac{\text{Ending inventory in current-year dollars}}{\text{Ending inventory in base-year dollars}}$$

Base-year dollars refers to the specific price level for the pool in effect at the beginning of the year in which the firm adopted LIFO.

When this index is multiplied by the increase in inventory for the year as measured in base-year dollars, the result is the increase in inventory in current costs—the layer added to DV LIFO ending inventory.

A firm adopts DV LIFO at the beginning of the current year (Year 1). The beginning inventory under FIFO is $2,000 at cost. The FIFO ending inventory for Year 1 is $3,200. The price index in Year 1 is 1.10.

Beginning inventory (BI) = $2,000
Ending inventory (EI) = $3,200
} **$1,200 Difference**

Price-level index = 1.10* → 10% Inflation

**Note, price-level index = ending inventory in current-year dollars / ending inventory in base-year dollars. 1.10 = $3,200 / 2,909*

First, convert FIFO ending inventory to ending inventory at base-year cost:

$$\frac{\text{FIFO EI}}{\text{Price-level index}} = \$3{,}200/1.10 = \$2{,}909 \text{ EI @ base year \$}$$

→ **$2,909** EI @ beginning of year prices OR base year $ (Base year = year started DV LIFO)

Second, compute the change in inventory in base-year cost:

Adding layers	$2,909 =	EI @ beginning of year prices OR base year $
	(2,000) =	Subtract base
Layer	**$ 909** =	Increase in inventory @ base year $

This result is important because it shows that there has been a *physical* increase in inventory for the year (because the measurement of the dollar is fixed at the base year). The $909 amount is the layer added in the current year at base-year cost. But LIFO must measure layers at current cost. The next step accomplishes this objective.

Third, compute the current-year layer at current-year costs:

Layer	$ 909 =	From above
	× 1.10 =	Multiply by inflation factor
Layer	**$1,000** =	Layer @ current costs

Finally, compute ending inventory under DV LIFO:

Layer	$1,000 =	From above
	+ 2,000 =	Still around (old inventory) @ base cost
EI	**$3,000** =	EI @ current cost

The balance sheet will report $3,000 of inventory. This consists of two layers: beginning inventory of $2,000 and the Year 1 layer of $1,000. The two layers reflect different price-level indices (1.00 and 1.10, respectively).

In **Year 2**, FIFO ending inventory is $4,025, and the price-level index is 1.15:

Ending inventory at base-year cost	$4,025 / 1.15	= $3,500
Increase in inventory at base-year cost	$3,500 − 2,909 (from Year 1)	= $591
Increase in inventory at current year cost	$591 × 1.15	= $680
Ending inventory under DV LIFO	$680 + 3,000 (from Year 1)	= $3,680

COGS is computed as in any periodic inventory context: Ending inventory as computed for DV LIFO is subtracted from cost of goods available for sale. The result is COGS.

This process illustrates that DV LIFO first uses price-level indices to measure the inventory increase in base-year cost and then expresses each year's layer at current cost through the conversion index. The result is a DV LIFO ending inventory that is the sum of layers measured in current dollars for the period the layers were added.

This method is called the *double-extension method* because the ending inventory is extended at both base-year cost and ending current-year cost.

Inventory Estimation Methods

Overview

Companies often estimate ending inventory for a variety of purposes. For example, a company may use an estimate of ending inventory for internal purposes during interim periods when a physical count is prohibitively expensive or when inventory is destroyed as the result of a casualty. The **gross margin method** can be used only for estimation purposes. It may not be used for financial reporting of inventory. In contrast, the **retail inventory method** can be used both for internal decision purposes and for financial reporting of inventory.

Gross Profit (Margin) Method

Gross profit can be used to prepare interim financial statements or as an estimate if ending inventory is missing or destroyed. First, calculate an estimate of COGS by using the *historical gross profit percentage*, then back into ending inventory.

Office Inc. reported beginning inventory of 100,000 and purchases of 300,000. Assume that the company made sales of 300,000 during the period and earned a 40% gross profit margin. Determine Office's COGS and ending inventory.

100% of sales is split between a gross profit percentage (ie, how much profit the company earns on each unit) and a COGS percentage (ie, how much it costs the company to sell each unit).

Gross profit percentage is the portion of sales that the company gets to "keep":

$$\text{Gross profit \%} = \frac{\text{Sales} - \text{COGS}}{\text{Sales}}$$

The remaining portion of sales is the COGS percentage:

$$\text{COGS \%} = \frac{\text{COGS}}{\text{Sales}}$$

Here, the gross profit margin is 40%. Therefore, COGS must be 60% of sales (100% of sales = 40% profit and 60% COGS). COGS will be $180,000 (60% × $300,000). If COGS is $180,000, ending inventory is $220,000 (see calculation below).

Beginning inventory	100,000
+ Purchases	300,000
Goods available for sale	400,000
(COGS)	(180,000)
Ending inventory	220,000

Retail Inventory Method

The **retail inventory method** is a means of estimating ending inventory by relying on the relationship between the cost of inventory and the sales price.

Under the retail inventory method, companies track inventory costs (eg, beginning inventory, purchases) in both cost and retail (ie, sales) dollars. Sales, markups, markdowns, theft losses, and employee discounts during the year are recorded at retail dollars. At the end of each period, the company converts ending inventory from retail dollars back to cost dollars by using a cost-to-retail percentage. This percentage represents the cost portion of each sales dollar.

Net markups and net markdowns are included in the calculations of the retail inventory method:

- Net markups are calculated as markups − markup cancellations
- Net markdowns are calculated as markdowns − markdown cancellations

The cost-to-retail percentage calculation is dependent on the cost-flow assumption applied (eg, LIFO, FIFO, average cost). For example, in the conventional retail method (used for FIFO and average cost), the percentage calculation includes net markups but excludes net markdowns. However, in the LIFO retail method, the cost-to-retail percentage includes both net markups and net markdowns but excludes beginning inventory.

Conventional Retail Inventory Method

For illustration purposes only

	Cost	Retail
Beginning inventory + purchases	$10,000	$16,000
+ Purchases	26,000	43,500
+ Freight in	15,000	-
+ Net markups	-	25,500
Goods available for sale	**$51,000**	**$85,000**
− Net markdowns		(6,000)
Sales price of goods available for sale		$79,000
− Losses and employee discounts		(1,000)
− Sales at retail		(60,000)
Ending inventory in retail dollars		$18,000

Percentage
$51,000 / $85,000
= 60%

Ending inventory in cost dollars $18,000 × 60% = **$10,800**

Lower of Cost or Market and Lower of Cost or Net Realizable Value

Representative Task (Application): Use the lower of cost and net realizable value or the lower of cost or market approach to calculate the carrying amount of inventory.

Regardless of the choice of inventory costing method, a company must account for declines in the market value of unsold inventories (ASC 330). Two methods of inventory valuation exist:

- **Lower of cost or market (LCM)** applies only to inventory accounted for under the *LIFO or retail inventory methods.*
- **Lower of cost or net realizable value (LCNRV)** applies to all other inventory methods.

Lower of Cost or Market (LCM) and
Lower of Cost or NRV (LCNRV)

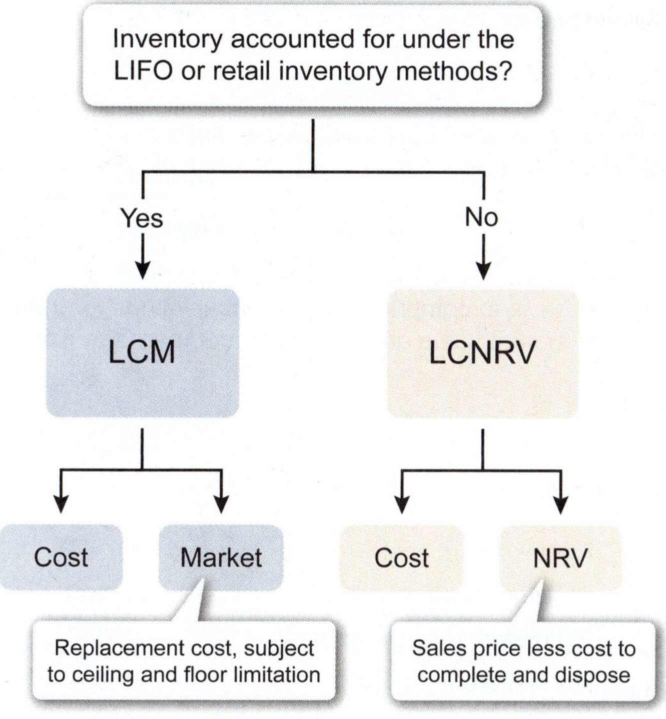

NRV = Net realizable value

Regardless of the costing or valuation method used, if the prices of goods in inventory have been consistently:

- *Rising*, then the valuation will usually be at *cost*
- *Falling*, then the valuation will usually be at *market value*

Inventory is initially recorded at historical cost. If the valuation of inventory indicates that the inventory value is below cost, then a loss must be recorded to lower the inventory value. **Losses are recognized immediately** on the income statement. Once inventory is written down, there is **no recovery** from the write-down until the units are sold.

Loss on inventory (market decline)	XX	
Inventory		XX

Lower of Cost or Market (LCM)

Lower of cost or market (LCM) compares the historical cost (ie, purchase price) with the current market value. Although market value is usually **replacement cost**, it is subject to a ceiling and floor limitation as follows:

- The **ceiling** is NRV, or Sales price − Costs to complete the inventory − Disposal costs, which is the maximum amount that may be reported as market
- The **floor** is NRV − Profit margin and is the lowest amount that may be reported as market

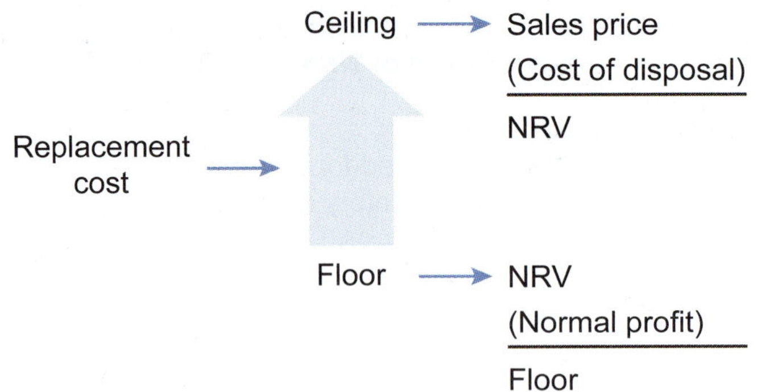

A shortcut to determine market value is to compare the numerical values for the replacement cost, ceiling, and floor. The middle value is the market value and should be compared to historical cost to determine if a loss must be recorded.

Assume the following facts:

Replacement cost	100,000
Estimated selling price	120,000
Estimated selling expenses	30,000
Normal profit margin	20,000

From the above information, we can determine the normal, ceiling, and floor amounts for market:

Normal: Replacement cost	100,000
Ceiling: Net realizable value	90,000
Floor: NRV − normal profit margin	70,000

Because the ceiling is the middle number, it is the market value. $90,000 will then be compared to historical cost to determine the lower of cost or market. If historical cost is greater than $90,000, the value of the inventory will be written down, and a loss will be recorded.

Lower of Cost or NRV (LCNRV)

Under **lower of cost or net realizable value (LCNRV)**, the amount to be used as the market value will always be NRV. If the NRV is lower than the original cost, the inventory must be written down, and a loss will be recorded.

Assume that a company owns inventory with the following valuation:

Historical cost	100,000
Estimated selling price	99,000
Replacement cost	88,000
Costs of completion, disposal, and transportation	9,000

The company will compare historical cost of $100,000 to NRV of $90,000 ($99,000 selling price − 9,000 costs of completion, disposal, and transportation). NRV is less than cost; therefore, the inventory must be written down to $90,000. The company will record the following:

Loss on inventory	10,000	
Inventory		10,000

LIFO and retail inventory methods	All other inventory costing methods
LCM – Lower of: • Cost = Original cost • Market = Middle of three numbers: ○ Net realizable value (NRV)—Ceiling ○ Replacement cost ○ NRV less normal profit margin—Floor	**LCNRV** – Lower of: • Cost = Original cost • NRV = Sales price – Cost of disposal

Losses on purchase commitments related to inventory are covered in the FAR Contingencies and Commitments chapter.

Inventory Rollforward

Representative Task (Analysis): Prepare a rollforward of the inventory account balance using various sources of data and information.

A **rollforward** is a high-level, summary method to review periodic activity in related accounts. For inventory, a rollforward starts with the beginning balance of inventory and lists all activity that increased or decreased the account during the period (ie, monthly, quarterly, or annually), resulting in the ending balance. The inventory rollforward includes purchases and cost of goods sold and any additional adjustments needed to correctly present the inventory balance in the financial statements.

Analysis-level tasks are typically tested in a task-based simulation (TBS). Below is an example of a TBS that might be encountered on the CPA exam for inventory.

Example

Wolf LLC sells one product, which it purchases from various suppliers. Wolf uses the FIFO inventory costing method and has a perpetual inventory system (a physical inventory count is performed at the end of each year). Prepare Wolf's rollforward for April of Year 5. Exhibits and additional information are given first, then the solution will follow.

Exhibit 1: April sales information

Sales by Quarter			Consignment Sales	
Date sold & shipped*	**Units sold**	**Net sales in dollars**	**Units sold**	**Net sales in dollars**
6-Apr	400	$ 6,400		
10-Apr	1,100	17,600		
13-Apr			500	$ 9,000
19-Apr	1,800	28,800		
28-Apr	500	8,000		
Totals	**3,800**	**$ 60,800**	**500**	**$ 9,000**

**All sales are FOB shipping point.*

Exhibit 2: April purchases information

Purchases					Consignment Inventory	
Date ordered & shipped	**Date received***	**Units purchased**	**Unit cost**	**Total cost**	**Date**	**Units received**
5-Apr	9-Apr	800	$9.10	$ 7,280	Beginning inventory	200
7-Apr	11-Apr	1,600	8.80	14,080	2-Apr	400
15-Apr	20-Apr	900	8.50	7,650	25-Apr	130
30-Apr	2-May	1,500	9.00	13,500		
Totals		4,800		$ 42,510	**Totals**	**730**

**All purchases are FOB destination.*

Additional Information:

- The balance of the March ending inventory is 1,000 units at $10 per unit
- Wolf is the consignee in a consignment inventory agreement with Jackal Inc. Wolf sells the consigned product for $18 each and receives commission of $3 per unit sold
- At the end of April, Wolf determined that the replacement cost of its inventory was $3,970. The company also estimated that it could sell the inventory for $6,000 with disposal costs of $1,855. Wolf's normal profit margin is $400

Solution:

Wolf's Inventory Rollforward, April Year 5

Beginning balance	$10,000
Purchases	29,010
Cost of goods sold (COGS)	(34,760)
Valuation adjustment	(105)
Ending balance	$ 4,145

Beginning balance: In the additional information, March ending inventory (ie, April beginning inventory) is given at 1,000 units at $10 per unit for a total cost of $10,000.

Purchases: According to the Purchases exhibit, the total cost of the 4,800 units purchased in April Year 5 is $42,510. However, all purchases are purchased *FOB destination*. Although 1,500 units (worth $13,500) were purchased and shipped on April 30, these units did not arrive until May 2. As title of these items has not yet passed to Wolf as of the end of April, these units are excluded from Wolf's inventory. **Total purchases are $29,010** ($42,510 − $13,500).

Wolf also reports consignment inventory in the Purchases exhibit. Per the additional information, Wolf is a consignee in the consignment arrangement with Jackal. Although Wolf has possession of these goods, the company does not own these goods. Therefore, consignment inventory is excluded from Wolf's inventory.

Cost of goods sold: Wolf uses the FIFO inventory costing method. The first units purchased are the first units sold.

Wolf will first sell the units that are already in its April beginning inventory. Once all beginning inventory units are sold, Wolf will then sell the inventory that it received on April 9. Once all inventory received on April 9 is sold, Wolf will then sell the inventory that it received on April 11. Once all inventory received on April 11 is sold, Wolf will then sell the inventory that it received on April 20.

Using this methodology, **Wolf's COGS is $34,760**. The following schedule lists Wolf's cost of goods sold based on each sale:

			Source					COGS	Source remaining units	
Beginning inventory		1,000 units at $10								
Apr. 6	Sold	400 units	Beginning inventory	400	×	$ 10.00	=	$ 4,000	600 units	(1,000 – 400)
Apr. 9	Received	800 units at $9.10								
Apr. 10	Sold	1,100 units	Beginning inventory	600	×	$ 10.00	=	$ 6,000	0 units	(600 – 600)
			Received Apr. 9	500	×	$ 9.10	=	$ 4,550	300 units	(800 – 500)
Apr. 11	Received	1,600 units at $8.80								
Apr. 19	Sold	1,800 units	Received Apr. 9	300	×	$ 9.10	=	$ 2,730	0 units	(300 – 300)
			Received Apr. 11	1,500	×	$ 8.80	=	$13,200	100 units	(1,600 – 1,500)
Apr. 20	Received	900 units at $8.50								
Apr. 28	Sold	500 units	Received Apr. 11	100	×	$ 8.80	=	$ 880	0 units	(100 – 100)
			Received Apr. 20	400	×	$ 8.50	=	$ 3,400	500 units	(900 – 400)
								$34,760		

Valuation adjustment: Since Wolf uses the FIFO method, its inventory will be valued at LCNRV. The LCNRV rule compares cost (ie, purchase price) with NRV (sales price less costs required to complete the inventory and disposal costs).

Based on the other items in the rollforward, the ending inventory cost under FIFO (before any valuation adjustments) is $4,250. According to the additional information, Wolf could sell the inventory for $6,000 with disposal costs of $1,855. Therefore, the NRV is $4,145 ($6,000 sales price − $1,855 disposal costs). Because the NRV ($4,145) is lower than cost ($4,250), the inventory will be valued at the NRV ($4,145).

A valuation adjustment will be recorded for the $105 ($4,250 − $4,145) decline in value:

Loss on inventory due to market decline	105	
Inventory		105

Reconciliation of Inventory Subledger and General Ledger

Representative Task (Analysis): Reconcile and investigate differences between the subledger and general ledger for inventory to determine whether an adjustment is necessary.

Recall that the **general ledger** is the central **record-keeping** system for an entity's **accounting transactions**. Account balances in the general ledger are supported by **detailed account records** kept in separate subsidiary ledgers (ie, **subledgers**). General ledger balances are reported in the entity's financial statements (F/S).

It is important to make sure that the total of the items in the subledger matches to the corresponding account in the general ledger by performing a reconciliation that compares the subledger to the general ledger to identify any discrepancies. Generally, the reconciliation process follows these steps:

- Compare the ending balances of the general ledger to the subledger
- Identify any differences by confirming beginning balances (for balance sheet accounts), ensuring daily postings from the subledger to the general ledger match, and researching any nonrecurring or unusual transactions
- Investigate reasons for the differences. Typically, these are errors or items posted in the general ledger and not the subledger or vice versa
- Adjust the appropriate ledger
- Compare adjusted balances

Example

Bloom Inc. sells home furniture. Each month the inventory subsidiary ledger is reconciled to the general ledger. For the month of December, Year 3, Bloom reviews the postings to the inventory subledger and general ledger and investigates any differences.

Bloom Inc.
Inventory Subledger Detail (Unadjusted)
For the Period December 1, Year 3 to December 31, Year 3

Date	Item #	Transaction type	Item description	Unit cost	Quantity	Amount
30-Nov	**Balance**					567,000
2-Dec	002344	Purchase	Lounge chaise	680	15	10,200
	Balance					577,200
7-Dec	002350	Sale–INV#921	Wide dining table	1,050	1	(1,050)
	Balance					576,150
11-Dec	002122	Return on INV#865	High-top table set	410	2	(820)
	Balance					575,330
15-Dec	002986	Sale–INV#922	Bookcase	275	3	(825)
	Balance					574,505
21-Dec	002345	Purchase	Patio set	2,340	5	11,700
	Balance					586,205
24-Dec	002125	Purchase	Queen bed frame	790	10	7,900
	Balance					594,105
26-Dec	002225	Purchase	Medium wardrobe	540	20	10,800
	Balance					604,905
29-Dec	002478	Purchase	Loveseat	500	10	5,000
31-Dec	**Balance**					609,905

Difference between subledger and general ledger = $4,800 ($609,905 − 605,105)

Bloom Inc.
General Ledger

Account: Inventory				**Account number: 400**
Date	Description	Debit	Credit	Balance
1-Dec	Beginning balance	567,000		567,000
2-Dec	Purchase	10,200		577,200
7-Dec	Sale		1,050	576,150
15-Dec	Sale		825	575,325
21-Dec	Purchase	11,700		587,025
24-Dec	Purchase	7,900		594,925
26-Dec	Purchase	10,800		605,725
28-Dec	Inventory on consignment		5,620	600,105
29-Dec	Purchase	5,000		605,105
31-Dec	**Totals and ending balance**	612,600	7,495	605,105

The first step in the monthly reconciliation between the inventory subledger and general ledger is to compare the ending balances. For December, Year 3, Bloom discovers that there is a $4,800 discrepancy.

Next, Bloom identifies the differences. Bloom notes that the beginning balances agree between the inventory subledger and general ledger. However, there are the following differences:

- The $820 return to supplier of the high-top table sets (INV #865) is missing from the general ledger
- The $5,620 removal of inventory on consignment is missing from the subledger
- The $5,000 purchase of loveseats on December 29, Year 3, is incorrectly included in the subledger and general ledger

$820 return of high-top table sets:

From: Inventory@BloomInc.com
To: Bryan@BrySuppy.com
Sent: December 11, Year 3
Subject: Return

Hello,

Thank you for speaking with us this afternoon. As discussed, we are sending back the two high-top table sets that arrived damaged. We just shipped them out, and would like a full refund ($820) for these items.

Please let us know if you need any additional information.

Sincerely,
Inventory Department

The return on INV #865 was posted to the inventory subledger but not the general ledger. Per the above email, Bloom returned the damaged inventory to a supplier on December 11.

While researching the missing posting, Bloom discovers that the entry in the inventory subledger was not posted to the general ledger because the accounting manager did not review and approve the transaction. To correct this, the posting will be processed, and the $820 return will be reflected in the general ledger.

$5,620 reversal of inventory on consignment:

From: Accounting@BloomInc.com
To: Inventory@BloomInc.com
Sent: December 28, Year 3
Subject: Inventory on Consignment

Hello,

Thank you for discussing our inventory records this afternoon. We now understand that $5,620 of inventory was not sold, but rather represents goods that Bloom is holding on consignment for Leaf Co. As we are so close to year-end, we will make a topside adjustment so that this is accurately reflected in our accounting records.

Please let me know if you need anything else from me.

Thank you,
Accounting Department

Earlier in the year, inventory on consignment of $5,620 was inadvertently included in Bloom's accounting inventory records. Inventory held on consignment by a consignee (here, Bloom) should not be included in the consignee's inventory as the consignee does not own the inventory. Per the above email, on December 28, the accounting department made a topside (ie, manual) adjustment directly to the general ledger to save time. However, the subledger was never updated to reflect this adjustment. To correct this, the $5,620 inventory on consignment will be removed from the subledger.

$5,000 purchase of loveseats:

Invoice

Supplier Ltd.
789 Decker Drive
San Francisco, CA 94016

Invoice # 1999
Date Dec. 29, Year 3

Bill to:
Bloom Inc.
101 Fine Avenue
San Diego, CA 91911

Item	Quantity	Price per unit	Amount
Loveseat	10	$500.00	$5,000.00

Subtotal	$5,000.00
Fees/discounts	$0.00
Total	$5,000.00

***Terms of shipping:**
Supplier Ltd. does not ship to P.O. boxes
Shipping timeline is 5–7 business days after order is received.
All goods are shipped FOB destination.

Bloom purchased 10 loveseats (costing $5,000 total) from Supplier Ltd. on December 29. This purchase was included in Bloom's inventory at December 31, Year 3. However, per the above invoice, Supplier Ltd. ships all goods FOB destination and goods take five to seven business days to ship after the order is received. Since the goods were ordered on December 29, Bloom would not have received them by December 31. Because title of the goods will not transfer to Bloom until the goods are received, these loveseats should not yet be included in Bloom's inventory. Bloom will adjust both the subledger and general ledger for this error.

Once all adjustments and correcting journal entries are recorded, Bloom compares the adjusted balances of the inventory subledger and the general ledger to ensure that the balances are reconciled.

Task

Complete the below reconciliation. Round all amounts to the nearest whole dollar. Enter positive adjustments as positive whole numbers and negative adjustments as negative whole numbers.

Inventory subledger original balance		General ledger original balance	
Inventory on consignment		Return of high-top table sets	
Loveseat purchase		Loveseat purchase	
Inventory subledger adjusted balance		**General ledger adjusted balance**	

Solution

Inventory subledger original balance	$609,905	General ledger original balance	$605,105
Subtract inventory on consignment	(5,620)	*Subtract* return of high-top table sets	(820)
Subtract loveseat purchase	(5,000)	*Subtract* loveseat purchase	(5,000)
Inventory subledger adjusted balance	**$599,285**	**General ledger adjusted balance**	**$599,285**

The adjusted balance in the inventory subledger and general ledger is $599,285. The corrected inventory subledger and general ledger are below:

Bloom Inc.
Inventory Subledger Detail (Adjusted)
For the Period December 1, Year 3 to December 31, Year 3

Date	Item #	Transaction type	Item description	Unit cost	Quantity	Amount
30-Nov	**Balance**					567,000
2-Dec	002344	Purchase	Lounge chaise	680	15	10,200
	Balance					577,200
7-Dec	002350	Sale–INV#921	Wide dining table	1,050	1	(1,050)
	Balance					576,150
11-Dec	002122	Return on INV#865	High-top table set	410	2	(820)
	Balance					575,330
15-Dec	002986	Sale–INV#922	Bookcase	275	3	(825)
	Balance					574,505
21-Dec	002345	Purchase	Patio set	2,340	5	11,700
	Balance					586,205
24-Dec	002125	Purchase	Queen bed frame	790	10	7,900
	Balance					594,105
26-Dec	002225	Purchase	Medium wardrobe	540	20	10,800
	Balance					604,905
28-Dec		Adjustment	Inv. on consignment			(5,620)
31-Dec	**Balance**					599,285

Subledger and general ledger agree

Adjusted inventory balance = $599,285

Bloom Inc.
General Ledger

Account: Inventory				**Account number: 400**
Date	**Description**	**Debit**	**Credit**	**Balance**
1-Dec	Beginning balance	567,000		567,000
2-Dec	Purchase	10,200		577,200
7-Dec	Sale		1,050	576,150
11-Dec	Return		820	575,330
15-Dec	Sale		825	574,505
21-Dec	Purchase	11,700		586,205
24-Dec	Purchase	7,900		594,105
26-Dec	Purchase	10,800		604,905
28-Dec	Inventory on consignment		5,620	599,285
31-Dec	**Totals and ending balance**	607,600	8,315	599,285

FAR 10
Property, Plant, and Equipment

FAR 10: Property, Plant, and Equipment

10.01 Property, Plant, and Equipment: Fixed Assets

Overview

Representative Task (Application): Calculate the gross and net property, plant and equipment balances and prepare journal entries.

Property, **plant**, **and equipment (PP&E)**, also called fixed assets or long-lived assets, are tangible assets acquired for long-term use in the normal course of business. They are not for resale and are generally subject to depreciation. To be included within the PP&E accounts, an asset needs to meet the following conditions: (1) be currently used in operations, (2) have a useful life extending more than one year beyond the balance sheet date, and (3) have physical substance.

Categories within PP&E

Account	Description
Plant and Equipment	• Buildings, machinery, and equipment • Finite useful life
Land	• Any plot of land on which a company has constructed facilities specifically related to primary business operations* • Examples include the site of manufacturing facilities, administrative offices, and storage warehouses • Indefinite life; therefore, not depreciated *(only PP&E item not depreciated or amortized)*
Land Improvements	• Differs from land in that it has a finite useful life and is depreciated • Examples include parking lots, fencing, external lighting, and some landscaping
Natural Resources	• Will produce income until all natural resources are extracted and sold • Examples include gravel pits, coal mines, tracts of timber land, and oil wells
Leasehold Improvements	• Includes improvements to leased property, such as retail stores or office space • The lessee can depreciate the leasehold improvement over the useful life of the improvement or the life of the lease (whichever is shorter)

If land is held for investment purposes or for future development, it is* ***excluded* *from plant assets because it is not currently a productive asset.*

Capitalized Cost

Costs Capitalized upon Acquisition of PP&E

The initial capitalized cost of PP&E includes two components: (1) **the acquisition cost** and (2) the **get-ready costs**. The acquisition cost is either the cash paid for the asset on the acquisition date or the present value of future cash payments if the asset is bought on a payment plan. The get-ready costs include all costs incurred to get the asset on the company's premises and ready for use (eg, setting up and testing of new machinery).

The list price of a plant asset is $30,000. The purchaser makes a $10,000 down payment and issues a two-year, non-interest-bearing note for the remainder. The note calls for a single lump-sum payment of $20,000 to be made at the maturity of the note. The market rate of interest on such notes is 10%. The present value of a single payment of $1 received two years in the future at 10% is 0.82645. Determine the entry that should be recorded by the purchaser when the plant asset is acquired.

The entry to record the plant asset is as follows:

Plant asset ($10,000 + 16,529)	26,529	
Cash		10,000
Note payable ($20,000 × 0.82645)		16,529

The note is recorded at present value. The list price of plant assets should not be used for valuation of assets. The list price is mainly a starting point for negotiations between the buyer and seller. Subsequent to acquisition, interest expense is recognized as the note approaches maturity.

Other, less common acquisition transactions may include the following: (1) issuing equity securities, in which case the acquisition cost is the fair value (FV) of the security or the FV of the asset acquired, and (2) receiving donated assets, in which case the assets received in donation are recorded at their FV.

The general rule for **capitalizing expenditures related to the acquisition of PP&E** is similar to the rule for capitalizing costs to inventory. All expenditures necessary to bring the asset to its intended condition and location are capitalized.

Acquisition Costs and Get-Ready Costs	Cost of Land
• Purchase price • Legal fees • Delinquent taxes • Title insurance • Transportation (freight-in) • Installation • Test runs • Sales taxes	• Purchase price (including any existing buildings to be demolished) • Surveying • Clearing, grading, and landscaping • Costs of razing or demolishing an old building are added to the land cost • Proceeds from the sale of any scrap (eg, old bricks) are subtracted from the land cost

A piece of land with an existing building on it is acquired, with the following facts applying:

Purchase price	$300,000
Cost of razing old building	50,000
Sale of scrap from clearing old building	8,000

The cost of the land is $300,000 + $50,000 − $8,000 = $342,000. Notice that nothing is allocated to the old building, since it is being demolished. No benefits are being derived from the old building, so the matching principle indicates that no cost should be allocated to it.

Lump-Sum Purchases

In a lump-sum purchase, **multiple assets** are acquired for a **single price**. If a group of fixed assets (eg, land with a building) is acquired in a single transaction, the total negotiated price is **allocated** to the individual assets acquired. This allocation is based on the *respective FVs* of the individual assets acquired.

Allocation of asset values with lump-sum purchase

$$\text{Individual asset allocated value} = \frac{\text{Individual asset appraised value}}{\text{Total assets appraised value}} \times \text{Lump-sum (total cost)}$$

A building and land were acquired for the lump sum of $600,000. The only available information related to the value of the assets is the tax appraisal, which allocates $100,000 to the land and $400,000 to the building. Determine how the lump-sum payment should be allocated to each asset.

The total tax value is $500,000. Therefore, allocation of the payment should be based on the following:

Item	Appraisal value	Calculation	Allocation %
Land	$100,000	$100,000 / $500,000	20%
Building	$400,000	$400,000 / $500,000	80%
Total	$500,000		100%

The entry to record acquisition of the property is as follows:

Land (20% × $600,000)	120,000	
Building (80% × $600,000)	480,000	
Cash		600,000

If land is acquired along with a depleting asset, such as oil in the ground, then the land is normally allocated its estimated residual value, assuming that all oil has been removed, and the remainder is allocated to the oil itself. One complication, however, is that the cost of the property includes all costs of acquisition and preparation of the property for drilling, as well as any estimated restoration costs for the property following the completion of drilling.

Costs Capitalized during the Life of the Plant Asset

An expenditure will either be **capitalized or expensed:**

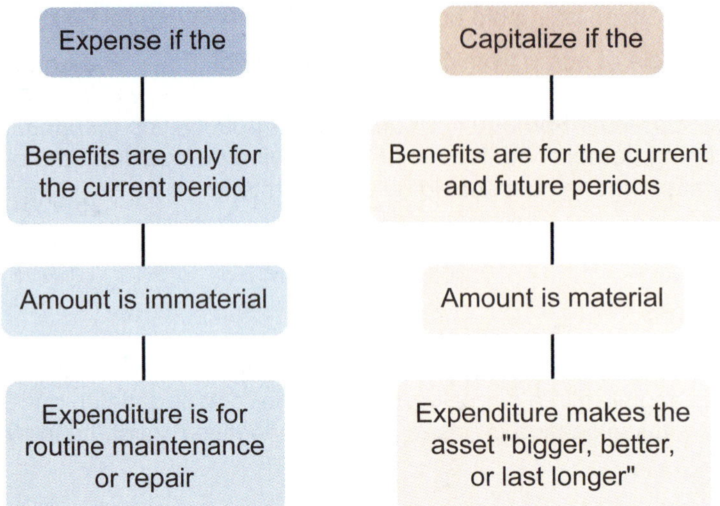

"Bigger, better, or last longer" means that the expenditure gives the asset increased or improved functionality, makes it a better product, or gives it a longer life.

Examples of "Bigger, Better, or Last Longer"	
Scenario	**Example**
The estimated useful life of the asset is extended beyond the original estimation	A major overhaul of a bread oven in a commercial bread bakery that extends the life of the oven beyond the original estimate
The asset becomes more efficient or productive, meaning it can produce higher quantities or operate at a lower cost	A new laser-based product sorter is added to a machine, replacing human efforts to sort out defective products and thereby speeding up the process
Quality of the asset's output is improved	Upgrades to equipment for a textile entity, which enable it to produce a sheet with a higher thread count

If part of an asset is **replaced** and the old part is identifiable (ie, the company maintained records of the old part's cost and accumulated depreciation), the replacement is accounted for as if the old part was sold and replaced with the new part. The old part is removed from the books, a loss is recorded for the old part's remaining depreciation, and the new part is added.

If the old part is *not* identifiable, the accounting depends on whether the new part enhances the asset or increases the asset's remaining useful life. If the asset is enhanced, the new part is capitalized to the asset. If the asset's useful life is extended, the new part is recorded as a decrease to accumulated depreciation (ie, accumulated depreciation is debited).

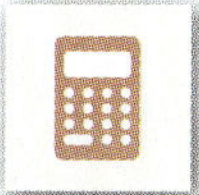

The boiler of a large office building is replaced with a more efficient boiler at a cost of $65,000. The useful life of the building is unaffected, but the new boiler will reduce energy costs significantly. The cost of the old boiler was $40,000, and its accumulated depreciation (A/D) subsidiary ledger account reflects a balance of $35,000. Determine the entry to record the replacement.

Because the company maintained records related to the cost and A/D of the old boiler, the replacement is accounted for as if the old boiler was sold and the new boiler was purchased. The entry to record the replacement is as follows:

Accumulated depreciation	35,000	
Loss on replacement	5,000	
Boiler		40,000

Boiler	65,000	
Cash		65,000

Capitalized Interest

When a company **constructs a fixed asset**, capitalized costs include the following:

- Direct labor
- Direct materials
- Overhead charges
- Construction period interest

Interest cost is typically expensed in the period incurred. However, when a company constructs a fixed asset, the interest cost incurred *during* the construction period is considered a get-ready cost and is, therefore, capitalized. Interest capitalization exemplifies the matching principle as the benefit of the constructed asset will be over its useful life.

The justification for interest capitalization is that, had the construction not taken place, the funds used in construction could have been used to reduce interest-bearing debt. Therefore, the amount capitalized is considered the **avoidable interest** (ie, interest that would have been avoided had the construction not taken place). In a sense, the construction caused this amount of interest, which, therefore, should be included in the cost of the asset constructed.

Interest incurred on construction loans and nonconstruction loans should be included, but only to the extent that the funds have been spent on construction. The following table shows assets eligible for capitalization of interest costs:

Capitalization of Interest Costs	
Capitalize Interest Costs	**Do not Capitalize Interest Costs**
• Asset is constructed for company's own use, or • Asset is manufactured for resale resulting from a special order	• Inventory that is manufactured in the ordinary course of business

Interest is capitalized during periods in which *all three* conditions are met:

- Qualifying expenditures have been made (eg, cash payments, transfers of other assets, or the incurrence of interest-bearing debt)
- Activities that are necessary to get the asset ready for its intended use are in progress (ie, construction is proceeding)
- Actual interest cost is being incurred

Interest cost is only capitalized **during** the construction period. Interest incurred before and after the construction period is expensed.

The **amount** of capitalized interest (ie, avoidable interest) is equal to:

Weighted average accumulated expenditures (WAAE) × Interest rate

Remember that the capitalized interest is the measure of the amount of debt, on an annual basis, that could have been avoided had the construction not taken place. This may include interest on other (non-construction-related) debt. The amount of capitalized interest **should never exceed the actual interest cost incurred**:

Capitalized Interest on Self-Constructed Assets

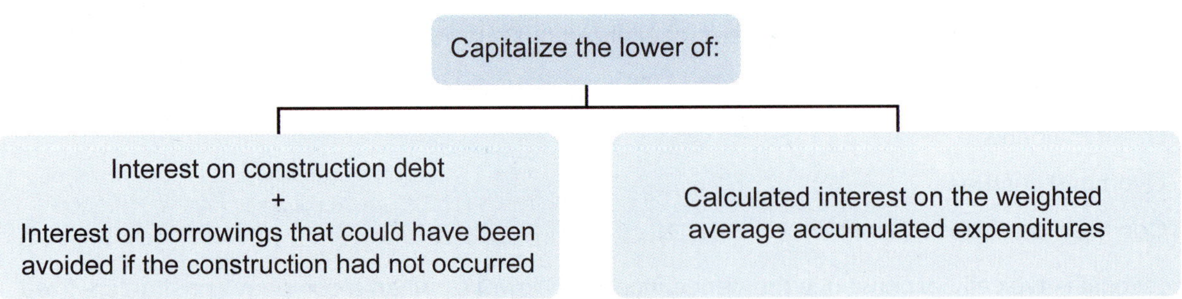

Determining the WAAE

To calculate the **WAAE**, expenditures must be weighted for the number of months they are outstanding in the capitalization period and then added together.

The **months outstanding** refers to the number of months between the date of the expenditure and the end of the capitalization period. The **capitalization period** is often 12 months, but it could be less if, for example, construction begins or ends during the year.

Computation of Weighted Average Accumulated Expenditures

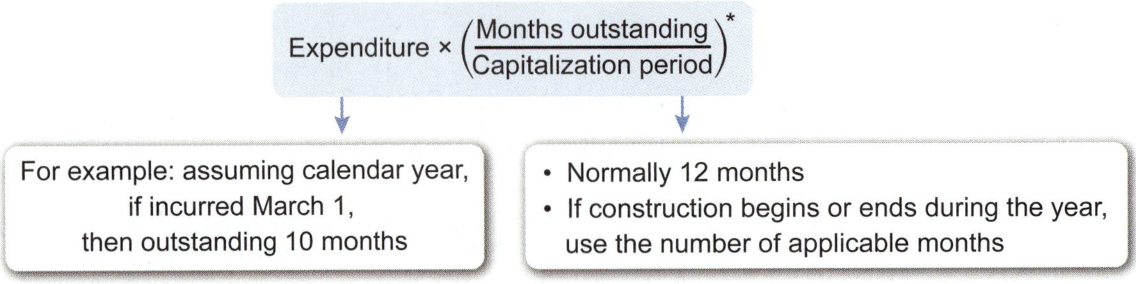

**If expenditures each month are the same amount (ie, expenditures are made uniformly throughout the period), this calculation is mathematically equivalent to the entire year's expenditures being made halfway through the period, (ie, the total year's expenditures × 1/2).*

There are three expenditures during Year 1, occurring on the first of the month in January, April, and December for $100,000, $300,000, and $360,000, respectively. Calculate the WAAE.

The WAAE would be calculated as follows:

1/1/Year 1	$100,000	×	12/12	=	$100,000
4/1/Year 1	$300,000	×	9/12	=	$225,000
12/1/Year 1	$360,000	×	1/12	=	$30,000
			WAAE	=	$355,000

Determining the Interest Rate

GAAP *does not* limit capitalized interest to specific construction loan interest. Rather, the more general concept of avoidable interest is used. Two ways of computing total interest to be capitalized are allowed:

- **Weighted average method:** Interest is capitalized using the weighted average rate on all interest-bearing debt
- **Specific method:** Interest is capitalized on specific construction loans first. Then, if needed, interest is capitalized on all other debt, based on the average interest rate for that debt

The interest rate is adjusted for the fraction of the year the debt is outstanding. If new interest-bearing debt is incurred during an interest capitalization period, the interest rate reflects the period that the debt was outstanding

Lilly Inc. began construction of a building in January for the company's own use. Lilly spent $100,000 in qualifying expenditures by year-end. Expenditures were made evenly throughout the period. Debt outstanding for the entire year was as follows:

	Principal	**Annual interest**
10% construction loan	$30,000	$3,000 ($30,000 × 10%)
Other debt, average interest rate 8%	$60,000	$4,800 ($60,000 × 8%)
Total	$90,000	$7,800

Determine the amount of interest to be capitalized under the weighted average and specific methods.

First, Lilly will determine the WAAE. Here, since the $100,000 expenditures were made evenly throughout the period, WAAE is calculated as $100,000 × 1/2, or $50,000.

Next, Lilly will calculate the amount of interest to be capitalized under each method.

Under the **weighted average method:**

The interest rate used is calculated as the total interest incurred on all debt, divided by total principal of all debt. Here, the interest rate is 8.67% ($7,800 / $90,000).

Capitalized interest = $50,000 WAAE × 8.67% interest rate = $4,335

$4,335 is less than actual interest incurred of $7,800. Therefore, the capitalized interest is $4,335. The remaining $3,465 ($7,800 − $4,335) is recorded as interest expense.

Under the **specific method:**

The interest on the specific construction loan is capitalized first. Then interest is capitalized on all other debt, based on the other debt's average interest rate. Here, the interest capitalized is $4,600:

Interest rate		WAAE		Capitalized interest
10%	×	$30,000*	=	$3,000
8%	×	$20,000*	=	$1,600
		$50,000		$4,600

**The specific method first uses the construction loan. The principal amount of that loan is only $30,000. But $50,000 (WAAE) of debt could have been retired. The additional $20,000 of debt (to sum to the $50,000 WAAE) is the portion of the nonspecific debt that could have been retired.*

$4,600 is less than actual interest incurred of $7,800. Therefore, the capitalized interest is $4,600. The remaining $3,200 ($7,800 − $4,600) is recorded as interest expense.

Interest capitalized compounds over several periods. The interest capitalized in Year 1 is included in WAAE for Year 2, thus increasing the amount of interest capitalized in Year 2. Interest is, therefore, compounded and included in the asset account.

Capitalized Interest vs. Interest Expense

As depicted in the previous example:

- When WAAE is less than total interest-bearing debt, reported interest expense for the period is the *difference between total interest cost and the amount of interest capitalized*
  - Here, because WAAE is less than total debt, not all debt could have been avoided
- When WAAE is greater than total interest-bearing debt, *all* interest cost is capitalized, and there is no reported interest expense for the period
  - Here, all debt could have been avoided had construction activities not taken place

Mather Co. began construction on a project on January 1, Year 6, with a construction payment of $100,000 to the contractor. One additional payment of $120,000 was made on July 1, Year 6. Debt outstanding during Year 6 (entire year) included the following:

- 5%, $120,000 construction loan
- 6%, $20,000 note payable unrelated to construction
- 4%, $30,000 note payable unrelated to construction

Determine the amount of interest to be capitalized under the weighted average and specific methods.

First, Mather will determine the WAAE. Here, WAAE is calculated as follows:

[$100,000 × (12/12)] + [$120,000 × (6/12)] = $160,000

Next, Mather will calculate the amount of interest to be capitalized under each method.

Under the **weighted average method:**

The applicable interest rate is calculated as total interest incurred on all debt, divided by total principal of all debt:

$$\frac{(5\% \times \$120{,}000) + (6\% \times \$20{,}000) + (4\% \times \$30{,}000)}{\$120{,}000 + \$20{,}000 + \$30{,}000} = 4.94\%$$

Capitalized interest is calculated as follows:

$160,000 WAAE × 4.94% interest rate = $7,904

Actual interest incurred is $8,400. Interest expense is $496 ($8,400 − $7,904).

Remember, the maximum amount of interest capitalization allowed is the *actual interest incurred.* If WAAE had been greater than the amount of total debt (ie, greater than $170,000), then all interest incurred during the period ($8,400) would have been capitalized. Under the **specific method:**

The average interest rate on the nonconstruction loans is calculated as follows:

$$\frac{(6\% \times \$20{,}000) + (4\% \times \$30{,}000)}{\$20{,}000 + \$30{,}000} = 4.8\%$$

Capitalized interest is calculated as follows:

(5% × $120,000 construction loan) + (4.8% × $40,000 other loans*) = $7,920

**$160,000 WAAE − $120,000 first allocated to construction loan = $40,000 allocated to other loans*

If WAAE had been less than the amount of the construction loan (ie, less than $120,000), then only the construction loan interest would be capitalized (up to the amount of WAAE).

If WAAE had been greater than the amount of total debt (ie, greater than $170,000), then all interest incurred during the period ($8,400) would have been capitalized.

Interest capitalized in one period becomes part of WAAE in the next. Using the above example (weighted average method), the balance in the construction in process (CIP) account at the end of the first period is $227,904 ($100,000 construction payment + $120,000 construction payment + $7,904 capitalized interest).

The next year, the calculation of WAAE will begin with $227,904 (12/12), with the payments during the second year receiving the appropriate rate for the period of time in the project. Thus, the $7,904 of interest capitalized the previous period will be part of the base on which interest is capitalized the next period.

Depreciation Methods

Overview

Depreciation is a systematic and rational allocation of capitalized plant asset cost to different reporting periods. The term **systematic** implies that the allocation is not random but, rather, is made on an orderly basis. The term **rational** means that by appealing to the way the asset is used, the process can be supported. The process of depreciation matches the cost of the plant asset to periods in which the asset is used to generate revenue.

Depreciation is *not:*

- A process of valuation
- A reflection of the decline in the market value of the asset
- A measure of the amount of the asset that has been "used up"

Depreciation is simply the amount allocated to the period based on the method chosen by the firm.

The **book value** (BV) of a depreciable plant asset is calculated as follows:

Original cost − Accumulated depreciation

The BV is the amount of original cost yet to be depreciated. If the BV equals the market value, this is only coincidental.

The amount of **depreciation** recognized each period is affected by the following four factors:

1. Capitalized cost
2. Estimated useful life
3. Estimated salvage value (the cost of the asset not subject to depreciation—that is, the portion of initial cost expected to be returned at the end of the asset's useful life)
4. Method chosen

Several methods of depreciation are acceptable under GAAP. They can be categorized into two basic types: (1) nonaccelerated methods and (2) accelerated methods.

Nonaccelerated Depreciation Methods

The **straight-line method** (SL) is commonly used. It allocates the cost equally over the useful life of the asset. The **depreciation expense** is calculated as follows:

$$\frac{\text{Cost} - \text{Salvage value}}{\text{Useful life}} = \text{Depreciation expense}$$

Depreciation is recorded with the following adjusting entry:

Depreciation expense (I/S)	XX	
Accumulated depreciation		XX

Contra-asset account (reduces asset)

An asset costing $22,000 with a salvage value of $2,000 and a useful life of five years is depreciated $4,000 each year using the SL method ($22,000 − $2,000) / 5.

The **units of production** (UOP) method defines the life of the asset and its depreciation rate in terms of the units of output. Annual depreciation varies depending on the number of units produced during the year as compared to the total estimated output. There is no expectation that depreciation will be the same amount each year.

Depreciation expense may be calculated as follows:

Units of production depreciation

$$\text{Depreciation expense per unit} = \frac{\text{Cost} - \text{Salvage value}}{\text{Total units in asset's life}}$$

Depreciation expense for year = Depreciation expense per unit × Units produced during year

An asset costing $22,000 with a salvage value of $2,000 and a useful life of five years is depreciated using the units of production method. The asset is expected to produce 1,000 units. In a given year, 300 units are produced. The constant rate is $20 per unit [($22,000 − $2,000) / 1,000]. Depreciation for the given year is $6,000 (300 units × $20).

Accelerated Depreciation Methods

Accelerated methods of depreciation are used when more of the asset's cost is depreciated in earlier years than in later years.

The rationale for using an accelerated method is that it results in better **matching** because the asset is more productive in earlier years. Also, using an accelerated method can minimize loss due to obsolescence. Because an asset is depreciated more quickly, the BV in later years is lower, and therefore, a loss from obsolescence would be smaller. Using an accelerated method can also help **even out expenses**. Because repairs and maintenance in the earlier years are typically lower, by taking more depreciation earlier on, the total expenses (depreciation, plus repairs and maintenance) would stay more constant over time.

The **double-declining balance** (DDB) method is a depreciation rate that is **twice the straight-line rate** applied against the BV of the asset. For example, if an asset were to be used for five years, then the straight-line depreciation rate would be 20% (1/5) per year. It follows that the double-declining balance depreciation rate would be 40% (20% × 2).

Importantly, when applying the DDB method, the salvage value is ignored in the annual calculation of depreciation. Rather, the asset is depreciated to the salvage value. This means that the final year of depreciation is often a plug figure to set the asset value equal to the salvage value.

Depreciation expense Yr 1

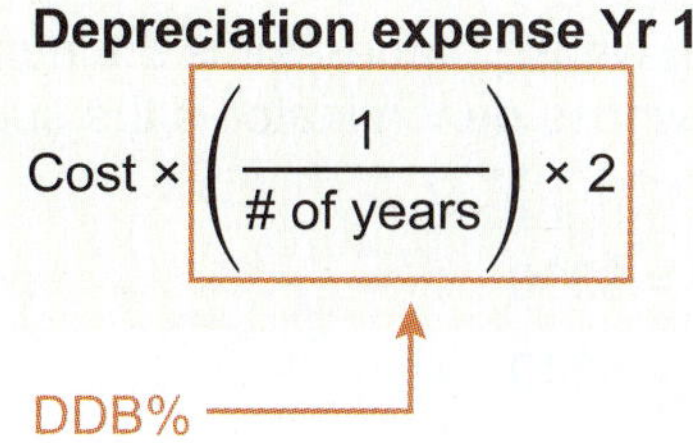

Depreciation expense Yr 2

(Cost − Depreciation expense Yr 1) × DDB%

Sum of the years digits (SYD) is an accelerated depreciation method that is considered less aggressive than the DDB method. To determine the SYD rate, the numerator is the number of years left in the asset's useful life, while the denominator is the sum of the years in the asset's useful life.

$$(\text{Cost} - \text{Salvage value}) \times \left(\frac{\text{\# of years left in asset's life}}{\text{Sum of years in asset's life}} \right) = \text{Depreciation expense}$$

Assuming a three-year asset, the numerator would be 3 in Year 1, 2 in Year 2, and then 1 in Year 3. The denominator in all years would be 3 + 2 + 1 . This can also be calculated as $[n \times (n + 1)] / 2$, where n = *useful life*. The rate of depreciation each year is as follows:

Year	Rate
Year 1	3 / 6
Year 2	2 / 6
Year 3	1 / 6

To calculate depreciation expense each year, the applicable rate is multiplied by the cost, less the salvage value.

Comprehensive Depreciation Example

The data for a machine is provided below. Calculate depreciation expense for the first two years using the SL, UOP, SYD, and DDB methods.

Purchase date	1/1/Year 1
Cost	$1,000
Estimated useful life	5 years
Estimated salvage value	$100
Estimated total output	1,000 units
Year 1 output	250 units
Year 2 output	300 units

SL depreciation allocates the depreciable basis (cost − salvage) over the useful life:

- Year 1: $1,000 cost − $100 salvage = $900 basis / 5 year life = $180
- Year 2: $1,000 cost − $100 salvage = $900 basis / 5 year life = $180

UOP depreciation multiplies the depreciable basis by a fraction whose numerator is the current output and whose denominator is the estimated total output.

- Year 1: $900 basis × 250 current output / 1,000 total output = $225
- Year 2: $900 basis × 300 current output / 1,000 total output = $270

SYD depreciation multiplies the depreciable basis by a fraction whose numerator is the number of the years left in the asset's life as of the beginning of the year and whose denominator is the sum of the number of years in the asset's life.

- Year 1: $900 basis × 5 / (1 + 2 + 3 + 4 + 5) = $900 × 5 / 15 = $300
- Year 2: $900 basis × 4 / (1 + 2 + 3 + 4 + 5) = $900 × 4 / 15 = $240

DDB depreciation multiplies the BV (cost − A/D) at the beginning of each period by a fraction that is double the straight-line depreciation rate*

- Year 1: $1,000 cost × 2 / 5 year life = $400
- Year 2: $1,000 cost − $400 A/D = $600 BV × 2 / 5 = $240

**Other declining balance approaches work the same way as the double-declining balance approach, except that the multiplier of the straight-line rate is different.*

Partial Period Depreciation

In computing depreciation expense for partial periods, it is necessary to determine the depreciation expense for the full year and then prorate the depreciation expense for the periods involved. This process continues throughout the asset's useful life.

When an asset is bought on a date other than the first of the fiscal year, depreciation in the year of acquisition needs to consider the fractional time period for all methods except the UOP method (which is based on output rather than passage of time).

Assume the same facts applied as in the previous example, except that the purchase date was 7/1/Year 1.

Since the asset was purchased in the middle of the year, the first year's depreciation is based on one-half of a year, and the second year's depreciation may be affected as well.

SL depreciation:

- Because the asset was purchased halfway through the year, only half the amount of depreciation is taken in Year 1. Year 1 depreciation is $90 ($180 × 1/2)
- Year 2 depreciation, $180, remains unchanged

UOP depreciation:

- Depreciation is unchanged because it is based on output rather than the passage of time

SYD depreciation:

- Because the asset was purchased halfway through the year, only half the amount of depreciation is taken in Year 1. Year 1 depreciation is $150 ($300 × 1/2)
- Year 2 depreciation is calculated as follows: $900 basis × 4.5* / (1 + 2 + 3 + 4 + 5) = $900 × 4.5 / 15 = $270

**Using SYD, the numerator is the amount of life remaining at the start of the year. For a five-year asset that is six months old, the remaining life is four and a half years at the start of the second year.*

DDB depreciation:

- Because the asset was purchased halfway through the year, only half the amount of depreciation is taken in Year 1. Year 1 depreciation is $200 ($400 × 1/2). This impacts the amount of A/D used in the Year 2 calculation
- Year 2 depreciation is calculated as follows: $1,000 cost − $200 A/D = $800 BV × 2 / 5 = $320

Group or Composite Depreciation

Group or composite depreciation is a system that applies the straight-line method to a collection of assets rather than to individual assets.

- **Group** refers to a collection of assets that are *similar* in nature, are fairly homogeneous, and have approximately the same useful lives.
- **Composite** refers to a collection of assets that are *dissimilar* in nature, are fairly heterogeneous, and have different useful lives.

A/D records are not maintained by asset; rather, only a control account is used to accumulate depreciation. **When one of the assets in the group is sold**, gains and losses are not recorded. The entry to dispose of an asset plugs the A/D account.

	Debit	Credit
Cash	20	
Accumulated depreciation	80	
Loss	NONE	
Asset		100
Gain		NONE

Under the **composite method** of depreciation, a building that is furnished with tables, chairs, and other items might elect to determine a weighted average life for all the furnishings and depreciate the total over this life. In the first year, the company determines the individual depreciation amounts for the items, totals them, and then divides this amount into the total cost to determine an average life that is used from that point forward. The savings in bookkeeping effort can be enormous.

A company acquires a desk, chair, and lamp to furnish an office. These items will be of approximately equal usefulness each year, with no salvage at the end of their individual lives:

Item	Cost	Estimated life in years	Annual depreciation
Desk	$1,000	10	$100
Chair	200	5	40
Lamp	100	4	25
Total	$1,300	7.88	$165

Under the composite approach, the furnishings for the office are carried on the depreciation schedule at a single cost of $1,300 and depreciated over a life of 7.88 years ($1,300 / $165).

Natural Resources and Depletion

While assets like PP&E have limited useful lives, some assets get "used up." Mining companies and other companies in *extractive industries* will buy or otherwise obtain rights to real property that is expected to have some kind of natural resource, such as oil, minerals, precious metals, or other commodities.

When a **natural resource** is acquired, the amount capitalized is the sum of three different types of costs:

1. **Acquisition costs:** The amount paid to acquire the rights to explore for undiscovered natural resources or to extract proven natural resources
2. **Exploration costs:** The amount paid to drill or excavate or any other costs of searching for natural resources
3. **Development costs:** The amount paid after the resource has been discovered but before production begins

Furthermore, a firm must choose between two methods of *accounting for exploration costs*:

1. The **successful-efforts method**, in which only the cost of successful exploration efforts is capitalized to the natural resources account; any unsuccessful efforts are expensed. This method best reflects the definition of an asset because only those efforts used to locate the resource are capitalized to the natural resource account.
2. The **full-costing method**, in which all costs of exploring for the resource are capitalized to the natural resources account. Note: The total amount capitalized cannot exceed the expected value of resources to be removed. This method reflects the matching principle as it capitalizes all costs until the natural resource produces revenue through sale of the inventory.

After resources are discovered on the property, the cost to **develop** the property to enable extraction of the resource is capitalized to the natural resources account. Development costs pertain to facilities that will not be removed when the project is finished. Removable assets such as drilling equipment and vehicles are recorded in their own separate accounts as plant assets.

Capitalized costs are initially recorded in the natural resources account. Over time, as the resource is used, depletion is recorded in inventory:

Inventory	XX	
Accumulated depletion—natural resources		XX

Depletion expense is then charged to cost of sales based on the units sold. Depletion is recognized using the following process:

Calculation of Cost Depletion: Activity Method	
Step 1: Volume in units	Units remaining to be extracted at beginning of year*
Step 2: Depletion cost per unit	Depletion base** / Units from Step 1
Step 3: Depletion (charged to inventory)	Per-unit cost from Step 2 × Units *extracted*
Depletion expense (transferred from inventory when sold)	Per-unit cost from Step 2 × Units *sold*

**For the first year, this equals total units to be extracted.*

***Depletion base for the first year is total cost, less salvage value. In subsequent years, this amount is reduced by depletion taken previously.*

The natural resource account is presented as a **noncurrent asset**. The property associated with the natural resource is not classified as land because the land is not held as a building site but, rather, for access to its natural resources.

Some firms classify the natural resource as an intangible asset because they have purchased the rights to utilize the land and do not own the land itself. These "mineral rights" are an intangible asset. Once extracted, the natural resource noncurrent asset is transferred to resource inventory, a current asset.

Disposal of Fixed Assets

Representative Task (Application): Calculate gains or losses on the disposal of long-lived assets to be recognized in the financial statements.

When a company disposes of a fixed asset, it will typically remove the original cost and A/D, record any amounts received or due as a result of disposal, and recognize a gain or loss for the difference. The gain or loss is reported in continuing operations as part of other items.

Rose Co. owns a machine with an original cost of $10,000 and a carrying amount of $3,000. The machine is sold for $2,500 cash. Determine the entry to record the sale.

The entry is as follows:

Cash		2,500	
Loss on sale ($3,000 – $2,500)		500	
Accumulated depreciation		7,000	
Machinery and equipment			10,000

Involuntary Conversion

Disposals include *destruction of property* as well as seizure by government entities as a result of condemnation or eminent domain actions. The accounting for these events is **the same as voluntary sales**, and GAAP does not allow deferral of gains or losses as a result of subsequent replacement of such property. The loss on abandonment or conversion is an ordinary loss and part of continuing operations on the income statement (I/S).

On 9/15/Year 1, a fire destroyed a client's warehouse. The warehouse had an original cost of $1,000,000, and A/D on the date of destruction was $225,000. The client anticipates receiving $1,200,000 from the insurance company. Removal of debris cost $20,000. On 1/20/Year 2, the insurance company issued a check to the client for $1,200,000, and a new warehouse was built and completed on 6/30/Year 2 at a cost of $1,300,000. Determine the entries to be recorded in Year 1 and Year 2 related to the fire.

In Year 1, the entries to account for the effects of the fire are as follows:

Account	Debit	Credit
Accounts receivable (from insurance company)	1,200,000	
Accumulated depreciation	225,000	
Involuntary conversion gain		405,000
Warehouse		1,000,000
Cash		20,000

In Year 2, the collection of the insurance payment and construction of the new warehouse result in the following entries:

Account	Debit	Credit
Cash	1,200,000	
Accounts receivable (from insurance company)		1,200,000
Warehouse (new)	1,300,000	
Cash		1,300,000

In determining the A/D balance at the time of a disposal, the asset should reflect any depreciation in the current period prior to time of disposal. Also, in determining the gain or loss, all costs associated with the sale should be included.

If an asset that is part of a group being depreciated under the composite method is sold or removed from service before the entire group has been fully depreciated, determining the asset's cost and A/D may be impossible. In this case, the BV of the group is simply reduced by net proceeds (if any) resulting from disposal, and no gain or loss is recorded.

Impairment of Long-Lived Assets Used in Operations

Representative Task (Application): Calculate impairment losses on long-lived assets to be recognized in the financial statements.

Impairment of long-lived assets held for use occurs when the carrying amount of an asset is not recoverable and a write-off is needed. Impairment testing must be completed when any of the following occur:

Indicators of Impairment	
Significant decrease in the FV of the asset	Significant change in the way the asset is used or physical change in the asset
A change in laws, regulations, or the business climate that would adversely affect use of the asset	Significantly higher than expected costs involved with the construction or acquisition of an asset
Incurred or projected negative operating income or cash flows from the asset	The entity decides to sell the asset before the end of its expected life

Impairment testing applies to asset groups as well as to individual assets. The impairment is applied proportionately to all long-lived assets in the asset group.

The process of determining an impairment loss is as follows:

1. Review events or changes in circumstances for possible impairment. If events or changes are identified, further testing is required.
2. If the review indicates impairment, apply the **recoverability test:**

   If the **sum of the expected future undiscounted net cash flows** from the long-lived asset is **less than the BV of the asset**, an impairment has occurred.

   Importantly, the recoverability test is a conservative test and does not calculate a present value using discounted cash flows but, rather, uses only undiscounted cash flows.

3. The **impairment loss** is:

   The excess of the **BV over FV** of the asset.

   The FV is the market value or the present value of future *discounted* cash flows.

Note that estimated *future cash flows* are used to determine if impairment has occurred (ie, Step 2), but the asset is adjusted to its *estimated FV*, **not** estimated future cash flows, once the determination has been made (ie, Step 3). The impairment loss, which appears on the I/S in income from continuing operations, may ***not* be restored** for an asset *held for use*.

Impairment of Fixed Assets

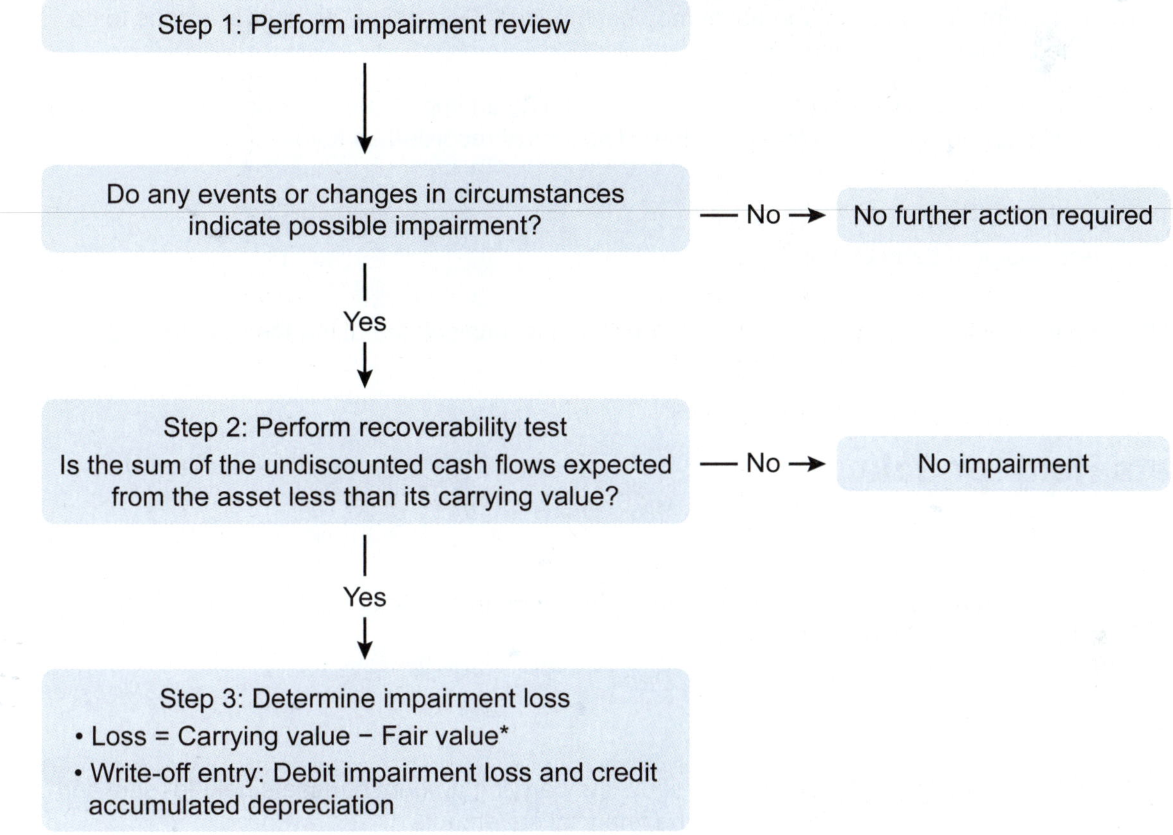

**The FV is either the market value or the present value (ie, the discounted expected future cash flows) of the asset.*

The entries to record the impairment loss and subsequent depreciation expense are as follows:

Impairment loss: subsequent depreciation expense

Entry to record impairment loss

Loss on impairment (I/S)	XXX	
Accumulated depreciation—asset (B/S)		XXX

Update new reduced carrying value

Carrying value = Cost − New accumulated depreciation

Compute new depreciation expense (straight-line method)

$$\frac{\text{Cost} - \text{Salvage value}}{\text{Remaining life}}$$

An asset has a BV of $600, expected future net cash flows of $580, and a market value of $525. Recent events indicate that the asset may be impaired. Determine the journal entries to be recorded related to the impairment.

Since the $580 expected cash flow is less than the $600 BV, an impairment has occurred. The amount of the loss is $75 ($600 BV − $525 market value). The loss is recorded as follows:

Impairment loss (I/S)	75	
Accumulated depreciation		75

After the impairment loss is recorded, future depreciation is recalculated using the new $525 BV.

Assets Held for Sale

Representative Task (Application): Determine whether an asset qualifies to be reported as held for sale in the financial statements.

Representative Task (Application): Adjust the carrying amount of assets held for sale and calculate the loss to be recognized in the financial statements.

Criteria for Held for Sale Classification

There are six criteria for determining when an asset is considered **held for sale**:

- A **plan to sell the asset** has been committed to by people with the authority to do so
- The asset is **available for immediate sale** in its present condition
- Action to complete the plan for disposal has been initiated, and a buyer is **actively being sought**
- The sale is probable and expected to be **completed** and to qualify for recognition **within one year**
- The **price** at which the asset is being marketed is **reasonable**
- It is **unlikely** that significant **changes** will be made to the plan or that it will be withdrawn

All criteria must be met for the accounting provisions to apply. Otherwise, the asset is considered in use.

Accounting for Assets Held for Sale

When an asset is classified as held for sale, it is reclassified on the balance sheet (B/S). The asset is removed from PP&E, reported in **current assets** or **other assets**, and described as held for sale.

The asset is recorded at the **lower** of the asset's **BV** and its **net realizable value** (NRV), which is the estimated selling price, less costs of disposal. If the NRV is lower, it becomes the new BV, and an impairment loss is recognized on the I/S in continuing operations. If the old BV is lower, it remains the BV and no loss is recognized.

Assets held for sale are **not depreciated**. However, if held for another period, increases or decreases in the NRV can be recognized. An asset held for disposal **can be written up or down** in future periods as long as the write-up is not greater than the carrying amount of the asset before the impairment.

A plant asset (cost $100,000; A/D $40,000) has a current FV of $30,000 at the end of Year 4. Management has decided to sell the asset as soon as possible during the next reporting period. The estimated direct cost to sell is $5,000. The six criteria for determining whether the asset is held for sale have been met. Determine the loss to be recorded on the asset in Year 4.

In Year 4, the BV of the asset is compared to the asset's NRV:

$100,000 cost − $40,000 A/D = $60,000 BV

$30,000 FV − $5,000 cost to sell = $25,000 NRV

The asset is reported at the lower of BV and NRV. In this case, the asset will be reported at $25,000, or NRV. As such, a loss will be recorded for $35,000 ($60,000 BV − $25,000 NRV) to write the asset down to the NRV.

Assume that, at the end of Year 5, the asset remains unsold. The FV is now $20,000, and estimated direct cost to sell is $12,000. Determine the additional loss to be recorded on the asset in Year 5.

The asset will be adjusted for changes in NRV. The NRV is now $8,000 ($20,000 FV − $12,000 cost to sell). The NRV decreased by $17,000 ($25,000 − $8,000) during Year 5. Therefore, an additional $17,000 loss will be recorded in Year 5.

Assume that, instead, the FV had risen to $70,000, and estimated cost to sell remained at $5,000. NRV has increased from $25,000 to $65,000, an increase of $40,000. The maximum gain allowed is the amount of the previous loss (in this case, $35,000). Therefore, the asset would be written back up to $60,000 (the BV immediately before the initial impairment), and a gain of $35,000 would be recognized.

Comparison of Long-Lived Assets Used in Operations vs. Held for Sale

Long-lived assets used in operations and held for sale are accounted for as follows:

Long-Lived Assets used in Operations vs. Held for Sale

	Used in Operations	**Held for Sale**
Original Valuation	Historical cost	**Lower** of carrying value or fair value, less disposal costs* when reclassified
Impairment Loss	Carrying value – Fair value	Carrying value – Fair value
Restoration of Carrying Value	None allowed	Allowed up to carrying value **before** the reclassification
Depreciation Allowed	Yes	No

**Equivalent to net realizable value*

PP&E Rollforward

Representative Task (Analysis): Prepare a rollforward of the property, plant and equipment account balance using various sources of information.

A **rollforward** is a high-level, summary method to review periodic activity in related accounts. For PP&E, a rollforward starts with the beginning balance of PP&E and lists all activity that increased or decreased the account during the period (ie, monthly, quarterly, or annually), resulting in the ending balance. The PP&E rollforward includes additions, disposals, depreciation, and any additional adjustments needed to correctly present the PP&E balance in the financial statements.

Analysis-level tasks are typically tested in a task-based simulation (TBS). Below is an example of a TBS that might appear on the CPA exam for PP&E.

Example

Merchant Company is a consulting firm. Merchant prepares a rollforward of PP&E each year. Using the information and exhibits below, prepare Merchant's rollforward at December 31, Year 7. Exhibits and additional information are given first, and then the solution will follow.

Task: Prepare Merchant's rollforward at December 31, Year 7.

Fixed Asset Rollforward, Year 7

Asset	Automobiles	Buildings	Equipment	Land
Gross:				
Beginning balance				
+ Additions				
− Disposals				
Ending balance				
Accumulated depreciation:				
Beginning balance				
+ Additions				
− Disposals				
Ending balance				
Net ending balance				

Exhibits

Exhibit 1: PP&E report as of December 31, Year 6

Account: 600 Property, plant and equipment Retrieval date: 12/31/Year 6

Asset group	Description	Historical costs/basis	Method of depr.	Total depr.
A	Automobiles – 5 yr life	26,000	200% DB	6,552
B	Buildings – 25 yr life	1,800,000	150% DB	394,650
C	Equipment – 20 yr life	1,225,000	SL	281,280
D	Land	250,000	N/A	–
		3,301,000		**682,482**

Exhibit 2: Invoice from supplier

Invoice

Supplier Inc.
123 Budd Court
Buffalo, NY 14201

Invoice # 2099
Date July 1, Year 7

Bill to:
Merchant Company
156 Penn Street
Philadelphia, PA 19019

Item	Product code	Quantity	Price per unit	Amount
Equipment	101	20	$2,560.00	$51,200.00
Equipment	221	10	$1,900.00	$19,000.00
Equipment	435	35	$1,280.00	$44,800.00

Subtotal	$115,000.00
Delivery fees	$2,300.00
Installation fees	$3,500.00
Total	$120,800.00

Exhibit 3: Email from fixed assets acctg. manager

From: FixedAssets@MerchantCo.net
To: Controller@MerchantCo.net
Sent: December 11, Year 7
Subject: Important Transactions

Hello,
As requested, here are the costs related to the land and building purchase:

On January 3 of this year, the land and building were acquired together for $1,470,000. Based on property tax records, the assessed values of the land and building were $276,000 and $644,000, respectively.

I also wanted to recap our earlier conversation regarding the company automobile, just to ensure that we are on the same page. As you know, during the year, Merchant sold our last remaining company automobile. On October 1, Merchant sold the automobile (which had an initial cost of $26,000) for $8,500. The automobile had incurred a total of $9,360 of depreciation at the time of sale. $2,808 of this depreciation occurred during Year 7.

Please let me know if you need any additional information.

Sincerely,
Sally, Fixed Assets Accounting Manager

Solution

Fixed Asset Rollforward, Year 7

Asset	Automobiles	Buildings	Equipment	Land
Gross:				
Beginning balance	$26,000	$1,800,000	$1,225,000	$250,000
+ Additions	–	1,029,000	120,800	441,000
− Disposals	(26,000)	–	–	–
Ending balance	$ 0	$2,829,000	$1,345,800	$691,000
Accumulated depreciation:				
Beginning balance	$ 6,552	$ 394,650	$ 281,280	–
+ Additions (depreciation expense)	2,808	146,061	64,270	–
− Disposals	(9,360)	–	–	–
Ending balance	$ 0	$ 540,711	$ 345,550	–
Net ending balance	$ 0	$2,288,289	$1,000,250	$691,000

Automobiles

Per the fixed asset manager's email (Exhibit 3), the automobile was sold on October 1 for $8,500. The initial cost of the asset, $26,000, is removed from the books. During the year, the automobile incurred depreciation of $2,808. This depreciation is recorded as follows:

Depreciation expense	2,808	
Accumulated depreciation—Automobiles		2,808

The A/D at the time of sale is $9,360 ($6,552 in prior years + $2,808 in current year). This is also removed from the books. The entry to record the sale is as follows:

Cash	8,500	
Accumulated depreciation—Automobiles	9,360	
Loss on sale	8,140	
Automobiles		26,000

Land and Buildings

Per the fixed asset manager's email (Exhibit 3), the land and building were acquired as a lump-sum purchase for $1,470,000. Therefore, the purchase price must be allocated to each item on the basis of the assessed values:

Item	Assessed Value	Calculation	Allocation %
Land	$276,000	$276,000 / $920,000	30%
Building	$644,000	$644,000 / $920,000	70%
Total	$920,000		100%

The entry to record the acquisition is as follows:

Land (30% × $1,470,000)	441,000	
Buildings (70% × $1,470,000)	1,029,000	
Cash		1,470,000

The buildings are depreciated as follows:

Historical cost—Dec. 31, Year 6	$1,800,000
A/D—Dec. 31, Year 6	(394,650)
Net BV—Dec. 31, Year 6	1,405,350
Building acquired—Jan. 3, Year 7	+ 1,029,000
Subtotal	$2,434,350
150% declining rate (1/25 × 1.5)	× 6%
Year 7 depreciation expense	$146,061

The entry to record the depreciation expense on buildings is as follows:

Depreciation expense	146,061	
Accumulated depreciation—Buildings		146,061

Land is not depreciated.

Equipment

Merchant purchased equipment for $115,000 (before additional fees). Delivery costs, $2,300, and installation costs, $3,500, are capitalized to equipment as well. The total cost of the equipment is $120,800 ($115,000 + $2,300 + $3,500). The entry to record the acquisition of the equipment is as follows:

Equipment	120,800	
Cash		120,800

The new equipment was acquired on July 1. Therefore, only six months of depreciation will be recorded for the new equipment. The total depreciation expense in Year 7 is calculated as follows:

Historical cost—Dec. 31, Year 6	$1,225,000	
Straight-line depreciation rate (1/20)	× 5%	
Year 7 depreciation expense for old equipment	$ 61,250	Year 7 depreciation expense
Equipment acquired—July 1, Year 7	120,800	
Straight-line depreciation rate (1/20) for 6 months	× 2.5%	$64,270
Year 7 depreciation expense for new equipment	$ 3,020	

The entry to record the depreciation expense on equipment is as follows:

Depreciation expense	64,270	
Accumulated depreciation—Equipment		64,270

Reconciliation of PP&E Subledger to General Ledger

Representative Task (Analysis): Reconcile and investigate differences between the subledger and general ledger for property, plant and equipment to determine whether an adjustment is necessary.

The **general ledger** is the central **record-keeping** system for an entity's **accounting transactions**. Account balances in the general ledger are supported by **detailed account records** kept in separate subsidiary ledgers (ie, **subledgers**). General ledger balances are reported in the entity's financial statements.

The subledgers provide more **granular details** for specific types of transactions, like customer accounts, vendor accounts, and fixed assets. The total of the subledger each period should match the total reported in the general ledger. Subledgers help organize and control transaction-level data that flows into financial statements.

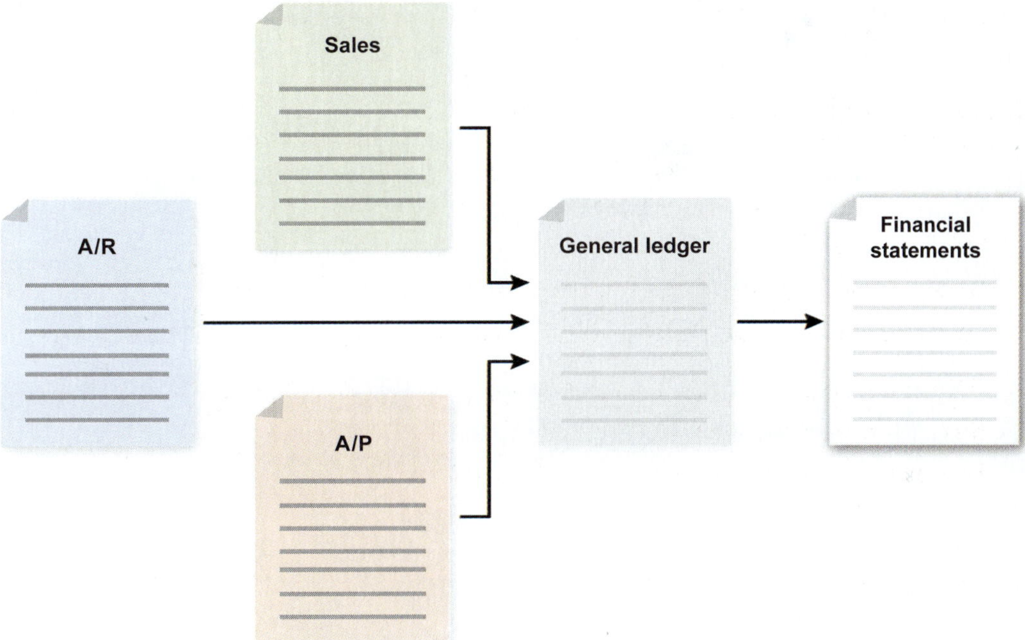

Generally, the reconciliation process follows these steps:

- Compare the ending balances of the general ledger to the subledger
- Identify any differences by confirming beginning balances (for B/S accounts), ensuring that daily postings from the subledger to the general ledger match, and researching any nonrecurring or unusual transactions
- Investigate reasons for the differences. Typically, these are errors or items posted in the general ledger and not the subledger or vice versa
- Adjust the appropriate ledger
- Compare adjusted balances

A reconciliation of the PP&E subledger to the general ledger follows the same methodology as shown in other chapters (eg, Trade Receivables, Inventory). For additional examples of PP&E reconciliation TBS, refer to the question bank.

FAR 11
Investments

FAR 11: Investments

11.01 Investments Overview

The FAR exam blueprint organizes investments by how they are accounted for. Representative tasks on reporting financial assets at fair value are grouped together, and representative tasks on reporting financial assets at amortized cost are grouped together. However, for learning purposes, this text will cover investments in debt securities first, and then investments in equity securities. The following text still contains all relevant content for accounting for investments in debt and equity securities. It is simply presented in a different order than in the FAR exam blueprint.

Representative Task (Remembering & Understanding): Identify investments that are eligible or required to be reported at fair value in the financial statements.

Representative Task (Remembering & Understanding): Identify investments that are eligible to be reported at amortized cost in the financial statements.

Representative Task (Application): Calculate the carrying amount of investments measured at fair value (excluding impairment).

Representative Task (Application): Calculate the carrying amount of investments measured at amortized cost and prepare journal entries (excluding impairment).

Representative Task (Application): Calculate investment income to be recognized in net income for investments measured at fair value and prepare journal entries.

Representative Task (Application): Calculate impairment losses to be recognized on applicable investments reported at fair value in the financial statements.

Representative Task (Application): Calculate impairment losses to be recognized on investments reported at amortized cost in the financial statements.

Entities may decide to invest in the securities of other entities. The accounting for an investment by the acquiring entity depends on various factors, including whether the investment is an equity or debt security, the intent of the investor, the amount held, and whether the investment has a readily determinable fair value.

Securities fall into two basic categories:

	Definition	Examples
Debt Securities	Securities that represent the right of buyer/holder (creditor) to receive from the issuer (debtor) a principal amount at a specified future date and, generally, to receive interest as payment for providing use of funds	• Bonds • Notes • Convertible bonds • Redeemable preferred stock
Equity Securities	Securities that represent ownership interest or the right to acquire or dispose of ownership interest	• Common stock • Preferred stock • Stock warrants • Call/put options

Questions on the CPA exam may provide information regarding the characteristics of a security and ask that you determine whether the security is an equity or debt security. Questions also may ask that you identify the characteristics of a security that gives ownership or rights to ownership. Pay close attention to the distinguishing characteristics, as those characteristics dictate the accounting method used for that security.

For example, redeemable preferred stock may seem like an equity security, but since it is redeemable (usually by the issuing entity for a set value), it is classified as debt because it has a set principal payment as well as a contractually determined stream of cash flows (dividends), similar to the interest on debt.

The concepts of **recognition** and **realization** are important with regard to investments.

Recognition is an accounting concept. It means that the company has *reported the item on its financial statements* (F/S). Recognized gains or losses occur when a gain or loss related to an investment (or other item) is recorded (recognized) in the F/S, regardless of whether the investment has been sold. For example, a gain or loss from the change in the *value* of an equity or debt security (ie, an unrealized gain or loss) may be recognized but not realized.

Realization is an economic concept. It means that there is a culmination of the earnings process and cash or other consideration is given or received. A *realized* gain/loss occurs when the investment (or other item) is *sold* (or otherwise disposed of). The difference between the cash or other consideration received and the carrying value of the investment is a realized gain or loss. An *unrealized* gain or loss occurs from holding an investment. As mentioned above, unrealized gains and losses may be *recognized but are not realized.*

Fair Value Option

In addition to those items that are required to be measured at fair value (FV), an entity can *elect* to report some or all of its **financial instruments** (ie, financial assets and liabilities) at their FV. A financial instrument is defined as *cash*, evidence of an *ownership interest* in an entity, or certain *contracts*. When the FV option is elected, the eligible item will be measured at its FV on each balance sheet date, and **unrealized gains and losses are reported in income**.

If an entity decides to elect the FV option, the entity may apply that option to any qualifying financial instrument, without being required to apply it to others, including those that are similar. An election may be made only when a financial asset or liability is acquired or in other limited circumstances, referred to as "election dates." Likewise, once elected, the FV option is permanent and may only be discontinued on a subsequent election date.

Some of the specific applications of the FV option include the following:

- An investment that otherwise qualifies for the **equity method** is reported at FV on each balance sheet date, increases or decreases are recognized as unrealized gains or losses on the *income statement*, and dividends received are recognized as *income*. In other words, the FV option overrides the equity method
- **Held-to-maturity (HTM) securities** continue to be accounted for at amortized cost, recognizing interest income under the effective interest method. In addition, the carrying value is adjusted to FV on each balance sheet date with the increase/decrease recognized as a component of *net income*
- **Available-for-sale (AFS) debt securities** are reported at FV on each balance sheet date, as already required. However, unrealized gains or losses are reported as a component of *net income* instead of other comprehensive income (OCI)

11.02 Investments in Debt Securities

Overview

The accounting and reporting of an **investment in debt securities** depends on management's **intent for holding** the debt security. In addition, an important factor in the valuation of the debt security is whether there is a **readily determinable FV**.

There are three types of debt securities:

Marketable Debt Securities			
Security	**Classification**	**Balance Sheet Measurement**	**Holding Gains and Losses**
Trading	Investor buys and sells within a short period of time to earn a profit	Fair value	Reported in net income
Available-for-sale	All other securities not classified as trading or held-to-maturity	Fair value	Reported in other comprehensive income
Held-to-maturity	Investor has intent and ability to hold until the due date for repayment	Amortized cost	N/A

For all classifications of the investments in debt securities, any **dividend or interest income** is reported in current-period earnings (ie, net income). The amortization of any premium or discount is also included in current-period earnings.

Upon acquisition of an investment in debt securities, the company must document the classification of the investment into one of three categories: trading, AFS, or HTM. The company should review these classifications annually to determine if a change is warranted.

Trading Securities

Trading securities are debt investments that a company acquires with the intent to make a profit by buying and selling within a short period of time (eg, days, months).

Trading securities are measured and reported at FV, with the changes in the FV recorded in **net income**. The securities are initially recorded at the price paid (typically this is the market value or the present value of the security's future cash flows as of the date of the investment). The securities are then adjusted to the market value (ie, FV) at the end of each period.

Balance Sheet

Trading securities are reported on the balance sheet at **FV**, typically as a **current asset**. A valuation account (contra or adjunct) typically is not used when the debt security is classified as trading. A debt security classified as trading is one that will be sold in the near term and is highly liquid.

Income Statement

As the market value of trading securities fluctuates, **unrealized** gains or losses (ie, holding gains or losses) are recorded in net income. If the securities are sold or disposed of, **realized** gains or losses are recorded in net income as well. Interest income (net of any amortization of a premium or discount) is also recorded in net income.

Trading Securities: Unrealized and Realized Gains and Losses

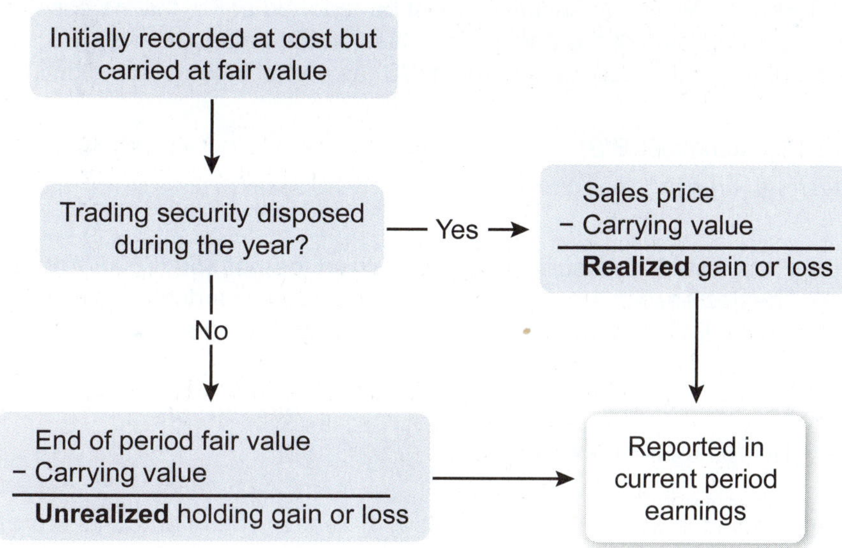

Statement of Cash Flows

Cash flows associated with trading investments in debt securities typically are presented in the statement of cash flows as **operating activities**. The very nature of trading securities indicates that part of the entity's operations is to regularly buy and sell securities. If the trading investments are not part of the entity's core operations, then those cash flows are classified as investing activities.

Impairments

There are **no impairment losses** on trading securities, as these securities are recorded at FV and unrealized gains or losses are already included in net income.

Company A acquires bonds of Company B with a cost and face value of $100. Company A intends to sell the bonds. They are being held in anticipation of an increase in value due to an expected decrease in market interest rates. The following information relates to cost and market values.

Purchase price, 1/1/Year 1	$100
Fair value, 12/31/Year 1	$140
Fair value, 12/31/Year 2	$ 90

Company A sells the securities for $120 on 1/1/Year 3. Determine the journal entries that Company A should record at 1/1/Year 1, 12/31/Year 1, 12/31/Year 2, and 1/1/Year 3.

Since Company A intends to sell the bonds once the value increases, the securities are classified as trading securities. They will be reported at FV on the balance sheet, and unrealized and realized gains and losses will be reported in net income.

When Company A purchases the securities on 1/1/Year 1, the company will record the following:

Investment in trading securities	100	
Cash		100

At 12/31/Year 1, the **FV is now $140**, resulting in an unrealized **gain of $40** ($140 FV at 12/31/Year 1 – $100 paid at 1/1/Year 1). Since the securities must be reported at FV, the increase in the securities' value increases the carrying value of the trading securities on the balance sheet (B/S). The corresponding unrealized gain is reported on the income statement (I/S) as part of income from continuing operations:

Investment in trading securities **(B/S)**	40	
Unrealized gain **(I/S)**		40

At 12/31/Year 2, the **FV is now $90**, resulting in an unrealized **loss of $50** ($90 FV at 12/31/Year 2 – $140 FV at 12/31/Year 1). The decrease in the securities' FV is recorded as a decrease in the carrying value of the trading securities on the B/S, and an unrealized loss is reported on the income statement:

Unrealized loss **(I/S)**	50	
Investment in trading securities **(B/S)**		50

The income statement effect is $40 in Year 1 and ($50) in Year 2. These amounts represent the current-year effects only since they are both income statement items. The investment in trading securities account will have a debit balance of $90 ($100 + $40 – $50).

At 1/1/Year 3, the company sells the securities for $120. The company will record a realized gain of $30 ($120 selling price – $90 value on B/S), and the trading securities will be taken off the books:

Cash **(B/S)**	120	
Investment in trading securities **(B/S)**		90
Realized gain on sale of trading securities **(I/S)**		30

Available-for-Sale Securities

Available-for-sale (AFS) securities are debt instruments that do not fit the definitions of HTM or trading securities.

Like trading securities, AFS securities are measured and reported at **FV**. The securities are initially recorded at the price paid (typically the market value or present value of the security's future cash flows, as of the date of the investment). The securities are then adjusted to the market value (ie, FV) at the end of each period.

However, unlike trading securities, **unrealized** gains and losses associated with changes in the FV are recorded as unrealized holding gains or losses in **other comprehensive income** (OCI). Similar to trading securities, **realized** gains and losses are recorded in **net income**.

For AFS securities, a balance sheet valuation account will be used to adjust the carrying amount of the securities to the FV. AFS securities are reported as **current or noncurrent assets**, depending on management's intent. AFS securities are presented in the statement of cash flows as an **investing activity**. Interest income (net of any amortization of a premium or discount) is also recorded in net income.

To adjust the value of AFS securities, do the following:

1. Determine the FV of the AFS security
2. Determine the carrying value of the AFS security
3. If the FV is *greater* than the carrying value, recognize an **unrealized holding gain in OCI**
4. If the FV is *less* than the carrying value, recognize an **unrealized holding loss in OCI**. The security must be assessed for **impairment**, and as a result, a loss may be reported in net income as well (see below)

On 1/1/Year 1, Company C acquires securities from Company D for $1,000 and classifies them as AFS debt securities. On 12/31/Year 1, the FV of the securities has increased to $1,500. Determine the journal entry that Company C would record at 1/1/Year 1 and 12/31/Year 1.

When the company purchases the securities **on 1/1/Year 1**, the company will record the following:

Investment in AFS securities	1,000	
Cash		1,000

At 12/31/Year 1, the **FV is now $1,500**, resulting in an unrealized **gain of $500** ($1,500 FV at 12/31/Year 1 − $1,000 paid at 1/1/Year 1). Since the securities must be reported at FV, the increase in the securities' value will be reflected in a valuation account on the B/S. The corresponding unrealized gain is reported in OCI:

Investment in AFS securities – unrealized gains valuation account **(B/S)**	500	
Unrealized gain **(B/S - OCI)**		500

The total value of the securities at 12/31/Year 1 is now $1,500.

Impairments and Credit Loss

Impairment is tested by comparing the FV of the AFS security to the security's **amortized cost**. If the FV is *less than the amortized cost*, the security is **impaired**. Any portion of this impairment that relates to credit risk (ie, credit loss) is recognized on the income statement. However, any portion that relates to market risk results in an unrealized gain or loss recognized in OCI.

If impairment has occurred and the entity does not intend to sell (or is not more likely than not required to sell) the security before recovery of the amortized cost, the entity must determine how much of the impairment is due to credit loss and how much is due to other factors. Impairment due to **credit loss** is recorded in **net income**. Impairment due to **other factors** (ie, not credit loss) is recorded in **OCI**.

The following flowchart depicts the process of recording impairment for AFS debt securities:

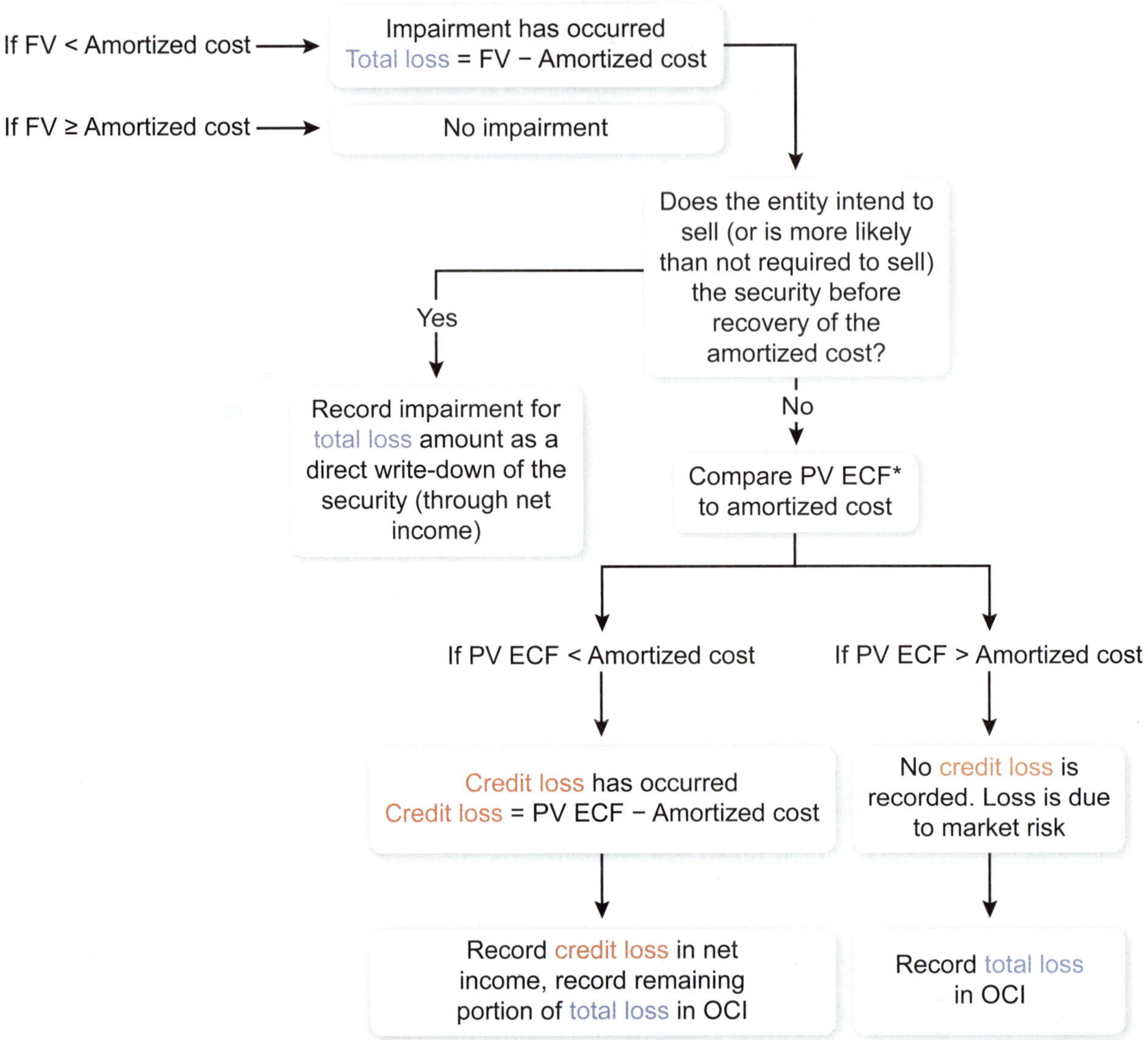

**PV ECF = Present value of expected cash flows*

The amount of credit loss is limited to the total loss amount (ie, FV − amortized cost). Therefore, even if *credit loss is greater than the total loss*, credit loss recognized cannot exceed the total loss amount. If *credit loss is less than the total loss*, the total loss will be split between credit loss (recorded in net income) and noncredit loss (due to market factors, recorded in OCI).

If impairment has occurred and the entity *does* intend to sell (or is more likely than not required to sell) the security before recovery of the amortized cost, any valuation accounts are eliminated and the security is written down to its FV. The incremental impairment loss is reported in net income.

On 1/1/Year 1, HB Corp. purchased $1,000,000 in bonds. HB classified the investment as AFS. At 12/31/Year 1, the bonds have a FV of $900,000. HB determined that it can only expect to receive $920,000 in cash flows going forward. HB does not intend to sell the security, and it is not more likely than not that it will be required to sell the security. Determine the journal entries that HB should record at 12/31/Year 1 related to the bonds.

Because the $900,000 FV is less than the $1,000,000 amortized cost, the bonds are impaired. Total impairment loss is $100,000 ($900,000 − $1,000,000).

HB must determine what portion of the loss, if any, relates to credit loss. PV of expected cash flows ($920,000) is less than the amortized cost ($1,000,000); therefore, an $80,000 credit loss ($920,000 − $1,000,000) has occurred. This credit loss will be reported as follows:

Credit loss expense **(I/S)**	80,000	
Investment in AFS securities – allowance for credit losses **(B/S)**		80,000

The $20,000 remainder of the total loss ($100,000 total loss − $80,000 credit loss) is noncredit related and will be reported as follows:

Unrealized loss **(B/S − OCI)**	20,000	
Investment in AFS securities – unrealized losses valuation account **(B/S)**		20,000

Now assume that HB determined that it can only expect to receive $850,000 in cash flows going forward.

Total impairment loss is still $100,000. The PV of expected cash flows ($850,000) is now $150,000 less than the amortized cost ($1,000,000). Therefore, a $150,000 credit loss has occurred. Here, credit loss ($150,000) exceeds the total impairment loss ($100,000). The amount of credit loss recorded cannot exceed the impairment loss. HB can only record a credit loss of $100,000:

Credit loss expense **(I/S)**	100,000	
Investment in AFS securities – allowance for credit losses **(B/S)**		100,000

Remember, the first step is comparing FV to amortized cost. If FV is greater than or equal to amortized cost (eg, in the prior example, if FV were greater than or equal to $1,000,000), no impairment or credit loss will be recorded, *even if PV of expected cash flows was less than amortized cost*. Rather, a gain may need to be recorded through OCI.

At each reporting date, the entity must reassess if there has been any additional decline in FV attributed to credit loss and, if so, adjust the allowance for credit loss. The adjustment will result in additional credit loss expense or a reversal of credit loss expense. The **reversal** of a credit loss is *limited to the balance* in the allowance for credit loss account. The balance cannot drop below zero.

Sale or Disposal

When an AFS security is disposed of or sold, any gain or loss from the sale should be recognized. Any related unrealized holding gain or loss on securities sold that is in accumulated other comprehensive income (AOCI) at the date of sale is reversed out of AOCI and recognized in income.

Bail Corp. bought AFS securities during Year 1. The following information relates to cost and market values:

	Purchase price	Market value at 12/31/Year 1	Market value at 12/31/Year 2
Security A	$25,000	$27,000	
Security B	$9,000	$10,000	$6,000

Bail sold Security A on 1/1/Year 2 for $31,000.

Determine the unrealized gain or loss that Bail will report on the Year 2 statement of comprehensive income and the AOCI that Bail will report on the Year 2 balance sheet.

Security A:

At 12/31/Year 1, Bail would have reported an unrealized gain of $2,000 ($27,000 − $25,000) in OCI and a valuation account on the balance sheet. The carrying value of the securities at 12/31/Year 1 was $27,000.

When the security is sold, the unrealized gain must be reversed out of OCI, and a $6,000 gain must be recognized for the difference between the $31,000 sales price and the $25,000 cost of the securities. The journal entry at 1/1/Year 2 is as follows:

Account	Debit	Credit
Cash **(B/S)**	31,000	
Unrealized gain **(B/S − OCI)**	2,000	
Investment in AFS debt securities **(B/S)**		25,000
Investment in AFS securities – valuation account **(B/S)**		2,000
Realized gain **(I/S)**		6,000

Security B:

At 12/31/Year 1, Bail would have reported an unrealized gain of $1,000 ($10,000 − $9,000) in OCI and a valuation account on the balance sheet. The carrying value of the securities at 12/31/Year 1 was $10,000.

At 12/31/Year 2, Bail will report an unrealized loss of $4,000 ($6,000 market value at Year 2 − $10,000 carrying value at Year 1) in OCI and a valuation account on the balance sheet. The carrying value of the securities at 12/31/Year 2 is $6,000.

Net Impact:

The unrealized loss reported on the Year 2 statement of comprehensive income will include only the adjustments that occurred in Year 2:

Unrealized gain reversed out of OCI − Security A	(2,000)
Unrealized loss in OCI − Security B	(4,000)
Total unrealized loss on Year 2 statement of comprehensive income	(6,000)

Recall that OCI closes to AOCI. Year 2 AOCI reported on the balance sheet is a running total of all transactions that have impacted OCI. Security A's net impact to AOCI is zero. An unrealized gain was recognized, then reversed out. Security B initially increased AOCI with an unrealized gain of $1,000 but then decreased AOCI with an unrealized loss of $4,000. The net impact of Security B on AOCI is a $3,000 loss ($4,000 − $1,000).

Held-to-Maturity Securities

Held-to-maturity (HTM) securities are investments in debt securities that an entity has both the intent and ability to hold until maturity. Even if the securities are sold before maturity, they can still be considered HTM if the sale meets the following conditions:

- The sale is near enough to the maturity date that interest rate risk is substantially eliminated as a factor in pricing
- The sale occurs after the investor has collected (through periodic payments or prepayment) a substantial portion (at least 85%) of the principal outstanding at the acquisition date

In the rare case that these securities are not held to maturity, an ordinary gain/loss results on disposal. This would be true, for example, when the issuer of the debt securities exercises a call provision, compelling the investor to redeem them early. If the future exercise of a call provision on a purchased callable debt security is considered likely, any premium is required to be amortized over the period from purchase through the expected exercise date.

Balance Sheet

HTM securities are **initially recorded at cost** and then **carried at amortized cost** (ie, face amount, net of unamortized discount or premium). The difference between the cost and the face/maturity value is amortized over the life of the security, using the *effective rate method* (discussed in the FAR Debt chapter). Since HTM securities are not going to be sold, fluctuations in market price are disclosed but not recorded. There are **no unrealized gains or losses** with respect to HTM securities.

HTM securities are generally considered **noncurrent assets** unless the maturity date is less than one year from the balance sheet date. Any *allowance for credit losses* is reported separately from the amortized cost of the financial asset on the balance sheet.

Income Statement

Interest income (net of any amortization of discount or premium) is recorded in net income. Any change in the allowance for credit losses will be reported on the income statement as either **credit loss expense** or reversal of credit loss expense.

Statement of Cash Flows

The cash effects of purchases (outflows) and sales or redemptions (inflows) of HTM securities are classified as **investing activities** on the statement of cash flows.

On January 1, Evans Inc. purchased a bond with a face value of $250,000 and a stated interest rate of 5%, at a price of 97 (ie, 97% of face value). Interest is payable on June 30 and December 31. Evans intends to hold the investment until maturity and does not elect the FV option. Determine the initial carrying value at January 1.

Bond investments have a **stated interest rate** (eg, 5%) that does not change with market conditions. When a bond's stated rate is less than the market rate, the bond is priced at a **discount**. When a bond is sold at less than face value (eg, 97%), it has been issued at a discount. The discount is amortized by the investor using the effective interest method over the term of the security.

Evans purchased a $250,000 bond at 97% for $242,500 ($250,000 × 97%). There is a $7,500 discount ($250,000 face value − $242,500 purchase price) on the bond when purchased. Therefore, initial carrying value is $242,500 ($250,000 − $7,500).

Evans will record the following:

Investment in held-to-maturity securities	250,000	
Unamortized discount		7,500
Cash		242,500

Impairments

Impairment on HTM securities is reported in accordance with the current expected credit loss (CECL) model. The CECL model measures expected credit losses for the financial asset as of each balance sheet date and is based on historical experience, current conditions, and reasonable (and supportable) forecasts.

At each balance sheet date, an **allowance for credit loss** is estimated and *deducted from the amortized cost basis* of the HTM security. The allowance will result in a reported value that represents the net amount that the entity expects to collect. The allowance is a contra account to the HTM security, and the corresponding credit loss expense is recognized in earnings.

A company has a $100,000 HTM investment with an unamortized premium of $2,775 and an allowance for credit loss of $1,500. The net amount reported on the balance sheet would be the following:

Investment in held-to-maturity securities	$100,000
Unamortized premium	2,775
Allowance for credit losses	(1,500)
Net investment in held-to-maturity securities	$101,275

GAAP does not require reporting entities to use a specific method to calculate the allowance for credit losses. Instead, various methods can be used, including discounted cash flow (DCF), loss-rate, roll-rate, and probability of default/loss given default, among others. The **DCF** approach is often used to calculate the allowance for credit losses. Under the DCF approach, similar to AFS securities, credit loss is calculated as the *difference between amortized cost and the present value of expected cash flows.*

At each reporting date, the entity reestimates the amount expected to be collected and adjusts the allowance for credit loss. The adjustment will result in additional credit loss expense or a reversal of credit loss expense. The reversal of a credit loss is limited to the balance in the allowance for credit loss account. The balance cannot drop below zero.

If an HTM security is deemed to be uncollectible, it is written off.

During Year 1, a company pays $100,000 for a six-year bond with a face value of $100,000. The company classifies the bond as an HTM security, and the bond has an annual interest rate of 5.5%. However, shortly after the bond is acquired, the company estimates that it will only be able to collect $4,000 each year in interest, plus the $100,000 principal at maturity. The company uses the DCF model to record credit losses.

PV factor of an annuity at 5.5% for 6 years: 4.99553

PV factor of $1 at 5.5% for 6 years: 0.72525

Determine the journal entry that the company will record at the end of Year 1 to recognize the impairment.

Under the DCF model, credit loss (impairment) is recorded for the excess of amortized cost over the present value of future cash flows. Here, there is no discount or premium, so amortized cost is equal to the face value of the bond ($100,000).

The company estimates that it will be able to collect $4,000 in interest each year and the $100,000 principal at maturity. The PV of the interest payments is $19,982.12 ($4,000 × 4.99553), and the PV of the principal is $72,525 (100,000 × 0.72525).

Total PV = $19,982.12 + 72,525 = $92,507.12

Credit loss = PV − Amortized cost = $92,507.12 − 100,000 = ($7,492.88)*

The company will record the following:

Credit loss expense **(I/S)**	7,493	
Investment in HTM securities – allowance for credit losses **(B/S)**		7,493

**This amount is rounded to 7,493 in the journal entries.*

Reclassifications

Reclassifications (ie, transfers) of marketable debt securities result from changes in management's intentions. Securities may be transferred from one category to another, and the accounting treatment will vary depending on the old and new classifications.

Securities are treated as if they are being sold from the portfolio they are leaving, then repurchased at the current market price into the portfolio they are entering. The investment in the new category will be reported on the **balance sheet at FV**. However, the treatment of any unrealized holding gain (loss) depends on the new category of the security:

Reclassifications (Transfers) of Debt Securities		
Type of Transfer	**Revalued at**	**Treatment of Unrealized Holding Gains or Losses**
To trading	Fair value	Recognized in earnings
From trading		N/A (has already been recognized and is not reversed)
From AFS to HTM		Recognized in OCI Transferred to AOCI and amortized over remaining life
From HTM to AFS		Recognized in OCI

AFS = available-for-sale; AOCI = accumulated other comprehensive income; HTM = held-to-maturity; OCI = other comprehensive income

Summary of Accounting for Investments in Debt Securities

The following is a summary of the accounting for investments in debt securities:

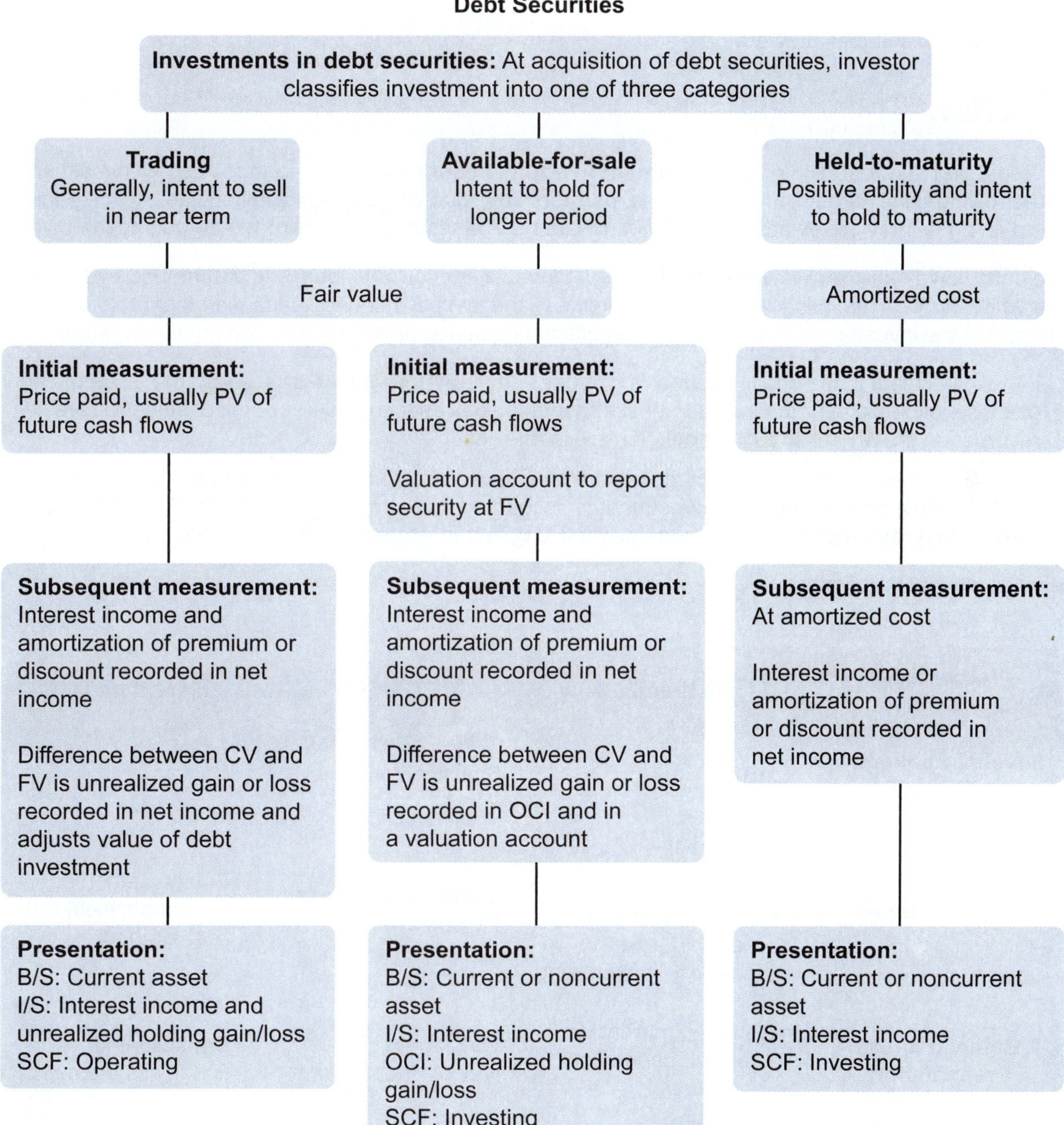

Note: Realized gains and losses on trading and AFS debt securities are recognized in net income.

11.03 Investments in Equity Securities

Overview

The accounting and reporting of an **investment in equity securities** applies to those equity investments (or other ownership interests) in corporations, partnerships, joint ventures, and limited liability companies. Ownership rights may be rewarded with dividends, but dividends are not required to be paid to the owners.

Since equity ownership provides **voting rights**, the level of economic influence is determined by the impact of the voting rights. The voting rights are a guideline to the level of influence because other factors may contribute to the investor's ability to exercise significant influence or control over the equity investee.

- If the investment in the equity security is **nominal (ie, less than 20% ownership)**, the investor cannot exercise influence over the investee. Investments in equity securities with nominal influence are recorded at FV when there is a readily determinable FV
- If the investment in the equity security provides the investor **significant influence (ie, 20%–50% ownership)**, the investment is accounted for using the equity method (covered below). Alternatively, the investor can elect to use the FV option to account for the investee

The following table presents an overview of equity securities:

Percentage Equity Ownership	Less than 20%	20%–50%	More than 50%
Level of Economic Influence	Nominal	Significant	Control
Valuation Basis	• FV, if FV is readily determinable • If there is no readily determinable FV, cost less impairment	Equity method, unless FV option elected	Equity method or (in some cases) cost method
Balance Sheet Presentation	Investment, current or noncurrent, depending on intent to hold	Investment, typically noncurrent	Consolidated financial statements

Consolidations (ie, accounting for equity investments where the investor holds more than 50% ownership) are covered in detail in the FAR General-Purpose Financial Reporting: For-Profit Business Entities chapter.

Investments in Equity Securities Reported at Fair Value

When an owner holds less than 20% ownership, investments in equity securities with *readily determinable FV* are required to be reported at **FV**, with changes in FV recognized in **net income**. If the FV is not readily determinable, either the adjusted cost method or practical expedient method is used (discussed later).

The FV of an equity security is the price that *would be received to sell the security* in an orderly transaction between market participants. The securities are initially recorded at the price paid and are adjusted to the market value (ie, FV) at the end of each period. The initial recognition will include the purchase price and any costs directly related to the purchase (eg, brokerage fees, transfer fees). Initial recognition will include transaction costs, but subsequent measurement of the investment is at FV *excluding* transaction costs.

Similar to a trading debt security, as the market value of the equity securities fluctuates, **unrealized** gains or losses (ie, holding gains or losses) are recorded in net income. If the securities are sold or disposed of, **realized** gains or losses are recorded in net income as well. Interest income and **dividends** declared and/or received are recorded in net income.

Less than 20% Ownership in Equity Securities

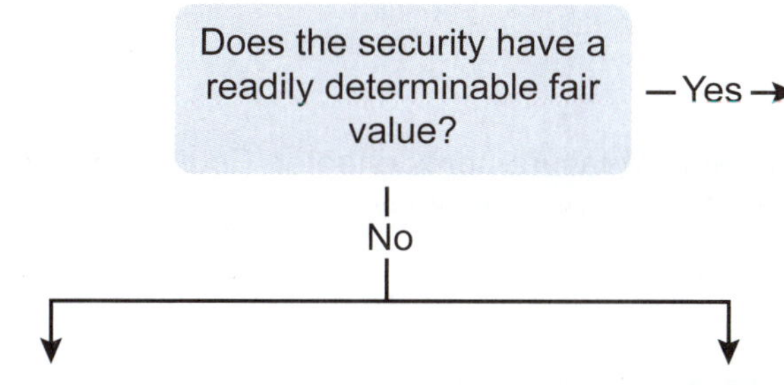

- Fair value method (report at fair value on balance sheet)
- Report dividends, unrealized and realized gains (losses) in net income

- Adjusted cost method (elected)
- Valued at cost – impairment losses

- Practical expedient method
- Use fair value calculated consistent with an investment company

Equity securities recorded at FV through earnings are reported as **current or noncurrent assets** on the balance sheet (depending on management's intent for holding the equity security for the short term or long term). The presentation of the cash flows associated with the purchases and sales of equity securities should be classified on the basis of the nature and purpose for which the securities were acquired. In general, the classification of cash flows would be **investing activities**, unless the purpose of the entity's equity transactions is part of its normal operations (ie, a financial institution), in which case the classification would be operating activities.

There is **no impairment loss** related to equity securities recorded at FV through earnings because all fluctuations in the securities' value (ie, unrealized gains and losses) are already reported in earnings.

The journal entries to record an investment reported at FV are as follows:

Journal Entries for Fair Value Method
(less than 20% ownership)

Purchase Investment		
Investment	XXX	
Cash		XXX

Investor Receives Stock Dividend
No entry made; increase number of shares

Investor Receives Cash Dividend		
Cash	XXX	
Dividend income (I/S)		XXX

I/S = income statement

FV measurement is covered in the FAR Fair Value Measurements chapter. Equity securities recorded at FV through net income follow the FV measurement rules.

Dean Co. purchases 1,000 shares (5% ownership) of Key Co. for $49,000, plus $1,000 of brokerage fees. Determine Dean's entry to record the purchase.

Initial recognition of equity securities recorded at FV through earnings includes the $49,000 purchase price and $1,000 of costs directly related to the purchase. Dean will record the following:

Equity investment in Key Co.	50,000	
Cash		50,000

Assume that Key declares and pays a dividend of $0.50 per share. Determine Dean's entry to record dividend income.

For equity securities at FV, dividend income is recorded in net income. Dean's share of dividends is $500 (1,000 shares × $0.50). Dean will record dividend income as follows:

Cash	500	
Dividend income		500

At the end of the reporting period, the value of Key's shares is $51 per share. Determine Dean's entry to record the necessary adjustment to the investment's FV.

The equity securities will be adjusted to FV, and an unrealized gain (or loss) will be recognized in net income. Total FV of the investment should be reported at $51,000 (1,000 shares × $51 per share), and the current carrying value is $50,000. A $1,000 ($51,000 − $50,000) unrealized gain will be recognized in net income. Dean will record the following:

Equity investment in Key Co.	1,000	
Unrealized gain on investment (I/S)		1,000

Note: A balance sheet valuation account may be used to reflect changes in FV.

During the next reporting period, Dean sells the investment in Key for $59,000. Determine Dean's entry to record the sale.

The equity securities will be taken off the books, and a realized gain will be recorded through net income. Dean will record the following:

Cash	59,000	
Realized gain on investment (I/S)		8,000
Equity investment in Key Co.		51,000

Accounting for equity investments reported at FV is similar to accounting for trading debt securities. In both cases, the investments are reported at FV, and both unrealized and realized gains/losses are recognized in net income. Impairment is not recognized.

Contractual sale restrictions imposed on an equity security recorded at FV are not considered when measuring the FV of equity securities. Entities cannot recognize a contractual sale restriction as a separate unit of account (ie, as a contra-asset or separate liability).

Investments in Equity Securities Reported at Cost

Accounting for investments in equity securities where the owner holds less than 20% ownership and the FV of the security is not readily determinable is as follows:

Less than 20% Ownership in Equity Securities

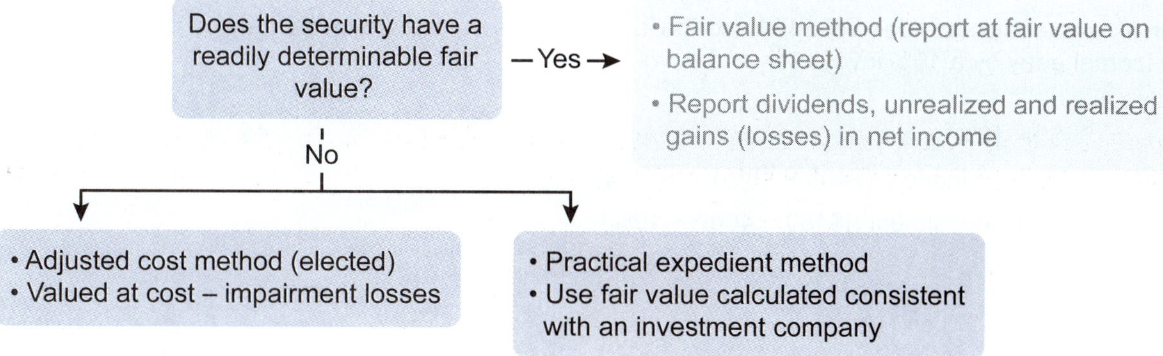

Practicability Exception

When an owner holds less than 20% ownership and there is **no readily determinable FV**, an entity can elect a practicability exception to FV measurement for investments in an equity security. Often, the investor uses the practicability exception because the investee is a privately held company. The practicability exception allows the investor to **carry the equity investment at cost** because readily determinable FV cannot be practically obtained.

In some cases, an entity will have an equity interest in another entity that reports its **net asset value** (NAV) per share. As a **practical expedient**, such an investment may be reported at the published NAV per share. Election of the practicability exception applies only to equity investments that *do not qualify for using NAV as the **practical expedient*** for FV.

The practicability exception can be made on an investment-by-investment basis, but once elected, it must be *applied consistently* to that investment as long as the investment meets the criteria. The investor must reassess annually whether the equity investment still qualifies for the practicability exception. For example, if the investee becomes a public company and FV is determinable, the equity security will need to be accounted for at FV, with changes in FV recognized in net income.

When an equity security's FV is not readily determinable, the entity should first determine if NAV per share (ie, the practical expedient) is provided. If NAV per share is not provided, the security qualifies for the practicability exception and the entity will report the investment at cost.

Adjusted Cost Method

Under the practicability exception, entities can elect to report investments on the balance sheet at:

Cost − Impairment losses

This is called the **adjusted cost method**.

The initial purchase of the equity security is **recorded at the investor's cost**. **Dividends** received by the investor from the investee are recorded like normal dividends (similar to equity securities reported at FV). Cash is collected and dividend income is recognized in net income. When the investee earns money, no journal entry is recorded.

For equity securities reported at cost and equity securities reported at FV, the dividend received may be greater than the investor's share of the investee's income since acquisition. If this is the case, the excess distribution is considered to be a *return of capital*, and the dividend received is recorded as a reduction of the investment.

If an investee paid a dividend of $450 and the income earned since the investment date was only $400, the journal entry by a 10% investor is as follows:

Cash ($450 × 10%)	45	
Dividend income ($400 × 10%)		40
Equity investment ([$450 − 400]) × 10%)		5

Impairments

Each reporting period, an entity must consider **qualitative factors** in assessing whether its investment is impaired. The qualitative assessment is similar to what is completed for long-lived assets, goodwill, and indefinite-lived intangible assets. The following factors should be considered in the evaluation of a potential impairment:

- A deterioration in earnings, financial position, credit rating, asset quality, or business prospects
- Changes in the regulatory, economic, or technological environment
- Changes in the market conditions relevant to the entity's geographical area or industry
- A bona fide offer to purchase the entity, or a completed auction process, for less than the carrying amount of the net investment
- Factors affecting the investee's ability to continue as a going concern

If the factors indicate that the equity security is impaired, an **impairment loss is recorded**. The impairment loss is measured as the **excess of carrying value (CV) over FV of the equity security**. Since this equity security does not have a readily determinable FV, the FV will need to be estimated based on valuation models. The impairment loss is *recorded in net income*, and the *FV becomes the new basis* of the equity investment.

An equity investment was purchased for $150,000 and is carried at cost using the practicability exception. The investment does not qualify to use NAV as a practical expedient. Subsequent factors indicate that there may be an impairment. A valuation model was employed, and it was determined that the FV of the equity investment is $128,000.

Since impairment is indicated, an impairment loss will be recorded. The loss will be recorded at the excess of CV over FV, which, in this case, is $22,000 ($150,000 CV − $128,000 FV). The security will be written down to its FV on the balance sheet.

Impairment loss	22,000	
Equity investment carried at cost		22,000

The equity investment is now reported at $128,000 on the balance sheet.

An impairment loss cannot be reversed unless there are observable price changes in a similar or identical security, as described in the next section.

Adjustments Based on Observable Transactions

When the investor elects the practicability exception and carries the investment in the equity security at cost, the investor must also make a "reasonable effort" to determine if there are known (or can be reasonably known) price changes that should be made to the equity security.

The investor should make an effort to monitor any observable price changes in transactions of the *same issuer* for any security that is similar or identical to the equity security being held. To determine if the security is similar or identical to the one being held, the investor should look at the rights and obligations of the security. Examples of rights and obligations are voting rights, distribution rights, preferences, and conversion features.

Changes in the observable prices in similar or identical securities may indicate that the investor should make an adjustment to the equity security being held as an investment.

If the equity investment was impaired and, subsequently, an observable transaction for a similar or identical security indicates an increase in value, the investor may adjust the investment to match that increase in value. The adjustment would be a FV adjustment, with an unrealized gain reported on the income statement.

Sale or Disposal of Equity Securities Reported at Cost

Upon the sale of an equity security carried at cost, an entity will record a realized gain or loss on the income statement. The realized gain or loss is the difference between the carrying value and the selling price.

An equity investment is carried at cost on a company's books. The investment is reported at $137,000. The company sold the investment for $140,000. Determine the entry that the company would record to report the sale.

The company will record a realized gain of $3,000 ($140,000 − $137,000). The investment will be removed from the books, and cash collected will be recorded. The entry will be recorded as follows:

Cash	140,000	
Realized gain on investment (I/S)		3,000
Equity investment carried at cost		137,000

11.04 Investments in Equity Securities: The Equity Method

Representative Task (Remembering & Understanding): Identify when the equity method of accounting can be applied to an investment.

Representative Task (Application): Calculate the carrying amount of equity method investments and prepare journal entries (excluding impairment).

Overview

When the investor has **significant influence** over the operating and financing activities of the investee, the investor uses the **equity method accounting.** The entity can also elect to use the FV method instead.

Significant influence is presumed if the investor **owns 20%–50% of the investee's voting stock**. The figure 20% is a guideline. There are circumstances under which the investor can exert significant influence with less than 20% ownership, and there are circumstances under which the investor cannot exert significant influence, even with 20% stock ownership. The following are indicators that the investor *has significant influence* even though ownership is less than 20%:

Factors to Consider Regarding an Investor's Significant Influence over an Investee (PERMIT)

- Participation in policy-making processes
- Extent of ownership in relation to the concentration of other shareholdings
- Representation on the board of directors
- Material intra-entity transactions
- Interchange of managerial personnel
- Technological dependency

The following are indicators that the investor *will not have significant influence* even though ownership exceeds 20%:

- The investee opposes investment
- There is a standstill agreement between the investor and the investee (ie, the investor cannot acquire more stock and other attempts to exert significant influence are unsuccessful)
- Significant influence or control is exercised by shareholders other than the investor
- The investee is in bankruptcy or legal reorganization and under the control of the courts

- The investee is a foreign entity that operates under foreign government restrictions that preclude exercise of significant influence
- The investor lacks information for use of equity method (very rare)
- The investor cannot obtain representation on the investee board of directors

Significant influence is not just a bright-line rule. Various factors must be used to determine if the investor can exert significant influence over the investee.

Typically, on the CPA Exam, when it is stated that the investor has significant influence over the investee, the investor will use **equity method accounting** *unless* the question says that the FV option is elected.

If the FV option is elected, the investor must apply it consistently. Under the FV option, the investment is carried at FV, with changes in FV recorded in net income (similar to an equity security reported at FV, previously discussed).

Control is presumed when there is **greater than 50% ownership of voting stock**. Here, the investor is the parent of the investee, and the parent will consolidate the investee for financial reporting purposes. The parent company may use a variety of methods (including the equity method) to account for the investment in its subsidiary. However, since the parent will *consolidate* the subsidiary for financial reporting purposes, the method used by the parent company is irrelevant, as the equity investment is eliminated upon consolidation.

Accounting at Acquisition

Under the equity method, the initial investment in the securities is **recorded on the balance sheet at the price of the equity securities**. The equity method investment is typically recorded as a **noncurrent** asset. *All other costs* related to the purchase of the equity security are *expensed* because they are not considered an attribute of the investee. These other costs (sometimes referred to as direct costs) include finder's fees, audit fees, and legal fees related to the acquisition.

The journal entry at acquisition is as follows:

Equity method investment	XXX	
Cash (or other consideration)		XXX

At the time of initial investment, the investor must also do the following:

- Determine the **book value** of the investee's assets and liabilities at the date of investment
- Determine the **FV** of the assets and liabilities of the investee at the date of investment; assets and liabilities of the investee are valued at FV
- Determine goodwill:

Goodwill = Consideration transferred − Net FV of the identifiable assets and liabilities

The components of the purchase of a significant equity investment are shown below:

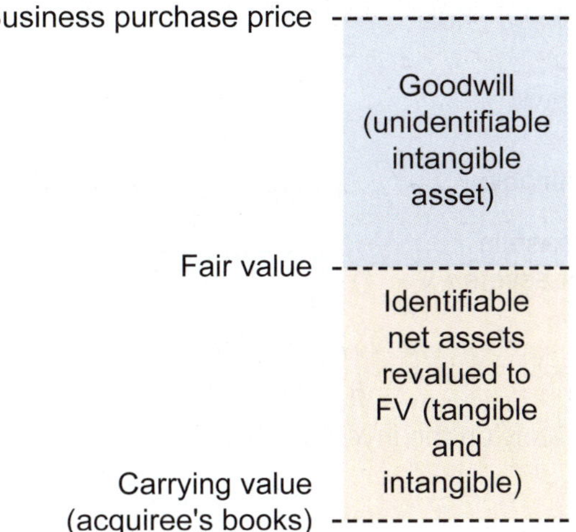

At acquisition, the investee's net assets are revalued to **FV**. If the investor paid more than the FV of the net assets, the difference between the purchase price and the FV of the identifiable net assets is goodwill.

An investor's equity method investment is reported in a single line (initially at cost) on the investor's balance sheet. At acquisition, the investor will not record any impact from the identified basis differences or equity method goodwill. However, the investor will track goodwill, basis differences, and the impact on equity earnings in future periods.

P Company (P) acquired 20% of S Corp. (S) on July 1 for $500,000. S's net book value (Assets − Liabilities) = $2,000,000. The FV of S's plant assets is $300,000 more than the book value, and the assets have a remaining useful life of five years.

Determine the entry to record the equity investment.

Equity method investments are initially recorded at cost. P paid $500,000 for its investment in S. Therefore, the initial journal entry is as follows:

Equity method investment	500,000	
Cash		500,000

Determine the amount of equity method goodwill.

Goodwill is the excess of the purchase price over the FV of S's net assets. The FV of S's assets is $2,300,000 ($300,000 more than its book value of $2,000,000). P owns 20% of S; therefore, P's share of this FV is $460,000 ($2,300,000 × 20%). P paid $500,000 for this investment. Goodwill is $40,000 ($500,000 − $460,000).

	100%	20%
Purchase price		$500,000
Goodwill		40,000
Identifiable FV	2,300,000 × 20% =	460,000
Increase in plant assets FV	300,000 × 20% =	60,000
CV	2,000,000 × 20% =	400,000

Goodwill is not recorded separately on the investor's balance sheet. Rather, it is baked into the equity method investment line.

Accounting after Acquisition

After the date of acquisition, the investor does the following:

1. Recognizes its share of the investee's net income or loss
2. Recognizes its share of the investee's dividends
3. Accounts for any difference between the cost of its investment in the investee and the book value of the investee's net assets it acquired

Equity method accounting affects both the investor's investment account (on the balance sheet) and the income recognized from the investee by the investor (on the income statement).

Reporting Investor's Share of Investee Income (Loss)

As the investee reports earnings, the investor's share of the earnings is recognized. It is reported as equity in earnings on the income statement (with a corresponding entry to equity method investment on the balance sheet) and is equal to:

Investor's ownership percentage × Investee's earnings

This is a component of continuing operations and should exclude the investor's share of any intercompany profits/losses in assets (eg, in inventory, etc.).

If the investee reports net income, the following entry is made:

Equity method investment	XXX	
Equity in earnings (I/S)		XXX

If the investee reports net loss, the following entry is made:

Equity in losses (I/S)	XXX	
Equity method investment		XXX

If investee losses reduce the investment to zero, the investor should discontinue applying the equity method unless the investee's imminent return to profitability is assured. If the investee later returns to profitability, the investor should resume applying the equity method when the investor's share of net income equals its share of net losses that were not recognized during the equity-method suspension period.

If the investor elects to use the FV option to report an investment that would otherwise be accounted for using the equity method, the investor *does not* recognize its share of the investee's results of operation. The investee's results of operation are assumed to be reflected in the change in FV of the investment (which is recognized in net income).

Reporting Investor's Share of Investee Dividends

The investor recognizes its proportionate share of investee dividends as a reduction in its investment in the investee on the balance sheet (with a corresponding entry to cash or dividends receivable). It is equal to:

Investor's ownership percentage × Investee's dividends

Dividends received are considered a reduction of the investment account and **do not appear on the income statement**. The entry made by the investor when the investee declares/pays a cash dividend would be as follows:

Cash or dividends receivable	XXX	
Equity method investment		XXX

If the investor elects to use the FV option to report an investment that would otherwise be accounted for using the equity method, the investor recognizes the investee's cash dividends as dividend income in earnings.

Adjusting for Differences between Cost and Book Value

The **excess of the cost of the investment over book value** is not reported separately on the financial statement; it is included in the investment. Nevertheless, it will have an impact on the subsequent reporting of income by the investor. This impact *depends on the nature of the asset* causing the difference.

When the FV of net assets is greater than the CV at acquisition, this difference often relates to **depreciable and amortizable assets**. For depreciable and amortizable assets, differences will be depreciated/amortized against the reported equity in investee income based on the appropriate life of the asset.

- Depreciation/amortization is only recorded as it relates to identifiable depreciable/amortizable assets. Nondepreciable assets (eg, land) are not depreciated

The depreciation/amortization entry is as follows:

Equity in earnings	XXX	
Equity method investment		XXX

The investor does not debit expense but reduces the amount of income picked up from the investee and reduces the carrying amount of the investment.

When the price paid is greater than the FV of net assets, the difference relates to **goodwill**. For goodwill, the amount initially recorded will later reduce reported income in periods in which impairment losses are recognized. *Goodwill is not amortized* (unless the exception for private companies to amortize goodwill over 10 years is applied).

Any **outstanding differences** will be written off against reported income at the time the asset is sold or otherwise disposed of.

Adjusting for the difference related to depreciable/amortizable assets is necessary for reporting the investor's true share of the investee's earnings. For example, an equity method investee owns a building that had a book value of $50,000 on the date of acquisition. However, on that date, the FV of the building was $1,000,000. Therefore, when determining the purchase price of the shares, the investor would include the building's FV of $1,000,000 rather than its book value of $50,000.

The investee's depreciation expense will be based on the book value of $50,000. The investor, on the other hand, has paid the equivalent of its share of $1,000,000 and has to depreciate the difference.

Summary

The basic journal entries recorded under the equity method are as follows:

Investor's Entries under the Equity Method

Purchase Investment		
Investment in investee (cost)	XXX	
Cash		XXX
Record Cash Dividends Received		
Cash	XXX	
Investment in investee		XXX
Record % of Investee's Earning		
Investment in investee	XXX	
Equity in earnings − investee (I/S)		XXX
Record Adjustment for Excess FV over CV		
Equity in earnings − investee (I/S)	XXX	
Investment in investee		XXX

I/S = income statement

The above journal entries translate to the T-accounts related to the equity method as follows:

Equity Method: Impact of Investee Transactions

Investment (Balance Sheet)		Equity Investment Earnings (Income Statement)	
Purchase price	Amortization of FV in excess of CV	Share of investee's net loss	
Share of investee's net income			Share of investee's net income
	Share of investee's net loss	Amortization of FV in excess of CV	
	Dividends		
Ending balance			

Peach Company paid $300,000 on 7/1/Year 1 to acquire 30% of Sand Company's stock. At the time, Sand's net book value was $850,000. The FV of Sand's net assets was $50,000 more than the book value. The difference between net book value and FV related to a machine that has a remaining useful life of five years.

Sand earned net income of $400,000 evenly throughout Year 1. In addition, Sand paid dividends of $100,000 on 12/31/Year 1.

Determine the entry to record the equity investment.

The components of Peach's purchase are shown below:

	100%	30%
Purchase price		$300,000
Goodwill		30,000
Identifiable FV	900,000 × 30% =	270,000
Increase in net assets FV	50,000 × 30% =	15,000
CV	850,000 × 30% =	255,000

Equity method investments are initially recorded at cost. Peach paid $300,000 for its investment in Sand. Therefore, the initial journal entry at 7/1/Year 1 is as follows:

Equity method investment	300,000	
Cash		300,000

Determine the equity method entries recorded by Peach at the end of Year 1.

Peach will record its share of Sand's earnings. Since Peach invested in Sand in July (six months into the year), Peach will only report its share of six months of Sand's income. Peach will report $60,000 ($400,000 NI × 6/12 × 30%) of income:

Equity method investment	60,000	
Equity in earnings		60,000

Peach will also record its share of Sand's dividends. Sand paid dividends of $100,000. Peach's share is $30,000 ($100,000 × 30%):

Cash	30,000	
Equity method investment		30,000

Finally, Peach will record a portion of depreciation of the excess FV. The excess FV of the assets over CV was $50,000 (attributable to a machine with a useful life of five years). Peach's share of this excess is $15,000 ($50,000 × 30%). Therefore, one full year of depreciation is $3,000 ($15,000 / 5 years). However, as Peach invested in Sand on July 1, Peach will depreciate only six months of the excess FV ($1,500 = $3,000 × 6/12).

Equity in earnings	1,500	
Equity method investment		1,500

Note: Equity method goodwill of $30,000 ($300,000 paid − $270,000 Peach's share of FV) exists. However, no journal entries are made associated with the goodwill.

Impairments

An investor is required to assess its equity method investment (including goodwill) for impairment when circumstances suggest that the investment's carrying amount may be impaired. An investor records an impairment loss in earnings when the **FV of the investment is less than the CV** and the decline is determined to be **other than temporary**. The entry to record an impairment loss is as follows:

Equity in earnings	XXX	
Equity method investment		XXX

Purchase or Sale of an Equity Method Investment

If prior ownership with no significant influence is followed by additional purchase of equity shares, resulting in significant influence, then the entity will switch from FV to equity method accounting. A change to the equity method accounting is accounted for **prospectively**.

In a sale of all or part of an investment accounted for using the equity method, the equity method accounts are first updated to date of sale by recording the following:

- Investor's share of the investee's income or loss to date of sale
- Investor's share of the investee's dividends declared or paid to the date of sale
- Investor's depreciation or amortization of the excess cost over book value to date of sale

A **gain or loss** on the sale will be realized for the difference between selling price and carrying value (CV) of the equity investment sold:

- If selling price is *greater* than carrying value, a *gain* is realized
- If selling price is *less* than carrying value, a *loss* is realized

If the sale is not for the entire investment and results in the investor **losing significant influence over the investee** (eg, less than 20% ownership), the remaining investment should be *accounted for at FV*, with any difference between the carrying amount of the remaining investment and its FV recognized as a gain or loss in current income.

Equity Method Disclosures

When the equity method is used to report investments in common stock, the following disclosures are appropriate:

- The name and percentage of ownership for each equity method investee
- The name of any investee in which the investor owns 20%–50% of the voting stock not accounted for using the equity method and the reason for that treatment
- The name of any investee in which the investor owns less than 20% of the voting stock accounted for using the equity method and the reason for that treatment
- Any difference between the carrying amount of the investment and the investor's share of the underlying claim to net assets and how that difference is treated
- When a bargain purchase gain is recognized, the amount of the gain recognized, the line item where the gain is recognized, and a description of the transaction that resulted in the gain
- When there is a quoted market price for the common stock, the market value of each investment
- When the equity method is used for investments in corporate joint ventures that are material to the investor, summary information about the assets, liabilities, and results of operation of those joint venture investees
- Possible effects of conversion or exercise of outstanding securities (eg, options, convertible securities) on the investor's ownership claim

Summary of Accounting for Investments in Equity Securities

The following is a summary of the accounting for investments in equity securities:

Equity Investments

Investments in equity securities: are measured at FV with changes in FV recognized in net income, except for those with no readily determinable FV, or that result in consolidation, or that are accounted for under the equity method of accounting.

< 20% ownership (**passive**)

Cost method

Cost method is used when there is no readily determinable FV and the **practicability exception is elected.**

Applies only to equity investments that <u>do not qualify</u> for using net asset value (NAV) as the practical expedient for FV.

Initial measurement: Investor's cost.

Subsequent measurement: Cost is reduced for any impairment, (+/–) price changes from any observable transactions for an identical or similar investment. Dividends received are income.

FV through net income

FV through net income is used when there is a readily determinable FV.

Initial measurement: Investor's cost.

Subsequent measurement: Change in FV is reported as an unrealized holding gain or loss in net income until sold. Dividends received are income. Sale of security: Realized gain or loss is difference between last FV measurement and selling price.

Presentation: B/S: Current or noncurrent, depending on management's intent for holding.

≥ 20-50% ownership (**significant influence**)

Equity method of accounting is used when there is significant influence and FV election is not made.

Initial measurement: Investor's cost.

Subsequent measurement: Equity method accounting which reflects investor's share of investee's earnings and dividends. Adjust for FV increment at the date of acquisition.

Presentation: B/S: Noncurrent (generally) I/S: Equity method income. Dividends are NOT income, but a reduction of the equity investment.

> 50% ownership (**control**)

Investor uses equity or cost method to account for investee. For reporting, consolidated F/S must be prepared.

Separate F/S of the investor and investee are maintained. The investor's stand-alone F/S are not in compliance with GAAP until consolidated.

Presentation: Consolidated F/S.

11.05 Investor Stock Dividends, Splits, and Rights

Stock Dividends

Stock dividends are additional shares of an investee stock that an investor receives. Unlike a cash dividend, a stock dividend is not income but *additional ownership* of the entity. When the stock dividend is received, the investor *adjusts the per share (not total) carrying value* of the equity investment. The investor will own additional shares, and therefore the stock dividend will reduce the per share cost basis of the stock. No journal entry is needed unless the new securities are in a different class.

Upon sale of the shares (in part or total), the shares will be removed at the new per share carrying value, and any **gain or loss** will be the difference between the selling price and the new per share value.

Duke Corp. held the following equity investment in Hike Corp.

Investment in Hike Corp.	$100,000
Original number of shares	1,000
Per share value ($100,000 / 1,000)	$100

Hike declared a 10% stock dividend. Determine the new value per share.

Duke would receive an additional 100 shares (1,000 shares × 10%). The new value per share is $90.90 ($100,000 / [1,000 original shares + 100 new shares]). No journal entry is made. The total carrying value of the investment remains at $100,000; only the per share carrying value has changed.

Stock Splits

In a **stock split**, an investor receives additional shares of the equity investee's stock. An example would be a two-for-one split (double the number of shares is owned but at the same value). When received, a stock split is not income but is *additional ownership* of the entity. Just as with stock dividends, when the stock split is received, the investor adjusts the *per share (not total) carrying value* of the equity investment. The investor will own additional shares, and therefore the stock split will reduce the per share cost basis of the stock. No journal entry is recorded for a stock dividend or a stock split.

When the stock subsequently is sold, the investor would recognize a **gain or loss**.

Stock Rights

A **stock right** gives the investor the privilege (right) to purchase additional shares of an investee at a specific price (strike price) within a specific time. Like stock dividends and splits, stock rights are not income when received.

If the strike price is less than the FV of the stock, the stock right has a value (in-the-money). The value of the right is determined by allocating the carrying value of the investment between the shares of stock owned and stock rights received based on their relative FV. If the per share FV of the stock right is known, the total value of the rights is as follows:

$$\frac{\text{FV of one right}}{\text{FV of stock without right + FV of one right}} \times \text{CV of investment} = \text{Total value of rights}$$

$$\frac{\text{Total value of rights}}{\text{Number of rights received}} = \text{Per share value of rights}$$

Crab Inc. purchased 100 shares of stock from Shrimp Inc. at a price of $24 per share. During the year, Shrimp issued a stock right for each existing share when the FV of the stock was still $24 per share and the FV of the right was $6 per right. Determine the entry that Crab should record to reflect the stock right.

The initial CV of the investment is $2,400 (100 shares × $24 per share). The total value of the rights is calculated as follows:

$$\frac{6}{(24 + 6)} \times \$2{,}400 = \$480$$

Crab will record the following:

Account	Debit	Credit
Equity investment in stock rights	480	
Equity investment in Shrimp Inc.		480

FAR 12
Intangible Assets

FAR 12: Intangible Assets

12.01 Intangible Assets

Overview

Representative Task (Remembering & Understanding): Identify the criteria for recognizing intangible assets in the statement of financial position and classify intangible assets as either finite-lived or indefinite-lived.

Intangible assets refer to a company's assets that **lack physical substance** and provide economic benefits through the rights and privileges associated with their possession. They may have finite or indefinite lives. **Finite-lived assets** have an identifiable useful life or, in some situations, a specific legal life. **Indefinite-lived assets** have no legal, regulatory, contractual, competitive, or other limits on their life. "Indefinite" means that there is no foreseeable limit on the period of time over which the intangible is expected to provide cash flows.

The FAR exam covers *finite*-lived intangible assets (eg, legal rights and identifiable intangibles), while the Business Analysis and Reporting (BAR) exam covers *indefinite*-lived intangible assets (eg, research and development and unidentifiable intangibles [goodwill]). Only finite-lived intangibles are *amortized*.

Examples of Finite-Lived Intangible Assets		
Type	**Description**	**Period**
Patents	Protection for product and process ideas resulting from R&D	Maximum 20-year life; amortized over useful or legal life (whichever is shorter)
Copyrights	Protection of artistic works, including books, recordings, and computer software	Life of the creator, plus 70 years; amortized over useful life
Franchises	Operation of a business unit under contractual arrangements with another party	Amortized over useful life of related contract

Trademarks provide the exclusive use of an identifying name for a product or process. Although trademarks often have a defined legal life, they can typically be renewed every ten years, so they are considered indefinite-lived intangible assets. However, any external acquisition costs associated with trademarks are capitalized and amortized over the trademark's useful life.

Carrying Values

Representative Task (Application): Calculate the carrying amount of finite-lived intangible assets reported in the financial statements (initial measurement, amortization and impairment) and prepare journal entries.

Initial Carrying Amount

Intangibles are either acquired from other parties or internally developed. An **acquired intangible** is capitalized if either:

- The benefit of the asset is obtained through contractual or other legal rights (as in a patent), or
- The intangible is otherwise separable (ie, can be sold, transferred, licensed, rented, or exchanged, regardless of the acquirer's intent to do so [eg, customer lists]).

In general, the initial carrying amount (ie, capitalized cost) is determined similarly for all acquired intangible assets: purchase price, plus legal and administrative expenditures associated with obtaining the assets and **successfully** protecting them against infringement. If a legal defense of an intangible asset is **unsuccessful**, all costs should be **expensed** since no legal benefit exists in that case.

A firm paid $45,000 on 1/1/Year 1 for a patent. On 2/1/Year 1, the firm won an infringement lawsuit concerning the patent. Legal costs amounted to $15,000. Determine the journal entry that should be recorded at 2/1/Year 1.

Since the legal defense was successful, the firm will capitalize the legal costs as part of the patent:

Account	Debit	Credit
Intangible asset — patent	15,000	
Cash		15,000

The carrying amount of the patent on the balance sheet is now $60,000 ($45,000 + 15,000). If the defense of the patent had been unsuccessful, the legal costs would have been expensed immediately.

Internally developed intangibles are expensed immediately if they are not specifically identifiable, have indeterminate values, or are inherent in a continuing business. Firms must expense the amount of internal expenditures devoted to the development of intangibles. The only costs related to internally developed intangibles that are capitalized are registration fees and legal costs paid to outsiders.

Amortization

In general, finite-lived intangible assets are **amortized** straight-line over their useful lives. When a range of useful lives is possible, the **shortest** option should be used. This is consistent with the **conservatism** principle of overestimating expenses when dealing with transactions involving uncertainties.

Several factors can influence the determination of useful life, including expected use of the asset; legal, regulatory, or contractual provisions; obsolescence, competition, or other economic factors; or expected maintenance expenses. If a useful life cannot be determined, the intangible asset is considered indefinite and, therefore, is not amortized.

Amortization Expense of an Intangible Asset with a Finite Useful Life

$$\text{Amortization expense} = \frac{\text{Cost} - \text{Residual value}}{\text{Useful life}}$$

A company paid $80,000 at the beginning of Year 1 for a patent with a fair value of $90,000 and remaining legal life of 10 years. The company signed a contract to sell the patent for $15,000 at the end of Year 5. Determine the carrying amount of the patent that should be reported on the balance sheet at the end of Year 2.

In this scenario, the fair value of the patent is distractor information. The fair value is not capitalized because amortization expense cannot be matched to an economic benefit that was not purchased and may not be realized. The patent is initially recorded at the cost of **$80,000**, and $80,000 is used in the numerator of the amortization expense calculation.

The residual value is similar to a salvage value used in the calculation for depreciation expense. Since the company is contracted to sell the patent in the future, the future selling price of **$15,000** is the residual value.

Patents are amortized over their useful or legal life (whichever is shorter). The company is contracted to sell the asset in **five years**, so that is the period used to calculate amortization expense. The remaining legal life is irrelevant.

Each year, amortization on the patent is $13,000:

$$\frac{\$80{,}000 - \$15{,}000}{5 \text{ years}} = \$13{,}000$$

At the end of Years 1 and 2, the journal entry to record the amortization expense is as follows:

Amortization expense	13,000	
Intangible asset—patent		13,000

At the end of Year 2, the carrying amount of the patent to be reported on the balance sheet is the cost, less the total amortization expense, or $80,000 − ($13,000 × 2 years) = **$54,000**.

Testing for Impairment

Intangibles are subject to impairment testing. Since finite-lived assets are amortized, they are only evaluated for impairment (ie, a decline in the recorded value of the asset) if events or conditions indicate the likelihood of impairment. If there is no indication, no further testing is required. If, however, events or conditions indicate that the asset is likely impaired, the **recoverability test** is applied to determine if (but not how much) impairment has occurred.

The recoverability test compares an asset's *undiscounted expected future net cash flows with its carrying amount.* If the carrying amount is *higher* than expected future net cash flows, the intangible asset is impaired. The impairment loss to be recorded is the excess amount of the asset's carrying value over its fair value.

Impairment Testing for Intangible Assets with *Finite Lives*

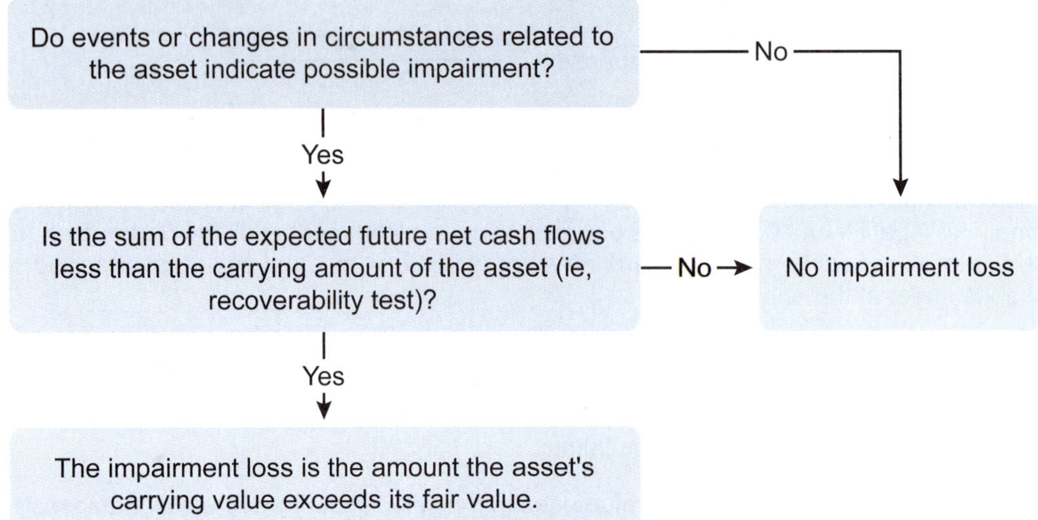

Zee Company recorded the following information pertaining to a copyright in Year 1:

Carrying value	$33,000
Fair value	$16,000
Expected future net cash flows	$25,000

During Year 1, conditions indicated that the copyright was likely impaired Determine the impairment to be recorded on the copyright.

First, Zee will compare the expected future net cash flows (undiscounted) to the carrying value. The expected future net cash flows ($25,000) are less than the carrying value ($33,000), so impairment has occurred.

Second, Zee will record an impairment loss for the amount that the asset's carrying value ($33,000) exceeds its fair value ($16,000). Zee will record an impairment loss of $17,000 ($33,000 − $16,000).

Purchased Software and Cloud Computing Arrangements

Representative Task (Application): Calculate the carrying amount of purchased software and cloud computing arrangements reported in the financial statements (initial measurement, amortization and impairment) and prepare journal entries.

Purchased Software

An entity may purchase software for internal use and implement the software with **no customization** (ie, buy and use off the shelf). These costs are **capitalized and amortized** over the expected useful life of the software.

Alternatively, an entity may purchase software and **customize it** so that the software fits the entity's unique needs. The accounting for modified software follows the criteria for research and development costs. That is, the stage of the modification of the software dictates whether the costs are expensed or capitalized and when amortization commences:

- The costs incurred to modify the software to the point of technological feasibility are expensed as incurred. The costs incurred after technological feasibility but before the software is put to use are capitalized as an intangible asset.
- The capitalized costs of the modified software intended for internal use are amortized over the expected useful life of the software.

Costs associated with the maintenance of the software (often referred to as a servicing agreement) are expensed as incurred.

Cloud Computing Arrangements

Entities often utilize software in a **cloud computing arrangement** (ie, a hosting arrangement). This means that the entity does not have physical possession of the software but has use of the software on the cloud.

When an entity enters a cloud computing arrangement, an analysis is performed to determine whether some or all of the arrangement represents a software license. The arrangement **contains a software license** if both of the following are true:

- The customer has the contractual right to take possession of the software at any time during the hosting period, without significant penalty.
  - "Significant penalty" means that the customer can take delivery without incurring significant costs and can use the software separately, without a significant reduction in utility or value.
- It is feasible for the customer either to run the software on its own hardware or to contract with another party unrelated to the vendor to host the software.

If the entire arrangement is considered a **software license**, the entire cost, including the present value of future payments, is treated as an **intangible asset** and accounted for similarly to other licenses. It will be capitalized, and a determination will be made as to whether it has a finite useful life and should therefore be amortized.

If the arrangement does **not** include a software license, the entire amount is treated as a **service contract**, with the expense recognized in the period in which the benefit is derived, similar to other service expenses for an entity.

If the arrangement represents a **combination**, the total cost will be **allocated** between the software license and the service contract.

Cloud Computing—Asset or Expense?

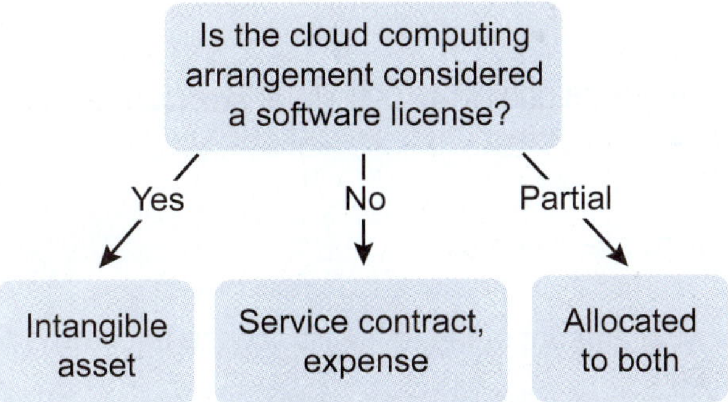

Implementation Costs

Both licensing arrangements and service contracts that are provided via a cloud computing arrangement will have **implementation costs** (ie, costs incurred to set up the hosting arrangement). To determine which implementation costs are capitalized and which are expensed, the entity follows the same guidance used when capitalizing other intangibles.

Internal and external costs to research, develop, or obtain the software are at the preliminary stage and therefore are expensed as incurred. Examples include costs for coding, testing, and converting old data into new systems.

- Internal and external costs to **implement** the software for use (ie, implementation costs) can be **capitalized**. Implementation includes fees to customize or configure the software, as well as payroll costs of employees directly associated with implementation during the development phase.
- Once the software is in use, costs can no longer be capitalized and must be expensed in the period incurred.

When the cloud computing arrangement is a **license**, the implementation costs are **capitalized** to the software intangible asset and **amortized** as part of the software asset.

When the cloud computing arrangement is a **service agreement**, the implementation costs are **capitalized** as a prepaid asset. The costs are not capitalized as an intangible asset (because there is no intangible asset) but are prepaid as part of the service agreement. The implementation costs are expensed over the life of the service agreement.

At the beginning of Year 3, a company signed a five-year contract for a cloud computing arrangement. The company will pay a total of $690,000, which includes a one-time charge of $140,000 in Year 3 for the necessary software license. The rest of the total will be paid evenly over the life of the contract. The company does not yet have plans to renew the contract after the initial agreement expires. Prepare the necessary journal entries for Year 3 and determine the carrying amount of any assets to be reported on the balance sheet at the end of Year 3.

$140,000 of the arrangement is paid for a software license. This amount will be capitalized as an intangible asset. The remaining $550,000 ($690,000 − $140,000) is treated as a service contract and expensed in the period in which benefit is derived. Here, the contract is for five years. Therefore, $110,000 of expense ($550,000 / 5 years) will be recognized each year.

To initially record the software license and service contract in Year 3, the company will record the following:

Intangible asset—software license	140,000	
Cloud computing expense	110,000	
Cash		250,000

Each year, the company will record $28,000 ($140,000 / 5) of amortization expense on the software license:

Amortization expense	28,000	
Intangible asset—software license		28,000

At the end of Year 3, the carrying amount of the software license to be reported on the balance sheet is $140,000 − $28,000 = **$112,000.**

FAR 13
Payables and Accrued Liabilities

FAR 13: Payables and Accrued Liabilities

13.01 Payables and Accrued Liabilities

Overview

Representative Task (Application): Calculate the carrying amount of payables (eg, accounts payable, dividends payable) and accrued liabilities (eg, accrued wages, accrued vacation, accrued bonuses, self-insurance liabilities) and prepare journal entries.

According to the FASB Concepts Statements, a **liability** is a present obligation of an entity to transfer an economic benefit. A liability has two essential characteristics:

1. It is a present obligation.
2. The obligation requires an entity to transfer or otherwise provide economic benefits to others.

Liabilities are classified in two ways, as current liabilities (discussed here) or noncurrent liabilities (see FAR Debt chapter). Liabilities can be definite (ie, arising from a contract or obligation that exists at the balance sheet date) or contingent (ie, contingent on an event that may or may not occur after the balance sheet date). Note: For the discussion of contingent liabilities, see FAR Contingencies and Commitments chapter.

Current liabilities are *due within one year* or due within the operating cycle of the business, whichever is longer. All other liabilities are **noncurrent** (also called long term). Liabilities are presented on the balance sheet in increasing order of maturity.

Liability Classifications	
Current Liabilities	**Noncurrent Liabilities**
• Settled with a current asset (eg, cash) or another liability (eg, note refinanced with bonds) • Settled within the longer of one year or the operating cycle	• All liabilities that are not classified as current liabilities
Examples: • Accounts payable • Salaries (or wages) payable • Dividends payable • Income taxes payable • Unearned revenue • Current portion of long-term debt	**Examples:** • Notes/bonds payable • Deferred tax liability • Short-term debt refinanced to long-term debt • Noncurrent portion of finance lease

Accounts Payable

Accounts payable (also called trade payables) generally represent amounts due to vendors resulting from the purchase of merchandise. These payables are typically for a short duration, usually 30–60 days.

Accounts payable are recognized at the time of purchase or at the time that services are received by the business entity. If a payable involves the purchase of merchandise, the payable should be recognized when the merchandise is included in the company's inventory.

Merchandise suppliers often offer discounts for prompt payment of accounts. For example, the terms of the payable may be 2/10, n/30. This means a 2% discount is applied if the account is paid within 10 days, and the remaining balance is due within 30 days.

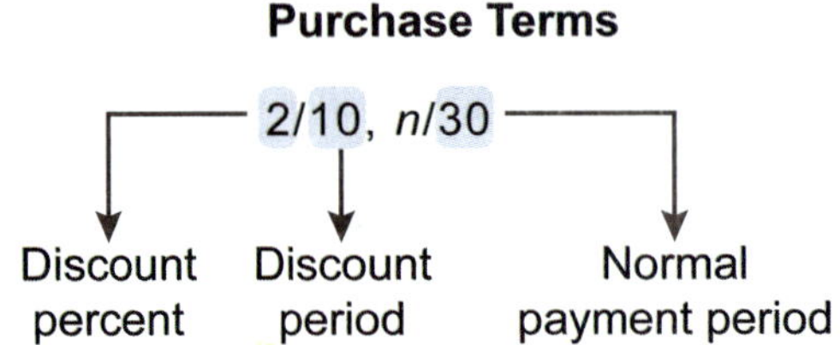

When discounts on accounts payable are offered, purchasing firms can choose to use the **gross method** or the **net method**. Under the gross method, purchases are recorded at their full purchase price; then, if the discount is taken, it is considered a reduction of cost of sales. Under the net method, purchases are recorded as if the discount will be taken; then, if the discount is not taken, the discount lost may be considered an expense (eg, interest expense).

On May 4, Year 3, a company purchased supplies with a cost of $10,000 and terms 2/10, net 30. Half of the invoiced amount was paid on May 12. The remaining balance was paid on June 2.

Prepare the journal entries for these transactions using both the gross method and the net method.

Gross Method			**Net Method**		
Record purchase of supplies (terms 2/10, net 30)					
Supplies	10,000		Supplies	9,800	
Accounts payable		10,000	Accounts payable		9,800
Payment of first half of the invoiced amount (May 12, within discount period)					
Accounts payable	5,000		Accounts payable	4,900	
Purchase discount		100	Cash		4,900
Cash		4,900			
Payment for second half of the invoiced amount (June 2, after discount period)					
Accounts payable	5,000		Accounts payable	4,900	
Cash		5,000	Purchase discount lost	100	
			Cash		5,000

Under the **gross method**, the purchase is initially recorded for the full $10,000 amount. Then, a $5,000 payment ($10,000 × 1/2) is made within the discount period. The 2% discount, here for $100 ($5,000 × 2% discount), is recorded when the first payment is made. The remaining $5,000 is not paid until after the discount period, so the full $5,000 payment amount is recorded when paid.

Under the **net method**, the purchase is initially recorded for $9,800, as if the 2% discount will be taken ($10,000 − [$10,000 × 2% discount]). When the company pays the first invoice within the discount period, the entry is recorded for $4,900. However, when the second payment is made after the discount period, the company fails to take advantage of $100 of purchase discount ($5,000 × 2% discount). This is recorded as purchase discount lost (an expense).

Dividends Payable

Dividends are considered a current liability when they are **declared**, whether they pertain to common stock or preferred stock. Dividends in arrears (ie, unpaid dividends) on cumulative preferred stock are not a liability but must be disclosed in the notes to the financial statements.

The journal entries related to dividends payable are as follows:

When cash dividends are declared:		
Dividends or Retained earnings*	XX	
Dividends payable		XX

**Companies may record dividends in a separate account or in the retained earnings account for internal tracking purposes. If the company records dividends in a separate dividends account, the account is closed to retained earnings at the end of each period.*

When cash dividends are paid:		
Dividends payable	XX	
Cash		XX

On March 1, Year 2, the board of directors of a company declared a $0.50 dividend on its 5,000 shares, payable to shareholders of record on March 15 to be paid on April 2. Record the journal entries related to these dividend transactions.

When the dividends are declared, the following will be recorded:

March 1	Dividends or Retained earnings (5,000 shares × $0.50)	2,500	
	Dividends payable		2,500

When the dividends are paid, the following will be recorded:

April 2	Dividends payable	2,500	
	Cash		2,500

Note: The dividend record date (here, March 15) is the date on which a shareholder must own shares to be eligible for a dividend payment. No transaction takes place on this date. It is simply used to determine which shareholders receive payment and which shareholders do not. Therefore, March 15 does not require an entry.

Accrued Liabilities

When an expense is **incurred but not yet paid**, the company will record an **accrued liability** (along with the corresponding expense).

On March 31, Year 3, a company received a utility bill for $936 covering the service period March 1 to March 25, with a payment due date of April 5. Also on March 31, the company prepaid rent for $685, the monthly rental fee covering the period April 1 to April 30.

Determine the entries that the company will record at March 31, Year 3, related to these transactions.

The company will accrue $936 for the utility bill. This bill relates to services that have already been performed (ie, an expense that has already been incurred). However, the company has not yet paid for these services. At March 31, the company owes $936; therefore, a liability is recorded.

Utilities expense	936	
Accounts payable		936

The company will record a prepaid asset (ie, prepaid rent) of $685. When an expense is incurred before cash is paid, an accrued liability is recorded. Here, cash has been paid *before* the expense was incurred. The company will record a prepaid asset of $685 and expense this asset ratably over the rental period.

Prepaid rent	685	
Cash		685

Accrued liabilities are often recorded as an **adjusting entry** to update account balances at the end of an accounting period.

Company A has a December 31 year end. During the year, Company A had the following loan transactions:

- Transaction 1: Borrowed $400,000 from First Bank on April 1. Principal and interest are due upon maturity in one year. The interest rate is 12%.
- Transaction 2: Borrowed $100,000 from Second Bank on September 30, by signing a six-month, $112,000, zero-interest-bearing note.

What amount of interest expense must be accrued for each of these transactions?

Each period, the company will record interest expense on its loans. In general, for interest-bearing loans, interest expense is calculated as the principal, multiplied by the applicable interest rate, multiplied by the time outstanding. For non-interest-bearing loans, the implicit interest expense is calculated as the face value of the loan, less the cash actually borrowed, multiplied by the time outstanding.

If, at the end of the period, the company has not yet paid the interest expense, it will be accrued as interest payable. This is the case in transaction 1 (because interest payment is not due until maturity) and transaction 2 (because it is a zero-interest-bearing note, and therefore, implicit interest recorded is actually paid as part of the principal).

Thus, the transactions are accounted for as follows:

Transaction 1: Interest expense of $36,000 = ($400,000 × 12%) × 9/12 ← Portion of time outstanding
Transaction 2: Interest expense of $6,000 = ($112,000 − 100,000) × 3/6 ←

Interest expense ($36,000 + 6,000)	42,000	
Interest payable		42,000

Unearned revenue (an accrued liability) results when cash is received in advance of providing any product or services.

Company B is contracted to install custom drapes for a home owner for $45,000. Prior to beginning any work, Company B requires the home owner to provide a 25% down payment.

Determine the journal entry that is required to record the receipt of the down payment.

The down payment is received by the company in advance of any work being performed. As a result, the $11,250 down payment ($45,000 × 25%) is considered to be unearned revenue. When the services are performed, the unearned revenue will be recognized as revenue ratably over the service period.

Cash	11,250	
Unearned revenue (liability)		11,250

Sales taxes are collected by the company on behalf of the taxing authority (eg, county, city, or state). Between the collection and submission of the tax, the company has an accrued liability to the taxing authority.

Egg Company made cash sales during June in the amount of $375,000 (not including sales tax). The sales are subject to an additional 6% sales tax, which Egg collected. Egg has not yet remitted the sales tax payments to the county's revenue department (ie, taxing authority).

Determine the entry that would be recorded for sales tax payable.

Cash ($375,000 × 1.06)	397,500	
Sales tax payable ($375,000 × .06)		22,500
Sales revenue		375,000

Accrued Salaries (Wages)

Salary expense (also called wage expense) is incurred when employees perform services, regardless of when the employees are paid. At the end of each reporting period, a liability is recorded (ie, accrued salaries payable or accrued payroll) for salaries earned by employees but not yet paid to them.

To determine the salary expense incurred in a pay period, the salary expense per day is multiplied by the number of workdays in the month. A corresponding liability is recorded for salary expense incurred but not yet paid.

Fill Inc.'s employees are paid $20,000 every other Friday for the 10 workdays then ending. The last payroll paid was on Friday, December 23, Year 1. Determine the journal entry that Fill should record to accrue salaries at December 31, Year 1.

December, Year 1						
SUN	MON	TUE	WED	THU	FRI	SAT
				1	2	3
4	5	6	7	8	9	10
11	12	13	14	15	16	17
18	19	20	21	22	23 $20,000 paid	24
25	26	27	28	29	30	31

The employees' pay per workday is $2,000 ($20,000 / 10 workdays). At December 31, employees have worked for five days (December 26–30) but have not yet been paid for this work. Therefore, Fill owes the employees $10,000 ($2,000 per day × 5 days). The company will record the following entry on December 31:

Salaries expense	10,000	
Accrued salaries payable		10,000

Similarly, **deferred compensation** is created when an employee's (eg, executive's) contract promises *future compensation based on services performed in the present*. A company's obligation to provide the future payments accrues as the employee provides service to the company (ie, remains employed).

If the contract requires the executive to provide services for more than one year, the company must systematically accrue the cost of the payments during the time the executive provides service (ie, matching).

Payroll Tax Liabilities

Payroll tax liabilities result from the employee's and employer's share of certain taxes. The Federal Insurance Contributions Act (**FICA**) requires payroll tax on *employee pay* with a matching contribution from *employers* to fund Social Security and Medicare. The Federal Unemployment Tax Act (**FUTA**) and State Unemployment Tax Act (**SUTA**) require *employers* to pay federal and state unemployment tax.

As employers, firms incur current **payroll-related liabilities** from two different sources:

- **Employer** taxes paid, including the employer share of FICA, FUTA, and SUTA. The employer recognizes a **payroll tax expense** for these costs (liabilities are also recognized as the costs have not yet been paid)
- When **employees** earn wages, an employer must deduct from those wages the applicable amount of income tax withholding and the employee share of FICA. These amounts deducted from the employee's gross wages are **liabilities** until they are remitted to the government (as the employer is just acting as a collector for the government)
    - The employer will also recognize **wage expense** for the employee's net wages

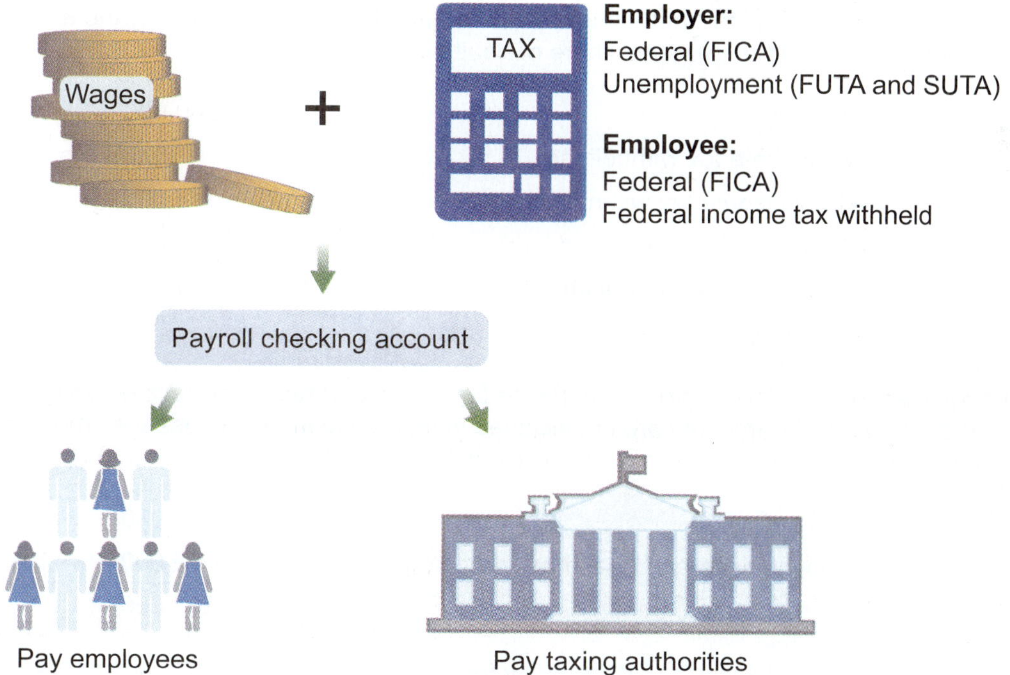

An employer reported gross payroll of $60,000 for the month of November (gross pay limits for some employees have been exceeded). Relevant information for the salaries follows:

- Health insurance premiums: $3,000, 1/3 paid by employees
- FICA tax: 7.65% each for employee and employer, only $40,000 of gross pay subject to tax
- State income tax withholding: $2,000 (based on withholding tables)
- Federal income tax withholding: $18,000 (based on withholding tables)
- SUTA: 5%, only $20,000 of gross pay subject to tax
- FUTA: 1%, only $20,000 of gross pay subject to tax

Based on the tax rates and information provided, prepare the payroll-related journal entries.

The employer will withhold income tax from the employees, to be paid to the state and federal government later, for $2,000 and $18,000, respectively. The employer will also deduct the employees' share of FICA tax from the employees' paychecks, to be paid to the federal government later, for $3,060 ($40,000 limit × 7.65%). Finally, the employer will accrue a liability for both its portion and the employees' portion of the employees' health insurance.

Account	Debit	Credit
Salary or wage expense	62,000**	
State income tax withholding payable		2,000
Federal income tax withholding payable		18,000
FICA tax payable		3,060
Health insurance payable		3,000
Cash (net pay) or wages payable (net)		35,940*

*Cash (net pay) or wages payable (net) is how much the employer will actually pay the employees (after considering taxes and employees' share of health insurance):

Gross pay	$60,000
State income tax withholding	(2,000)
Federal income tax withholding	(18,000)
FICA tax	(3,060)
Employees' share of health insurance ($3,000 × 1/3)	(1,000)
Cash (net pay) or wages payable (net)	$35,940

** Salary or wage expense is the employer's expense for wages and the employer's portion of employee health insurance. Note: tax amounts are not included in this calculation because the employer simply remits the tax to the government. No expense is incurred related to the employees' portion of the taxes.

Gross pay	$60,000
Employer's share of health insurance ($3,000 × 2/3)	2,000
Salary or wage expense	$62,000

The employer will also record liabilities for the employer's portion of FICA, FUTA, and SUTA tax, with a corresponding entry to payroll tax expense (as this is the amount of tax the employer owes to the government).

Account	Debit	Credit
Payroll tax expense	4,260	
FICA tax payable ($40,000 limit × 7.65%)		3,060
FUTA tax payable ($20,000 limit × 1%)		200
SUTA tax payable ($20,000 limit × 5%)		1,000

Accrued Vacation Pay

In addition to regular pay, many employees are entitled to future **compensated absences**, such as vacation. Generally, a company will report a liability for vacation pay if all four of the following conditions are met:

Requirements to Accrue Vacation Pay

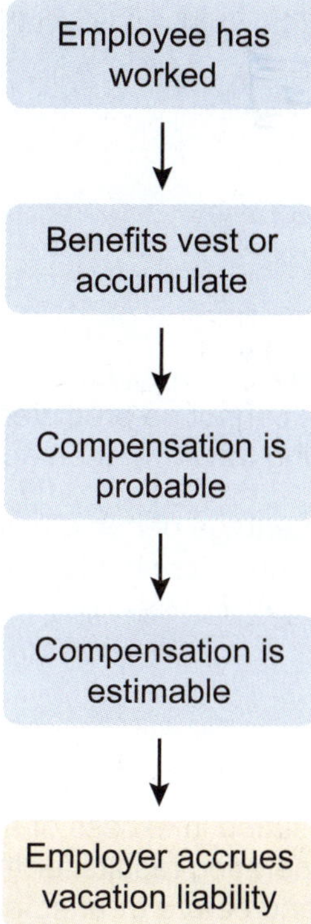

When employees have performed services, the employees are typically allotted a specific number of days off with compensation, which should be computed at the wage rate expected to be in effect when these days are utilized. If wage rates are adjusted, the liability should also be adjusted.

The recognition of costs is required if the vacation days *accumulate or vest*. **Accumulation** means that days not taken in the current period may be used in a future period. Accumulated vacation days are almost certain to be used by an employee at some time if they are in danger of losing them. **Vesting** means that days not used will be paid in cash at the time of the employee's termination of service with the company.

The journal entries to record accrued vacation are as follows:

Accrued Vacation Journal Entries

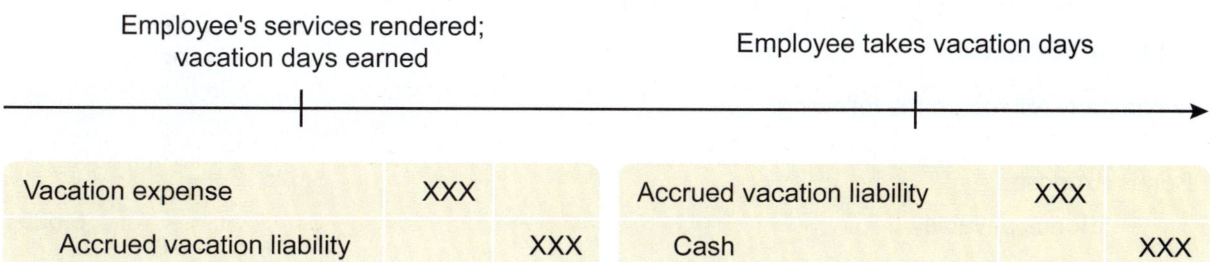

A company pays its employees an average of $100 per day. There are 50 unused vacation days at 12/31/Year 1, which accumulate but do not vest. The company is giving a 10% raise to all employees, effective 1/1/Year 2. Determine the amount that the company should accrue for vacation liability.

The vacation must be accrued because all four required conditions have been met: (1) the employees have worked, (2) the benefits accumulate, (3) the compensation is probable, and (4) the amount can be estimated. The amount of the accrual will be based on an average pay of $110 per day ($100 × 110% wage increase) because the 10% raise will be in effect when the days are utilized. The accrual is $5,500 ($110 per day × 50 unused days).

Vacation expense	5,500	
Accrued vacation liability		5,500

Compensated absences also include **sick pay**. Accumulated sick pay benefits may not be accrued, because the event causing payment (illness) cannot be predicted. However, if unused sick pay benefits are **routinely paid** to employees (eg, upon leaving the firm), then accrual is required because the benefits **vest**.

Companies often estimate that a certain percentage of benefits earned each year will *not* be paid (because the employees will let the benefits lapse). Companies should only report compensated absences liability for the benefits *expected to be paid*.

Accrued Bonuses

A **bonus** is an additional amount of compensation in excess of a base salary. Frequently, liabilities related to bonus compensation are dependent on operating results for the accounting period. The bonus may be based on income before or after the bonus and before or after income tax effects.

With bonus calculations, there are often two unknown variables. An equation can be used to help solve these questions.

An employee's bonus is based on operating income after income taxes but before deducting the bonus. Operating income before bonus and taxes is $90,000, the bonus rate is 10%, and the tax rate is 40%. Record the journal entry for bonus payable.

Let *B = bonus*, *T = tax amount*. The bonus is calculated as follows:

Step 1: B = 10% × ($90,000 − T)

Step 2: T = 40% × ($90,000 − B)

Step 3: B = 10% × ($90,000 − [40% × ($90,000 − B)])

Step 4: B = $5,625

The company will record the following:

Bonus expense	5,625	
Bonus payable		5,625

Note: Multiple-choice questions may require a calculation such as the one above. To save time, instead of solving for B, each answer choice can be plugged into the Step 3 formula. The answer that computes correctly is the correct answer.

Self-Insurance Liabilities

Companies often use insurance to protect them from exposure to various types of risk. However, a company may instead choose to bear the risk itself and set aside funds as a form of **self-insurance**. Self-insurance is essentially no insurance.

A company will generally take on self-insurance risk for one of the following reasons:

- The type of coverage needed is not available
- The company believes it can administer the insurance coverage at a lower cost

A company may self-insure related to insurance policy deductibles, liabilities that are not covered under insurance due to policy requirements, etc.

Self-insured amounts should be estimated and recorded according to ASC 450. The liability that a company records is based on the total cost for both asserted and unasserted claims. The journal entry to record self-insurance is as follows:

Estimated or actual loss	XX	
Estimated or actual payable		XX

Liabilities from Exit or Disposal Activities

Representative Task (Application): Identify and calculate liabilities arising from exit or disposal activities (eg, one-time termination benefits, severance arrangements) and determine the timing of recognition in the financial statements.

When a company engages in activities to **exit or dispose** of a division or product line, a liability is *generally* recognized in the period incurred. The commitment to an exit or disposal plan, by itself, is insufficient to recognize a liability. Recall that a liability should only be recognized when both of the following conditions are met:

- The company has a present obligation
- The obligation requires the company to transfer or otherwise provide economic benefits to others

On the **balance sheet**, the liability associated with an exit or disposal activity is initially measured at fair value, *except for* liabilities for one-time employee termination benefits that incur over time. Revisions resulting from changes in estimates (eg, timing changes, cash-flow updates) are accounted for by adjusting the liability for the cumulative effect of the change during the period that the change is made.

- If employees who were expected to be terminated during the minimum retention period are retained and render service beyond the retention period, the previously recognized liability should be adjusted to an amount based on the fair value as of the termination date (ie, the amount that would have been recognized)
- Changes resulting from the passage of time cause an increase in the carrying amount of the liability and recognition of an expense (eg, accretion expense)

On the **income statement**, costs associated with an exit or disposal activity may be reported as part of discontinued operations or as income from continuing operations, if the activity is not related to a discontinued operation.

Examples of costs associated with exit or disposal activities include the following:

- Involuntary employee termination benefits
- Costs to terminate a contract that is not a capital lease
- Costs to consolidate or close facilities and relocate employees

One-Time Termination Benefit

A **one-time termination benefit** arises if the termination plan meets certain criteria and has been **communicated to employees**. It is accrued when all of the following criteria are met:

- Management commits to a plan of termination
- The plan identifies the number of employees to be terminated, their job classifications or functions and their locations, and the expected completion date
- The plan establishes the benefits that employees will receive upon termination and the amount of benefits that they will receive if they are involuntarily terminated
- It is unlikely that significant changes to the plan will be made or that the plan will be withdrawn

The amount and timing for recognition of a liability for one-time employee termination benefits depend on the following:

- Whether employees are required to render service until they are terminated in order to receive the termination benefits
- If employees are required to render service until they are terminated, whether employees will be retained to render service beyond a minimum retention period (typically 60 days)

Recognition of a Liability for One-Time Employee Termination Benefits

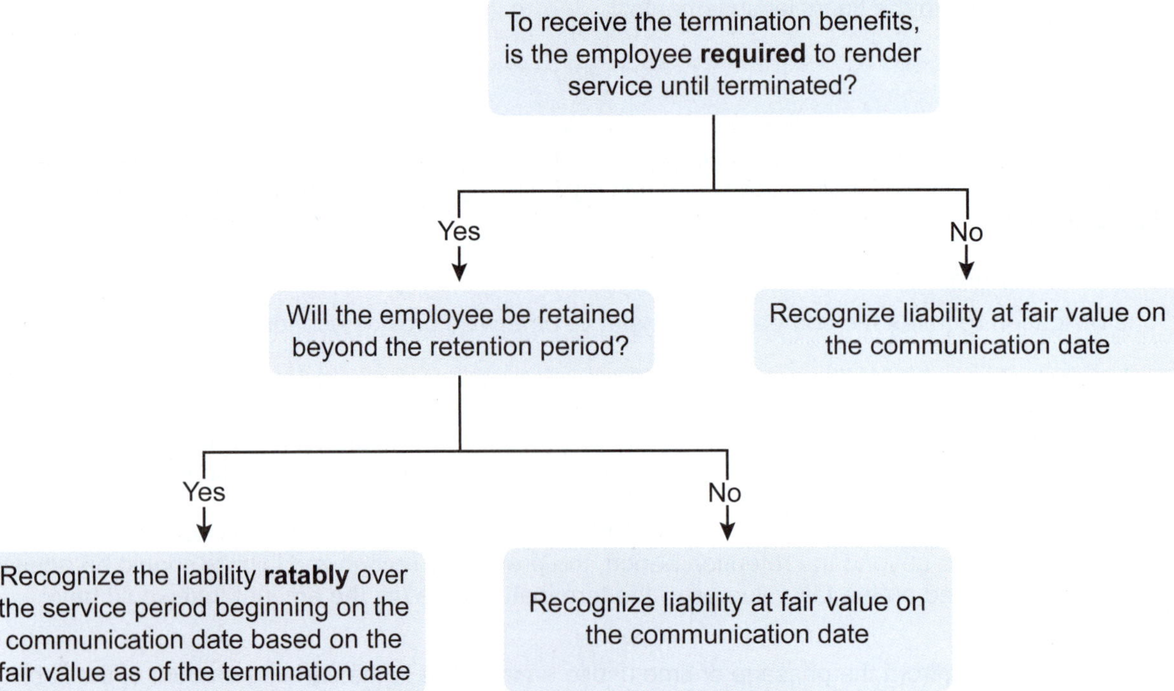

A company has operations in four cities in Texas and plans to cease operations in one of those cities. The 100 employees who currently work at that location will no longer be needed. The employees are notified that they will be terminated in 120 days. Employees are *not* required to render services until terminated. Each employee will receive a termination benefit payment of $8,000, which will be paid on the date that an employee ceases rendering service during the 120-day period.

Assume that all of the criteria for a one-time termination benefit have been met. Determine how the liability will be recognized.

Because the employees may cease to render service at any time during the 120-day period (ie, rendering services until termination is not required), the **liability** would be recognized at fair value on the communication date in the amount of **$800,000** (100 employees × $8,000 termination benefit).

A company plans to shut down a manufacturing facility in 16 months and terminate any remaining employees at the facility. Employees who remain until the facility is shut down will receive a one-time stay bonus. Each employee who stays and renders service for the full 16-month period will receive as a termination benefit payment of $10,000, which will be paid six months after the termination date. If an employee decides to leave before the facility is shut down, the employee will not be eligible to receive any of the termination benefit. Based on a present value calculation, the fair value of the liability as of the termination date is estimated to be $962,240.

Assume that all of the criteria for a one-time termination benefit have been met. Determine how the liability will be recognized.

Employees are *required* to render service and will be retained beyond the retention period; therefore, the **liability is recognized ratably** in each month for the next 16 months (ie, future service period) in the amount of **$60,140** ($962,240 / 16 months).

After eight months, the number of employees who have left voluntarily exceeds the original estimate. Based on revising the expectations, the company adjusts the fair value of the liability as of the termination date to $769,792.

Based on these revised estimates, determine the amount that should be recognized for the liability.

If the $769,792 estimate were initially used, a **liability of $48,112** ($769,792 / 16 months) *would have been recognized* for each month of the service period.

An adjustment to the existing liability must be recorded based on the revised estimate. Given the original estimate, a total liability of $481,120 ($60,140 × 8 months) has been recognized to date and should be reduced to $384,896 ($48,112 × 8 months). A $96,224 ($481,120 − 384,896) adjustment should be made to the existing liability.

A liability of $48,112 should be recognized in each month for the remaining service periods.

Severance Arrangement

A **severance arrangement** is a specific benefit plan for involuntary termination benefits. If the benefits are part of an *ongoing written or substantive plan* (ie, a severance arrangement) rather than related to a one-time benefit arrangement, the severance benefit is accrued when it is **probable and reasonably estimated**.

Many companies have a written postemployment benefit plan for involuntarily terminated employees. If this plan is mutually understood by employer and employee, then such benefits are accrued when payment is probable and reasonably estimable.

If no such written plan exists but a history of paying these types of severance benefits exists, such benefits can still be accrued when payment is probable and reasonably estimable. Otherwise, any termination benefits would be accounted for as a one-time termination benefit when payments are agreed on.

In general, severance benefits provided pursuant to an ongoing plan (ie, a severance arrangement) are accrued when probable and reasonably estimable. One-time termination benefits cannot be accrued until the terms of the benefit arrangement have been communicated to the affected employees and may need to be spread over a future service period through the termination date.

Asset Retirement Obligations

Representative Task (Remembering & Understanding): Recall the recognition and measurement requirements for asset retirement obligations.

An asset retirement obligation (ARO) is a legal obligation associated with the retirement of a tangible, long-lived asset. AROs are expected to be paid at the end of the period of usage. Examples of AROs include the following:

- Cost of dismantling an asset
- Removal of an asset
- Site reclamation
- Nuclear decommissioning
- Closing mines

The costs are incurred at the end of the asset's life but are capitalized when they become estimable, often at the beginning of the asset's useful life.

An ARO should be initially recorded as a liability at **fair value**. This is the amount at which the obligation could be settled today. If fair value cannot be determined, an estimate should be made based on the **present value of the expected future costs** using credit-adjusted risk-free rate of return.

The journal entry to initially record the ARO is as follows:

Long-lived asset	XXX	
ARO liability		XXX

Each year, the ARO liability is increased based on the discount rate. This increase is reported as accretion expense. Accretion is the growth of the liability over time so that when the liability is satisfied, it is reported at its total nondiscounted value.

When the ARO is initially recorded, total depreciation or depletion over the long-lived asset's life increases by the amount of the ARO capitalized. Each year, the net book value of the long-lived asset declines through depreciation or depletion.

The following flowchart can be used in accounting for AROs:

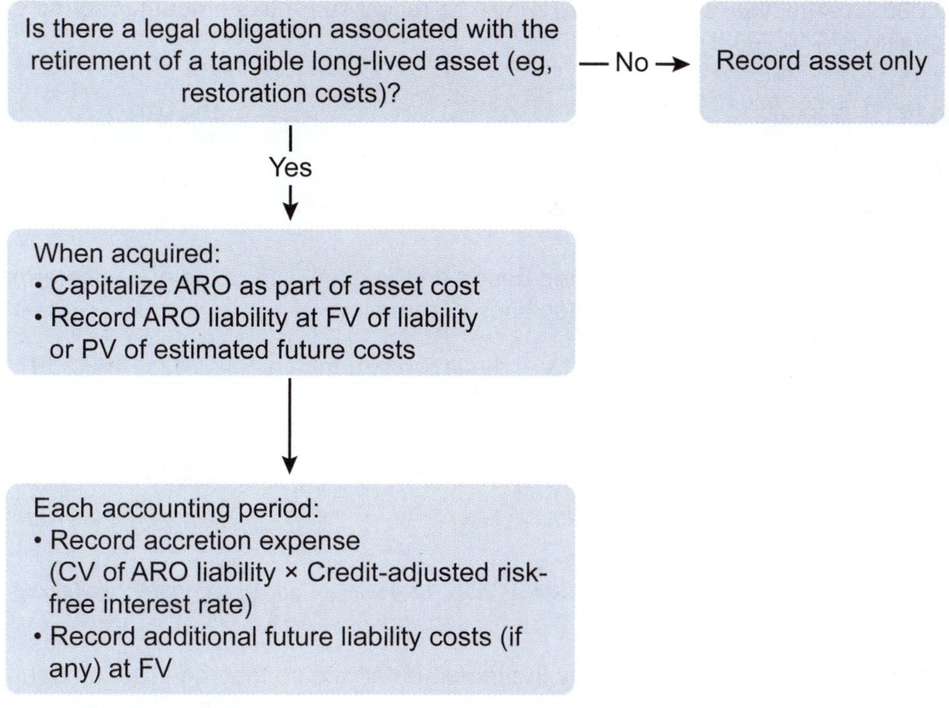

Certain disclosures are required with AROs. These disclosures include the following:

- Description of the obligation and related asset
- Description of how fair value was determined
- The funding policy
- A reconciliation of the beginning and ending carrying value

On 1/1/Year 1, a firm opened a mine with a capitalized cost of $400,000 (before considering any ARO). After the firm is done operating the mine, the firm is legally required to close the mine for the safety of the surrounding community and to reclaim the land for environmental purposes. Operations are expected to cease at the end of Year 12, at which time the closing and reclamation costs will be incurred.

It is estimated that it will cost approximately $20,000 to close the mine and reclaim the land.

Assume that a discount rate of 6% is considered appropriate and that the present value of $1 at 6% for 12 years is 0.496969. Determine the initial entry that the firm will record related to the mine.

Amounts in the solution below are rounded for simplicity.

The $20,000 of costs to close the mine and reclaim the land have a present value (ie, an estimated fair value) of $20,000 × 0.496969 = $9,939. An ARO will be recorded for this amount. The mine will have a total carrying value of $409,939:

Mine ($400,000 + 9,939)	409,939	
Cash		400,000
ARO liability		9,939

Each period, straight-line depletion is recorded based on the useful life of the mine. Determine the entry that the firm will record in Year 1 related to depletion of the mine.

The mine has a useful life of 12 years; therefore, depletion expense is $34,162 ($409,939 / 12 years) each year:

Depletion expense	34,162	
Accumulated depreciation		34,162

Note: The annual depletion expense includes $828 ($9,939 / 12 years) of depletion on the capitalized closing and reclamation costs.

Each period, the ARO liability is increased by the incremental rate so that the initial amount recorded in the ARO account grows to its future value. Determine the entry that the firm will record in Year 1 related to this increase.

The ARO will accrete at a rate of 6% per year. In the first year, this will lead to accretion expense of $596 ($9,939 × 6%).

Accretion expense	596	
ARO liability		596

At the end of Year 12, the mine will be fully depleted (ie, the carrying value will be zero), and the ARO will have a carrying value of $20,000. When the company pays the costs to close the mine and reclaim the land, the following journal entry will be recorded:

ARO liability	20,000	
Cash		20,000

The T-account for AROs is as follows:

Asset Retirement Obligation	
	Beg. balance
Payments to satisfy obligation	New obligations at FV
	Adjustment for accretion expense to increase to future value
	End. balance

FV = fair value

Reconciliation of Subledger to General Ledger

Representative Task (Analysis): Reconcile and investigate differences between the subledger and general ledger for accounts payable and accrued liabilities to determine whether an adjustment is necessary.

Recall that the **general ledger** is the central **record-keeping** system for an entity's **accounting transactions**. Account balances in the general ledger are supported by **detailed account records** kept in separate subsidiary ledgers (ie, **subledgers**). General ledger balances are reported in the entity's financial statements (F/S).

Example

Tastie Bakery & Deli, Inc., hires an accounting firm to audit Tastie's financial statements as of October 31, Year 3. You are the staff accountant tasked with ensuring that accounts payable are accurately reported. Evaluate the supporting documentation, investigate differences, and reconcile the accounts payable subledger to the general ledger. Exhibits are given first, and then the solution will follow.

Exhibits

Exhibit 1: Unadjusted Accounts Payable Subledger

Tastie Bakery and Deli, Inc.
Accounts payable by vendor subledger detail (unadjusted)

For the period October 1, Year 3 to October 31, Year 3

Date	Inv #	Vendor	Total invoice	Due date	Balance due	Payment date	Payment	Balance
9/30								1,250
10/1	18942	Best Food Service	1,895	10/11	0	10/11	1,895	1,250
10/1	18942	Best Food Service	1,895	10/11	1,895			3,145
10/7	1452	Creamy Dairy	5,015	11/7	5,015			8,160
10/15	63995	Paper Products	985	10/25	0	10/25	985	8,160
10/27	28866	Spices and More	750	11/8	750	10/31	500	8,410
10/30	19001	Best Food Service	5,500	11/10	5,500			13,910
10/31	652	Service Distributors	950	11/9	950			14,860

Exhibit 2: Excerpt from Unadjusted General Ledger

Tastie Bakery and Deli, Inc.
General ledger excerpt (unadjusted)

Date	Description	Debit	Credit	Balance
Oct 1	Beginning balance			1,250
Oct 1	Invoice 18942		1,895	3,145
Oct 7	Invoice 1452		5,015	8,160
Oct 11	Payment 18942	1,895		6,265
Oct 15	Invoice 63995		985	7,250
Oct 25	Payment 63995	985		6,265
Oct 30	Invoice 19001		5,500	11,765

Exhibit 3: Email Regarding Best Food Service

From: AccountsPayable@Tastie.com
To: StaffAccountant@AccountingFirm.com
Sent: November 4, Year 3
Subject: Duplicate Invoice

Staff Accountant:

As requested in your last email, we investigated invoice #18942 from Best Food Service further. We can confirm that this invoice was accidentally posted twice to the accounts payable subledger on October 1, Year 3. The transaction should only be posted once. The single posting to the general ledger for $1,895 is correct. We will make the correction to the accounts payable subledger as soon as possible.

Accounts Payable

Exhibit 4: Email Regarding Spices And More

From: AccountsPayable@Tastie.com
To: StaffAccountant@AccountingFirm.com
Sent: November 5, Year 3
Subject: Spices and More Invoice

Staff Accountant:

Thank you for reaching out regarding the Spices and More invoice. As mentioned in our conversation earlier today, Spices and More is a new vendor for Tastie. It appears that the $750 new vendor invoice (#28866) and $500 payment on this invoice were not included in the posting to the general ledger. This was the result of a processing error, and we truly apologize for the error.

Accounts Payable

Exhibit 5: Email Regarding Service Distributors

From: AccountsPayable@Tastie.com
To: StaffAccountant@AccountingFirm.com
Sent: November 6, Year 3
Subject: AP Cutoff

Staff Accountant:

We appreciate you bringing the issue with invoice #652 to our attention. We believe that the cutoff for month-end accounts payable transactions was one day too early. Transactions were transferred to the general ledger as of October 30, rather than October 31. As a result, the general ledger did not include the invoice from Service Distributors in the amount of $950. We apologize for the error.

Accounts Payable

Task: Reconcile the accounts payable subledger to the general ledger. Complete the below reconciliation by selecting the necessary adjustments in columns B and D and entering the necessary adjustment amount in columns C and E. Enter positive values as positive whole numbers and negative values as negative whole numbers.

Possible adjustments are listed in the menu below:

Select An Option Below:

- Add duplicate invoice 18942
- Add invoice 63995
- Subtract debit memo
- Subtract payment on invoice 28866
- Subtract invoice 652
- Add credit memo
- Subtract duplicate invoice 18942
- Add invoice 652
- Subtract invoice 63995
- Add invoice 28866

A	B	C	D	E
B	Accounts payable subledger original balance	$14,860	General ledger original balance	$11,765
C				
D				
E				
F	Accounts payable subledger adjusted balance		General ledger adjusted balance	

Steps to Completing the Task

It is important to make sure that the total of the items in the subledger matches to the corresponding account in the general ledger by performing a reconciliation that compares the subledger to the general ledger to identify any discrepancies. Generally, the reconciliation process follows these steps:

- Compare the ending balances of the general ledger to the subledger
- Identify any differences by confirming beginning balances (for balance sheet accounts), ensuring that daily postings from the subledger to the general ledger match, and researching any nonrecurring or unusual transactions
- Investigate reasons for the differences. Typically, these are errors or items posted in the general ledger and not the subledger or vice versa
- Adjust the appropriate ledger
- Compare adjusted balances

Identify Differences

There is a $3,095 discrepancy between the ending balances at October 31, Year 3:

Balance per unadjusted subledger	$14,860
Balance per general ledger	11,765
Difference	$3,095

Because the beginning balances agree between the subledger and general ledger at October 1, identify the differences in transactions that occurred during the month:

- The accounts payable subledger records two identical invoices (invoice 18942) for Best Food Service.
- The accounts payable subledger records invoice 28866 for Spices and More in the amount of $750 and a subsequent payment of $500. This invoice and payment do not appear on the general ledger
- The accounts payable subledger records invoice 652 for Service Distributors in the amount of $950. This invoice does not appear on the general ledger

Investigate Reasons and Adjust Ledgers

Exhibits 3, 4, and 5 provide more information regarding the differences. To rectify this discrepancy, the following adjustments are required:

Adjustments to subledger:

Subtract duplicate invoice 18942: The email from the accounts payable department regarding Best Food Service (Exhibit 3) confirms that the duplicate posting was made in error. Therefore, the amount of the duplicate posting, $1,895, needs to be subtracted from the subledger.

Adjustments to general ledger:

Add invoice 28866: The email from the accounts payable department regarding Spices and More (Exhibit 4) confirms that the entry was missing from the general ledger due to a processing error. Therefore, the amount of $750 needs to be added to the general ledger.

Subtract payment on invoice 28866: The email from the accounts payable department regarding Spices and More (Exhibit 4) confirms that the invoice and payment were not recorded on the general ledger due to a processing error. Therefore, the amount of $500 needs to be subtracted from the unadjusted general ledger to account for the payment on invoice 28866.

Add invoice 652: The email from the accounts payable department regarding Service Distributors (Exhibit 5) confirms that the entry was missing from the general ledger due to a cutoff error. Therefore, the amount of $950 needs to be added to the general ledger.

Completed Reconciliation:

A	B	C	D	E
B	Accounts payable subledger original balance	$14,860	General ledger original balance	$11,765
C	Subtract duplicate invoice 18942	(1,895)	Add invoice 28866	750
D			Subtract payment on invoice 28866	(500)
E			Add invoice 652	950
F	Accounts payable subledger adjusted balance	$12,965	General ledger adjusted balance	$12,965

Compare Adjusted Balances

Tastie Bakery and Deli, Inc.
Accounts payable by vendor subledger detail (adjusted)
For the period October 1, Year 3 to October 31, Year 3

Date	Inv #	Vendor	Total invoice	Due date	Balance due	Payment date	Payment	Balance
9/30								1,250
10/1	18942	Best Food Service	1,895	10/11	0	10/11	1,895	1,250
10/7	1452	Creamy Dairy	5,015	11/7	5,015			6,265
10/15	63995	Paper Products	985	10/25	0	10/25	985	6,265
10/27	28866	Spices and More	750	11/8	750	10/31	500	6,515
10/30	19001	Best Food Service	5,500	11/10	5,500			12,015
10/31	652	Service Distributors	950	11/9	950			12,965

Tastie Bakery and Deli, Inc.
General ledger excerpt (adjusted)

Date	Description	Debit	Credit	Balance
Oct 1	Beginning balance			1,250
Oct 1	Invoice 18942		1,895	3,145
Oct 7	Invoice 1452		5,015	8,160
Oct 11	Payment 18942	1,895		6,265
Oct 15	Invoice 63995		985	7,250
Oct 25	Payment 63995	985		6,265
Oct 27	Invoice 28866		750	7,015
Oct 30	Invoice 19001		5,500	12,515
Oct 31	Payment 28866	500		12,015
Oct 31	Invoice 652		950	12,965

Reconciling differences for **accrued liabilities** involves a similar process. Accrued liabilities often also require a review of journal entries (eg, accruals for interest payable, adjustments to unearned revenue).

FAR 14
Debt (Financial Liabilities)

FAR 14: Debt (Financial Liabilities)

14.01 Notes and Bonds Payable

Representative Task (Application): Calculate the carrying amount of notes and bonds payable and prepare journal entries.

Representative Task (Application): Calculate the interest expense attributable to notes and bonds payable reported in the financial statements (eg, discounts, premiums, debt issuance costs).

Bonds Payable

A **bond** is a debt security issued to investors willing to lend money to the issuer for a certain period of time. In return, the issuer promises to pay interest over the life of the bond and repay the principal (ie, par value) when the bond matures.

Bonds are classified by characteristics, including the following:

Bond Classifications	
Maturity Pattern	• Term bond: single maturity date at end of term • Serial bond: matures in stated amounts at regular intervals
Secured vs. Unsecured	• Debentures: backed by borrower's general credit • Collateralized: backed by specific assets
Ownership	• Registered: issued to specific owner • Bearer (coupon bonds): not registered
Redemption	• Callable: bonds can be repurchased by issuer before maturity • Convertible: bonds can be converted into equity securities at the option of the buyer • Sinking: bonds can be repurchased in limited quantities periodically at specified prices

To account for a bond, the following information must be known:

- **Face (or maturity) value:** The amount to be paid to the bondholder at maturity. This is also called the bond principal
- **Stated (or coupon) interest rate:** The contractual rate listed in the bond. This is the rate at which the bond pays cash interest
- **Interest payment dates:** The dates that the bond pays cash interest

- **Yield (or market or effective) rate:** The rate that investors demand to earn for loaning their money. This rate is also the rate of return for comparable bonds (it is determined by the market)
- **Issuance date:** The date that the bonds are issued
- **Maturity date:** The date that the maturity value is paid, the end of the bond term
  - The time from the issuance date to the maturity date is called the **bond term**

The portion of a bond payable that will not be paid within the upcoming year is classified as a **noncurrent liability** on the balance sheet. The portion that will be paid within the upcoming year is classified as a **current liability**.

Selling Price

The **selling price of a bond** is equal to the present value (PV) of future cash flows from the bond's principal and interest. This is the amount of cash that the bond issuer will receive today (also called bond proceeds). In calculating the PV, the **market interest rate** is used. Interest rates and time periods should reflect the schedule of the bond. Interest rates are typically expressed annually and will need to be adjusted. For example, if interest on a bond is due semiannually:

Interest rate is calculated as:	Time period is calculated as:
Annual rate / 2	Years × 2

To calculate the PV of the principal, the PV of $1 should be used. To calculate the PV of the interest, the PV of an annuity should be used.

- If the interest is due at the *beginning* of each period, the PV of an annuity due (or annuity in arrears) is used
- If the interest is due at the *end* of each period, the PV of an ordinary annuity is used

Interest Expense

Interest expense on debt is recorded in the period incurred (time period the debt was outstanding). Interest rates on debt are (by default) expressed as annual rates, even if the term of the debt is less than one year. Under the effective interest method, periodic interest expense is calculated as follows:

Bond payable outstanding balance × Market rate × Time (eg, fraction of year elapsed)

To reflect proper matching, interest expense that has been accrued but not yet paid on bonds payable is recorded each reporting period.

Bonds Issued at Par

If the stated interest rate is equal to the market interest rate, the bonds are **issued at par** (or face value). There is no discount or premium on the bond payable. Interest expense recorded in the financial statements (F/S) will be equal to the amount of interest paid (or payable) each period.

On 1/1/Year 1, Michigan Co. issued a 10%, $1,000,000 bond due in four years. Interest on the bond is due semiannually (on June 30 and December 31). The yield rate is also 10%.

- PV of $1 at 5% for eight periods*: 0.6768394
- PV of annuity at 5% for eight periods*: 6.4632128

Determine the journal entries that Michigan would record on 1/1/Year 1 and 6/30/Year 1.

The PV of future payments is calculated based on cash interest and principal. Cash interest is equal to the face value × stated rate. Each period, the bond pays $50,000 interest ($1,000,000 × 5%*). The bond returns the principal of $1,000,000 at maturity.

PV of future payments:

Principal	$1,000,000 × 0.6768394	≈	$ 676,839
Interest	$50,000 × 6.4632128	≈	323,161
			$1,000,000**

For bonds that are issued at par, the **PV of future payments is equal to the face value**.

**Because the bond pays semiannually, the interest rate used is 5% (annual rate of 10% / 2), and the time period used is eight (four years × 2).*

***Amounts have been rounded for simplicity.*

On 1/1/Year 1, Michigan will record the following:

Cash	1,000,000	
Bonds payable		1,000,000

Interest:

Each period, Michigan will **pay cash interest and record interest expense**. Because the bond is issued at par, interest expense equals the amount of cash paid.

Date	Carrying value	×	Interest rate	=	Interest expense	Cash payment
6/30/Year 1	$1,000,000	×	5%	=	$50,000	$50,000
12/31/Year 1	$1,000,000	×	5%	=	$50,000	$50,000
6/30/Year 2	$1,000,000	×	5%	=	$50,000	$50,000

For bonds issued at par, the carrying value on the balance sheet does not change each period.

On 6/30/Year 1, Michigan will record the following:

Interest expense	50,000	
Cash		50,000

This is the same entry that will be recorded each period until the end of the bond term. At the end of the bond term, Michigan will repay the principal amount of $1,000,000.

Bonds Issued at a Discount or Premium

Issued at a Discount

When bonds are issued, they have a stated coupon rate that remains constant over the bond's life. For bonds to be competitively priced with investments providing better returns, the price is adjusted to effectively yield the market rate.

This creates an inverse relationship between market interest rates and bond prices. As market rates increase, the bond price decreases, and vice versa.

- When the stated rate is below the market rate (ie, 12% market rate > 10% coupon), it is priced at a **discount**
- When the stated rate is greater than the market rate (ie, 10% coupon > 8% market rate), it is priced at a **premium**

For example, if a bond has a stated rate of 10% and the market rate is 12%, the seller essentially has to put the bond "on sale" (like any other commodity) to be competitive. The seller *discounts* the selling price to make the 10% rate effectively yield a 12% return. Otherwise, their bonds would not be purchased by anyone.

On 1/1/Year 1, Michigan Co. issued a 10%, $1,000,000 bond due in four years. Interest on the bond is due semiannually (on June 30 and December 31). **The yield rate is 12%.**

- PV of $1 at 6% for eight periods*: 0.6274124
- PV of annuity at 6% for eight periods*: 6.2097938

Determine the journal entry that Michigan would record on 1/1/Year 1.

The PV of future payments is calculated based on cash interest and principal. Each period, the bond pays $50,000 interest ($1,000,000 × 5%). The bond pays $1,000,000 at maturity. Note: the cash interest paid did not change from the previous example; because the interest paid is based on the stated rate (and not the market rate), it is not impacted by the market rate and is the same every period.

The cash interest and principal are then discounted at the *market* rate:

PV of future payments:

Principal	$1,000,000 × 0.6274124	≈	627,412
Interest	$50,000 × 6.2097938	≈	310,490
			937,902**

**The yield rate must be used in the PV calculations. Here, the PV factors are different from the previous example because the yield rate has changed.*

***Amounts have been rounded for simplicity.*

The discount is equal to the difference between the face value and the PV of future payments. Here, because the face value is greater than the PV of future payments, the bond is issued at a discount:

$1,000,000 face value − 937,902 PV of future payments = $62,098 discount

The bond is issued at a discount; this means the bond is paying less interest than the market rate. The seller essentially treats the bond like a "discount product" (eg, a used car) and charges less than other bond sellers. The seller will not recognize a loss at the point of sale; rather, the interest expense will be greater every year, so that the "loss" is spread ratably over the bond life.

On 1/1/Year 1, Michigan will record the following:

Cash	937,902	
Discount on bonds payable	62,098	
Bonds payable		1,000,000

The noncurrent liability section of the balance sheet immediately after issuance would disclose the following:

Bonds payable	$1,000,000
Less: Discount on bonds payable	(62,098)
Net bonds payable	$ 937,902

The bond payable is reported as a noncurrent liability because the principal will not be repaid for four years. The bonds payable account is measured at face value. The discount (or premium) accounts are contra (or adjunct) accounts that reduce (or increase) the net liability to the present value.

Issued at a Premium

On 1/1/Year 1, Michigan Co. issued a 10%, $1,000,000 bond due in four years. Interest on the bond is due semiannually (on June 30 and December 31). **The yield rate is 8%.**

- PV of $1 at 4% for eight periods*: 0.7306902
- PV of annuity at 4% for eight periods*: 6.7327449

Determine the journal entry that Michigan would record on 1/1/Year 1.

The PV of future payments is calculated based on cash interest and principal. Each period, the bond pays $50,000 interest ($1,000,000 × 5%). The bond pays $1,000,000 at maturity. Note: the cash interest paid did not change from the previous example; because the interest paid is based on the stated rate (and not the market rate), it is not impacted by the market rate and is the same every period.

The cash interest and principal are then adjusted to reflect the market rate:

PV of future payments:

Principal	$1,000,000 × 0.7306902	≈	730,690
Interest	$50,000 × 6.7327449	≈	336,637
			1,067,327**

**The yield rate must be used in the PV calculations. Here, the PV factors are different from the previous example because the yield rate has changed.*

***Amounts have been rounded for simplicity.*

Here, because the face value is less than the PV of future payments, the bond is issued at a premium:

$1,000,000 face value − 1,067,327 PV of future payments = $67,327 premium

The bond is issued at a premium; this means the bond is paying more interest than the market rate. The seller essentially treats the bond like a "premium product" (eg, a luxury car) and charges more than other bond sellers. The seller will not recognize a gain at the point of sale; rather, the interest expense will be less every year, so that the "gain" is spread ratably over the bond life.

On 1/1/Year 1, Michigan will record the following:

Cash	1,067,327	
Premium on bonds payable		67,327
Bonds payable		1,000,000

The noncurrent liability section of the balance sheet immediately after issuance would disclose the following:

Bonds payable	$1,000,000
Plus: Premium on bonds payable	67,327
Net bonds payable	$1,067,327

Amortization of a Discount or Premium: Effective Interest Method

The discount or premium on a bond issue is **amortized** over the bond term. At the maturity date, the book value of the bond issue must equal face value because that is the amount paid to retire the bonds.

Under GAAP, the amortization of premiums and discounts is accomplished through the use of the **effective interest method**. However, companies are allowed to employ the **straight-line amortization method**. The straight-line method is acceptable only if the *results do not depart materially from the effective interest method*.

Under the effective interest method, interest expense aligns with the carrying value of the bond each period. Under the straight-line method, interest expense is constant each period:

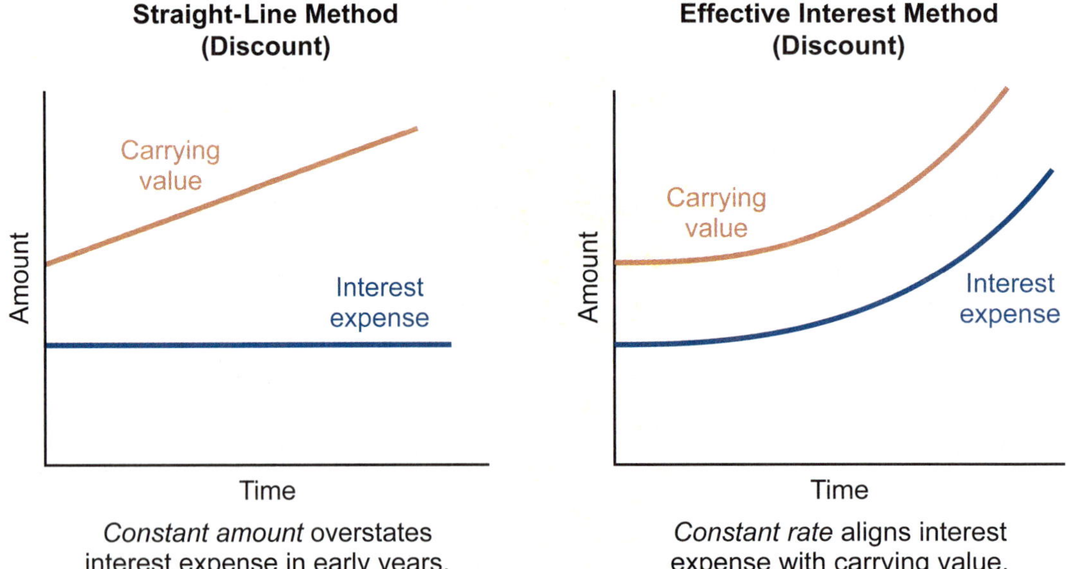

Constant amount overstates interest expense in early years.

Constant rate aligns interest expense with carrying value.

This section covers the effective interest method, and the following section will cover the straight-line method.

On the CPA exam, students are typically asked to amortize the discount or premium using the effective interest method.

As previously mentioned, the amount of cash interest payment on a bond never changes. Interest payable is used in place of cash when the amount of interest for a period has been incurred but not yet paid. Under the effective interest method, when a bond is issued at a discount or premium, **interest expense** changes every period. Interest expense correlates with a bond's carrying value and is calculated as follows:

Bond Interest Expense: Effective Interest Method

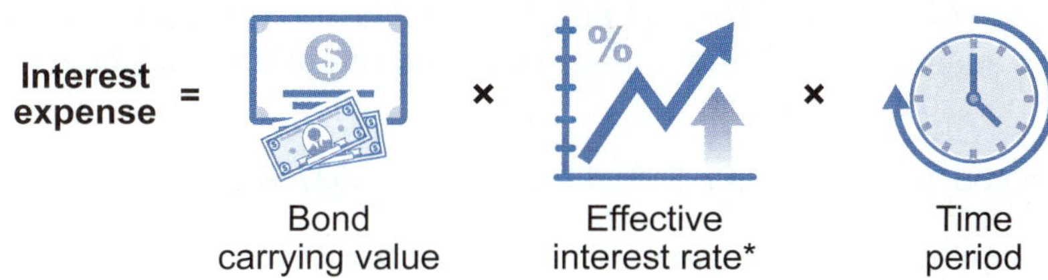

Also called yield or market rate

The market rate at issuance is used to compute interest expense. The rate is not changed after issuance because it represents the true interest rate over the bond term.

The calculated interest expense is then compared to the cash interest paid to calculate the **amortization of the discount or premium**. The amortization of discount or premium is a "plug" figure.

Amortization of a Discount

For a bond issued at a discount, amortization is calculated as follows:

Bond Discount Amortization: Effective Interest Method

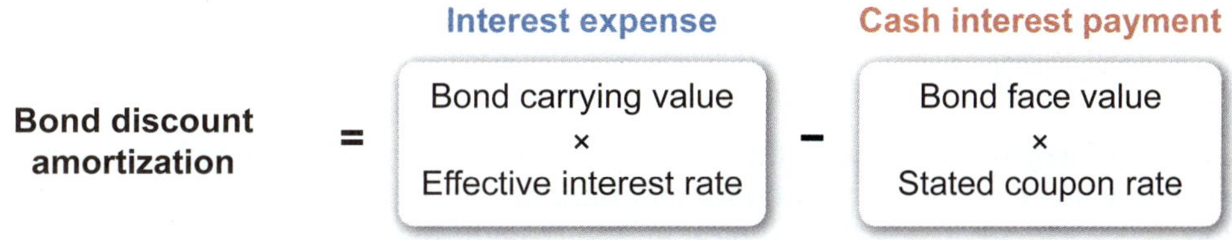

Each period, the **discount amortization** chips away at the unamortized discount account on the balance sheet. The unamortized discount is a **contra account** to bonds payable on the balance sheet. Therefore, the carrying value of the bond is equal to the face value—the unamortized discount. As the discount is amortized, the unamortized portion decreases until, at the end of the bond term, the carrying value of the bond is equal to the face value.

The discount is effectively added to the carrying value of the bond at each reporting period.

Each period, the following journal entry will be recorded:

Interest expense	XX	
Discount on bonds payable		XX
Cash		XX

The unamortized discount is initially recorded as a debit (it is contra account to the bond payable). When the unamortized discount is credited each period, the carrying value of the bond increases.

The initial discount represents additional interest because the borrower must pay back more at maturity than they initially received from bondholders. For bonds issued at a discount, **interest expense is greater than the interest payment** (in total and each period). Total interest expense over the bond term is calculated as follows:

Cash interest paid + Discount

Assume the same facts from the previous discount example:

On 1/1/Year 1, Michigan Co. issued a 10%, $1,000,000 bond due in four years. Interest on the bond is due semiannually (on June 30 and December 31). **The yield rate is 12%**. Michigan uses the effective interest method to amortize the discount.

Recall that the calculated selling price (ie, PV) of the bonds is $937,902.

Determine the journal entries that Michigan would record on 6/30/Year 1 and 12/31/Year 1.

The bond amortization schedule is calculated as follows:

	A	B	C	D	E	F
Date	**Beginning Carrying Value**	**Interest Rate**	**Interest Expense**	**Cash Payment**	**Amortization**	**Ending Carrying Value**
			A × B		C − D	A + E
6/30/Year 1	$937,902	6%	$56,274	$50,000	$6,274	$ 944,176
12/31/Year 1	$944,176	6%	$56,651	$50,000	$6,651	$ 950,827
6/30/Year 2	$950,827	6%	$57,050	$50,000	$7,050	$ 957,877
12/31/Year 4	$990,566	6%	$59,434	$50,000	$9,434	$1,000,000*

**Amounts have been rounded for simplicity.*

Each period, the amortization is added to the carrying value of the bond. For example, at 6/30/Year 1, the bond's carrying value (before accounting for that period's amortization) is $937,902. Amortization is then calculated as $6,274. On the balance sheet at 6/30/Year 1, the ending bond carrying value would be reported as $944,176 ($937,902 + $6,274).

As the discount is amortized (and the unamortized portion decreases), the bond's carrying value gradually increases over time until, at the end of the bond term, it is $1,000,000.

On 6/30/Year 1, Michigan would record the following:

Interest expense	56,274	
Discount on bonds payable		6,274
Cash		50,000

On 12/31/Year 1, Michigan would record the following:

Interest expense	56,651	
Discount on bonds payable		6,651
Cash		50,000

Each entry recognizes a different amount of interest expense and a different amount of discount amortization. However, the ratio of interest expense to beginning carrying value is constant and equals the effective interest rate.

Amortization of a Premium

For a bond issued at a premium, amortization is calculated as follows:

Bond Premium Amortization: Effective Interest Method

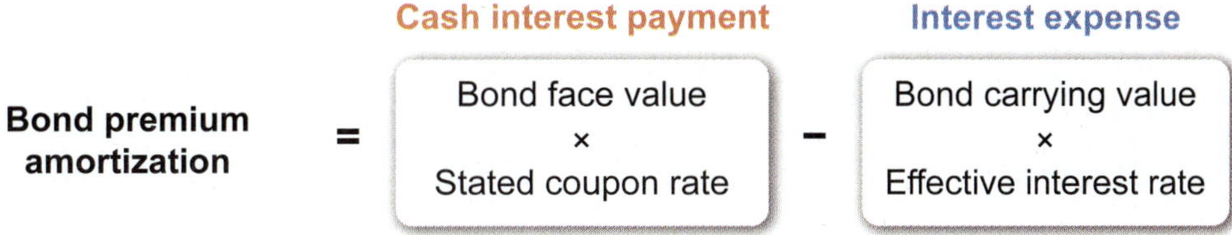

Each period, the **premium amortization** chips away at the unamortized premium account on the balance sheet. The unamortized premium is an adjunct account to bonds payable on the balance sheet. Therefore, the carrying value of the bond is equal to the face value + the unamortized premium. As the premium is amortized, the unamortized portion decreases until, at the end of the bond term, the carrying value of the bond is equal to the face value.

The premium is effectively subtracted from the carrying value of the bond at each reporting period.

Each period, the following journal entry will be recorded:

Interest expense	XX	
Premium on bonds payable	XX	
Cash		XX

The unamortized premium is initially recorded as a credit (it is an adjunct account to the bond payable). When the unamortized premium is debited each period, the carrying value of the bond decreases.

The initial premium represents a reduction in interest because the borrower must pay back less at maturity than they initially received from bondholders. For bonds issued at a premium, **interest expense is less than the interest payment** (in total and each period). Total interest expense over the bond term is calculated as follows:

Cash interest paid − Premium

Assume the same facts from the previous premium example:

On 1/1/Year 1, Michigan Co. issued a 10%, $1,000,000 bond due in four years. Interest on the bond is due semiannually (on June 30 and December 31). **The yield rate is 8%**. Michigan uses the effective interest method to amortize the discount. Recall that the calculated selling price (ie, PV) of the bonds is $1,067,327.

Determine the journal entries that Michigan would record on 6/30/Year 1 and 12/31/Year 1.

The bond amortization schedule is calculated as follows:

	A	B	C	D	E	F
Date	**Beginning Carrying Value**	**Interest Rate**	**Interest Expense**	**Cash Payment**	**Amortization**	**Ending Carrying Value**
			A × B		**D − C**	**A − E**
6/30/Year 1	$1,067,327	4%	$42,693	$50,000	$7,307	$1,060,020
12/31/Year 1	$1,060,020	4%	$42,401	$50,000	$7,599	$1,052,421
6/30/Year 2	$1,052,421	4%	$42,097	$50,000	$7,903	$1,044,518
12/31/Year 4	$1,009,615	4%	$40,385	$50,000	$9,615	$1,000,000*

**Amounts have been rounded for simplicity.*

Each period, the amortization is subtracted from the carrying value of the bond. For example, at 6/30/Year 1, the bond's carrying value (before accounting for that period's amortization) is $1,067,327. Amortization is then calculated as $7,307. On the balance sheet at 6/30/Year 1, the ending bond carrying value would be reported as $1,060,020 ($1,067,327 − $7,307).

As the premium is amortized (and the unamortized portion decreases), the bond's carrying value gradually decreases over time until, at the end of the bond term, it is $1,000,000.

On 6/30/Year 1, Michigan would record the following:

Interest expense	42,693	
Premium on bonds payable	7,307	
Cash		50,000

On 12/31/Year 1, Michigan would record the following:

Interest expense	42,401	
Premium on bonds payable	7,599	
Cash		50,000

Each entry recognizes a different amount of interest expense and a different amount of discount amortization. However, the ratio of interest expense to beginning carrying value is constant and equals the effective interest rate.

Amortization of a Discount or Premium: Straight-Line Method

The **straight-line method** can be used when the results don't differ materially from the effective interest method. Under the straight-line method, **amortization is the same each period** and is calculated as follows:

$$\frac{\text{Discount or premium}}{\text{Number of periods}}$$

Interest expense is a "plug" figure. The bond's carrying value is adjusted each period by the amount of the discount or premium. Regardless of the method used, the same total amount of discount or premium is amortized. At maturity, the total amortization will be the same under both methods.

Assume the same facts from the previous discount example:

On 1/1/Year 1, Michigan Co. issued a 10%, $1,000,000 bond due in four years. Interest on the bond is due semiannually (on June 30 and December 31). **The yield rate is 12%**. Michigan uses the **straight-line method** to amortize the discount.

Recall that the calculated selling price (ie, PV) of the bonds is $937,902, and the discount is $62,098.

Determine the journal entries that Michigan would record on 6/30/Year 1 and 12/31/Year 1.

Each period, the discount will be amortized by $7,762 (rounded):

$$\frac{\$62{,}098}{8\text{ periods}} \approx \$7{,}762$$

The bond amortization schedule is calculated as follows:

	A	B	C	D	E
Date	**Beginning Carrying Value**	**Cash Payment**	**Amortization**	**Interest Expense**	**Ending Carrying Value**
				B + C	**A + C**
6/30/Year 1	$937,902	$50,000	$7,762	$57,762	$ 945,664
12/31/Year 1	$945,664	$50,000	$7,762	$57,762	$ 953,426
6/30/Year 2	$953,426	$50,000	$7,762	$57,762	$ 961,188
12/31/Year 4	$992,236	$50,000	$7,762	$57,762	$1,000,000*

**Amounts have been rounded for simplicity.*

Recall that, when a bond is issued at a discount, interest expense is greater than cash paid. Therefore, the interest expense is equal to the cash payment plus amortization. Similar to the effective interest method, as the discount is amortized, the bond's carrying value gradually increases over time until, at the end of the bond term, it is $1,000,000.

On 6/30/Year 1, Michigan would record the following:

Interest expense	57,762	
Discount on bonds payable		7,762
Cash		50,000

On 12/31/Year 1, Michigan would record the following:

Interest expense	57,762	
Discount on bonds payable		7,762
Cash		50,000

Each entry recognizes the same amount of interest expense and the same amount of discount amortization.

Amortization of a premium under the straight-line method is calculated in a similar manner. However, interest expense is calculated as cash payment *minus* amortization. This is because, with a bond premium, interest expense is *less than* cash paid. Additionally, each period amortization is effectively *subtracted from* the carrying value.

The straight-line method should not be used in either of the following circumstances:

- The term to maturity is long, and there is more than a minor difference between the market and stated rates
- There is a very significant difference between the market and stated rates, regardless of the length of the term

Remember the relationship between interest expense and cash payments:

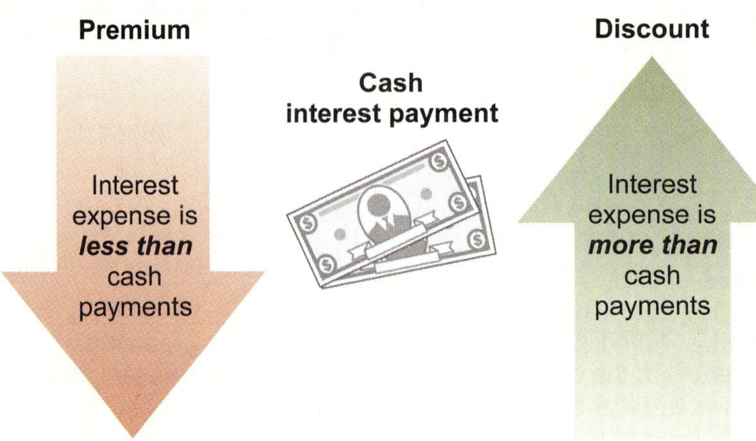

Zero Coupon Bonds

Zero coupon bonds pay no interest (ie, the coupon rate is zero). The accounting for these bonds remains the same, except that no cash is paid during the bond term. The entire amount of interest is included in the face value (similar to a non-interest-bearing note, covered below). GAAP requires that interest is **imputed** on the bond.

On January 1, Year 1, Indiana, Inc., issued $400,000 zero coupon bonds to yield 5%. The bonds mature in 20 years.

PV of $1 at 5% for 20 periods: 0.37689

Determine the journal entries to be recorded by Indiana at 1/1/Year 1 and 12/31/Year 1.

PV of future payments:

$400,000 × 0.37689 ≈ $150,756

Here, because the face value is *significantly more* than the PV of future payments, the bond is issued at a deep discount:

$400,000 face value − 150,756 PV of future payments = $249,244 discount

In order to sell a bond that pays no interest, the seller must significantly decrease the price of the bond so that, effectively, there is a return to the buyer. Here, the buyer pays $150,756 and holds the bond for 20 years with no interest. However, at the end of the 20 years, the buyer receives $400,000 (ie, much more than what they paid initially).

On 1/1/Year 1, Indiana will record the following:

Cash	150,756	
Discount on bonds payable	249,244	
Bonds payable		400,000

Although no interest is paid, in order to abide by the matching principle, interest expense will still be recorded over the life of the bond. Interest expense in the first and second year is calculated as follows:

	A	B	C	D	E	F
Date	Beginning Carrying Value	Interest Rate	Interest Expense	Cash Payment	Amortization	Ending Carrying Value
			A × B		C − D	A + E
12/31/Year 1	$150,756	5%	$7,538	0	$7,538	$158,294
12/31/Year 2	$158,294	5%	$7,915	0	$7,915	$166,209

On 12/31/Year 1, Indiana will record the following:

Interest expense	7,538	
Discount on bonds payable		7,538

Note: The straight-line method would not be appropriate for this type of bond.

Bond Interest Accruals

Bond Issuance between Interest Dates

In some cases, the bond issuance date (ie, the date when the bonds are issued) is different from the bond date (ie, the date listed on the bond). If the bond date precedes the issue date, the purchase amount will include accrued interest because the buyer will receive the entire interest payment in the next scheduled payment. The total cash received by the company issuing the bonds (ie, the bond "proceeds") is calculated as follows:

Selling price of the bond + Interest (at the stated rate) accrued since the last interest date

By requiring the investor to pay the interest accrued since the last interest date, the issuing company can pay the usual amount of interest at the next interest date.

Delaware, LLC, issued $8,000 of 8% bonds on March 1, Year 1. The bonds pay interest each June 30 and December 31 and are dated January 1, Year 1. The yield rate is also 8%, and the bonds mature five years after the bond date.

Determine the entries to be recorded at March 1, June 30, and December 31, Year 1.

The interest paid each period is $320 ($8,000 × [8% / 2]). Because the bonds are issued two months into the first six-month period, 1/3 (ie, 2 months / 6 months) of periodic interest has already accrued at the time the bonds are actually issued:

$$\text{Accrued interest} = \$320 \times 1/3 \approx \$107$$

The bondholders paid Delaware this $107 as part of the bond purchase price. Delaware will pay the bondholders this $107 back as part of the first interest payment.

On March 1, Year 1, Delaware will record the following:

Cash ($8,000 + $107)	8,107	
Accrued interest payable		107
Bonds payable		8,000

On June 30, Year 1, Delaware will record the following:

Interest expense	213	
Accrued interest payable	107	
Cash		320

The cash paid in the first interest payment contains both interest expense and repayment of the accrued interest to the bondholders. The bonds were only outstanding for four months (March–June). Interest expense is still only based on the total time that the bonds were outstanding:

$$\$8{,}000 \times 8\% \times 4/12 \approx \$213$$

On December 31, Year 1, Delaware will record the following:

Interest expense	320	
Cash		320

Year-End Bond Interest Accrual

Interest payments on a bond are made at regularly scheduled intervals according to the bond's terms (eg, semiannually). The **interest payable** at year end is the interest **incurred but not yet paid** (based on the market rate under the effective interest method).

If the bond payment schedule does not align with the bond issuer's reporting period, interest payable will be recorded.

Maine Co. issued $900,000 of 6% bonds on January 1, Year 1. The bonds pay interest each April 1 and October 1. The yield rate is also 6%. The last day of Maine's reporting period is December 31.

Determine the entry to be recorded at December 31, Year 1, and April 1, Year 2.

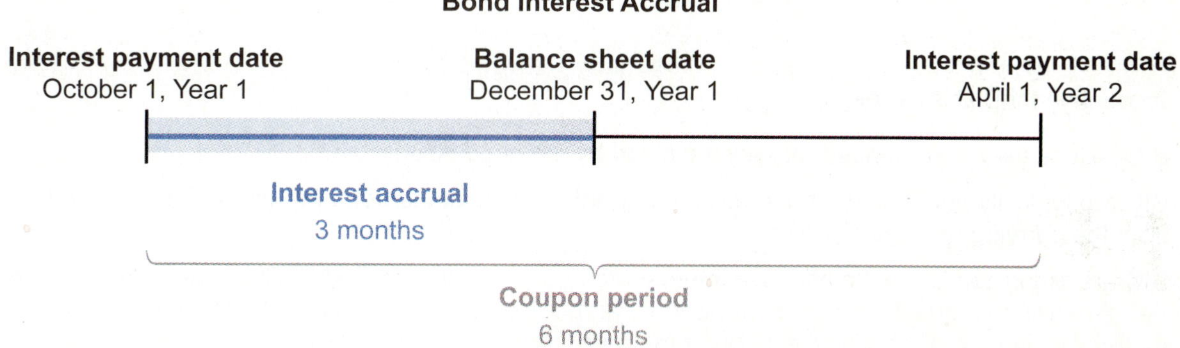

On April 1 and October 1, Maine paid $27,000 ($900,000 × [6% / 2]) of interest. On December 31, Maine will need to accrue interest payable for three months (October–December). This is the interest incurred but not yet paid as of year end:

$$\$900,000 \times 6\% \times 3/12 = \$13,500$$

On December 31, Year 1, Maine will record the following:

Interest expense	13,500	
Accrued interest payable		13,500

On April 1, Maine will pay the $27,000 of interest owed. $13,500 was already recorded as interest expense. The remaining $13,500 will be recorded as interest expense, and the payable will be reversed.

On April 1, Year 2, Maine will record the following:

Interest expense	13,500	
Accrued interest payable	13,500	
Cash		27,000

A year-end accrual would also take into account a prorated amount of discount or premium amortization.

Bond Issuance Costs

Bond issuance costs (BIC) are the various costs that a bond issuer incurs to bring the bonds to market. These costs include the following:

Bond Issue Costs
• Printing and engraving bond certificates • Legal and accounting fees • Underwriter commissions • Promotion costs (printing the prospectus) • Registration

The accounting for BIC is as follows:

- BIC reduce the net issuance proceeds received by the bond issuer
- BIC are typically added to the bond discount or netted against the bond premium. They are deductions from the carrying amount of the bond
- BIC are amortized using the effective interest method, according to GAAP. The straight-line method (ie, amortizing an equal amount each period) can be used to amortize BIC when the results don't materially differ from the effective interest method

Nevada Org. issued $20,000 of 8% bonds on January 1, Year 1. The bonds mature in five years and pay interest each June 30 and December 31. The yield rate is 6%, and the bonds sold for $21,706 (rounded). Nevada incurred $200 of debt issuance costs and uses the straight-line method to amortize the issuance costs and the premium.

Determine the entries to be recorded at January 1 and June 30.

The bond premium is $1,706 ($20,000 face value − $21,706 PV). The bond issuance costs will initially be netted against the bond premium. The journal entry at January 1, Year 1 is as follows:

Cash ($21,706 − $200)	21,506	
Premium and issuance costs ($1,706 − $200)		1,506
Bonds payable		20,000

Since Nevada uses the straight-line method, each period Nevada will amortize $150.60 of premium and issuance costs:

$$\frac{\text{Premium − bond issuance costs}}{\text{Number of periods}} = \frac{\$1,506}{\text{10 periods}} = \$150.60$$

The cash payment on the bonds is $800 each period ($20,000 × [8%/2]).

On June 30, Year 1, Nevada will record the following:

Interest expense (plug)	649.40	
Premium and issuance costs	150.60	
Cash		800

Bond Fair Value Option

Under the **fair value** (FV) option, certain assets and liabilities can be reported at FV, with unrealized gains and losses reported in earnings in the year they occur. This option reduces the accounting mismatch inherent in using FV for assets and a different measurement basis for liabilities. It also reduces earnings volatility because the effect of interest rate changes on assets such as investments in debt securities is opposite that on liabilities such as bonds payable.

If the firm makes the decision to elect the FV option, the election must be made on the date of issuance and is irrevocable. The option can be applied to all or a subset of debt instruments, even within the same type. If the FV option is chosen, the accounting proceeds as discussed above, but in addition, the firm increases or decreases the bond payable liability to FV using a FV adjustment account. FV is the quoted market price of the security. If that is not available, the current market rate of interest on similar debt instruments is used to estimate FV.

The required change in the FV adjustment account for the period (in order to report the bond at FV) is recognized as an unrealized gain or loss.

- If the required FV adjustment has increased, the firm recognizes an unrealized loss. The amount required to pay off the liability relative to the book value under the effective interest method at the balance sheet date has increased
- If the required FV adjustment has decreased, the firm recognizes an unrealized gain

Notes Payable

Notes payable are written promises to pay an amount of money on a specified future date. Notes can be classified as **current** (if due within one year) or **noncurrent** (if due within more than one year).

Current notes payable are reported at the amount due when they mature. Noncurrent notes are reported at the present value (PV) of future payments, discounted at the prevailing interest rate at time of issuance.

Similar to bonds, there are two rates of interest relevant to notes payable:

- Stated rate (ie, the contractual rate listed in the note), which determines the cash interest payments
- Yield or market rate (ie, the rate on notes of similar risk and term)

If the two rates are equal, the note is issued at face value. If the stated rate is below the market rate, the note is issued at a discount. If the stated rate is greater than the market rate, the note is issued at a premium.

The **issue price** or proceeds are equal to the PV of future cash flows. The total **interest expense** over the note term equals the difference between the total payments required under the note and the principal amount. Total interest expense comprises cash interest paid over the term plus the discount or minus the premium.

Periodic interest expense and amortization of the discount or premium for notes are computed in the same manner as for bonds. The effective interest method is preferred, but the straight-line method can be used if it does not yield materially different results.

Notes Issued in Exchange for Goods or Services

Goods or services received in exchange for a note are recorded at one of the following:

- The fair value of the note
- The fair value of the goods or services
- The present value of the note using a fair interest rate

Regardless of how the goods or services are valued, the difference between that amount and the note's face value is considered a discount or premium.

Note Payable Journal Entry Example

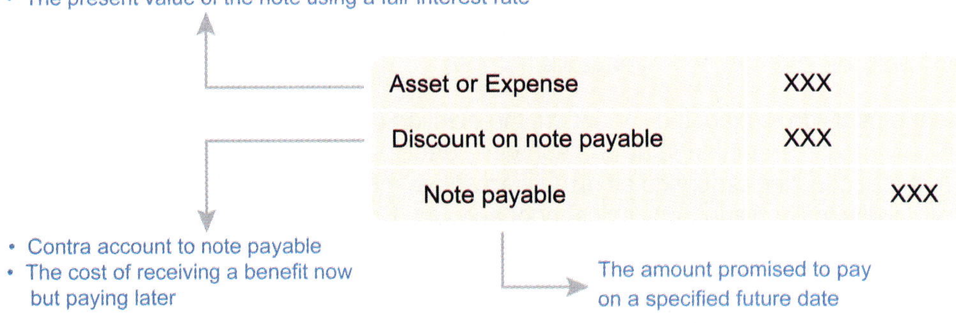

Year-End Interest Accrual

Similar to a bond, interest payments on a note are made at regularly scheduled intervals according to the note's terms (eg, semiannually) and are paid at the note's stated rate. The **interest payable** at year end is the interest **incurred but not yet paid** (based on the market rate under the effective interest method). If the note payment schedule does not align with the note issuer's reporting period, interest payable will be recorded.

If a note does not have a stated rate but interest is imputed, interest payable will still be recorded.

A company with a calendar year end issued a note on May 1 with payment dates of February 1 and August 1. At December 31, interest would be accrued at the market rate for the five months between August 1 and December 31. This interest has been incurred but not yet paid.

Note Interest Expense

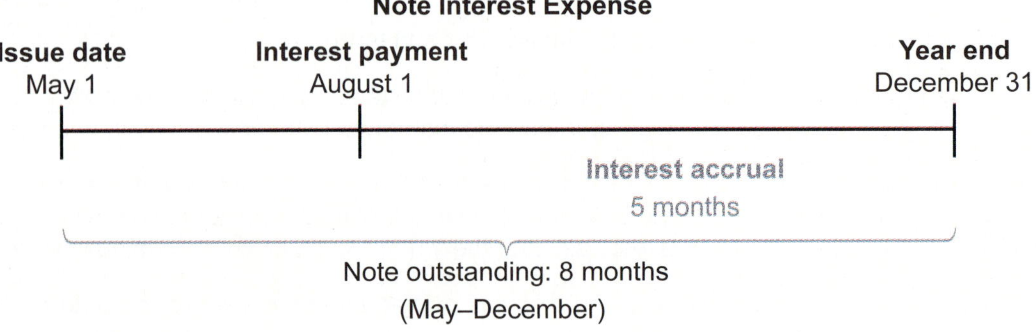

**Interest payment dates: February 1 and August 1*

Non-Interest-Bearing Notes

An **interest-bearing note** is one with a stated interest rate. A **non-interest-bearing note** is one that lacks a stated annual rate (ie, face rate or discount rate) of interest but does bear interest. Although an interest rate is not stated, a lender expects the borrower to pay for the use of its money (ie, interest). These notes are recorded at the PV of future cash flows; GAAP requires the use of an **imputed rate** equivalent to the market rate.

On July 1, Year 1, Washington, Inc., purchased a used plant asset by issuing a two-year, $10,877 face value note. The note pays no cash interest. The plant asset has a market value of $9,500. The implied market rate of interest is 7%.

The PV of $1 at 7% for two periods is 0.87344.

Determine the journal entries that Washington would record at July 1 and December 31, Year 1.

Washington will impute interest onto the note at a rate of 7%.

PV of future payments: $10,877 face value × 0.87344 ≈ $9,500

The asset is initially recorded at its market value of $9,500. The difference between the asset's market value of $9,500 and the $10,877 face value of the note is the $1,377 discount.

At July 1, Year 1, Washington will record the following:

Plant assets	9,500	
Discount on note payable	1,377	
Note payable		10,877

The net carrying value of the note is equal to the plant asset's market value.

The interest expense and amortization of the discount is calculated as follows:

Date	Interest Rate	Interest Expense/ Amortization	Net Carrying Value
7/1/Year 1	7%	$ 0	$ 9,500
7/1//Year 2	7%	$665	$10,165
7/1/Year 3	7%	$712	$10,877*

**Note payable − discount = $10,877 − 1,377 = $9,500* (italic)

At December 31, Year 1, the note has accrued interest expense of $332.50:

$665 × 6/12 months = $332.50

However, the interest is not actually paid, as it was bundled into the amount of the note. Therefore, the discount is adjusted (ie, amortized) each period. The net amount of the note payable increases over time.

At December 31, Year 1, Washington will record the following:

Interest expense	332.50	
Discount on note payable		332.50

Installment Notes

An **installment note** is one that requires the borrower to repay the lender in specified amounts at specified time intervals. Similar to an auto loan or a mortgage payment, repayment to the lender includes a portion of the note's principal and interest each period.

If noncurrent notes are payable in installments, the principal amounts that are due within the next year are reported as current liabilities, called **current portion of long-term debt**.

Hawaii Co. makes four annual loan payments to Guam, Inc., The payments are for $5,000 each. There is no stated rate of interest. The prevailing interest rate for a note of this type is 10%. The present value of the loan payments at 10% for four periods is $15,850.

Determine the journal entries that Hawaii would record for the first and second payments.

Since the note has no stated rate of interest, Hawaii will impute interest at the market rate of 10%. Each $5,000 payment will be allocated to principal and interest.

The initial carrying value of the loan is the loan's PV of $15,850. The discount is $4,150 ($20,000 face value − $15,850 PV).

Each payment is allocated between interest and principal as follows:

Payment	Interest Rate	Interest Expense	Cash Payment	Principal Paid	Net Carrying Value
1	10%	$1,585	$5,000	$3,415	$12,435
2	10%	$1,244	$5,000	$3,756	$ 8,679
3	10%	$ 868	$5,000	$4,132	$ 4,547
4	10%	$ 455	$5,000	$4,545	0*

**Amounts have been rounded for simplicity.*

For the first payment, Hawaii will record the following:

Interest expense	1,585	
Note payable	3,415	
Cash		5,000

For the second payment, Hawaii will record the following:

Interest expense	1,244	
Note payable	3,756	
Cash		5,000

Refinancing Current Liabilities

Current liabilities are obligations that will be settled within one year or the operating cycle, whichever is longer. In general, the maturing (ie, current) portion due of any long-term debt is an example of a current liability.

However, if an entity plans to **refinance a short-term obligation** to longer than one year, the obligation is reclassified from current to long term if the **intent and ability** to refinance can be demonstrated:

Refinancing Short-Term Obligations to Long-Term Obligations

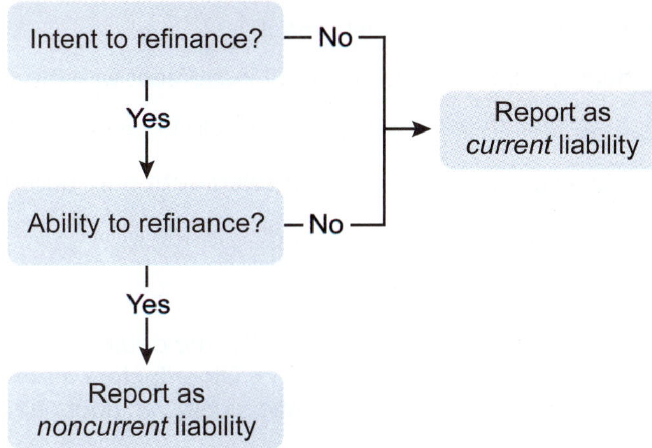

This reclassification is important because it affects **financial ratios** and provides information to financial statement users about an entity's capacity to pay its most pressing obligations.

Many firms have a preference for classifying liabilities as noncurrent rather than current to improve their reported liquidity position and reduce the perceived immediate riskiness of the firm. Refinancing on a current basis is of no help here, but if a current liability is **refinanced on a long-term basis**, the classification of a current liability can be successfully changed to noncurrent without extinguishing the original liability.

On January 1, Year 7, Bulldog Corp. reports a current note payable that matures on April 1, Year 7. The note is payable to an equipment dealer. Bulldog reports on a calendar year end. Determine if the original note would be reclassified from current to noncurrent in the following scenarios:

- Scenario 1: Bulldog signs a refinancing agreement with a lender. The agreement requires the lender to pay the original note in return for a note from Bulldog due after December 31, Year 8. Bulldog is informed that the lender is not financially capable of honoring the note.
- Scenario 2: In March, Year 7, Bulldog issues shares of common stock to the equipment dealer in full payment of the note.
- Scenario 3: In February, Year 7, Bulldog issues another note payable maturing in Year 9 to replace the original note.

In scenario 1, the note would not be reclassified. Bulldog has the intent to refinance but lacks the ability to refinance.

In scenario 2, since Bulldog issued the shares before the balance sheet date, there is no liability to be reclassified. The note has already been settled through the issuance of common stock.

In scenario 3, since Bulldog issued another long-term note to replace the original short-term note, the note is reclassified to long term.

Troubled Debt Restructuring

Representative Task (Remembering & Understanding): Understand when a change to the terms of a debt instrument qualifies as a troubled debt restructuring.

A change to a debt instrument may include the following:

- Amending the terms or cash flows of a debt instrument
- Exchanging an existing debt instrument for a new debt instrument with the same lender
- Repaying an existing debt obligation and issuing new debt to the same lender

These changes in debt instruments are classified as a **troubled debt restructuring** (TDR) if:

- The borrower is experiencing **financial difficulty**; and
- The lender grants the borrower a **concession**.

To determine if the debtor is **experiencing financial difficulty**, the debtor should consider if its creditworthiness has deteriorated since the debt was issued. Other factors that indicate financial difficulty include inability to repay old debt, declaring bankruptcy, and significant doubt as to whether the debtor will continue to be a going concern.

A lender is deemed to have **granted a concession** when the effective borrowing rate on the restructured debt is less than the effective borrowing rate on the original debt. There are three ways to restructure debt in a TDR:

Troubled Debt Restructuring Options	
Transfer of Property	• Debtor transfers an asset and removes the asset from the books
Transfer of Equity Interest in Debtor	• Debtor records equity as if issued for its fair value with increases to common stock and APIC
Modification of Debt Terms	• Interest rate is reduced • Due date of one or more payments is delayed • Face amount, accrued interest, or both are reduced

When TDR occurs through **transfer of property** (ie, transfer of assets), two gains (or losses) may be recorded:

- A restructuring gain is recognized for the excess of the carrying value of the debt over the fair value of the asset transferred in settlement
- A gain or loss on transfer of the asset is recognized for the difference between the asset's fair value and its carrying value

When the TDR occurs through a **transfer of equity:**

- A restructuring gain is recognized for the excess of the carrying value of the equity and the fair value of the equity transferred in settlement

When a TDR occurs by **modifying the terms of the debt**, the **sum of the total future cash payments** under the new terms for the debtor is compared with the **existing debt's carrying value** to determine a restructuring gain or loss.

- If the future payments are *less* than the carrying value, the debtor is relieved of a portion of the debt and will record a restructuring gain

Examples of modification of debt terms under a TDR include the following:

- A reduced interest rate or payment amount, allowing the debtor to make payments as the payments are due
- Delayed due date for one or more payments, giving the debtor more time to obtain the resources necessary to repay the debt

Modification of Terms and Extinguishment of Debt

Representative Task (Remembering & Understanding): Recall the criteria to classify a change to a debt instrument as either a modification of terms or an extinguishment of debt.

If the borrower concludes that change to a debt instrument does not meet the TDR criteria, then the borrower must determine if the change should be accounted for as a **modification of terms or an extinguishment of debt**.

Debtors must determine if the **change in the debt terms is considered to be substantial**. To determine if the change in the debt terms is considered to be substantial, the *PV of the new loan's cash flows is compared to the PV of the old loan's cash flows.*

If there is at least a **10% difference** between these two figures, the change in debt terms is considered to be substantial (and is, therefore, an extinguishment). If the difference is less than 10%, the change in debt terms is not considered to be substantial (and is, therefore, a modification of terms).

Bond Retirement

Companies often extinguish their debt through bond retirement. Bonds are issued and retired as part of financing ongoing operations. When a bond is retired at maturity, any discount or premium and bond issuance costs are fully amortized. The final payment extinguishes the liability at its maturity value, which is also the net liability amount at maturity. No gain or loss is recognized.

Firms may retire their debt at any time (before maturity) unless the debt agreement prohibits it. An issuer may choose to retire its outstanding debt when interest rates change or if it has excess cash reserves. The amount paid to retire debt early reflects the current yield rate and may be different from the book value of the debt on the retirement date.

When debt is redeemed prior to maturity, the difference between its carrying value and the amount paid is reported as a **gain or loss** on the issuer's income statement as part of continuing operations.

Treatment of Debt on Financial Statements	
Debt principal	Liability recorded on balance sheet
Interest	Expense recorded on income statement over life of debt
Premium/discount	Amortization recorded on income statement over life of debt
Early extinguishment*	Gain or loss recorded on income statement at time of extinguishment

**Retirement*

To account for bond retirement, take the following steps:

1. Record interest expense and amortization of the discount or premium or bond issuance costs to the date of extinguishment. Accrued interest from the most recent interest payment date will be included in the amount paid to retire the bond.
2. Remove the related bond accounts at their remaining amounts (face value, unamortized discount or premium, and any unamortized bond issuance costs).
3. Record the gain or loss by comparing the new carrying value (from step 1) to the cash paid to redeem the bond:

Gain or Loss on Bond Redemption/Retirement	
Step 1: Determine Bond Carrying Value	Bonds payable (face value) + Unamortized bond premium *or* − Unamortized bond discount − Unamortized bond issue costs = **Bond carrying value**
Step 2: Compare Carrying Value to Cash Paid	**Bond carrying value** − Cash paid to redeem bonds = **Gain** or **loss** on bond redemption **Gain** = Carrying value > Cash paid **Loss** = Carrying value < Cash paid

$10,000 of bonds were issued 5/1/Year 1 at 91. The bonds mature on 12/31/Year 6. Bond issuance costs of $680 were incurred on issue, and the straight-line method is used to amortize both the discount and bond issuance costs. The bonds pay interest each December 31. On 1/1/Year 4, 60% of the bonds were retired at 97. Determine the entry to record retirement of the bonds.

The bonds were issued at 91% of face value, or $9,100 ($10,000 × 91%). The total original discount was $900 ($10,000 face value − $9,100 PV). The bond term is five years and eight months, or 68 months. The bonds are retired when three years (or 36 months) remain in the bond term.

Unamortized discount:

The discount is amortized straight-line over 68 months. Each month, the discount is amortized for $13.24, rounded ($900 discount / 68 months). When 60% of the bonds are retired, 36 months remain in the bond term. Therefore, **$286 of unamortized discount** is included in the bond carrying value:

60% of bonds × $13.24 monthly amortization × 36 months remaining = $286 unamortized discount

Unamortized bond issuance costs:

Similarly, bond issuance costs are amortized straight-line over 68 months. Each month, the issuance costs are amortized for $10 ($680 issuance costs / 68 months). When the bonds are retired, **$216 unamortized issuance costs** are included in the bond carrying value:

60% of bonds × $10 monthly amortization × 36 months remaining = $216 unamortized issuance costs

Loss:

The loss is the excess of the cash paid (here, 97% of face value) over the carrying value of the bonds. The face value of the bonds being retired is $6,000 ($10,000 total face value × 60% of bonds being retired).

Cash paid	$6,000 face value × 97%	$5,820
Carrying value	$6,000 face value	
	− $286 unamortized discount	
	− $216 unamortized issuance costs	
		5,498
Loss		$ 322

The entry recorded at 1/1/Year 4 is as follows:

Bonds payable	6,000	
Loss	322	
Bond discount		286
Bond issuance costs		216
Cash		5,820

14.02 Debt Covenant Compliance

Overview

Representative Task (Application): Perform debt covenant calculations as stipulated in a debt agreement to ascertain compliance.

Covenants are **legally enforceable promises** made by a debtor (ie, borrower) to its creditors (ie, lenders). These promises are set forth in the contract related to the debt. A covenant also describes the responses available to the lender if certain events or conditions occur (eg, the borrower's current ratio falls below a certain level). The covenant may allow the lender to call the debt (demand immediate payment) if the borrower commits any violations.

Covenants can be established either unilaterally by the lender or through negotiation between lender and borrower. A description of the covenant must be **disclosed in the notes** to the borrower's financial statements.

The borrower must periodically demonstrate **compliance** with the covenants. The frequency is set at the time of borrowing and varies according to the perceived riskiness of the borrower. For example, demonstration of compliance might be required monthly for a troubled line of credit. Covenants are periodically revisited and modified as the borrower's financial health and macroeconomic conditions change. At a minimum, adjustments should be considered annually.

Attributes Used in Covenants

Financial Measures

Many different financial measures are used in debt covenants. Typically, minimum or maximum values are specified in the agreement, and any reported values outside the required limits are a violation.

Minimum levels are often specified for the following:

Examples of Minimum-Level Debt Covenants	
Measure	**Formula**
Current ratio	$\frac{\text{Current assets}}{\text{Current liabilities}}$
Working capital	Current assets − current liabilities
Interest coverage ratio	$\frac{\text{EBITDA*}}{\text{Interest expense}}$
Income measures	Eg, net income before tax, net income, EBITDA

** EBITDA = Earnings before interest, tax, depreciation, and amortization*

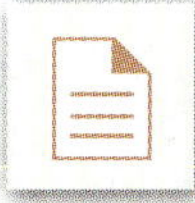

For example, a debt covenant specified that the debtor must maintain a current ratio of 1.2 or greater. This is a minimum-level debt covenant. If the debtor's current ratio were below 1.2, the debtor has violated the covenant. The creditor then has the right to respond in the specific ways defined in the contract.

Debt covenants may specify that minimum levels of assets or retained earnings must be maintained as well. **Maximum** levels are often specified for the following:

Examples of Maximum-Level Debt Covenants	
Measure	**Formula**
Debt to equity ratio	$\frac{\text{Total liabilities}}{\text{Total equity}}$
Total debt ratio	$\frac{\text{Total liabilities}}{\text{Total assets}}$

Debt covenants may specify that the company cannot exceed a maximum amount of interest expense or total debt.

Transaction Restrictions

Covenants also may describe a restriction on the borrower's transactions during the debt term for the protection of the lender. Some examples of transaction restrictions include the following:

- Limiting declaration of dividends or purchases of treasury shares to a specific amount or prohibiting them altogether
- Limiting additional borrowings—a leverage covenant may limit total debt to some multiple of an earnings variable, such as EBITDA; alternatively, the firm may be required to maintain a minimum specified interest coverage ratio if additional debt capital is acquired
- Prohibiting the borrower from voluntarily reducing net assets (weakening the balance sheet) or taking any action that might impede the ability to service the debt
- Prohibiting risky investments or expansion projects

Debt Rating Minimums

A covenant also may require the firm to maintain a minimum debt rating. Two rating agencies commonly used are Standard & Poor's Corporation and Moody's Investor Services.

For example, a borrower may be required to maintain an S&P rating of A or better for compliance with the covenant.

Debt Ratings		
Ranking	**S&P**	**Moody's**
Highest	AAA	Aaa
High	AA	Aa
Medium	A	A
Minimum	BBB	Baa

Compliance

Ensuring compliance with covenants is an **ongoing** task for many borrower firms. Both management and the audit committee continuously monitor the financial condition of the firm so that adjustments can be made in time to avoid situations that could cause a violation.

Periodic **internal self-evaluation** precedes the formal compliance review that involves the lender. All administrative requirements pertaining to the covenant within the debt agreement, including progress reports, should be fulfilled on a timely basis. Capital budgeting and other planning processes within the firm consider the potential effects on debt covenant compliance.

A periodic internal sensitivity analysis is performed to determine the leeway available on key factors used in the covenant, within current operations. The firm determines how much room it has to alter its tactics and strategies and continue to comply with its covenants.

Operating Strategies

Companies employ **operating strategies** in hopes of maintaining compliance. Relevant strategies available to the borrower are implied by the covenant. For example, if the covenant requires a limitation or elimination of dividends, then that strategy must be followed to avoid a violation. When dividends are impacted, the firm should communicate the reason for and scope of the impact to its shareholders.

Companies can improve operating results (and, thus, maintain compliance) through improving products and services, enhancing marketing, encouraging innovation, seeking the best management talent, avoiding risk, etc. **Leverage**, if allowed under the covenant, should be used sparingly and only if the forecasted increased profitability is sufficient to warrant increased debt.

Increasing **liquidity** is another aspect that helps improve compliance with several types of covenants (eg, those involving the current ratio or working capital). **Refinancing debt** from short term to long term is another strategy that would assist the borrower in complying with this type of covenant.

Before making any operating decisions that could alter the financial metrics, a borrower should analyze the impact of its options and determine which will improve compliance or perhaps cause a violation with the loan covenant.

Beta Co. has a loan covenant requiring it to maintain a current ratio of 1.5 or better as of year end. As Beta approaches year end, it has the following balances (in millions):

Cash	$ 10	Current liabilities	$135
Accounts receivable	$ 90		
Inventory	$100		

1. Calculate Beta's current ratio.

   Beta's current ratio is 1.48 (200 current assets / 135 current liabilities). This is below the minimum required by the debt covenant.

2. Of the following options, determine which action Beta should take in order to maintain compliance with the debt covenant by year end:

   Option 1: Sell $10 million in inventory and deposit the proceeds in the entity's checking account

   Option 2: Borrow $10 million short term and deposit the funds in the entity's checking account

   Option 3: Sell $10 million in inventory and pay off some of its short-term creditors

Option 1 decreases inventory by $10 million and increases cash by $10 million, so total current assets and current liabilities are **unchanged**, which means the current ratio is unchanged. Beta remains in **noncompliance**.

Option 2 increases both current assets (cash) and current liabilities by $10 million, resulting in a new current ratio of (200 + 10) / (135 + 10) = **1.45**, so Beta remains in **noncompliance**.

Option 3 decreases both current assets (inventory) and current liabilities by $10 million, resulting in a new current ratio of (200 − 10) / (135 − 10) = **1.52**. Beta should take this action to be **in compliance**.

Accounting Choices

Where GAAP allows a **choice** or leeway in estimation of certain variables, the borrower may consider choosing the methods that contribute to maintaining compliance with the debt covenant.

Although net income is not a formal variable in all covenants, higher earnings will contribute to a greater probability of compliance with many covenants. Choices such as FIFO, straight-line depreciation, longer useful lives for plant assets, higher recoverable costs for plant assets, the specific method of capitalizing interest, and others can help in this regard. However, the effect of choices on the *quality* of earnings must also be considered. Firms with low quality of earnings may suffer in the equity capital markets.

Some covenants compute compliance based on the accounting policies in effect at the time of the borrowing. In that case, improving a financial measure used in a debt covenant by changing an accounting policy may not actually improve debt covenant compliance.

Covenant Violations

Lender Response

The debt contract describes the actions that may be taken by the lender in the event of a covenant violation by the borrower. Typically, these are options rather than requirements.

If the covenant states that the debt can be **called** in the event of noncompliance, then the lender has the option to **demand immediate payment**. Other possible actions include increasing the interest rate, requiring the borrower to specify assets as collateral, accelerating the payment terms (other than immediate payment), reducing the amount available in a line of credit, and repossessing collateral.

In lieu of taking the above actions, the lender may instead place additional restrictions on the borrower. If a covenant is violated because of reduced earnings, for example, then the borrower may be prohibited from paying dividends or taking on more debt until the violation is cured. The lender may agree to renegotiate or restructure the debt. It may even take legal action against the borrower, such as a breach of contract lawsuit.

Borrower Strategies

The borrower may have few options after a covenant violation, depending on the response by the lender. Therefore, the borrowing firm should seek to **avoid a violation** and the potential negative impact on its operations. If a violation leads to a debt default, operations can be disrupted, access to the capital markets is hindered, higher borrowing costs and penalties may be incurred, and the borrower's going concern may be placed in doubt.

Lenders do not want borrowers to default. Covenant violations may attract scrutiny from bank examiners, which in turn may require an increase in a reserve against the possible loan loss. A default also raises the possibility that a loss is imminent.

Many borrowers are not in a position to pay the debt immediately and often request a **renegotiation** of the debt terms, enabling lower or deferred payments. A borrower may also ask for a **waiver** granting time to cure the violation or to void the violation. These requests are more likely when the reasons for the violation are beyond the immediate control of the borrower. General economic downturns and inflation often affect the borrower's earnings and liquidity and are potential factors to consider when requesting a waiver. For example, goodwill impairments due to declining stock prices can cause a parent firm's earnings to decline with no change in the parent's core operations.

The borrower may request **relief** from the covenant. This involves a request to either eliminate or weaken the covenant by amending the debt contract. For example, if the violated leverage covenant required debt to be less than five times EBITDA, the debtor may request to increase the multiple to six and a half. Such a change to the covenant may occur when the compliance review of the contract occurs or earlier, depending on the severity of the violation.

Borrower Balance Sheet Impact

Liabilities may be callable on demand (ie, require immediate payment) if a debt covenant is **violated**. In this case, if there is a violation, the liability is classified by the borrower as a **current liability** if there are no other relevant circumstances. However:

- If the violation is **waived** by the lender, then the liability is classified as a **noncurrent** liability
- If the lender grants a **grace period** to rectify the violation and it is **probable** that the borrower will rectify that violation within the grace period, then the liability is classified as a **noncurrent** liability

Wilsons Co. reported the following liabilities at December 31, Year 1:

Accounts payable—trade	$ 500
Short-term borrowings	$ 220
Loan from Bank X, current portion $100	$1,000
Loan from Bank Y, matures June 30, Year 2	$2,500
Loan from Bank Z, matures June 30, Year 3	$3,000

The loan from Bank Z was in violation of the loan agreement, and the creditor had not waived the rights for the loan. Determine the amount Wilsons should report as current liabilities at December 31, Year 1.

Accounts payable of $500 and short-term borrowings of $220 are both current liabilities. The current portion of the loan from Bank X, $100, is also part of current liabilities.

The loan from Bank Y matures within one year of the balance sheet date, so the entire balance of $2,500 is considered current.

Under normal circumstances, the loan from Bank Z would not be classified as current since it matures more than one year after the balance sheet date. However, Wilsons is in violation of the loan agreement, so Bank Z is able to call the loan, or require full payment immediately. Since the creditor had not waived the rights for the loan, the balance of $3,000 is included in the current liabilities calculation.

In total, Wilsons Co. should report current liabilities of $500 + $220 + $100 + $2,500 + $3,000 = **$6,320** at December 31, Year 1

FAR 15
Equity

FAR 15: Equity

15.01 Equity

Overview

Representative Task (Application): Prepare journal entries to recognize equity transactions in the financial statements (eg, equity issuance, stock dividends, stock splits, treasury stock, capital account activity in pass-through entities).

The **equity** accounts represent the residual interest in the net assets of an entity that remain after deducting its liabilities. There are two main categories of equity:

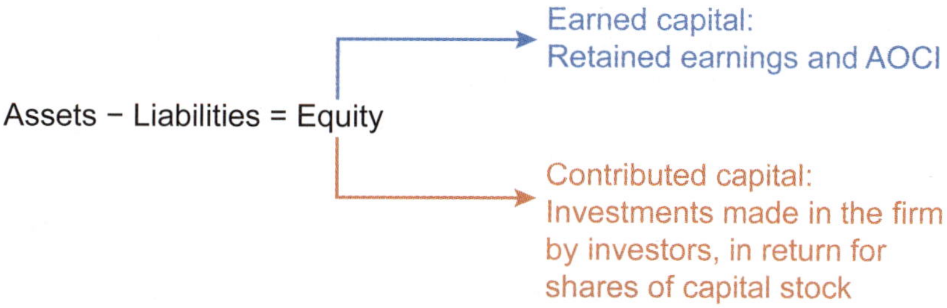

For a corporation, the major equity account types are the following:

- **Common stock:** The total par value of issued common stock
- **Preferred stock:** The total par value of issued preferred stock
- **Additional paid-in capital:** The amount received for stock issuances in excess of par value
- **Retained earnings:** The firm's net earnings to date less dividends to date, plus or minus other items including prior-period adjustments and certain accounting changes
- **Accumulated other comprehensive income:** The running total of all other comprehensive income items through the balance sheet date; this topic is covered further in the FAR chapter General-Purpose Financial Reporting: For-Profit Business Entities
- **Treasury stock:** Cost or par value of the common stock of a firm purchased by that firm, depending on the method used by the firm; this is a *contra* equity account

Common Stock

A corporation begins operations by issuing stock to raise funds. When the corporation is formed, a certain number of shares are **authorized to be issued**. This amount can be increased only by vote of the shareholders. Authorized shares are the maximum number of shares a company can issue per the firm's articles of incorporation.

Shares are further categorized into the following:

- The number of shares **issued** (ie, total shares that have been distributed by the company)
- The number of shares **outstanding** (ie, shares that are currently held by stockholders)
- The number of shares in the **treasury** (ie, shares repurchased by the issuing firm)

Issued shares = Outstanding shares + Treasury shares

Common stock typically has a **par value** or **stated value** assigned to it. The issue price of the stock, however, is almost always greater than the par value. This excess is recorded in additional paid-in capital (APIC) and is identified specifically as being from common stock.

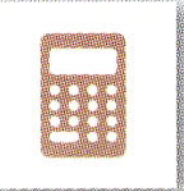

A corporation is authorized to issue 2,500 shares of $4 par value common stock. The corporation issues 2,000 shares for $10 per share. Determine the entry to record the stock issuance.

The entry to record issuance is as follows:

Cash (2,000 shares × $10 issue price)	20,000	
Common stock (2,000 shares × $4 par)		8,000
APIC—Common stock (2,000 shares × [$10 − $4])		12,000

If common stock has no par or stated value, there is no allocation between common stock and APIC; the entire amount is simply recorded in the common stock account.

Any **stock issuance costs** incurred are recoded as a reduction to cash and APIC.

If the stock is issued in exchange for property **other than cash**, recording of the transaction will be based on the **fair value** (FV) of the stock sold or the FV of the asset received, whichever can be most clearly determined. Stock may also be **issued to vendors** as payment for services. Here, an expense is recognized in the period that the services are provided. The value of the services is measured at the **FV** of the stock as this is a more objective measure (because billing rates for services can be negotiated).

Stock Issued with Other Securities

A **basket sale** occurs when two or more securities (eg, common stock and preferred stock) are bundled together and sold in a single transaction. The total amount received must be allocated to the individual securities sold:

Allocating Sales Price When Stock Is Issued with Other Securities		
Given Information	**Methodology**	**Mathematical Approach**
FV known for all securities	Relative FV method	To allocate sales price, use proportion of FVs to total FV
FV not known for all securities	Incremental method	Allocate known FVs to those securities, and allocate remaining sales price to other securities

Ten Co. issues 100 shares of $10 par value common stock and 50 shares of $12 par value preferred stock. The shares are issued as a unit for total consideration of $4,200. The market price of the common shares is $35, and the market price of the preferred shares is $30. Determine the entry that Ten would record related to the issuance of these shares.

Because the FV for both securities is known, Ten will use the relative FV method:

	FV	Proportional FV %	Proceeds	Allocated Proceeds
Common stock (100 shares × $35)	$3,500	70% ($3,500 / 5,000)	× $4,200	= $2,940
Preferred stock (50 shares × $30)	$1,500	30% ($1,500 / 5,000)	× $4,200	= $1,260
Total	$5,000	100%		$4,200

The entry to record issuance is as follows:

Cash	4,200	
Common stock (100 shares × $10 par)		1,000
APIC—Common stock ($2,940 − $1,000)		1,940
Preferred stock (50 shares × $12 par)		600
APIC—Preferred stock ($1,260 − $600)		660

If the market price for the preferred stock were unknown, the incremental method would be used. $3,500 of value would have been allocated to common stock first (100 shares × $35 market price). Then the remaining $700 ($4,200 − $3,500) would have been allocated to preferred stock.

Retired Stock

If stock is **repurchased and retired**, the accounts initially credited at the time of issuance are debited. If the repurchase price is *lower* than the original issuance price, the difference is credited to APIC from stock retirements. If the repurchase price is *higher*, the remainder is normally debited to retained earnings (after debiting any APIC that exists from previous stock retirements).

A company issued one share of $10 par value common stock for $13. The initial entry is as follows:

Cash	13	
Common stock		10
APIC—Common stock		3

If this share is **repurchased at $12** and retired, the repurchase price is lower than the issuance price. The difference will be credited to APIC from stock retirements. The entry is as follows:

Common stock	10	
APIC—Common stock	3	
APIC—Retired stock		1
Cash		12

If, instead, it is **repurchased at $15** and retired, the repurchase price is higher than the issuance price. The difference will be debited to retained earnings. The entry is as follows:

Common stock	10	
APIC—Common stock	3	
Retained earnings	2	
Cash		15

If the company had a balance in the APIC—Retired stock account from previous transactions, the debit to retained earnings would have been made to that account instead. If the difference, however, was greater than the balance in APIC—Retired stock, APIC—Retired stock would be reduced to zero, and the remainder would reduce retained earnings.

Stock Subscriptions

A company can obtain **stock subscriptions** from potential shareholders for new offers of the stock. When stock is sold on a subscription basis, the implication is that the selling price of the stock will be received in a series of payments from the shareholder. A down payment is often received at the time of the subscription. Then, once the full amount is received, the stock will be issued.

When the company obtains subscriptions, it will record the following:

Cash	Initial payment	
Subscriptions receivable*	Remaining payments	
Common stock subscribed		Par × # shares
APIC—Common stock		(Contract price − par) × # shares

**Note: Subscriptions receivable is a contra-equity account, not an asset.*

As subsequent payment is received, the company will record cash and reverse the subscriptions receivable. After the final payment, shares will be issued and reclassified from common stock subscribed to common stock.

A client is planning to issue one share of its $10 par value stock at $30 per share and obtains subscriptions from potential buyers. The buyers are required to make a $3 down payment with the subscription and pay the balance when the stock is issued to them. Determine the entries recorded when the subscription is initially made and when the balance is paid.

The entry when the subscription is taken out is as follows:

Cash	3	
Subscriptions receivable ($30 − $3)	27	
Common stock subscribed		10
APIC—Common stock ($30 − $10)		20

When the balance is paid and **stock issued**, the entry is as follows:

Cash	27	
Common stock subscribed	10	
Subscriptions receivable		27
Common stock		10

If a company does not issue stock within a certain time period after subscription, the potential investor is entitled to a **refund** of the down payment and **cancellation of the contract**. If the company failed to issue stock, the initial entry is simply reversed. The refund entry is as follows:

Common stock subscribed	10	
APIC—Common stock	20	
Cash		3
Subscriptions receivable		27

If, on the other hand, the **potential buyer** breaches the subscription contract and refuses to purchase it when available, the company is normally entitled to **keep the down payment** as an estimate of damages from breach. Rather than returning (ie, crediting) the cash, the company credits the down payment as APIC—Forfeited subscriptions. The cancellation is recorded as follows:

Common stock subscribed	10	
APIC—Common stock	20	
APIC—Forfeited subscriptions		3
Subscriptions receivable		27

If the shareholder **donates** stock back to the corporation, the entry would be as follows:

Treasury stock	X (at FV)	
APIC—Treasury stock		X

Stock Rights

Companies may issue securities that give the holders the right to buy shares of stock at an established price for a specific period of time. Examples of these securities are stock rights, which are often issued to existing shareholders; stock options, which are often issued to officers or employees; and stock warrants, which are often issued to bondholders.

Stock rights (sometimes called preemptive or subscription rights) are contractual rights held by existing shareholders to purchase a proportional share of new shares in the same class, to preserve their preexisting ownership percentage (prevent dilution of ownership).

If rights are given to existing shareholders, no entry is recorded at issuance of the rights or if the rights lapse. At exercise of the rights, the usual entry to record issuance of stock is made. The issue price is the exercise price as specified in the stock right.

Preferred Stock

Preferred stock has two advantages over common stock:

- **Dividends:** Preferred shareholders must be paid a dividend before the company is allowed to pay the common shareholders a dividend
- **Liquidation:** If the corporation liquidates, preferred shareholders must be paid before the common shareholders. Note: creditors are still paid before preferred shareholders

However, preferred stock typically does not provide voting rights for shareholders. That is, preferred shareholders are not participants in the major operating and financing decisions made by the company.

The **dividend preference** for preferred shares is based on a stated dividend rate that is computed on the par (or stated) value of the shares. Dividends are optional, however, and a company may decide not to pay any dividends at all in a particular year to any shareholders. The preferred shareholders have a dividend preference, not a dividend guarantee.

Juice, Inc., has two types of stock outstanding at 12/31/Year 6:

Type of Shares	Par Value	Shares	Total
10% Preferred stock	$100	4	$400
Common stock	$1	100	$100

$300 of dividends are declared. Determine the amount of dividends that will be paid to preferred and common shareholders.

The dividend on preferred shares is stated in dollar terms or as a percentage of par value. Juice has 10% preferred stock. This means that 10% of the total par value of the shares must be paid in dividends to preferred shareholders before any can be paid to common shareholders.

Of the $300 in dividends, the first $40 ($400 × 10%) must be paid to the preferred shareholders, based on the dividend preference. The remaining $260 ($300 − $40) is paid to the common shareholders.

Along with the stated annual preference, preferred shareholders may be paid additional amounts if the shares are of the following types:

- **Cumulative:** Dividends missed in earlier years must also be paid before the common shareholders receive anything
- **Participating:** If the common shareholders get a dividend that is a higher rate on its par value than the stated rate on the preferred shares, the preferred shareholders must get the same higher rate
- **Convertible:** The preferred shareholders have the option of converting their stock for common stock at a specified ratio
- **Callable:** The corporation has the option of repurchasing the preferred stock at a specified price
- **Preferred with warrants:** The warrants are convertible into shares of common stock

If preferred stock is **cumulative** and dividends for a year are not paid, then the dividends are considered to be **in arrears**. Dividends in arrears are not required to be paid but accumulate if unpaid. However, the liability for dividends in arrears is only recognized after a dividend is **declared**.

The cumulative feature of preferred stock simply means that, in the event of a dividend declaration, preferred shareholders are entitled to be paid the dividends in arrears before any distribution related to the current period occurs. **Undeclared dividends in arrears are disclosed in the footnotes**.

Assume that the company in the preceding example paid the same $300 in dividends in Year 6 but paid no dividends in the five years prior. Notwithstanding the preferred shareholders' preference, they received nothing in those years. Determine how much preferred shareholders will receive (1) if the preferred stock is *not* cumulative, (2) if it is cumulative, and (3) if it is *not* cumulative but is participating.

1. If the stock is *not* cumulative, the preferred shareholders will still only receive $40 ($400 × 10%). Since the stock is not cumulative, the dividends missed in Years 1 through 5 do not need to be paid.
2. If, however, the stock is cumulative, then the $40 preferences missed each year for five years result in $200 of dividends in arrears ($40 × 5 years) at 12/31/Year 5. In Year 6, when $300 is paid, the preferred shareholders will collect $240 and the common shareholders $60, determined as follows:

Amount	Shareholders	Reason
$200	Preferred	Dividends in arrears
$40	Preferred	Annual preference
$60 ($300 − $200 − $40)	Common	Remainder

3. If the preferred shares are *not* cumulative but are participating, the preferred shareholders will still receive more than their annual preference when $300 is paid in Year 6.

First, the preferred shareholders receive $40 as their annual preference. Next, the common shareholders are paid but only until they are *also* receiving 10%, or $10 ($100 × 10%), on their total par value.

The remaining $250 ($300 − $40 − $10) is allocated to the preferred and common shares based on their relative par values:

Type of Shares	Total Par Value	Percentage of Combined
Preferred	$400	$400 / $500 = 80%
Common	$100	$100 / $500 = 20%
Total	$500	100%

Thus, the preferred shareholders receive an additional $200 ($250 × 80%), and the common shareholders receive an additional $50 ($250 × 20%). The preferred shareholders receive $240 ($40 + $200), and the common shareholders receive $60 ($10 + $50).

In each case, the shareholders are receiving dividends equal to 60% of par value, so the preferred shareholders are fully participating in the large dividend.

When a company liquidates, **preferred shareholders are paid first**, based on the amount of their **liquidation preference**. Unless specifically stated, this is usually the same as the par value of the preferred shares. Remember, however, that a liquidating distribution is still a form of dividend, so preferred shareholders must also be paid dividends in arrears (if cumulative) on top of their liquidation preference. The remainder is paid to common shareholders. The remaining amount that each outstanding common share will receive is known as **book value (BV) per common share**.

$$\textbf{Book value per common share} = \frac{\text{Common stockholders' equity}}{\text{Common shares outstanding}}$$

Common stockholders' equity = (Total stockholders' equity) − (Amount due preferred stockholders)

Common shares outstanding = (Issued shares) − (Treasury stock shares)

The equity section of a company's balance sheet is as follows on 12/31/Year 1; no dividends have been paid in Year 1:

Account	Amount
8% Cumulative preferred stock: 5 shares authorized and issued, $100 par, $110 liquidation value	$500
Common stock: 5,000 shares authorized, 103 shares issued, $1 par	103
APIC	200
Retained earnings	223
Treasury stock, at cost: 3 shares, $12 cost	(36)
Equity	$990

Determine the amount and BV per share that preferred and common shareholders will receive in liquidation.

The preferred shares have a $110 liquidation value, so the preferred shareholders are entitled to receive their **liquidation preference of $550** ($110 liquidation value per share × 5 shares). Preferred stock is cumulative, but dividends have not been paid. Therefore, preferred shareholders are also entitled to **dividends in arrears of $40** ($500 total par × 8%). Preferred shareholders will receive $590 ($550 + $40) in total. The BV per share of preferred stock is $118 ($590 / 5 shares).

The common shareholders will receive the **remaining equity** of $400 ($990 − $590). This equity will be divided by the 100 common shares outstanding (103 shares issued − 3 shares repurchased as treasury stock). The BV per share of common stock is $4 ($400 / 100 shares).

Notice that the BV per share is based on the shares *outstanding*.

Additional Paid-In Capital (APIC)

There are many forms of APIC (contributed capital) that may be included in the stockholders' equity section of the balance sheet, including the following:

- **Common stock:** The portion of the issue price of common stock that exceeded the par (or stated) value of the shares
- **Preferred stock:** The portion of the issue price of preferred stock that exceeded the par (or stated) value of the shares
- **Retired stock:** Repurchase and retirement of shares at a price different from the original issue price
- **Treasury stock:** Related to treasury stock transactions under both the par value method and cost method
- **Warrants:** May be issued with bonds or preferred stock for the purchase of common stock, entitling the holder to purchase common stock at a fixed price; APIC is recorded for the amount allocated to the value of the warrants that are issued

Retained Earnings

Retained earnings are calculated as follows:

Net income to date − Dividends to date*

**+/− Other items including prior-period adjustments and certain accounting changes*

Retained earnings represent the **accumulated earnings** since inception of a company that have not been paid out to shareholders in the form of a dividend. At the end of each accounting year, net income is closed into retained earnings.

Retained earnings are assumed to be available for the payment of dividends. When a company faces contingent liabilities that may require large payments in the future or contractual obligations (eg, a clause in a loan agreement requiring appropriation), it will often **appropriate** a portion of the retained earnings to indicate to its shareholders its unavailability for dividend payments.

For example, if a company wishes to appropriate $100,000 of retained earnings for possible losses related to pending lawsuits, the entry is as follows:

Retained earnings—Unappropriated	100,000	
Retained earnings—Reserve for lawsuits		100,000

Unappropriated retained earnings are available for dividend declaration, while appropriated retained earnings are not.

Notice that the above entry has no impact on net assets, net income, or retained earnings. It is considered a disclosure on the face of the financial statements and is appropriate for contingencies involving reasonably possible costs or costs that are probable but not estimable. The above entry is not used for probable and estimable losses, as these should be accrued on the income statement and reduce net assets.

When the reserve is no longer needed, the above entry is reversed. This is appropriate whether or not the costs are actually incurred since the effects of the contingency will be reflected directly if and when they do result in losses.

Dividends

Retained earnings are periodically **reduced for dividends**. There are three dates relevant to each dividend:

- **Date of declaration:** The board of directors commits to the dividend
- **Date of record:** The shareholders as of this date are entitled to the dividend. This date is a cutoff point, used because it requires a certain amount of time to compile the list of shareholders as of a particular date
- **Date of payment:** Distribution is made to the shareholders of record

There are many types of dividends, including cash, stock, property, scrip, and liquidating. Each type has different impacts on retained earnings and stockholders' equity as well as different journal entries.

Types of Dividends

	Recorded At	Reduces Retained Earnings	Reduces Total Stockholders' Equity
Cash	Amount declared	Yes	Yes
Small Stock (Less than 20%–25%)	Fair value	Yes	No
Large Stock (Greater than 20%–25%)	Par value	Yes	No
Property	Fair value	Yes	Yes
Scrip	Amount declared	Yes	Yes
Liquidating	Amount declared	No	Yes

Cash Dividends

For **cash dividends**, the liability is recorded on the **date of declaration** with a debit to retained earnings and a credit to dividends payable. There is no journal entry on the date of record. Then, on the date of payment, dividends payable is debited and cash is credited.

Dividends are *not* recognized as an expense for the firm paying the dividends.

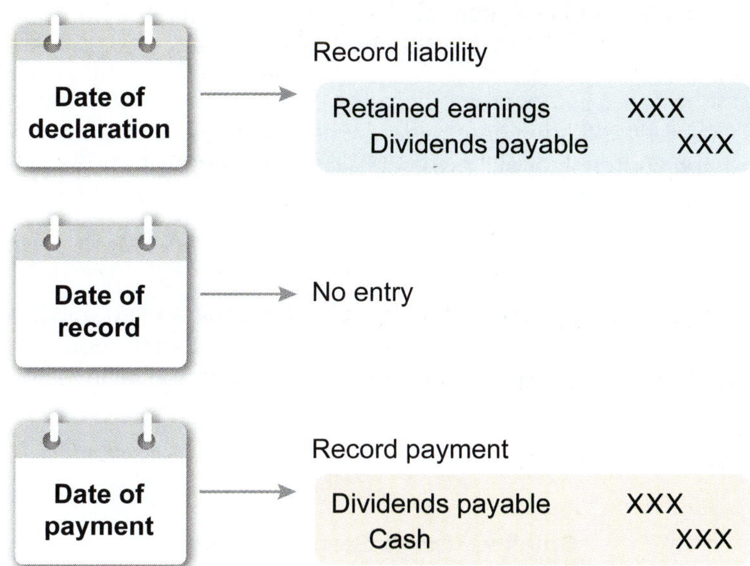

The board of directors at Pell Org. declares dividends totaling $500 on 4/1/Year 1, payable on 4/28/Year 1 to shareholders of record on 4/21/Year 1. Determine the related entries to be recorded.

The entries are as follows:

4/1/Year 1	Retained earnings	500	
	Dividends payable		500

This records the obligation. Identifying the actual payees doesn't change any account balances, so the next entry is on the **payment date:**

4/28/Year 1	Dividends payable	500	
	Cash		500

Stock Dividends

A **stock dividend** is a distribution by a firm of its stock to its shareholders in proportion to their existing holdings. Stock dividends are not actual distributions of assets from a company but represent transfers of capital from retained earnings to contributed capital accounts. Therefore, in relation to stock dividends, **no liability is recorded**.

Each investor simply holds more shares, but each share is worth proportionally less than before the dividend. Each investor maintains the previous ownership percentage, and total equity is unchanged.

If a firm has 10,000 shares of common stock outstanding and issues a 5% stock dividend, then 500 shares (10,000 shares × 5%) are distributed to the current shareholders at no cost to them.

If a specific shareholder owned 2,000 shares before the dividend, they would receive 100 shares (2,000 shares × 5%). Prior to the dividend, the shareholder owned 20% (2,000 shares / 10,000 shares) of the firm. After the dividend, the shareholder still owns 20% (2,100 shares / 10,500 shares) of the firm. There is no change in percentage ownership.

The effect of a stock dividend is to increase the number of shares issued and outstanding. Earnings per share are decreased by a stock dividend. Stock dividends are distributed to reduce the market price of the firm's stock (often because the stock price has become too high for potential investors) and also to reduce demand by shareholders for cash dividends.

There are two types of stock dividends:

Small vs. Large Stock Dividend

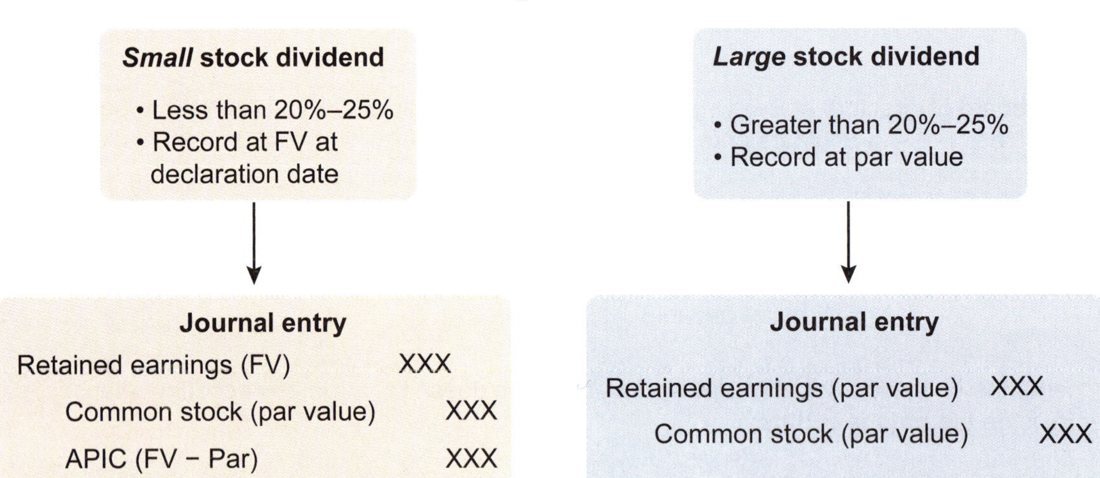

The reason for the difference is that the FV of the stock is not deemed to be a realistic estimate after a large stock dividend takes place since it will substantially reduce the selling price of the shares. Note that stock dividends between 20% and 25% generally do not appear on the CPA exam because it is difficult to determine which classification they should have.

Fox, Inc., has outstanding 100 shares of $10 par value stock with a fair market value of $30 per share. Determine the journal entries to be recorded (1) if a 5% stock dividend is declared and (2) if a 100% stock dividend is declared.

If a 5% stock dividend is declared and paid, five shares (100 shares × 5%) will be issued. Because it is a small stock dividend, the transaction is reported at the FV on the declaration date ($30 per share):

Retained earnings (5 shares × $30 per share)	150	
Common stock (5 shares × $10 par)		50
APIC—Common stock (5 shares × ($30 − $10))		100

If a 100% stock dividend is declared, 100 shares (100 shares × 100%) will be issued. Because it is a large stock dividend, the transaction is reported at par value ($10 per share):

Retained earnings (100 shares × $10 par)	1,000	
Common stock (100 shares × $10 par)		1,000

Stock Splits

A **stock split** is *not* a dividend. Rather, it is an adjustment to the par value and number of shares issued. Firms often split their shares to reduce the market price and make the shares available to a larger number of shareholders. A two-for-one stock split halves the par value and doubles the number of shares.

If a two-for-one stock split occurred on 200 shares of $30 par stock, the shares would be replaced by 400 shares (200 × 2) of $15 par ($30 / 2) stock. Total par value ($6,000) remains unchanged.

Since total par value is unchanged, no accounting entry is made. A firm may choose to record a memo entry. A reverse stock split does the opposite by reducing the number of shares outstanding and proportionally increasing the par value.

Comparison of a Stock Split and Stock Dividend

	Stock Split	**Stock Dividend**
Issued to Existing Shareholders	Yes	Yes
Treats New Shares as Outstanding for Entire Year	Yes	Yes
Based on Percentage of Existing Shares	No	Yes
Based on Splitting the Existing Shares	Yes	No
Decreases Par Value of Stock	Yes	No

Property Dividends

When a company pays a dividend in the form of **property** other than cash, this is known as a **dividend-in-kind**. Such dividends are treated as simultaneous sales of property and distributions of cash and result in gains or losses.

On the date of declaration, the dividends payable liability is recognized, and a gain (or loss) is recorded in order to bring the asset to FV. Then, on the date of payment, the FV of the asset is written off from the books.

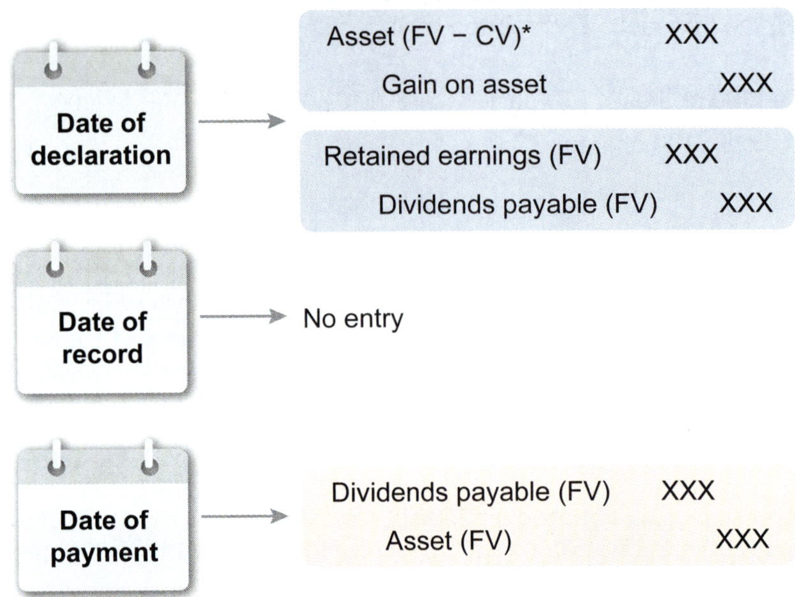

Rocco Co. declares a property dividend of land on 7/1/Year 1, payable on 7/15/Year 1. The land originally cost $300, is worth $800 on 7/1/Year 1, and is worth $820 on 7/15/Year 1. Determine the entries that Rocco should record on the declaration date and payment date.

On the declaration date, Rocco will record a liability and reduction to retained earnings for the FV of the land. Rocco will also write the land up to FV and record a gain of excess FV over CV. The entry on the declaration date is as follows:

7/1/Year 1	Retained earnings (FV)	800	
	Dividends payable (FV)		800
	Land ($800 – $300)	500	
	Gain on Land		500

On the payment date, Rocco will record payment on the liability and remove the asset from its books. The entry is as follows:

7/15/Year 1	Dividends payable	800	
	Land		800

Retained earnings are decreased by a net $300 ($800 from recording the dividend – $500 gain on land). This amount is equal to the BV of the land.

Note: The price appreciation after the declaration date is ignored, since the commitment to distribute the land effectively sells it.

Scrip Dividends

A company that is experiencing temporary cash-flow problems may still want to pay its shareholders a dividend. When this occurs, the company can choose to issue a **scrip dividend** (assuming adequate retained earnings). The most common form of scrip dividend is a **promissory note**. This assures shareholders that a dividend is forthcoming.

On the declaration date, a reduction to **retained earnings** and an increase in **notes payable** are recorded for the dividend, indicating that the company will pay its shareholders at a future date when funds become available. To compensate the shareholders for waiting to receive the dividend, the promissory note is usually **interest-bearing**. Therefore, on the payment date, the shareholders receive the dividend plus the total interest accrued on the note. Bear in mind that interest expense is recorded as incurred (ie, matching principle).

Recording Scrip Dividends

Date of declaration → Record notes payable

Retained earnings	XXX	
Notes payable		XXX

Date of record → No entry

Date of payment → Record payment and related interest expense

Notes payable	XXX	
Interest expense	XXX	
Interest payable*	XXX	
Cash		XXX

**If the time period covers more than one accounting period, any accrued interest is removed from the books*

A calendar-year company had sufficient retained earnings in Year 2 as a basis for dividends but was temporarily short of cash. It declared a dividend of $500 on April 1, Year 2, and issued promissory notes to its stockholders in lieu of cash. The notes, which were dated April 1, Year 2, had a maturity date of March 31, Year 3, and an 8% interest rate. Determine the entries that the company should record at April 1, Year 2; December 31, Year 2; and March 31, Year 3.

On April 1, Year 2, the company will record an entry to account for the scrip dividend declared:

Retained earnings	500	
Notes payable		500

Interest expense is computed from the date of declaration to the date of payment using the interest rate in the note. At December 31, Year 2, the company must accrue interest on the note. Interest expense is recorded for April through December ($500 × 8% × 9/12 months):

Interest expense	30	
Interest payable		30

On March 31, Year 3, when the notes mature, payment is made. The remaining $10 interest expense ($500 × 8% × 3/12 months) is recorded, and the notes payable and interest payable are reversed.

Notes payable	500	
Interest payable	30	
Interest expense	10	
Cash ($500 + $30 + $10)		540

Liquidating Dividends

When a dividend exceeds the balance of retained earnings prior to declaration, the amount of the dividend in excess of retained earnings represents a return of contributed capital and is known as a **liquidating dividend**. The liquidating portion of a dividend reduces an APIC account, rather than retained earnings, and must be disclosed.

Recording Liquidating Dividends

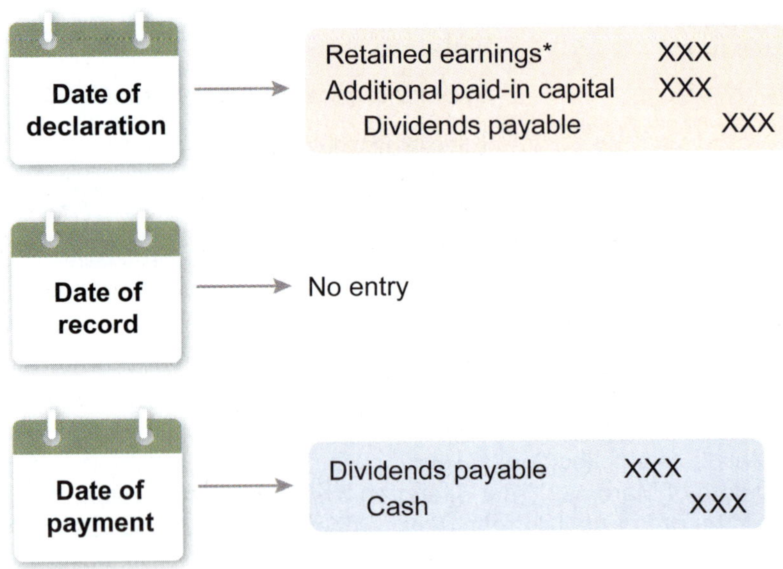

Debit limited to current balance.

The board of Lava, Inc., declares a $500 dividend on 4/1/Year 1; however, the balance in retained earnings is only $400 before recording the dividend. Determine the entry that Lava should record on the date of declaration.

Lava will first record the dividend as a reduction of retained earnings. Once the retained earnings account balance reaches zero, the remaining dividend will reduce the APIC account.

Retained earnings	400	
APIC	100	
Dividends payable		500

The liquidating portion of the dividends is $100.

Quasi-Reorganizations

In general, retained earnings may not be increased except when net income is closed into it. An exception is when a company has a **quasi-reorganization** (fresh start). Since new companies always begin with retained earnings of $0, a company with a deficit in retained earnings has the ability to eliminate that deficit by reorganizing as a new company. Accounting principles, therefore, allow a company to restate its accounts as if it had reorganized. This requires shareholder approval.

The steps to account for a quasi-reorganization are as follows:

1. Write assets down to market value, further reducing retained earnings (increasing the deficit).
2. Reduce APIC to absorb the retained earnings deficit.
3. Change value/number of shares. If needed, change par value or the number of shares of common stock to absorb the remaining deficit.

Sherbert Co. has the following balance sheet:

Assets	$10,000
Liabilities	4,000
Common stock ($1 par)	3,000
APIC	5,000
Retained earnings	(2,000)
Liabilities and stockholders' equity	$10,000

Sherbert determines that the assets have a market value of $6,000. Sherbert elects to reduce par value to accomplish a quasi-reorganization. Determine the entries that Sherbert will record in the quasi-reorganization.

First, Sherbert will write the assets down to their market value:

Retained earnings ($10,000 − $6,000)	4,000	
Assets		4,000

The retained earnings deficit is now $6,000 ($2,000 + $4,000).

Second, Sherbert will reduce APIC account down to zero:

APIC	5,000	
Retained earnings		5,000

The retained earnings deficit is now $1,000 ($6,000 − $5,000).

Finally, the common stock is reduced by $1,000 to absorb the remaining deficit. The new common stock balance will be $2,000 ($3,000 − $1,000). The new par value is calculated as follows:

$$\$2,000 = 3,000 \text{ shares} \times \text{New par value}$$

$$\text{New par value} = \$0.67$$

Common stock	1,000	
Retained earnings		1,000

The balance sheet immediately following the quasi-reorganization is as follows:

Assets	$6,000
Liabilities	4,000
Common stock ($0.67 par)	2,000
APIC	0
Retained earnings	0
Liabilities and stockholders' equity	$6,000

Treasury Stock

Treasury stock is stock that is repurchased by a firm but not retired. These treasury shares are *not paid dividends* and are *nonvoting*. They are considered **authorized and issued but not outstanding**. Treasury stock is a **contra-equity account**. No gain or loss is recorded in the income statement from the purchase, reissue, or retirement of treasury stock.

There are two options for recording treasury stock: *par value method* and *cost method*. Regardless of which method is used, total equity is reduced by the same amount. However, the balances of certain equity accounts are different under the two methods.

Par Value Method

Under the par value method, when treasury stock is **repurchased**, the following entries are recorded:

Treasury Stock: Par Value Method

Repurchase price < par value and original APIC-C/S		
Treasury stock (par value)	XXX	
APIC-C/S (original amt.)	XXX	
Cash		XXX
APIC-T/S		XXX

Accounts are decreased

Repurchase price > par value and original APIC-C/S		
Treasury stock (par value)	XXX	
APIC-C/S (original amt.)	XXX	
APIC-T/S*	XXX	
Retained earnings**	XXX	
Cash		XXX

C/S = common stock; T/S = treasury stock
**If exists from previous T/S transactions*
***If insufficient APIC-T/S*

Reissuances are treated as a regular issuance of common stock, except that the treasury stock account is credited, rather than common stock.

Treasury shares held under the par value method are **not** reported directly on the financial statements but **reduce the amount shown as common stock**.

1. Issue 700 Shares of $5 Par Common Stock at $20 Per Share		
Cash (700 × $20 sales price)	14,000	
Common stock (700 × $5 par)		3,500
APIC—Common stock (700 × ($20 − $5))		10,500

2. Repurchase 100 Shares at $16 Per Share (Less than Original Price): Par In, Par Out		
APIC—Common stock (100 × ($20 − $5))	1,500	
Treasury stock (100 × $5 par)	500	
Cash (100 × $16 repurchase price)		1,600
APIC—Treasury stock (100 × ($20 − $16))		400

3. Repurchase 100 Shares at $22 Per Share (Greater than Original Price): Par In, Par Out		
APIC—Common stock (100 × ($20 − $5))	1,500	
Treasury stock (100 × $5 par)	500	
APIC—Treasury stock* (100 × ($22 − $20))	200	
Cash (100 × $22 repurchase price)		2,200

**The APIC—Treasury stock account cannot have a net debit balance. After transaction 2, the APIC—Treasury stock account had a credit balance of $400. Therefore, the balance is sufficient to subtract the $200 resulting from transaction 3. If the amount were insufficient, retained earnings would be used.*

Under the par value method, the APIC—Common stock account is always reduced by the original amount received when the stock was issued. Treasury stock is always recorded at par.

4. Reissue 150 Shares at $18 Per Share		
Cash (150 × $18 sales price)	2,700	
Treasury stock (150 × $5 par)		750
APIC—Common stock (150 × ($18 − $5))		1,950

Under the par value method, when shares are retired, common stock is debited, and treasury stock is credited for the par value of the shares.

Cost Method

Under the cost method, when treasury stock is **repurchased** and **reissued**, the following entries are recorded:

Treasury Stock Transactions: Cost Method

Repurchased stock (recorded at cost)		
Treasury stock	XXX	
Cash		XXX

Reissued at a price *greater* than cost		
Cash	XXX	
Treasury stock		XXX
APIC-Treasury stock		XXX

Reissued at a price *less* than cost		
Cash	XXX	
APIC-Treasury stock	XXX	
Retained earnings*	XXX	
Treasury stock		XXX

No gain or loss recognized with any treasury stock transaction

Retired the stock		
Common stock	XXX	
APIC-Common stock	XXX	
Treasury stock		XXX
APIC-Treasury stock**		XXX

**Only if insufficient APIC-Treasury stock.*
***Only if original issue price is more than the cost of the treasury stock.*

Using this approach, the shares are recorded at cost and **reported separately on the financial statements** as the last account in stockholders' equity.

1. Issue 700 Shares of $5 Par Common Stock at $20 Per Share: Same as Par Value Method		
Cash (700 × $20 sales price)	14,000	
Common stock (700 × $5 par)		3,500
APIC—Common stock (700 × ($20 − $5))		10,500

2. Repurchase 200 Shares at $25 Per Share: Cost In, Cost Out		
Treasury stock (200 × $25 purchase price)	5,000	
Cash		5,000

There is no difference between shares repurchased below the original issue price or above it.

3. Reissue 50 Shares at $30 Per Share (Greater than Repurchase Price)		
Cash (50 × $30 sales price)	1,500	
APIC—Treasury stock (50 × ($30 − $25))		250*
Treasury stock (50 × $25)		1,250

**Excess of reissue price over repurchase price.*

4. Reissue 50 Shares at $18 Per Share (Less than Repurchase Price)		
Cash (50 × $18 sales price)	900	
APIC—Treasury stock*	250	
Retained earnings*	100	
Treasury stock (50 × $25)		1,250

**The total excess of repurchase price over reissue price is $350 (50 shares × ($25 − $18)). Recall that the APIC—Treasury stock account cannot have a debit balance. After transaction 3, the APIC—Treasury stock account has a $250 credit balance. The account is reduced to zero, and the remainder is debited to retained earnings.*

Sometimes firms retire their shares after purchasing them on the market, rather than treating them as treasury shares. Retired shares are placed back into the **authorized but unissued** category.

Remember that treasury stock is a contra-owner's equity account, not an asset. CPA exam questions in the past calling for the candidate to identify errors have listed treasury stock in the investment section of the balance sheet. These questions are solved by reducing the investment account by the amount recorded as treasury stock and reinstating the treasury stock account as a reduction from total equity.

Pass-Through Entities

Pass-through entities (eg, partnerships) account for equity differently than corporations do. Specifically, the equity section identifies the capital balances of **each partner** and does not distinguish between contributed capital and retained earnings. Additionally, a partnership isn't a taxable entity, so no provisions are recorded for current or deferred income taxes in the financial statements.

Historically, CPA exam questions have focused on the allocation of equity among partners in a pass-through entity.

Formation of a Pass-Through Entity

When forming a partnership, **each partner contributes assets** in exchange for a **partnership interest** that is recorded in the partner's capital account. Partner contributions are recorded as follows:

Treatment of Partner Contributions to a Partnership		
Item Contributed	**Valuation**	**Treatment**
Assets (eg, cash, building, equipment)	Fair value	Increases partner's capital
Noncash asset subject to a liability (eg, mortgage)	Asset's fair value *less* present value of liability	Increases partner's capital
Liabilities assumed by partnership	Present value	Increases partnership liabilities

Each partner's capital account is adjusted each period by the partner's share of profits and losses specified in the partnership agreement. The profit-sharing ratio *does not impact* the initial recording of capital.

Chase and Andrew formed a partnership on January 1, Year 1. Chase contributed cash of $60,000. Andrew contributed property with a tax basis of $25,000, an original cost of $30,000, and a FV of $45,000. The property is subject to a mortgage with a present value (PV) of $16,000. Determine what Chase's and Andrew's capital accounts should be at January 1, Year 1.

Chase's capital account equals $60,000 (ie, the FV of the asset on the day that it was contributed).

Andrew's capital account equals $29,000 ($45,000 FV of asset − $16,000 PV of mortgage assumed).

Allocation of Partnership Income (Loss) to Partners

In accordance with the partnership agreement, each partner is entitled to a portion of the partnership's net income/loss and to special allocations and allowances (eg, bonuses, salary allowances). Partners' accounts are credited for contributions and debited for distributions directly.

Income is allocated in three steps:

1. Partners may be **allocated interest** on the average capital balances they maintained during the year.

2. One or more partners may be allocated a **fixed salary** for services rendered to the partnership.
3. The **remaining income** or loss is allocated based on the partnership agreement or, in the absence of an agreement, equally.

Allocation of Partnership Net Income/Loss to Partners

Partnership net income/loss to be allocated	–	Special allocations (eg, bonuses) and allowances (eg, salary and interest) granted to individual partners	=	Remaining net income/loss to be allocated to partners*

**Allocated using established partner percentages*

A cash withdrawal to a partner represents a return of investment and does not impact the allocation of net income/loss. Instead, it reduces the capital account of the partner withdrawing the cash.

Abe, Bea, and Cy are equal partners in the ABC Partnership and maintained average capital balances during Year 1 of $50,000, $80,000, and $20,000, respectively. To encourage the partners to leave capital in the business, each partner is paid 10% on the capital balances they maintain. Bea is provided a $20,000 salary on top of profits. If partnership income during Year 1 totaled $71,000, determine the allocation of partnership income to Abe, Bea, and Cy.

The allocation is as follows:

	Abe	Bea	Cy	To Allocate
Capital balances	**$50,000**	**$80,000**	**$20,000**	
Income before interest allowance				$71,000
10% interest allowance	5,000	8,000	2,000	(15,000)
Subtotal				56,000
Bea's salary		20,000		(20,000)
Subtotal				36,000
Remainder allocated equally	12,000	12,000	12,000	(36,000)
Income/loss allocated	$17,000	$40,000	$14,000	–

Notice that the income allocated to each partner adds up to the total income earned by the partnership ($17,000 + $40,000 + $14,000 = $71,000).

Admission of a New Partner

The **admission of a new partner** to a business often requires a **reallocation** of the capital balances of both the new and old partners. Accounting for the admission depends on which of three methods is used: **bonus**, **exact**, **or goodwill**.

Bonus Method

If the **bonus method** is used to account for the admission, a reallocation of the capital balances of both the **new and old partners is required**.

The reallocation is based on the difference between the BV of the capital account acquired and the FV of the contribution. If the contribution is more than the capital's BV, a bonus is paid to the old partners; if less, then a bonus is paid to the new partner. The existing partners' old profit and loss ratio is used to allocate any bonus.

The DanDee partnership has two partners, Dan and Dee, who share profits on a 60:40 basis and have capital balances of $30,000 and $100,000, respectively. Lyon is admitted to a 1/6 interest in initial capital and profits in exchange for a $50,000 contribution to the partnership. The partnership has elected to use the bonus method to record the admission of Lyon into the partnership. Determine the entry to record the admission of Lyon.

The admission of a new partner using the bonus method is calculated as follows:

Admission of a New Partner Using the Bonus Method			
Step 1	Determine total partnership capital (BV)	Add the FV of new partner's contribution to existing partnership capital accounts	$30,000 + $100,000 + $50,000 = $180,000
Step 2	Determine new partner's share of total partnership capital	Step 1 × New partner's % of capital interest purchased	$180,000 × 1/6 = $30,000
Step 3	Determine amount of bonus	Difference between FV of contribution and Step 2	$30,000 − $50,000 = $20,000 bonus
Step 4	Determine who receives bonus (use old partners' profit/loss ratio to allocate)	If contribution > Step 2, bonus to old partners If contribution < Step 2, bonus to new partner	$50,000 contribution > $30,000 Bonus to old partners

Since the new partner's contribution ($50,000) is different from the new partner's share of partnership capital ($30,000), a $20,000 bonus exists. This bonus is allocated to the old partners because the new partner effectively gave more ($50,000) than what the share of partnership interest was worth ($30,000). The bonus is allocated to the old partners using their profit/loss ratio.

The entry to record the admission of Lyon into the partnership is as follows:

	Debit	Credit
Cash	50,000	
Capital – Dan ($20,000 × 60%)		12,000
Capital – Dee ($20,000 × 40%)		8,000
Capital – Lyon		30,000

Goodwill Method

The **goodwill method** is based on the **total value of the partnership implied** by the new partner's contribution. If the existing partners' capital accounts do not equal their pro rata share of the implied BV, goodwill is recorded for the difference. The **old partners'** capital balances are **increased** by the goodwill according to their old profit/loss ratios.

Assume the same facts as the previous example. However, the partnership now elects to use the goodwill method to record the admission of Lyon into the partnership. Determine the entry to record the admission of Lyon.

The admission of a new partner using the goodwill method is calculated as follows:

Admission of a New Partner Using the Goodwill Method			
Step 1	Determine the implied BV of the partnership	New partner's contribution ÷ New partner's ownership %	\$50,000 ÷ (1/6) = \$300,000
Step 2	Determine the old partners' share of implied BV	Implied value of partnership × Old partners' % ownership	\$300,000 × (5/6) = \$250,000
Step 3	Calculate goodwill	Old partners' share of implied value – Old partners' capital account balances	\$250,000 – \$130,000 = **\$120,000 goodwill**

The goodwill is allocated to the old partners using their profit/loss ratio.

The entry to record the admission of Lyon into the partnership is as follows:

Cash	50,000	
Goodwill	120,000	
Capital – Dan (\$120,000 × 60%)		72,000
Capital – Dee (\$120,000 × 40%)		48,000
Capital – Lyon		50,000

Exact Method

Occasionally, a partnership wishes to admit a partner and provide them with a certain fraction of initial capital **without recording either a bonus or goodwill** (exact method). Under the **exact method**, the old partners' capital accounts do not change; however, their percentage of ownership decreases. The value of the new partnership is based on the old partners' new percentage of ownership. The new partner must contribute an amount that will achieve the desired initial ownership percentage based on the new value of the total partnership capital.

Alpha and Beta are partners in a partnership. They share profits on a 70:30 basis and have capital balances of $45,000 and $60,000, respectively. Gamma is admitted as a new partner with a 20% interest. No goodwill or bonus is to be recorded. Determine the entry to record the admission of Gamma.

Since no goodwill or bonus is to be recorded, the exact method is used.

The entry to record the admission of Gamma into the partnership is as follows:

Admission of a New Partner Using the Exact Method			
Step 1	Determine the old partners' new % ownership in the new partnership	100% – New partner's % ownership	100% − 20% = 80%
Step 2	Determine the value of the new partnership capital	Old partners' capital accounts ÷ Old partners' new % ownership in the new partnership	($45,000 Alpha + $60,000 Beta) = $105,000 $105,000 ÷ 80% = $131,250
Step 3	Determine new partner's contribution	Value of new partnership capital × New partner's % ownership	$131,250 × 20% = $26,250

The entry to record the admission of Lyon into the partnership is as follows:

Cash	26,250	
Capital – Gamma		26,250

On the CPA exam, multiple-choice questions on the exact method may require a calculation such as the one above. To save time, instead of solving for the new partner's contribution, each answer choice can be plugged in.

Old partners' capital accounts
+ New partner's capital account (answer choices plugged)
Total capital accounts
× New partner's ownership percentage
New partner's capital account

The answer that computes correctly is the correct answer.

Retirement

When a partner **retires**, the partnership's assets and liabilities are adjusted to FV to determine the value of the retiring partner's interest. A retiring partner is entitled to be paid for their percentage of any increase in the net assets' FV that is credited to their capital account.

The **goodwill** method or the **bonus** method may be used to record the retirement:

Retirement of a Partner: Bonus vs. Goodwill Method

	Bonus	Goodwill
Excess amount paid to retiring partner over capital account	Recorded as bonus paid by remaining partners	Recorded as new goodwill
Capital accounts affected	Only the remaining partners	All partners (including retiring partner)
Impact on capital accounts	Reduced by % share of bonus based on *new* profit/loss ratios	Increased for % share of goodwill based on *old* profit/loss ratios

Note: The excess amount paid is never treated as an expense of the partnership.

The Bee El Tee Partnership's three partners share profits and losses equally and have capital accounts of $30,000, $100,000, and $50,000, respectively. Tee retires; the partnership's net assets are appraised at an amount $60,000 higher than BV, and Tee is then paid $80,000 at retirement. The partnership uses the bonus method to account for Tee's retirement. Determine the capital balances of the remaining partners, Bee and El, after Tee's retirement.

The capital balances are calculated as follows:

	Net Assets	Bee	El	Tee
Before retirement	$180,000	$30,000	$100,000	$50,000
Increase in FV of assets	60,000	20,000	20,000	20,000
Subtotal	240,000	50,000	120,000	70,000
Payment to Tee	(80,000)			(80,000)
Subtotal	160,000	50,000	120,000	(10,000)
Bonus		(5,000)	(5,000)	10,000
After retirement	160,000	45,000	115,000	–

After Tee's retirement, Bee's capital account is $45,000, and El's capital account is $115,000.

Liquidation

When a partnership **liquidates**:

- The noncash assets are sold,
- Any resulting gain or loss is allocated to the partners based on their profit/loss ratios, and
- The liabilities are paid.

The remaining cash is distributed based on the partners' updated capital accounts. If a partner owes money to the partnership (eg, a loan) and does not repay it, the unpaid balance reduces the cash distributed to that partner. If one partner has a deficit balance, it is allocated to the remaining partners based on their new profit/loss percentages.

The following condensed balance sheet is presented for the PB and Jay partnership. PB and Jay share in the profits and losses on a 60:40 basis:

Noncash assets	$400,000
Jay, loan	20,000
	$420,000
Accounts payable	$180,000
PB, capital	135,000
Jay, capital	105,000
	$420,000

The partners have decided to liquidate the partnership. The noncash assets are sold for $280,000. Determine the amount of available cash that should be distributed to each partner.

Cash will be distributed to each partner as follows:

1. Noncash assets are sold	$280,000 − $400,000 = ($120,000) loss
2. Loss is allocated to partners	PB: ($120,000) × 60% = ($72,000) Jay: ($120,000) × 40% = ($48,000)
3. Liabilities are paid	$280,000 − $180,000 = $100,000 remaining cash
4. Cash is distributed	PB capital: ($135,000 − $72,000) = $63,000 Jay capital: ($105,000 − $48,000) − $20,000 loan* = $37,000
Check figure: $63,000 + 37,000 = $100,000	

**Jay has not repaid the loan; therefore, it is reduced from the cash to be distributed to Jay.*

PB will receive $63,000 of cash, and Jay will receive $37,000 of cash.

In an **installment liquidation**, assets may be sold in stages. In the first stage, all assets not yet sold are written off as a total loss (because of the conservatism principle and since they aren't in cash form and cannot be used to pay partners yet). Any deficit reallocation is made as noted above.

FAR

Area III: Select Transactions

FAR 16
Accounting Changes & Error Corrections

FAR 16: Accounting Changes & Error Corrections

16.01 Accounting Changes & Error Corrections

Overview

Representative Task (Application): Calculate a required adjustment to the financial statements due to an accounting change (change in accounting principle or change in accounting estimate) or error correction and determine whether it requires prospective or retrospective application.

ASC 250 defines an accounting change as one of the following:

- Change in accounting principle
- Change in accounting estimate
- Change in reporting entity

The correction of an error in previous financial statements (F/S) is not an accounting change; however, the procedures for recording are the same as for accounting principle changes. Accounting changes and errors can be accounted for retrospectively, prospectively, or as a retroactive adjustment:

Accounting Changes

Type	Accounting Treatment	Examples
Change in accounting principle	Retrospective	• Inventory valuation method • Long-term contract revenue recognition (eg, over time instead of at a point in time)
Change in accounting estimate*	Prospective	• Credit losses • Inventory obsolescence • Sales returns and allowances • Salvage values of depreciable assets • Warranty obligations
Change in reporting entity	Retrospective	• Consolidated F/S** instead of individual F/S • Changing the specific subsidiaries presented in consolidated F/S
Error correction	Retroactive	• Change from cash basis (non-GAAP) to accrual basis (GAAP) • Mathematical errors

**A change that is both a principle and estimate change is accounted for as change in accounting estimate.*

***F/S = Financial statements*

Retrospective means that the change is applied to prior periods as if that principle had always been used. **Prospective** means that the change is applied to current and future periods only. **Retroactive** adjustment, also called **prior period** adjustment, is similar to retrospective adjustment but is specifically reserved for error changes only.

Change in Accounting Principle

A change in accounting principle includes the following:

Change in Accounting Principle

- A change from one generally accepted principle to another generally accepted principle when there are two or more acceptable alternative accounting treatments
- A change to a generally accepted principle when the current principle in use by the entity is no longer acceptable
- A change in the method of applying an accounting principle

Examples of changes in accounting principle include changes in inventory valuation methods (eg, LIFO to FIFO) and changes in long-term contract revenue recognition (eg, completed contract to percentage of completion).

A change from one GAAP method to another GAAP method is a change in accounting principle. A change from a non-GAAP method to a GAAP method is an error correction.

An entity may only change an accounting principle if either:

- The change is required as a result of an authoritative pronouncement or
- The entity can justify the change in that it is preferable

When new accounting standards that require a change in accounting principles are released, related authoritative pronouncements provide transition guidance indicating how the change is to be implemented. When provided, those guidelines are required to be followed.

A change in accounting principle, assuming no transition guidance is provided, is accounted for **retrospectively** as follows:

The company will determine the **cumulative effect** of the change by comparing reported retained earnings (R/E) to what R/E would have been if the new accounting principle had always been applied by the company.

The cumulative effect is reported as an adjustment to *beginning* R/E, net of tax, in the earliest period presented. Carrying amounts of impacted assets and liabilities are updated directly to reflect the change in the earliest period presented.

If comparative F/S are presented, the above changes to beginning R/E and impacted assets and liabilities flow through to all years presented. Any prior year F/S that are presented (ie, income statements and balance sheets) are restated to reflect the change.

On January 1, Year 4, MK Company changed its method of inventory valuation from weighted average to FIFO. Management believes that the FIFO method more accurately portrays the movement of goods and provides a better matching of revenues and expenses.

The change is also being made for tax purposes. The client's effective tax rate for all years is **40%**. Assume that comparative F/S are not being prepared.

Determine the adjustment that MK will record to reflect the change in inventory method.

Ending Inventory	Weighted Average	FIFO
Year 1	25,000	27,000
Year 2	30,000	34,000
Year 3	42,000	50,000

MK will **adjust inventory by $8,000** ($50,000 − $42,000) for the impact of the change and **retained earnings by $4,800** ([$50,000 − $42,000] × [1 − 0.4]) for the impact of the change, net of tax. MK will also record a **current income tax liability of $3,200** ([50,000 − 42,000] × 0.4) for the tax impact of the change.

MK will record the following journal entry on January 1, Year 4:

Inventory	8,000	
Retained earnings		4,800
Current income tax liability		3,200

If comparative F/S had been presented, MK would have reported an adjustment in the earliest period presented and restated inventory, income, retained earnings, and any other related accounts. These adjustments would flow through to all subsequent years.

Direct and Indirect Effects

A change in accounting principle has direct and indirect effects on the F/S:

Direct Effects	Indirect Effects
Recognized changes in assets or liabilities that are necessary to effect the change in accounting principle (eg, the change in inventory due to a change in cost flow assumption)	Changes in current or future cash flows resulting from making a change in accounting principle (eg, bonuses based on earnings)

Generally, the cumulative effect of the change (ie, the adjustment to R/E) should only include direct effects.

Exceptions

Impracticability exception: If it is impracticable to determine the cumulative effect to any of the prior periods, the new accounting principle is applied as if the change was made **prospectively**.

- For example, if a company changed inventory valuation from another inventory cost flow method to LIFO, it is impracticable to determine the cumulative effect of applying this change retrospectively because records of inventory purchases and sales are no longer available for all prior years. The change should be handled prospectively.

Inseparability exception: If a change in accounting principle is inseparable from a change in accounting estimate, it is accounted for as a **change in accounting estimate** (ie, handled prospectively).

- For example, a change in depreciation, amortization, or depletion method is considered to be both a change in accounting principle and change in accounting estimate. As such, it is accounted for as a change in estimate.

Change in Accounting Estimate

A **change in accounting estimate** is derived from new information and is a change that causes the carrying amount of an asset or liability to change or that changes the subsequent accounting for an asset or liability. Estimate changes are the most frequent type of accounting change.

Examples of changes in accounting estimate include changes in the following:

- Credit losses
- Inventory obsolescence
- Sales returns and allowances
- Depreciation methods used and/or salvage values of depreciable assets
- Warranty obligations

A change in accounting estimate is accounted for **prospectively**. The change is implemented in current and future periods and does not affect previous periods (ie, no effect on previously reported R/E).

On January 1, Year 5, Rose Company purchased a machine for $22,000. Rose initially implemented the double-declining balance method of depreciation and estimated that the machine would have a useful life of five years and a residual value of $2,000. Depreciation under the double-declining balance method in Year 5 was $8,800.

On January 1, Year 6, Rose received new information suggesting that the asset would provide more uniform benefits and for a longer period of time than initially expected. As such, Rose changed its method of depreciating the machine from double-declining balance to straight line and revised its estimates for useful life and salvage value.

The revised estimates as of January 1, Year 6, were a useful life of nine years and a residual value of $200. Determine the journal entry that Rose will record for depreciation expense at the end of Year 6.

The process to calculate revised depreciation expense is as follows:

Step	Description	Application to Example
1	Calculate previous depreciation expense	$8,800 (given)
2	Determine accumulated depreciation balance on date of change	$8,800 × 1 year = $8,800
3	Calculate current carrying value	$22,000 − 8,800 = $13,200
4	Calculate revised depreciation expense (use remaining estimated life here)	$\frac{(\$13,200 - 200)}{(9 \text{ years} - 1 \text{ year})} = \$1,625$

At the end of Year 6, Rose will record the following journal entry for depreciation expense:

Depreciation expense	1,625	
Accumulated depreciation		1,625

Change in Reporting Entity

A change in reporting entity results in F/S that are essentially those of a different reporting entity. A change in reporting entity is limited mainly to the following:

- Presenting consolidated F/S in place of individual F/S for each entity
- Changing the specific subsidiaries that comprise consolidated F/S
- Changing the entities included in combined F/S
- Changes between the use of the equity method of accounting and consolidation of a subsidiary, without a change in the ownership percentage of stock

A change due to new ownership, such as a business combination reported under the acquisition method, is not a change in reporting entity.

A change in reporting entity is applied **retrospectively**. All prior periods' F/S that are presented are modified to reflect the new reporting entity as if that had been the reporting entity as of the beginning of the earliest period presented.

When a change in reporting entity occurs, the changes affect virtually every account on the balance sheet and income statement. As such, computational problems on this type of change are generally beyond the scope of the CPA exam.

Error Correction

An error in prior period F/S is caused when correct information existed at the time the statements were prepared but a misstatement was made, causing erroneous recognition, measurement, or disclosure. It is presumed that the correct reporting could have been accomplished in the past.

Examples of error corrections include the following:

- Changes from non-GAAP to GAAP (eg, cash to accrual, credit losses direct write-off method to allowance method)
- Changes in estimates due to initial negligence or bad faith
- Mathematical errors
- Mistakes in applying GAAP (eg, failure to record depreciation expense)

If an error is discovered during the current year and the F/S have not been issued, then the error is corrected by recording the appropriate adjusting entry. If an error is discovered subsequent to F/S issuance, then a prior period adjustment (PPA) may be required.

Subsequent error correction is accounted for in a similar manner to a change in accounting principle. However, here, the term **retroactive adjustment** or **restatement** is used rather than **retrospective application** to distinguish voluntary principle changes from restatements due to errors.

Accounting for the error correction is dependent on the error's impact as well as the type of F/S being issued (ie, comparative vs. noncomparative):

Impact	**Balance Sheet**	**Net Income**		
F/S Issued		No comparative F/S	Comparative F/S	Comparative F/S
Error Presented			Period with error presented	Period with error not presented
Adjustment	Adjust account directly in earliest period presented	Cumulative prior period adjustment to beginning retained earnings (net of tax)* in current period F/S	Correct error directly in period with error	Cumulative prior period adjustment to beginning retained earnings (net of tax)* in earliest period presented

**If the error impacts OCI rather than net income, adjustment will be made to beginning AOCI (net of tax).*

Commonly tested errors impact the balance sheet. For example, failure to record depreciation expense in noncomparative F/S would impact the balance sheet (direct adjustment to accumulated depreciation and adjustment to beginning R/E).

When comparative F/S are issued, adjustments will flow through to all subsequent years presented. Any prior period F/S presented (ie, income statements and balance sheets) are restated to reflect the change.

Remember that changes in accounting principle are accounted for in a similar manner to error corrections.

On January 2, Year 4, Slip Inc. discovered that it had incorrectly expensed equipment that was purchased on January 2, Year 1, for $800,000. The equipment should have been depreciated straight line over ten years, with a salvage value of $15,000. Slip does not present comparative F/S. Determine the correcting entry that Slip will make on January 2, Year 4.

When the error was discovered, the equipment would have been depreciated for three years, resulting in accumulated depreciation of $235,500 ([$800,000 cost − 15,000 salvage value] / 10 year useful life × 3 years elapsed).

A prior period adjustment will be made to beginning retained earnings. Slip will record the following journal entry on January 2, Year 4:

Account	Debit	Credit
Equipment	800,000	
Retained earnings		564,500
Accumulated depreciation		235,500

Note: For purposes of this question, tax liability is disregarded.

Many accounting errors counterbalance or self-correct after a certain period of time if they are not corrected. These errors require no entry to correct R/E or any other current account balance after the error counterbalances. However, prior year F/S remain in error.

Impact of Accounting Changes and Error Corrections

Representative Task (Analysis): Derive the impact to the financial statements and related note disclosures of an identified accounting change or an error correction.

Required **note disclosures** for accounting changes and error corrections include the following:

Change in Accounting Principle	• Nature of and reason for change (including explanation of why new change is preferable) • Method of applying change • For current and prior periods adjusted retrospectively, the effect of the change on net income and any other affected F/S line item and per-share amounts • Cumulative effect of change on R/E as of the beginning of the earliest period presented • If retrospective application is impracticable, the reasons why and a description of alternative method used • Description of indirect effects of the change, including amounts recognized in the current period and related per-share amounts • Summaries of financial results (eg, major F/S subtotals for the previous ten years) as reported in the notes are also retrospectively adjusted for the change
Change in Accounting Estimate	• If change is material, effect of change on comprehensive income and per-share amounts
Change in Reporting Entity	• Nature of and reason for change • Effect of change on comprehensive income and related per-share amounts
Error Correction	• A statement that previously issued F/S were restated and nature of error • Effect of correction on each F/S line item and any per-share amounts for each prior period presented • Cumulative effect of the change on R/E as of the beginning of the earliest period presented • Pre- and post-tax effects of the correction on net income for each prior period presented

The section below provides an example that focuses on the impact of an error and subsequent error correction.

Lorch Company reported $900,000 of ending inventory at December 31, Year 1. During Year 3, Lorch discovered that Year 1 inventory was materially overstated. Assume that Lorch uses the periodic inventory method and determines year-end inventory through physical counts.

Task 1: Determine the effects of the error on the Year 1 and Year 2 F/S. For each line item, select the impact, if any, that the error had in each year. Choices are Overstate, Understate, and No effect.

Line Item	Year 1 Effect	Year 2 Effect
Inventory	**A. Overstate** B. Understate C. No effect	A. Overstate B. Understate **C. No effect**
Cost of goods sold	A. Overstate **B. Understate** C. No effect	**A. Overstate** B. Understate C. No effect
Net income	**A. Overstate** B. Understate C. No effect	A. Overstate **B. Understate** C. No effect
Retained earnings	**A. Overstate** B. Understate C. No effect	A. Overstate B. Understate **C. No effect**

Net sales		$XXX
COGS:		
Beginning inventory	$XXX	
Purchases	XXX	
Goods available for sale	$XXX	
Less: ending inventory	↑ (XXX)	
COGS		↓ (XXX)
Gross margin (profit)		↑ $XXX
Operating/nonoperating expenses		(XXX)
Net income		↑ **$XXX**

When transferred, will overstate retained earnings

There is an **inverse relationship** between ending inventory and COGS. When inventory is sold, COGS is expensed on the income statement. Thus, as inventory decreases (ie, is sold), COGS increases (an inverse relationship).

Therefore, when an inventory error occurs, it affects both the balance sheet and income statement amounts. The calculation of net income illustrates the relationships among these accounts. Under the periodic inventory method, COGS is determined by deducting ending inventory from goods available for sale (ie, beginning inventory + purchases). COGS is then deducted from net sales to determine gross profit. Finally, operating and nonoperating expenses are deducted from gross profit to determine net income. The interrelatedness of these accounts results in a cascade effect when an error occurs.

Year 1: The arrows in the above image depict Lorch's error. Here, in Year 1, **ending inventory is overstated**. Because ending inventory has an inverse relationship with COGS, overstating ending inventory results in **understating COGS**. There are amounts in the ending inventory account that should have been sent to the income statement as COGS but were not. Because COGS is deducted from net sales, an understated COGS results in **overstating gross profit and, therefore, net income**. The overstated net income is closed to retained earnings, resulting in an **overstated retained earnings** balance.

Year 2: At the end of Year 2, Lorch performs a physical count of inventory once again. This count is independent of Year 1; therefore, **ending inventory is correct**. Lorch then derives COGS using beginning inventory, purchases, and ending inventory. Although Year 2 ending inventory is correct, Year 2 beginning inventory (ie, Year 1 ending inventory) is overstated. Based on the COGS formula provided above, beginning inventory has a direct relationship with COGS; thus, overstating beginning inventory results in **overstating COGS**. When COGS is overstated, **net income is understated**.

Lorch's inventory count is correct at Year 2, meaning that Lorch accurately identified, in total, what was on hand and, therefore, what was sold. Combined Year 1 and Year 2 COGS and, consequently, combined Year 1 and Year 2 net income are correct. Retained earnings include aggregate net income, so **retained earnings at Year 2 are correct**.

Task 2: Determine the effect of the error on Lorch's **inventory turnover ratio** in Year 1 and Year 2. Select the impact, if any, that the error had on the inventory turnover ratio in each year. Choices are Overstate, Understate, and Indeterminable.

Ratio	Year 1 Effect	Year 2 Effect
Inventory turnover ratio	A. Overstate **B. Understate** C. Indeterminable	**A. Overstate** B. Understate C. Indeterminable

Inventory turnover ratio changes

$$\uparrow \text{Inventory turnover} = \frac{\uparrow \text{COGS}}{\downarrow \text{Average inventory}}$$

$$\downarrow \text{Inventory turnover} = \frac{\downarrow \text{COGS}}{\uparrow \text{Average inventory}}$$

The inventory turnover ratio is calculated as COGS / average inventory (ie, beginning inventory + ending inventory / 2).

Year 1: In Year 1, ending inventory (which, because we are in Year 1, is also equal to average inventory) was overstated and COGS was understated. An overstatement (ie, increase) in the denominator of a ratio, coupled with an understatement (ie, decrease) in the numerator, leads to an understatement (ie, decrease) in the ratio overall. The **inventory turnover ratio is understated**.

Year 2: In Year 2, ending inventory is correct and beginning inventory and COGS are overstated. The overstatement of beginning inventory leads to an overstatement (ie, increase) in the denominator. The overstatement of COGS leads to an overstatement (ie, increase) in the numerator. In general, an overstatement in both the numerator and denominator may have an indeterminable impact on the ratio. However, here, the overstatement of COGS (ie, the numerator) has a larger effect on the ratio.

Year 2 COGS and beginning inventory are overstated by the same amount (the amount for items that were sold during Year 1 but not reflected as sold until Year 2). The impact of the overstatement in the denominator is diluted, as beginning inventory is averaged with ending inventory. Meanwhile, COGS (ie, the numerator) still carries the entirety of the overstatement. The impact of the overstatement on the numerator is greater than that on the denominator; the **inventory turnover ratio is overstated**.

Task 3: Prepare the entry that Lorch would record in Year 3 to correct the Year 1 overstatement of inventory. For both the debit and credit line, select the appropriate accounts, if any, that Lorch would post to correct the error.

JE line	Account
Debit	A. Retained earnings B. Net Income C. Inventory D. Cost of goods sold **E. No entry needed**
Credit	A. Retained earnings B. Net Income C. Inventory D. Cost of goods sold **E. No entry needed**

Generally, inventory errors correct themselves after two years. At the end of Year 2, Lorch's ending inventory and retained earnings are correct. Starting in Year 3, beginning inventory (ie, Year 2 ending inventory) will be correct. Therefore, COGS and net income will also be correct. No adjustments are needed in Year 3.

If, in Year 3, Lorch presents comparative F/S, Lorch will need to restate Year 1 and Year 2 to reflect the correct balances for inventory, COGS, net income, and retained earnings.

The terms "overstate" and "understate" can add a layer of complexity when reasoning through a simulation. As you practice, consider simplifying the language provided; "overstated" can be replaced with "too high" and "understated" can be replaced with "too low."

FAR 17
Contingencies & Commitments

FAR 17: Contingencies & Commitments

17.01 Contingencies & Commitments

Contingencies

Representative Task (Remembering & Understanding): Recall the recognition and disclosure criteria used to identify commitments and contingencies.

Representative Task (Application): Calculate amounts of contingencies and prepare journal entries.

A **contingency** is an *existing condition* (at the balance sheet date) involving **uncertainty** as to the outcome and will be resolved when a future event occurs or fails to occur. There are two types of contingencies:

- **Contingent losses:** Recognition depends on the *probability* of those losses occurring
- **Contingent gains:** Not recognized until the underlying gain-causing event occurs (ie, the gains are realized)

Loss Contingencies

Examples of loss contingences include the following:

- Obligations related to product warranties
- Pending or threatened litigation
- Obligations related to product defects
- Threat of expropriation of assets

In assessing the probability of occurrence, **professional judgment** is employed to classify the probability into one of three categories. This assessment is performed by the entity's legal counsel. The categories include the following:

- **Probable:** The probability of occurrence is considered very high or a near certainty
- **Reasonably possible:** The probability of occurrence is neither very high nor remote. In other words, when probability of occurrence is considered along a spectrum of possibilities, the probability of occurrence is not at either end of the spectrum but is in the large middle section of the spectrum
- **Remote:** The probability of occurrence is considered to be very low or, as the name implies, remote

A determination is also made about the possibility of **estimating the amount of the contingency**. Either the amount of resulting gain or loss is reasonably estimable, or it is not. In addition, firms may be able to estimate a possible range of amounts for the gain or loss but unable to assign any amount in the range a higher probability of occurring than any other amount.

Probable Contingent Loss Accrual

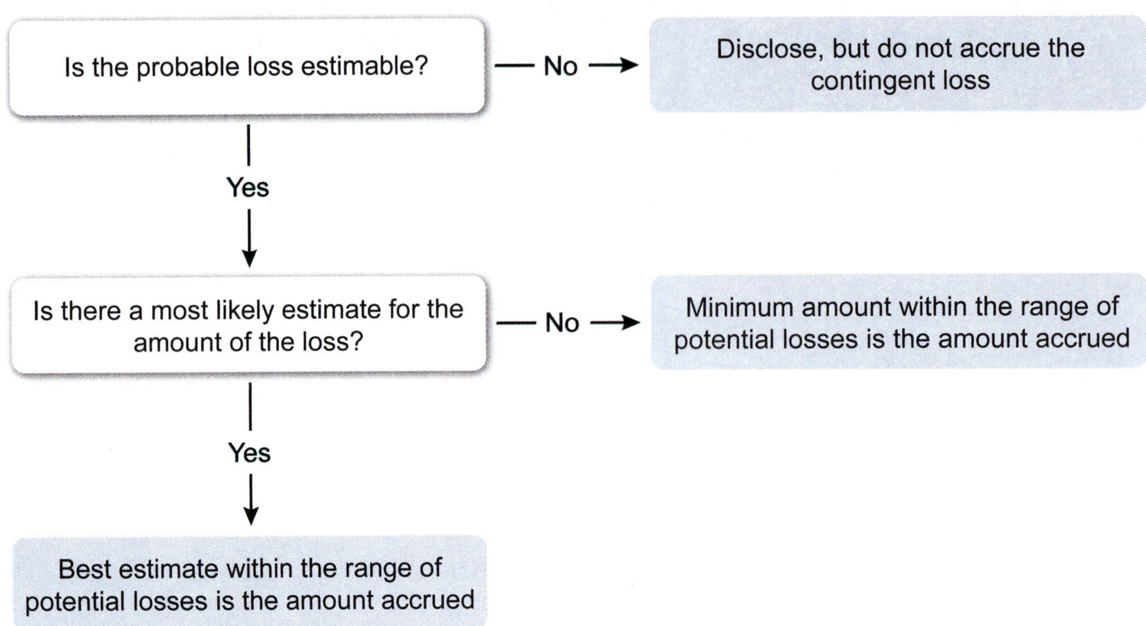

GAAP requires that if a contingent loss is both **probable and estimable**, then an estimated loss and estimated liability are recognized—that is, actually recorded in the accounts in the amount estimated. The guiding theoretical considerations here are *conservatism* and the definition of a liability.

Because the loss (asset decrease or liability increase) will most likely occur in the future and because the firm can estimate the amount, there is no reason to postpone the loss and liability recognition until it actually occurs. The general definition of a liability is met when the contingent liability is probable and estimable.

Often, in a lawsuit, there is a **range of probable loss**. When there is no amount within the range that is **most likely**, the lowest amount in that range is accrued as a contingent liability. If a range of values is given but one value in the range has a higher probability assigned to it than any other, the value with the higher probability is used to accrue the contingent liability.

GAAP Rules for a Loss Contingency

	Chance of Event	Disclose	Accrue	Range of Values
Remote	Unlikely to occur	No	No	N/A
Reasonably Possible	More than remote but less than probable	Yes	No	Disclose full range
Probable and Estimable	Likely to occur	Yes	Yes*	Accrue most probable amount or lowest amount in range
Probable and Not Estimable	Likely to occur	Yes	No	Disclose full range

**Report estimated loss on income statement and estimated liability on balance sheet.*

Assume that the Lion Company was sued during the last quarter of Year 8 because of an accident involving a vehicle owned and operated by the company. The case is expected to be settled in early Year 9.

After discussing the case with the company's legal representatives, it was decided that the company would probably lose the case, and the amount of damages could be reasonably estimated at $50,000. Determine the amount, if any, that should be recorded on the December 31, Year 8, financial statements.

Because the event is both probable and reasonably estimable, the entity will record the following entry for $50,000:

Estimated loss from pending lawsuit	50,000	
Estimated liability from pending lawsuit		50,000

Had the firm believed that the loss was only reasonably possible, the above entry would not be made. The lawsuit and possible loss would be discussed in the footnotes. Only a small percentage of contingent lawsuit losses are recognized.

Gain Contingencies

All **contingent gains** are **not recognized until** the underlying gain-causing event occurs. The conflicting treatment between probable contingent gains and losses is an application of *conservatism*. In other words, the recognition threshold for expected gains is higher than for expected losses. GAAP emphasizes conservatism when dealing with uncertainties because many F/S users prefer the risk of understated (not overstated) net income and net assets.

Gain Contingency	Disclose	Accrue
Remote = slight	No	No
Reasonably possible	Yes	No
Probable & estimable	Yes	No

Unasserted Claims and Assessments

Entities may be subject to future claims and assessments that have not yet been filed as of the balance sheet date. Examples include possible IRS actions against the entity for violations of tax law, EPA claims against the entity for environmental violations, and other events that have occurred as of the balance sheet date.

If, at the balance sheet date, it is not probable that a claim or assessment will occur or if the outcome is not expected to be unfavorable to the entity, then no recognition or disclosure is required.

If it is probable that a claim or assessment will occur and there is at least a reasonable probability that the outcome will be unfavorable to the entity, then the claim or assessment is treated as a contingency, even though no claim or assessment has been filed. The event before the balance sheet date that would trigger the claim or assessment (such as a previous year's tax return filing or environmental violation) must have occurred before the entity recognizes or discloses the contingency.

If the amount is estimable, the contingent liability is recognized. Otherwise, it is footnoted only.

Warranties

Products sold by the client often include warranties promising repairs or replacement for a limited time period. The actual loss or expense is contingent on a future event: customers making warranty claims. If the cost of the warranty can be reasonably estimated, the entity records a liability for the full amount in the year of sale.

Firms must disclose the accounting policy with respect to warranty accounting and disclose a schedule of the changes in the warranty liability for the period (increases due to expense, decreases due to claim service).

Assume that a client has cash sales of $10,000 in 20X1, its first year of operation. The products are covered by a two-year warranty, and the client estimates that costs equal to 1% of sales will have to be spent during the first year the warranty is provided and 3% of the sales during the second and final year the warranty is provided (warranty requests are expected to increase as the products age). Assume that the client has spent $60 on warranty repairs in 20X1.

The entry to record sales is as follows:

Cash	10,000	
Sales		10,000

At the same time, warranty costs estimated to total 4% of sales over the warranty periods are reported:

Warranty expense	400	
Estimated warranty liability		400

The amount spent on actual repairs is applied to the liability:

Estimated warranty liability	60	
Cash/parts inventory		60

Premiums

Premiums, such as coupons, are provided to encourage sales. The premium cost is charged to sales in the period(s) that benefit from the premium offer. Since premiums, such as coupons, may be redeemed over several reporting periods, the number of outstanding premiums is estimated at the end of each accounting period.

Fulton Cereal Company inaugurated a new sales promotional program. For every 10 cereal box tops returned to the company, customers receive a prize. Fulton estimates that only 30% of the cereal box tops reaching the consumer market will be redeemed. Additional information is as follows:

	Units	Amounts
Sales of cereal boxes	2,000,000	$1,400,000
Purchase of prizes	36,000	$ 18,000
Prizes distributed to customers	28,000	

Determine the amount that Fulton should recognize at the end of the year for the estimated cost of potential prizes outstanding.

Fulton has an estimated liability of **$16,000**. The estimated liability at the end of the year is the value of the prizes expected to be distributed, less the value of the prizes actually distributed.

Only 600,000 box tops (2,000,000 box tops × 30%) are expected to be redeemed. Because 10 box tops must be redeemed for one prize, 60,000 prizes (600,000 box tops / 10) are expected to be distributed. Only 28,000 prizes have been distributed. Thus, 32,000 more prizes are expected to be distributed. Each prize cost $0.50 ($18,000 / 36,000 prizes).

Number of box tops expected to be redeemed (2,000,000 × 30%)	600,000
Number of prizes expected to be distributed (600,000 / 10)	60,000
Prizes already distributed	(28,000)
Estimated prizes yet to be distributed	32,000
Estimated liability (32,000 × $0.50*)	**$16,000**

**$18,000 / 36,000 prizes*

Guarantees

There are many types of guarantees that an entity can provide. The more complex guarantees are beyond the scope of the CPA exam. However, the accounting and disclosure of the guarantee of another entity's indebtedness is something that the CPA candidate should understand.

Entities may guarantee the debt of an affiliate to help the affiliate obtain a loan or a line of credit. The guarantor must be ready to comply with the guarantee if the triggering event occurs (eg, default by the debtor whose debt is guaranteed by the guarantor).

The guarantor is **required to disclose** the following:

- The nature of the guarantee, the term of the guarantee, how the guarantee came into existence, and the triggering event
- The maximum future amount payable under the guarantee
- The carrying amount of the liability
- A description of recourse provisions or available collateral enabling the guarantor to recover the amounts paid under the guarantee, if any

If it is **probable** that the triggering event will occur and the guarantor will be required to pay under the terms of the guarantee, then the guarantor must accrue a liability associated with the guarantee.

Note Disclosure

Entities may have litigation pending that will result in a gain or loss in the future. Presentation of this contingency in the current F/S depends on how confident management and their legal counsel are in a potential settlement or judgment. The entity's attorneys will be sent an inquiry requesting an estimate of the outcome for each item in question.

The attorney's response also provides information such as the date of the occurrence and the potential monetary outcome for each pending legal action.

A sample note to the F/S is provided below:

Sample Note to Financial Statements Disclosing Contingency for Pending Litigation

Company X is in the restaurant business. During the past year, X was named the defendant in a lawsuit alleging personal injury resulting from a customer slipping and falling at one of its restaurants. Before year end, the plaintiff offered to settle the litigation for an amount in excess of $3 million. Management of X believes the matter will be resolved through arbitration with a possible loss in the range of $1 million to $1.5 million.

Commitments

Companies often commit (in a contract) to the purchase of materials to lock in the unit price of an item needed for production or resale in order to aid in cash flow budgeting and to protect against price increases. Sometimes the market price of the item declines below the contract price. The accounting for this price decline depends on whether the contract can be revised in light of the changing market conditions.

- **The contract can be modified:** The loss is required to be footnoted as a contingent liability but is not accrued in the accounts because the loss is not probable, given that the contract can be revised
- **The contract cannot be modified:** The loss must be accrued because the loss is probable and estimable. The inventory, when acquired, is recorded at market value, and a loss is recognized for the difference between the market value and the contract price

If the contract has not been executed as of the balance sheet date, the following adjusting entry is made:

Loss on purchase commitment	XXX	
Liability on purchase commitment		XXX

If the market price drops further in the second year, an additional loss is recognized when the contract is executed. Recoveries result in a gain, but only to the extent of the previously recognized loss.

In December, a firm contracted to purchase 200 units of prefabricated housing walls at $4,000 per wall. The contract is neither cancelable nor subject to revision. By December 31, the market price per wall had dropped to $3,900.

The adjusting entry at December 31 is as follows:

Loss on purchase commitment (200 × ($4,000 − $3,900))	20,000	
Liability on purchase commitment		20,000

In January, at payment date, if the market price had decreased to $3,850, the following entry would be made:

Liability on purchase commitment	20,000	
Loss on purchase commitment (200 × ($3,900 − $3,850))	10,000	
Inventory ($3,850 × 200)	770,000	
Cash		800,000

If the market price had been $3,950 at payment date, a gain of $10,000 would be recorded to partially offset the previously recorded loss and the inventory would be recorded at $3,950 per unit. If the market price exceeded $4,000 at payment date, a gain of $20,000 would be recorded to fully offset the previously recorded loss and the inventory would be recorded at $4,000 per unit, the original contract price. The contract price is the ceiling for recording the inventory. There is no floor.

Foreign currency commitments and hedge commitments are addressed in separate FAR chapters.

Recognition and Disclosure in Financial Statements

Representative Task (Analysis): Review supporting documentation to determine whether a commitment or contingency requires recognition and/or disclosure in the financial statements.

Example

Analysis-level tasks are tested with a task-based simulation (TBS) on the CPA exam. Some simulations, such as the one below, include **exhibits** that must be reviewed to extract information necessary to complete the TBS.

Directions

REV Co. is reviewing the accounting and disclosure requirements for its significant guarantees, commitments, and contingencies, including litigation, as of December 31, Year 3. The financial statements are expected to be available to be issued on February 10, Year 4.

Use the information in the exhibits to determine the amount, if any, to recognize and whether disclosure is required in REV's financial statements as of and for the year ended December 31, Year 3. Unless otherwise specified, assume that no amounts related to these guarantees, commitments, and contingencies, including litigation, have been recognized in the financial statements as of December 31, Year 3.

For each of REV's guarantees, commitments, and contingencies, do the following in the table below:

- Indicate in Column B whether disclosure is required by entering in the associated cell a "Yes" or "No," as appropriate
- Enter in Column C the asset or liability balance, if any, that should be recognized as of December 31, Year 3. Enter asset balances as positive whole dollars and liability balances as negative whole dollars. If no amount is required, enter a zero (0)

Exhibit (Supporting Documentation)

Letter from Outside Legal Counsel to REV Co. General Counsel

A&B, LLP
100 New Street
Town, NC 11115
January 31, Year 4

General counsel, REV Co.:

The following is an update on the matters for which we were retained to represent REV Co.:

- REV is a defendant in a $6,000,000 copyright infringement lawsuit brought by Beech Co. in October, Year 3. REV has offered $1,500,000 to settle the lawsuit, but Beech made a counteroffer of $5,000,000. The case is not expected to go to trial, and we believe that a loss is probable. As of the date of this letter, negotiations are ongoing. Although we cannot determine the exact amount of loss, we believe that a reasonable estimate of the loss is between $2,000,000 and $5,000,000. No amount within the range is a more likely outcome than any other amount.
- On September 15, Year 3, a $6,500,000 product liability lawsuit was brought against REV by a customer who sustained injuries while using one of REV's products. As of the date of this letter, we have completed our initial discovery and believe that the lawsuit is without merit. Given that the lawsuit lacks merit, we believe that the possibility that REV will be required to pay any amount to settle the lawsuit is remote.
- On December 1, Year 3, REV sued a competitor for $3 million as a result of a patent infringement. As of this date, we believe that it is probable that REV will prevail with a judgment of $500,000.

Sincerely,

Andrew J. Smith,
Andrew J. Smith
Lead Counsel, A&B, LLP

Answers and Explanations

	A	B	C
1	Event	Financial statement note disclosure required for Year 3?	Asset (liability) balance as of December 31, Year 3
2	Copyright infringement	Yes	($2,000,000)

The Letter from Outside Legal Counsel verified that a contingent liability is probable (ie, a liability was incurred as of December 31, Year 3) and that a range of potential loss amounts can be reasonably estimated. Therefore, disclosure is required to avoid misleading F/S users. When a range of probable potential loss estimates is available, the most likely amount to occur within the range is accrued. If no amount within the range is a better estimate than any other amount, the range's minimum amount (ie, $2,000,000) is accrued.

3	Product liability lawsuit	No	$0

The Letter from Outside Legal Counsel confirmed (as of December 31, Year 3) that the $6,500,000 product liability lawsuit brought against REV is without merit and that the possibility of loss is remote. Therefore, neither an accrual nor a disclosure in the F/S notes is required.

4	Patent infringement lawsuit	Yes	$0

Even though it is probable that REV will prevail in its lawsuit against a competitor, a gain contingency is not accrued because this might create a situation in which revenue is recognized before it is realized. Disclosure of the gain contingency is appropriate, but the company should not make any misleading implications as to the likelihood of the gain's realization.

FAR 18
Revenue Recognition

FAR 18: Revenue Recognition

18.01 Revenue Recognition

Overview

Representative Task (Remembering and Understanding): Recall concepts of accounting for revenue using the five-step model.

Under GAAP, all entities with contractual obligations to transfer goods or services to customers are subject to the revenue recognition standard, unless the contracts are accounted for under another set of standards (eg, leases and insurance contracts). The amount of revenue recognized represents the consideration that the entity **expects to receive** in exchange for those goods and services.

Process of Revenue Recognition

Revenues are recognized by applying a ***five-step process***.

Step 1. Identify the contract	• A contract is an agreement between parties that establishes enforceable rights and obligations • Contracts may be combined and accounted for as one contract or modified • All criteria for a contract must be met
Step 2. Identify the performance obligations	• A contract includes an obligation for a seller to transfer goods or services to a customer • The contract may contain a single or multiple obligations • If the goods or services are distinct, each promise is accounted for as a separate performance obligation
Step 3. Determine the transaction price	• The transaction price is the amount the seller expects to receive from the customer • The transaction price may be a fixed amount or include variable consideration (cash or other assets) • The transaction price is adjusted for any consideration payable to the customer and the time value of money, if needed
Step 4. Allocate the transaction price	• The transaction price is allocated to each performance obligation • A discount or variable amount may be included and allocated to performance obligations
Step 5. Recognize revenue	• Revenue is recognized at a point in time (eg, point of sale) when the performance obligation is satisfied, or • Revenue is recognized over time based on progress toward satisfying the performance obligation

Step 1. Identify Contracts with Customers

Representative Task (Application): Determine the amount and timing of revenue to be recognized using the five-step model and prepare journal entries.

A **customer** is defined as "a party that has contracted with an entity to obtain goods or services that are an output of the entity's ordinary activities in exchange for consideration."

A **contract** is an arrangement between two or more parties that creates legally enforceable rights and obligations. If either party can terminate the arrangement *without penalty* prior to either party's performance, it is not considered a contract. A contract will conform to four criteria:

- The parties have approved the provisions and have *committed to perform*
- The *rights* in the contract and the *payment terms* can be identified[1]
- The contract has commercial *substance*
- *Collection is probable* (ie, customer has the ability and intent to pay)

If all of the criteria are met, the arrangement is a contract with a bona fide customer and will be accounted for using the five-step process. The arrangement does not have to be reevaluated again unless there is a significant change in the facts and circumstances (eg, collection becomes unlikely) or the arrangement is modified.

If the arrangement does **not** meet all of the criteria, all amounts received will be recognized as a liability.

There is no requirement that the contract be in writing. It may be formal or informal, written or oral, and may even be implicit, based on the normal manner in which the entities or individuals act (ie, in certain industries or under specific circumstances).

Combining Contracts

In general, each contract is considered a separate accounting unit; thus, each contract is evaluated and accounted for separately. There are circumstances in which an arrangement with a customer appears to be numerous contracts, but in substance they are equivalent to a single contract. This may be done for a variety of reasons, but most provide the seller with the opportunity to accelerate or delay the recognition of revenue.

Contracts should be combined if one or more of the following criteria are met:

- Contracts are negotiated as a single package with a single commercial objective
- Price to be paid in one contract depends on the price or performance of other contracts (multiple deliverables)
- Goods/services promised in the contracts are a single performance obligation. The customer is unable to benefit from the goods/services received in one contract without the goods/services in the other

1 *FASB separates rights and payment terms into two separate criteria. Since rights and obligations go hand in hand, we combined them to reduce the number of criteria to remember.*

An entity is selling two identical machines using separate contracts, each of which has a normal sales price of $100,000. One is scheduled for delivery in the current fiscal period, and the other is scheduled for delivery in the next fiscal period.

The seller may attempt to accelerate revenue recognition by establishing a contract price of $150,000 for the machine to be delivered in the current period and only $50,000 for the one to be delivered in the next period.

However, the seller would not likely sell the second machine for $50,000 if the first one was not sold to the same customer for $150,000. Thus, the prices are interdependent, the contracts would be combined, and the two machines will be accounted for as two identical performance obligations that are part of a single contract. The total consideration of $200,000 will be allocated $100,000 to each machine.

Contract Modifications

A **contract modification** is a change in the scope and/or price of a contract that is approved by both parties. The modification may be in the form of an amendment, a change order, or a variation. It may be written, oral, or implicit from the behavior of the parties. Contract modifications are accounted for as follows:

Revenue Recognition for Contract Modifications*

Does the modification change the scope/price of the contract? — No → No change in existing contract

↓ Yes

Does the modification include additional goods/services that are distinct and have standalone selling prices? — Yes → New goods/services are a new, separate contract

↓ No

Does the modification make the remaining goods/services distinct from those already provided? — No → Update transaction price and measurement of performance obligation progress in existing contract

↓ Yes

Cancel existing contract and create a new contract

**Some modifications represent a combination of these alternatives.*

When a modification involves a change in the consideration in an unknown amount, the change will be estimated using the same approaches used to estimate variable consideration (discussed later).

Step 2. Identify Separate Performance Obligations

A contract will have at least one, and often more than one, **performance obligation**, which is an enforceable promise to transfer goods/services to a customer. Goods/services that are part of one performance obligation may be *either*:

- A single good/service or a bundle of goods/services; or
- A series of distinct goods/services that are substantially the same with the same pattern of transfer (eg, monthly cleaning service).

Performance obligations are identified at the inception of the contract. They may be explicitly stated in the contract or may be implicit due to the entity's business practices. If a contract has more than one performance obligation, each performance obligation should be allocated a portion of the transaction price and then accounted for separately.

Distinct performance obligations are those that meet *two criteria*:

- The customer must be able to benefit from the good or service on its own or together using other resources that are readily available to the customer
- The promise to transfer the good or service is separately identified from other promises in the contract

A good or service can be used on its own if it can be consumed, sold for more than scrap, or used for economic benefit. Resources are readily available if they are sold separately, by the same seller or others, or if the customer has previously acquired them.

Promises are *separately identifiable* in a contract if goods/services are promised separately, as opposed to promising to deliver goods/services on a combined basis, with promised goods/services being used as inputs. Other factors may indicate that promises are separately identifiable:

- The entity does not need to integrate the goods/services with others that are part of the contract
- Other goods/services are not significantly modified by the good or service in the contract
- Goods/services are neither highly dependent on nor highly interrelated with other goods/services in the contract

When goods/services are not material, it is not necessary to determine if they constitute performance obligations. In addition, an entity may elect to consider shipping and handling costs that are incurred after the control of goods has been transferred as a cost of fulfilling a promise, rather than as a separate promise.

A furniture dealer sells a kitchen table and a living room sofa to a customer. The kitchen table could be used without the sofa and vice versa. Thus, **each** piece of furniture would represent a distinct performance obligation.

A furniture dealer sells a unique tabletop and a base designed exclusively for that tabletop. Neither the tabletop nor the base can be used without the other.

In this case, neither would be a distinct performance obligation, but on a combined basis, they make up a **single** distinct performance obligation.

However, if the tabletop was a standard size and the customer could acquire a base from a variety of vendors, then the tabletop and the base would **each** be a distinct performance obligation.

Warranties

Warranties may be purchased separately or included in the purchase price of the goods to which the warranty relates. If the warranty may be **purchased separately**, it is a distinct performance obligation. Warranties are classified further as either *assurance-type* warranties or *service-type* warranties.

An **assurance-type warranty** protects the customer from obtaining a product that is not capable of performing at the level that the seller indicated that it would. These warranties are generally only available from the seller. To the seller, an assurance-type warranty represents a *contingent liability* that is probable and estimable and should be accrued in the period incurred— generally the period of sale.

A **service-type warranty** generally provides a customer with repairs in the form of parts and labor in addition to making certain that the product performs as promised. Service-type warranties may be required by law, may extend beyond the reasonable amount of time it should take to evaluate the product's performance, or may provide services that extend beyond making certain that the asset performs as expected.

- A service-type warranty is a separately identifiable promise in a contract
- A service-type warranty is a distinct performance obligation

A company sells washing machines to the public. To stimulate sales, the company provides a three-year warranty that will repair the machine, regardless of the cause of the malfunction.

- Each washing machine has a sales price, including the warranty, of $1,200. Although the company does not sell its machines without the warranty, an appliance store within a mile of the company's store sells the same washing machine for $950 on an "as-is" basis
- Each washing machine costs the company $600
- The company does sell three-year service contracts, comparable to the warranties, to owners of washing machines purchased from other dealers, at a sales price of $250
- The company estimates that it costs approximately $175 to service the warranty

For this transaction, determine the following:

- The type of warranty
- Performance obligations
- Revenue recognized

The warranty sold with the washing machines is classified as a service-type warranty because it obligates the company to perform repairs, if needed. Therefore, both the washing machine and the service-type warranty are distinct performance obligations. The revenue of $1,200 will be allocated based on the two performance obligations' relative standalone prices. The revenue allocated to the washing machine will be recognized upon satisfaction of the performance obligation (ie, the point of sale). The revenue allocated to the warranty will be recognized while the performance obligation is being satisfied over the three-year term.

Cash (or A/R)	1,200	
Sales revenue		950
Deferred revenue—warranty		250
Cost of sales	600	
Inventory		600

Option to Purchase Additional Goods or Services

In some cases, a contract with a customer may include an option to purchase additional goods or services at a **discount**.

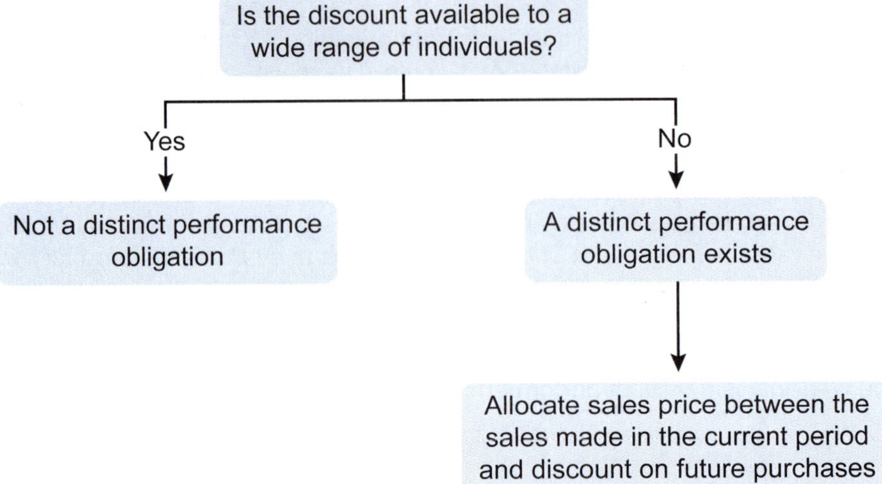

If a distinct performance obligation exists, the sales price is allocated between the following:

- **The value of the merchandise**, which will be equal to what it would be sold for if there was no discount on future purchases or any other benefits. The revenue is recognized upon satisfaction of the performance obligation, at the point of sale
- **The value of the future discounts**, which will be based on an estimate of the discounts expected to be applied adjusted to its present value. Revenue allocated to the future will be recognized while the performance obligation is being satisfied in the pattern in which the discounts are estimated to be taken or when it expires if it's a discount voucher

As part of a contract for the sale of a product for $100, an entity gives the customer a 40% discount voucher for future purchases up to $100 that is good for 30 days. The entity is also offering a 10% discount to all customers for the next 30 days. The 10% discount is not combinable with the 40% discount voucher. The entity estimates that there is an 80% chance that a customer will redeem the voucher and will, on average, purchase $50 of additional products.

Determine how the discount is applied. Then determine the allocation of the transaction price.

Since *all* customers will receive a 10% discount during the next 30 days, only the additional 30% discount constitutes a separate performance obligation.

The standalone selling prices and the resulting allocation of the $100 transaction price are calculated as follows:

Performance Obligation	Standalone Selling Price	
Product	$100	
Discount voucher	12	($50 avg. × 30% disc. × 80% probability)
Total	$112	

Performance Obligation	Allocated Transaction Price	
Product	$ 89	Recognize when control transfers (100/112 × 100)
Discount voucher	11	Recognize when redeemed/expired (12/112 × 100)
Total	$100	

Cash	100	
Revenue		89
Deferred revenue		11

Note: This example not only identified the performance obligations but also allocated the transaction price (discussed later).

Nonrefundable Prepayments

Generally, when **prepayments** are received (eg, customer buys a gift card), the entity should record a contract liability for the customer's unexercised rights to goods/services. However, when those prepayments are nonrefundable, they may be taken into income to the extent that the rights created by those payments are not expected to be redeemed by the customer (aka, breakage). Such payments are recognized in the following ways:

- As revenue in proportion to the pattern of rights exercised by customers if breakage is expected
- As revenue when the likelihood that the customer will exercise the rights becomes remote if breakage is not expected
- As a liability when the amounts are required to be remitted to a third party (eg, a government agency due to unclaimed property laws)

The beginning balance of a retailer's gift card liability (unearned revenue) for the current year is $4,600. During the year, $32,000 of gift cards were sold, and $28,000 of cards were used by customers to purchase goods at a 60% average gross margin percentage. From past experience, the firm estimates that 20% of the beginning gift card liability balance will be forfeited by customers.

Calculate the revenue and record the journal entries for these transactions.

Receipt of cash		
Cash	32,000	
Unearned revenue		32,000

Customer redemption		
Unearned revenue	28,000	
Sales revenue		28,000
Cost of goods sold	11,200	
Inventory (28,000 × 40%)		11,200

Forfeiture		
Unearned revenue	920	
Forfeited card revenue (4,600 × 20%)		920

The ending liability balance of $7,680 ($4,600 + $32,000 − $28,000 − $920) represents the remaining sales that could be recognized in the future on card redemptions. If forfeiture experience changes, the rate applied in the adjusting journal entry at year end uses the new rate (change in estimate). Eventually, all cash received from customers for gift cards is recognized as revenue, unless state law requires that the firm remit all or a portion of forfeited card receipts to the state.

Step 3. Determine the Transaction Price

The **transaction price** is the amount of consideration that the entity expects to be entitled to in exchange for transferring goods/services in a satisfactory manner, excluding amounts (such as sales taxes) to be collected on behalf of others. There are many factors that will affect the amount of revenue recognized, including the following:

- Whether the reporting entity is a principal or an agent in the transaction
- Whether variable consideration (eg, discounts, rebates, etc.) is exchanged
- Whether there are significant financing benefits associated with the transaction (ie, time value of money must be considered)
- Whether nonmonetary consideration (eg, shares of stock) is exchanged
- Whether the seller provides consideration to the customer
- Whether the seller provides the customer with a right of return

Principal versus Agent Considerations

When more parties than a seller and a buyer are involved in revenue-related transactions involving contracts with customers, the roles of the parties must be understood to determine the amount of revenue to be recognized by each party. A **principal** has the obligation to provide goods/services. An **agent** has the obligation to arrange for another party, the principal, to provide goods/services.

- When the seller is a principal in the transaction, the entire amount of revenue will be recognized, and amounts paid to third parties will be recognized as expenses or as a component of cost of sales
- When the seller is an agent, only the net amount of revenue to be retained after paying the principal is recognized

To distinguish between a principal and an agent, a significant factor to consider is **who has control** of the goods/services that are the subject of the contract before they are transferred to the customer.

- A principal controls goods/services before the transfer and may either satisfy the performance obligation or engage another to do so
- The fact that a party obtains control of the goods and immediately transfers them to a customer does not constitute control
- A principal has control of the following:
  - Goods or assets obtained from another party and transferred to the customer
  - Rights to a service to be provided by another party at the direction of the principal
  - Goods/services obtained from other parties to combine with other goods/services to satisfy a performance obligation (eg, chocolate and wine combined to create a gift basket)

- Indications of who has control of goods/services prior to transfer to the customer include the following:
  - Primary responsibility for providing goods/services to the customer
  - Risk of loss associated with inventory, both before delivery to the customer and after delivery to a customer, such as when a customer returns goods
  - Authority *to set prices* for the goods/services

Traveler's Treats is a website that sells vacations to customers on behalf of airlines and hotels. When a vacation is booked, both the airline and the hotel pay fixed-rate commissions to Traveler's Treats. The airline and the hotel provide the services directly to the customer. Traveler's Treats charges a fixed-rate commission of 3% for all services booked through its website. A customer books a $10,000 vacation. Determine which entity is the principal, which entity is the agent, and how much revenue the agent will record.

The airline and hotel are the principals, and Traveler's Treats is the agent.

Although the customer pays Traveler's Treats for the entire amount of the airline and hotel fees, only the commission portion is revenue to Traveler's Treats. By recording the commission only as revenue (as opposed to the entire amount paid by the customer for the hotel and the airline ticket), Traveler's Treats is using the net approach to recognize revenue as opposed to the gross method.

Traveler's Treats recognizes $300 in commission revenue ($10,000 × 3% commission).

Similar to the relationship between a principal and an agent, a seller may collect funds on behalf of a third party, such as when a sale is subject to state sales tax, which is collected by the seller and remitted to the taxing authority. These funds are not considered part of the consideration in a contract.

Variable Consideration

Variable consideration may result from discounts or rebates provided to buyers; credits, price concessions, or incentives; performance bonuses; or penalties. Variable consideration may also result from contingencies, such as the occurrence or nonoccurrence of a future event or a performance bonus based on achieving a milestone.

Variable consideration is a factor when either:

- The customer has a valid expectation that the seller will accept less than the contract amount in the form of a discount, rebate, refund, credit, or other price concession; or
- Facts indicate that the seller intended, as of the inception of the contract, to make a price concession.

Variable consideration is estimated at the inception of a contract and is included in the total consideration to be earned through the satisfaction of all performance obligations. The amount will be estimated, applying one of two approaches:

- Under the **expected value approach**, different amounts that will be obtained based on various levels of performance will each be assigned a probability, with the total of the probabilities equaling 100%. Each amount is multiplied by the probability of achieving it, and the total is the expected amount of variable consideration. The expected value method is used when an entity has many contracts with similar characteristics

Wesley Co. builds custom manufacturing equipment. Craig Co. engages Wesley to build a large piece of manufacturing equipment. The price of the equipment is $75,000. Craig agrees to pay an additional amount to Wesley if the equipment is delivered early; otherwise, the equipment is expected to be delivered by July 15. Wesley frequently enters into contracts with terms similar to this one. The table below lists the bonus amounts and probabilities of each delivery date:

If Wesley Delivers the Equipment by	Craig Will Pay Wesley a Bonus of	Probability of Equipment Delivery
June 30	$10,000	60%
July 5	$ 7,000	20%
July 10	$ 5,000	10%
July 15	$ 0	10%
		100%

Determine the transaction price based on the expected value method.

Because Wesley commonly enters into contracts such as this one with similar terms, Wesley should use the expected value method to estimate the transaction price. The expected value method uses a probability-weighted approach to estimate the total transaction price. In this case:

June 30 delivery	($75,000 + $10,000) × 60%	$51,000
July 5 delivery	($75,000 + $7,000) × 20%	16,400
July 10 delivery	($75,000 + $5,000) × 10%	8,000
July 15 delivery	($75,000 + $0) × 10%	7,500
Estimated total transaction price		**$82,900**

- Under the **most likely amount approach**, different outcomes are each assigned a probability such that the total of the probabilities equals 100% and the outcome with the greatest probability of occurrence is assumed to be the amount that is to be recognized. The most likely amount approach is used when an entity has two possible outcomes (eg, a performance bonus is earned or not)

Wesley Co. builds custom manufacturing equipment. Craig Co. engages Wesley to build a large piece of manufacturing equipment. The price of the equipment is $75,000. Craig agrees to pay an additional amount to Wesley if the equipment is delivered by June 30; otherwise, the equipment is expected to be delivered by July 15. If Wesley delivers the equipment by June 30, then Craig will pay Wesley a bonus of $10,000; otherwise, no bonus will be paid. Based on prior experience, Wesley's management estimates that there is a 70% likelihood that the equipment will be delivered by June 30.

Determine the transaction price based on the most likely amount approach.

Because there are two discrete outcomes, the most likely amount method should be used to determine the transaction price. There is a 70% likelihood that Wesley will make the delivery by June 30. The transaction price is **$85,000** ($75,000 for the equipment + $10,000 for the bonus) because the most likely outcome (ie, 70% likelihood) is that Wesley will deliver the equipment by June 30.

In a period in which cash receipts exceed the expected amount, the excess is reported as a refund liability.

The standard establishes a constraint on the amount of variable consideration that can be recognized. The constraint is designed to prevent an entity from recognizing revenues in one period only to be required to reverse it in a subsequent period. In applying the constraint, the entity should consider the likelihood and the magnitude of a potential reversal. Factors that increase the likelihood or the magnitude of a potential reversal include the following:

- Amounts that are susceptible to factors, such as market volatility, that are beyond the control of the entity
- Uncertainties that are not likely to be resolved for long periods
- Amounts due cannot be reliably anticipated due to a lack of experience or having experience that is not predictive
- The existence of a regular practice of making price concessions or changing terms and conditions
- The existence of a wide range of possible consideration amounts

Variable consideration is required to be reassessed each period such that the transaction price at the end of any given period reflects the circumstances at that time.

Time Value of Money

The **time value of money** is considered when measuring consideration if either the buyer or seller obtains a **significant financing benefit**. Such a benefit may be due to a provision of the contract or because of a time lag (ie, generally more than one year) between performance and payment.

Financing is considered significant when there is a difference between the amount of consideration and the cash price for the goods/services. The effect will depend on the time lag between performance and payment and prevailing interest rates.

When a financing component is included, it may be calculated using the discount rate that is applicable for separate financing transactions between the parties or the rate at which the present value of the consideration is equal to its equivalent cash price.

- The financing component is recognized as interest income or expense, separate from customer revenues
- Interest income or expense is only recognized to the extent that a contract asset or liability has been recognized

There is **no financing** component included in measuring consideration if:

- The customer paid in advance and the timing of performance is at the discretion of the buyer;
- Variable consideration is significant and is contingent on factors outside the control of the entity; or
- The difference between the amount of consideration and the cash price for the goods/services is due to factors other than financing, and the amount is commensurate with some factor, such as protection from nonperformance.

When the time between performance and payment is *expected to be one year or less*, no financing component is required.

Noncash Consideration

Noncash consideration (eg, shares of stock, other assets) is measured at **fair value**.

- When the fair value is not determinable, it will be measured by reference to the standalone selling price of goods/services exchanged
- Resources contributed by the customer to assist the entity in satisfying a performance obligation are accounted for as noncash consideration if the entity obtains control

Wolf Company sold goods to Frank Company for the rights to a patent. The fair value of the patent is $75,000. The inventory costs Wolf $40,000.

Determine the entry that Wolf should record related to the sale.

Wolf records the following journal entries associated with the sale:

Patent	75,000	
Sales revenue		75,000
Cost of goods sold	40,000	
Inventory		40,000

Because the goods were sold in exchange for noncash consideration (ie, rights to a patent), the revenue is reported at the fair value of the patent.

Consideration Paid to a Customer

Sellers may offer terms to incentivize buyers to pay quickly or to purchase a certain volume of goods. Contract terms may include a seller making a payment to a customer in cash or in the form of credit, coupon, rebate, or voucher.

When consideration paid to a customer is in exchange for distinct goods/services, it is accounted for as an asset or expense, as appropriate.

- If the amount paid exceeds the value of the distinct goods/services, the excess reduces the transaction price
- If the value of the goods/services cannot be determined, the entire payment reduces the transaction price

A reduction to the transaction price is recognized at the *later of* either:

- The recognition of revenue resulting from the transaction, or
- The payment of the consideration to the customer or the promise to do so.

An entity enters a contract with customer to sell $20 million of its products, but the customer wants a $2 million payment up-front to reconfigure shelf space in the retail store. How is the revenue recognized?

The $2 million payment to the customer reduces the $20 million transaction price to $18 million since the customer isn't providing a good or service in exchange for the $2 million. If the goods are to be transferred over 10 months, revenue of $1,800,000 [($20 million − $2 million)/10] will be recognized by the entity for each delivery.

	(in thousands)	
Cash or A/R	1,800	
Sales revenue		1,800
Cost of goods sold*	XX	
Inventory		XX

**The entity's cost for the products is not given.*

Nonrefundable Up-Front Fees

Nonrefundable up-front fees are often intended as compensation to the seller for an activity performed near the inception of the contract. Since amounts received are only recognized in income when a performance obligation has been satisfied, up-front fees are generally considered part of the total consideration and are allocated among distinct performance obligations.

For example, a health club membership fee is charged to cover the administrative costs of setting up the contract. The customer does not obtain anything of value at this point. Since the value to customer is the use of the facility, the membership fee is recognized over the course of the contract.

Sale with Right of Return

Goods may be sold under terms that allow the customer to **return the goods for a refund**. In this case, the entity recognizes revenue in an amount equal to the portion that is expected to be retained by the entity.

- Estimated amount of returns are recognized as a *refund liability*
- Right to recover goods from the customer (ie, receive goods back) is recognized as an *asset*
- Both the asset (right to recover goods) and liability (refund liability) accounts are removed when the customer requests a refund

Calculation of Net Sales Revenue

Gross sales revenue
− Sales returns
− Sales discounts
Net sales revenue

Assume that an entity sells the customer $100 of goods and the customer has 90 days to return the merchandise. The seller expects that 20% will be returned.

Determine the journal entry that the seller would record at the time of sale.

Account	Debit	Credit
Cash (or A/R)	80	
Right to recover goods	20	
Sales revenue		80
Refund liability		20

Expected returns are $20 ($100 × 20%). Thus, $80 is retained ($100 × 80%).

A right of return is **not** accounted for as a performance obligation. It is, instead, variable consideration that affects the amount the company expects to receive. The seller may offer a full or partial refund of any consideration paid, a credit to be applied against any amounts owed, or an exchange of the product for another product.

Step 4. Allocate Total Consideration

Most contracts cover a **single performance obligation** to which the entire transaction price is assigned. The performance obligation is satisfied, and the entity records revenue for the stated transaction price.

Walken Company sold and delivered 80 units of product to Timberlake Inc. for $5,000. The units cost $3,000. The 80 units of product represent a single performance obligation to which the entire $5,000 transaction price is allocated.

When the performance obligation is satisfied (ie, control of the 80 units of product transfers to Timberlake), then Walken recognizes revenue of $5,000 and records the following journal entries:

Cash or A/R	5,000	
Sales revenue		5,000
Cost of goods sold	3,000	
Inventory		3,000

Contracts may include **multiple performance obligations** but list only one transaction price. Here, the total consideration from a contract is allocated to all performance obligations in proportion to their standalone selling prices. The standalone selling price is the price the entity sells a good or service for separately in comparable transactions. If the good or service is sold separately, the entity has an *observable price*, which may be used as the best evidence of the standalone price.

Smith Company produces equipment and offers installation and training services to its customers. Westbrook Company enters into a contract with Smith for the following:

- Purchase of equipment
- Equipment installation
- Training on the equipment

Westbrook has the expertise to install the equipment and train its employees on the equipment but has chosen to contract Smith to complete those tasks. Smith and Westbrook agree to a total contract price of $1,200,000. In other sales transactions, Smith sells the equipment alone for $1,100,000 and offers installation services for $70,000 and training for $130,000. Installation and training services are performed when the equipment is delivered. The equipment costs Smith $900,000.

Assuming all criteria for the contract are met (ie, Step 1), calculate the revenue and record the journal entry for this transaction.

Identify the separate performance obligations (Step 2). There are three performance obligations in this contract: (1) provide equipment, (2) installation, and (3) training. Any one of the performance obligations could be purchased separately; thus, each is distinct. Westbrook is choosing to purchase each one in this contract.

Determine the consideration (Step 3). Smith and Westbrook agree to a total contract price of $1,200,000.

Allocate the transaction price to each performance obligation (Step 4). The transaction price is allocated using the relative proportion of the total standalone pricing represented by each performance obligation. The standalone prices are provided as follows:

	Standalone Price
Equipment	$1,100,000
Installation	70,000
Training	130,000
Total standalone price	$1,300,000

Westbrook calculates the proportion of the standalone price represented by each performance obligation.

	Standalone Price/Total	**Proportion**
Equipment	1,100,000/1,300,000	84.62%
Installation	70,000/1,300,000	5.38%
Training	130,000/1,300,000	10.00%
		100%

Westbrook allocates the total contract transaction price based on the proportions calculated.

	Total Contract Price		**Proportion**		**Contract Price Allocated**
Equipment	$1,200,000	×	84.62%	=	$1,015,440
Installation	1,200,000	×	5.38%	=	64,560
Training	1,200,000	×	10.00%	=	120,000
					$1,200,000

Recognize revenue (Step 5). Smith will make the following journal entries to recognize revenue and record costs of goods sold from this transaction.

Cash	1,200,000	
Sales revenue		1,015,440
Service revenue (installation)		64,650
Service revenue (training)		120,000
Cost of goods sold	900,000	
Inventory		900,000

- Service revenue is shown in two parts to correspond to the separate performance obligations. It could be recorded as one total credit to service revenue for both the installation and the training
- The cost to provide the installation and training would be reflected in the journal entry to record salaries expense for the period (not shown here)

However, if the good or service is not sold separately, then the standalone selling price must be estimated (as of the date of the *inception* of the contract) using one of the following *three approaches:*

- **Adjusted market assessment:** Evaluate the market and see what a customer might be willing to pay or look at competitors
- **Expected cost plus a margin:** Forecast expected costs and add an appropriate profit margin for that good or service
- **Residual value method:** Use only if either:
  - Some goods/services are sold for different amounts to different customers; or
  - The good/service has not previously been sold as a standalone product or service and a price has not yet been set.

An entity enters into a contract to provide a software license, installation, and three years of tech support as a bundle for $70,000. It uses the following information to determine standalone prices:

- The entity would normally sell the software license for $50,000
- The entity doesn't normally sell the installation, but its competitors sell it for $10,000
- The entity also doesn't have a price for the tech support. It estimates that it will cost the entity $32,000, and it would like to make a profit of 25% on top of that. So the standalone selling price for tech support is $40,000 ($32,000 × 1.25)

Thus, the total of the standalone selling prices is $100,000. Since the entity is selling the bundle for $70,000, this represents a $30,000 discount. Also, there is no observable evidence that indicates that the discount relates to any particular product; therefore, the discount will be allocated by allocating the total revenue to the different products on the basis of their relative standalone selling prices.

Product	Method Used	Standalone Selling Price	Allocation Calculation	Price Allocation
Software license	Observable price	$ 50,000	50/100 × 70,000	$35,000
Installation	Adjusted market assessment	10,000	10/100 × 70,000	7,000
Three years tech support	Expected cost plus margin	40,000	40/100 × 70,000	28,000
Total		$100,000		$70,000

Now assume all the same facts as in the last example, except that there is no observable price or other estimated price for the tech support. In this case, the price for the tech support will simply be the remaining amount of the transaction price after subtracting the two prices that are known/estimated.

Product	Method Used	Standalone Selling Price	Calculation	Price Allocation
Software license	Observable price	$50,000		$50,000
Installation	Adjusted market assessment	10,000		10,000
Three years tech support	Residual value	XX,XXX	70,000 − 50,000 − 10,000	10,000
Total		$70,000		$70,000

Discounts in General

Discounts, equal to the difference between the total of standalone sales prices and total consideration, are generally allocated proportionately among performance obligations. However, discounts may be allocated to some but not all performance obligations when four criteria apply:

- Each distinct good or service in the contract is also sold as a standalone good or service on a regular basis
- Some distinct goods and services are also sold as a bundle at a discount
- The discount on the contract is comparable to the discount on the distinct goods and services sold in a bundle at a discount
- If allocated to some but not all performance obligations, the residual approach is not applied until after the discounts have been allocated

Discounts in a Multiple Element Arrangement

In a *multiple element arrangement*, if a bundle of goods is sold at a discount and is also included in a bigger bundle with a discount that exceeds that of the smaller bundle, the discounts are allocated on a step basis.

- Step 1: First, the discount that applies to the smaller bundle will be allocated among the items in that bundle.
- Step 2: Next, the remaining discount is allocated among all items using:
    - The standalone sales prices for those items that were not included in the smaller bundle; and
    - The *adjusted* standalone sales prices (ie, standalone sales price − first discount) of the items in the smaller bundle.

A store sells recreational vehicles. The store offers a water package that consists of a jet ski with a normal standalone sales price of $2,900 and a motorized raft with a normal standalone sales price of $3,600. They can be purchased as a bundle for $5,525. In addition, the store sells a small off-road motorcycle with a normal standalone sales price of $2,800 and a snowmobile that has a normal standalone sales price of $3,000; these items are being bundled as the off-road package for a total of $5,220. The store also sells a larger bundle, consisting of all four items in its Sportsman's Package at a total cost of $10,100.

To determine how the $10,100 will be allocated, the discounts will be allocated on a step basis. The water package includes the jet ski with a normal standalone sales price of $2,900 and the motorized raft with a normal standalone sales price of $3,600, for a total of $6,500. With a bundle price of $5,525, there is a discount of $975 associated with that bundle, which is 15% of the total standalone sales prices. As a result, the discount on the jet ski will be 15% × $2,900, or $435, resulting in an adjusted standalone sales price of $2,465. The motorized raft will have a discount of 15% × $3,600, or $540, resulting in an adjusted sales price of $3,060 and a total for the water package of $2,465 + $3,060, or $5,525. Alternatively:

Water Package

Product	Standalone Selling Price	Allocation Calculation	Price Allocation (Step 1)	Discount
Jet ski	$2,900	2,900/6,500 × 5,525	$2,465	$435
Motorized raft	3,600	3,600/6,500 × 5,525	3,060	540
Total	$6,500		$5,525	$975

The off-road package consists of the motorcycle at $2,800 and the snowmobile at $3,000, for a total of $5,800. The bundle price is $5,220. There is a discount of $580, which is 10% of the total standalone sales price. Thus, the discount allocated to the motorcycle will be 10% × $2,800, or $280, resulting in an adjusted price of $2,520. The discount allocated to the snowmobile will be 10% × $3,000, or $300, resulting in an adjusted standalone sales price of $2,700. The total for the off-road package is $2,520 + $2,700, or $5,220. Alternatively:

Off-Road Package

Product	Standalone Selling Price	Allocation Calculation	Price Allocation (Step 1)	Discount
Motorcycle	$2,800	2,800/5,800 × 5,220	$2,520	$280
Snowmobile	3,000	3,000/5,800 × 5,220	2,700	300
Total	$5,800		$5,220	$580

The two packages combined would then be $5,525 + $5,220, or $10,745. Since the package can be purchased for $10,100, there is a discount of $645; this is 6% of $10,745. Thus, the additional discount to be allocated to the jet ski would be 6% × $2,465, or $148, adjusting the price to $2,317. The discount allocated to the motorized raft would be 6% × $3,060, or $184, resulting in an adjusted price of $2,876. The discount allocated to the motorcycle would be 6% × $2,520, or $151, resulting in an adjusted price of $2,369. The discount allocated to the snowmobile would be 6% × $2,700, or $162, for an adjusted price of $2,538. Thus, the total consideration would be allocated as follows:

Sportsman's Package

Product	Adjusted Standalone Selling Price	Allocation Calculation	Price Allocation (Step 2)	Discount
Jet ski	$ 2,465	2,465/10,745 × 10,100	2,317	$148
Motorized raft	3,060	3,060/10,745 × 10,100	2,876	184
Motorcycle	2,520	2,520/10,745 × 10,100	2,369	151
Snowmobile	2,700	2,700/10,745 × 10,100	2,538	162
Total	$10,745		$10,100	$645

Allocation of Variable Consideration

Variable consideration may relate to the entire contract or only part of it, such as one or more performance obligations or, more specifically, one or more goods/services:

- Variable consideration may relate to a single performance obligation, such as a bonus for timely performance
- Variable consideration may be an increase in the cost to be incurred in satisfying a performance obligation

Variable costs/revenues (ie, consideration) are generally required to be allocated to all performance obligations on the same basis as the allocation of other consideration. However, they may be allocated to specific performance obligations or specific goods/services if two criteria apply:

- The variable payment is associated with:
  - The entity's *efforts* to satisfy a specific performance obligation or to deliver a distinct good/service; or
  - The *outcome* from satisfying such obligation.
- Allocation of the entire amount of variable consideration is consistent with the objectives of the standard with regard to the allocation of transaction price to performance obligations (ie, the amount allocated is the amount the entity expects to be entitled to for that performance obligation)

Assume that a contract calls for granting the use of:

- License A for $800 (fixed amount); and
- License B for 5% royalties based on the customer's sales related to the license (variable consideration).

The royalties are expected to amount to $1,000.

Determine how the variable consideration would be allocated.

The variable consideration should be allocated to License B. Allocating the entire amount of variable consideration to License B makes sense because (1) it is related to the use of the license (ie, the outcome) and (2) the amount represents the consideration that the entity expects to receive for that particular performance obligation.

Price changes are dealt with similarly to variable consideration. The same criteria applied to variable consideration apply for purposes of allocating a price change to a specific performance obligation or good/service, but not the entire contract. Otherwise, a price change is allocated to all distinct performance obligations on the same basis as total consideration using standalone selling prices.

- Changes to standalone selling prices are not considered
- A price change may result in allocation to performance obligations that have already been satisfied. Portions allocated to performance obligations that have already been satisfied are taken into income immediately

Step 5. Recognize Revenue

Revenue is recognized **when** a performance obligation is satisfied (ie, at a point in time) or, in some circumstances, **as** it is being satisfied (ie, over time).

A performance obligation is considered satisfied when the entity has transferred the promised goods/services to the customer, which occurs at a **point in time** when the *customer has control* of those goods/services.

A **customer has control** over goods and services when the customer can:

- Direct the use of the goods/services;
- Prevent others from benefiting from them; and
- Obtain benefits from the goods/services in the form of cash flows (ie, inflows or savings).

O'Hara Corp. sold goods for $5,000 that had a cost of $3,000. The customer immediately accepted and took possession of the goods and paid for the goods using cash. O'Hara will record the following journal entries on the date of sale.

Cash	5,000	
Sales revenue		5,000
Cost of goods sold	3,000	
Inventory		3,000

When **control is uncertain**, other factors to consider include whether the customer has:

- Legal title to the goods
- Physical possession of the goods
- Significant risks and rights associated with ownership of the goods
- Accepted the goods

Revenue may be recognized at a *point in time* or *over a period of time:*

Criteria to Measure Revenue over a Period of Time

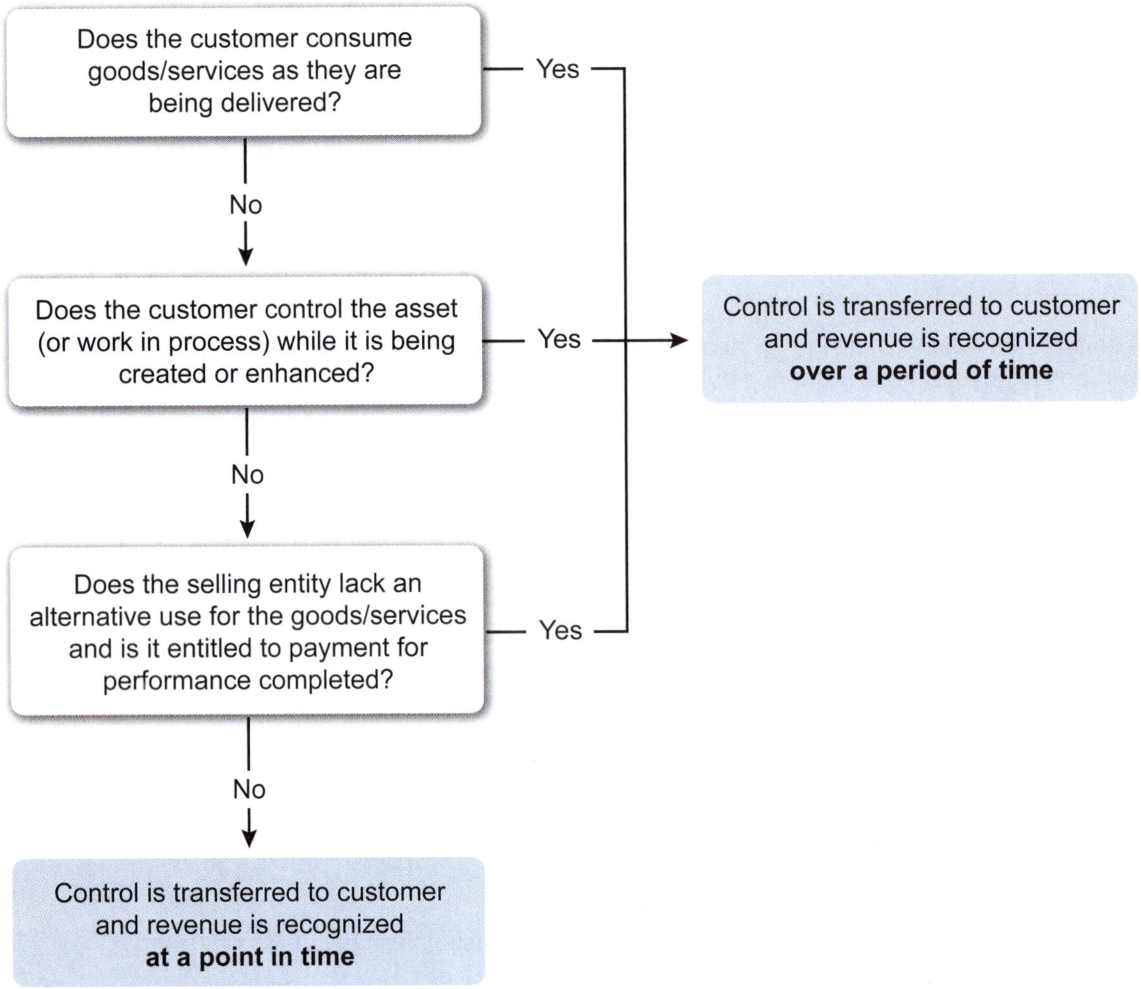

Certain performance obligations, by nature, are being **consumed as they are being delivered**. This is generally true of recurring services being provided to a customer, such as cleaning services.

Sometimes it is hard to determine whether goods/services are being consumed as they are being delivered. In such cases, one should ask, If another entity were engaged to complete the performance obligation, would it need to substantially reperform what the original entity completed? If yes, the customer has not been consuming the goods/services. If no, then the customer has been consuming the goods/services upon delivery.

In determining whether the **customer controls an asset** while it is being created or enhanced, the same criteria that are used to determine whether control has been transferred to the customer should be applied.

An asset is considered to **lack an alternative use** to the seller if the seller would be required to dispose of it at a substantial cost. For example:

- The entity would not be able to transfer the goods/services to another customer (perhaps due to unique design specifications), or it would incur a significant loss to do so
- Significant costs would be incurred to rework the asset for another use

Assuming that the contract was terminated for a reason other than the entity's inability to complete performance, the entity must also be entitled to payment for work completed to date. The amount should reflect the approximate selling price of the goods/services transferred. That is, the entity should be entitled to recover its costs, plus a reasonable profit; the profit, however, need not equal what would have been earned upon completion.

Recognizing Revenue while Performance Obligation is Satisfied

In order to recognize revenues **while** the performance obligation is being satisfied (ie, over time), there must be some means for measuring progress toward completion of the obligation. The two acceptable methods for measuring progress are the *output* method and the *input* method:

Measurement of progress on long-term contracts

Method	Input	Output
Objective	Calculate contract progress based on effort put forth by the entity	Calculate contract progress based on the value of the goods/services transferred to the customer up to that point
Examples	• Resources consumed • Labor hours expended • Costs incurred • Time elapsed • Machine hours used	• Surveys (eg, engineering studies) of the work completed • Appraisals of results achieved • Milestones reached • Time elapsed • Units produced or delivered

Licensing

When revenue is generated by granting a license to use intellectual property, the method used to recognize revenue will depend on the nature of the licensing arrangement—that is, whether it grants a *right to use* intellectual property or a *right to access* intellectual property.

- When a license grants the customer the **right to use** intellectual property (eg, a photo), it is assumed that the property is functional as is and that the licensor does not have any obligation to maintain the property; thus, revenue will be recognized at a point in time (ie, when the property is made available for use)
- When a **right to access** intellectual property is granted to a customer, the customer will have access to the property for a period of time, and the licensor will usually have an obligation to support or maintain the intellectual property during that time. Since the performance obligation largely consists of the duty to support and maintain the intellectual property over a period of time, revenue will be recognized over the term of the license

Consignment Arrangements

In a **consignment arrangement**, the consignor (owner of goods) uses the consignee's premises to sell its goods. No revenue is recognized by the consignor when it ships goods to the consignee, because no sale has yet taken place. The consignor includes unsold goods in its inventory even though they are on the consignee's premises, typically "moving" the goods from the finished inventory account to the inventory (consignments) account.

Consignment arrangement

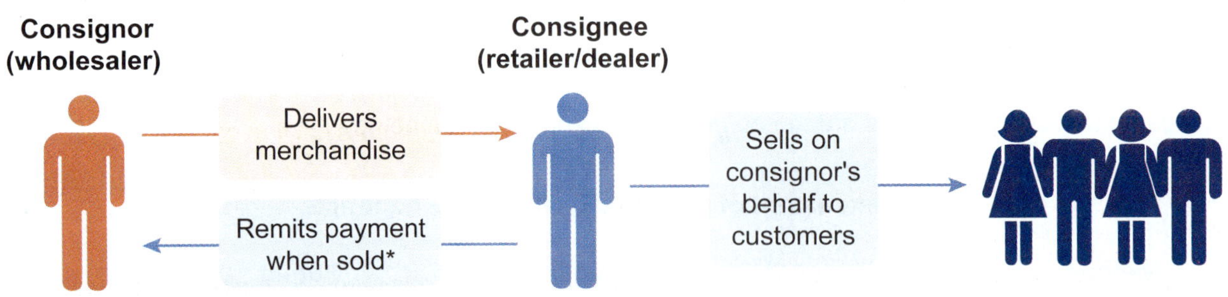

Less commission and reimbursable costs

When a retail customer purchases consigned goods on the consignee's premises, only then does the consignor recognize a sale. The consignee typically retains a percentage of each sale (its fee, a revenue) and remits the remainder to the consignor. The amount of revenue recognized by the consignor is the total sales amount. The consignee's fee is treated as an expense by the consignor (eg, commission expense).

The amount of any reimbursable expenses (eg, handling and advertising) incurred by the consignee is also withheld and recognized as an expense by the consignor.

Consignment arrangements are discussed further in the FAR Inventory chapter.

Onerous Performance Obligations

If, at any time, the expected cost of satisfying a performance obligation (or contract) is greater than the amount of revenue allocated, it is referred to as an onerous performance obligation (or contract). The entity will immediately recognize the expected loss and a corresponding liability. This applies to construction-type and production-type contracts (discussed further below).

Bill-and-Hold Arrangements

A contract with a **bill-and-hold** arrangement allows the seller to retain physical possession of the goods (ie, hold the goods) until the buyer is ready to receive the goods at a future point in time.

The seller may recognize revenue from the contract *before* transferring the goods to the buyer if the buyer has control of the goods and the following criteria are met:

- There is a substantive reason for the bill-and-hold arrangement (eg, the customer requested the arrangement because its facility does not have available space to receive the goods)
- The seller separates the product from the other inventory and identifies it as belonging to the customer
- The product is currently ready for transfer to the customer
- The product cannot be used by or directed to another customer

Accounting for Costs Incurred

Costs incurred in satisfying a performance obligation will be accumulated and reported on the income statement in the period in which the related revenues are recognized. Generally, costs of obtaining a contract will be recognized as expenses in the period in which they are incurred. Certain costs, however, should be capitalized.

- Recoverable incremental costs of obtaining a contract are capitalized until the related revenue is recognized on the income statement. For example, a land broker may pay to have land rezoned to increase the value of the property. These costs are incremental costs of obtaining the contract that should be capitalized because they will be recovered when the broker sells the property
- Certain costs are required by various standards to be capitalized, while others are required to be expensed
- Costs meeting all of the following criteria are required by the revenue recognition standards to be capitalized:
    - The costs relate directly to a contract that is in existence or a specific contract that is currently being negotiated
    - The costs generate or enhance resources that will be used to satisfy performance obligations in the future
    - The costs are expected to be recovered

Recovery of costs may be through collections of revenues on the contract if they were anticipated when the contracts were negotiated, or they might have resulted from changes made to the performance obligation that are reimbursable by the customer.

Deferred Revenue

Deferred revenues (ie, unearned revenues) are liabilities representing cash received for goods that have not yet been delivered or services that have not yet been performed. Recognition of revenue occurs when the firm provides the good or service, at which point the deferred revenue (liability) is reduced, often by making an adjusting journal entry.

In many cases, the contract need not be fully executed before some revenue is recognized. In these cases, the revenue is recognized based on the percentage of the total contract that has been provided.

Duration Magazine Inc. collects subscriptions in advance from customers. The beginning balance of deferred subscription revenue is $24,000. During the year, $87,000 of cash is collected. At the end of the year, the firm determined that the subscription value of magazines yet to be distributed is $37,000. Determine the amount of revenue earned during the year.

Beginning deferred subscription revenue	$24,000	
Plus: Increase in deferred subscription revenue	87,000	
Less: Decrease in deferred subscription revenue		← Solve for this
Ending deferred subscription revenue	$37,000	

Decrease in deferred revenue **$74,000** = $24,000 + $87,000 − $37,000

The adjusting entry to record the revenue earned and decrease the liability is as follows:

Deferred subscription revenue	74,000	
Subscription revenue		74,000

A tenant pays a building management firm $24,000 for two years' rent on August 1, Year 3. The rental period begins on August 1, Year 3, and the building management firm has a calendar fiscal year.

Provide the journal entries that the building management would record for Year 3.

Rent revenue earned during Year 3:

$24,000/24 months × 5 months (Aug. to Dec.) = $5,000

Year 3 entries:

Record receipt of cash			
August 1, Year 3	Cash	24,000	
	Deferred rental revenue		24,000

Year-end adjusting entry			
December 31, Year 3	Deferred rental revenue	5,000	
	Rental revenue		5,000

The ending balance in deferred rental revenue for 12/31/Year 3 is $19,000 ($24,000 − $5,000), of which $12,000 is a current liability (the portion relating to Year 4) and $7,000 is a noncurrent liability (the portion relating to Year 5).

Contract Assets

If the customer pays consideration before goods or services have been transferred to the customer, then the entity will record a contract liability (ie, deferred revenue) to represent its obligation to satisfy the performance obligation for which the customer has paid. However, if the **entity performs** by transferring goods or services to the customer *before* the customer pays consideration, then the entity may recognize a contract asset. A **contract asset** represents the entity's right to consideration. The right may be unconditional or conditional:

- An *unconditional* right to a contract asset occurs when an entity has earned the right to payment and is only waiting for the time to pass to receive payment. Accounts receivable represents an unconditional right to a contract asset. The entity has satisfied the performance obligation and is waiting to be paid
- A *conditional* right to a contract asset occurs when a company completes one performance obligation in the contract but must complete another performance obligation before it is entitled to consideration from the customer. Conditional rights to receive consideration should be reported as a contract asset

Hamilton Company entered into a contract with Burr Company to transfer two products to Burr for a sales price of $950,000. Delivery of Product 1 will occur first, and delivery of Product 2 will occur second. The contract requires the delivery of Product 2 before payment on Product 1 will be remitted. Product 1 has a sales price of $600,000, and Product 2 has a sales price of $350,000. Hamilton delivers Product 1 to Burr on April 2, Year 9, and delivers Product 2 to Burr on June 30, Year 9.

Provide the journal entries that Hamilton will record at April 2 and June 30, Year 9.

On April 2, Hamilton will record the conditional right to payment for Product 1:

Contract asset	600,000	
Revenue		600,000

On June 30, when Hamilton delivers Product 2 to Burr, Hamilton has an unconditional right to payment for both Product 1 and Product 2. Hamilton will record the following:

Accounts receivable	950,000	
Contract asset		600,000
Revenue		350,000

Long-Term Contracts

Representative Task (Application): Determine the recognition and subsequent measurement requirements for contract costs and prepare journal entries.

Many industries provide services that may require several accounting periods to complete. The **construction industry** is one example. Long-term contracts pose a unique revenue recognition problem because the work that generates the revenue is **performed over the term** of the contract. ASC 606 indicates that certain conditions must be met for the entity to recognize revenue while the performance obligation is **being satisfied**. Otherwise, revenues are recognized **upon satisfaction** of the performance obligation.

Revenue Recognition for Long-Term Contracts

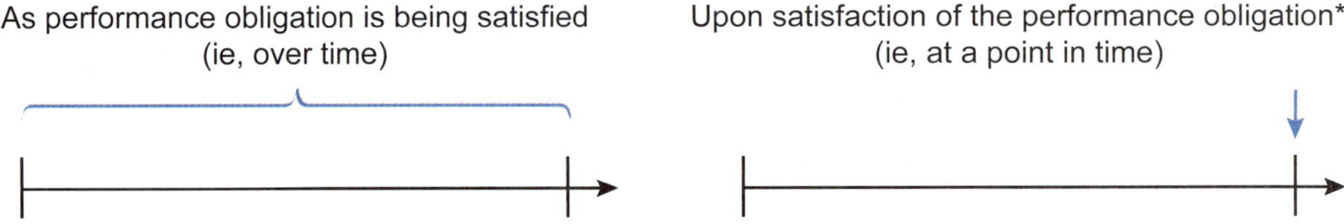

**Used for long-term construction contracts only if contracts fail to qualify for measurement over time*

Long-term construction contracts often allow the contractor to **bill the customer at intervals**, as it reaches various milestones in the project. These billings *do not* represent the amounts that should be recognized as revenue and are generally for amounts that are lower than what a payment would be for a proportionate amount of work completed on the contract. They are generally designed for the following purposes:

- To make certain that the customer has enough of an investment in the project to assure the contractor that the customer will meet its obligation to accept and pay the contractor
- To provide the contractor with working capital to enable the contractor to pay subcontractors and for materials, providing assurance to the customer that the project can be completed
- To make certain that the contractor has something to gain (ie, the remaining unpaid balance on the contract) by completing the contract on a timely basis

Costs of Obtaining and Fulfilling a Contract

Costs incurred in satisfying a performance obligation will be accumulated and reported on the income statement (I/S) in the period in which the related revenues are recognized.

- When recognizing revenues **while** the performance obligation is being satisfied (ie, the percentage-of-completion method), costs are charged against income *in proportion* to the revenues being recognized
- When revenues are recognized **upon** satisfaction of the performance obligation (ie, the completed-contract method), costs are recognized *upon the completion* of the contract in the same period in which revenues are recognized

The revenue recognition standards and the CPA exam no longer use the specific terms "percentage-of-completion method" and "completed-contract method," but the accounting under the new standards is so similar that this terminology is still used in practice.

Construction-in-progress (CIP) is an inventory account and a current asset. Although a contract may run for several years, the operating cycle of a construction firm is the length of its contracts. CIP is debited only when costs are incorporated into the project. Purchases of materials for the project are recorded in the materials account.

Billings on uncompleted contracts is a contra account to CIP. On the balance sheet, if the balance in CIP exceeds cumulative billings to date, the net difference is a current asset. If cumulative billings exceed the CIP balance, the difference is a current liability. By subtracting billings from CIP, the seller is transferring its equity in the project from the physical asset to the financial asset (to accounts receivable and then, ultimately, to cash).

Comparison of Percentage-of-Completion versus Completed-Contract Method

	Percentage-of-completion method	**Completed-contract method**
Revenue recognition	*Over time:* as construction is completed Appropriate portion of total revenue expected from the contract is recorded at end of each period on I/S	*At a point in time:* when construction is complete No profit/revenue entries are made until completion
	Billings and collections are recorded in B/S accounts	
Costs incurred	Charged against income in proportion to revenues recognized during period	Held in CIP account (B/S) until completion
	Anticipated losses recognized immediately on I/S	
Conditions for use*	1. Customer consumes benefits of asset(s) as they are delivered 2. Customer has *control* over asset(s) during creation or enhancement 3. Entity lacks alternative use for asset(s) and is entitled to payment for completion to date	Customer has *control* over asset(s)
Measuring progress*	*Output method:* % complete with respect to output (eg, milestones reached, units completed, etc.) *Input method:* % complete with respect to effort put in (eg, costs incurred, labor hours, etc.)	

**Previously discussed*

Percentage of Completion

The **cost-to-cost approach** of percentage of completion is an *input method*. Under this method, the *costs incurred to date* are compared to the *total estimated costs* of completing the performance obligations; the resulting ratio is considered the percentage complete.

The profit recognized in each period is determined on the accrual basis, taking into account the following:

- The estimated profit on the contract
- The portion of the contract completed (% complete)
- Any profit previously recognized

Accounting during Year

- Billings are added to *billings on uncompleted contracts* (ie, a contra account to CIP), and a receivable is recorded
- As cash is collected, the receivable is reduced
- As costs that qualify for capitalization are incurred (eg, when cash is spent on the project or when materials previously purchased are used in the project), they are added to CIP

All of the accounting during the year for percentage-of-completion and the completed-contract method is the same up to this point.

- Gross profit is added to CIP. Gross profit for the current period is calculated as follows:

Profitable Long-Term Contracts when Revenue is Recognized over Time

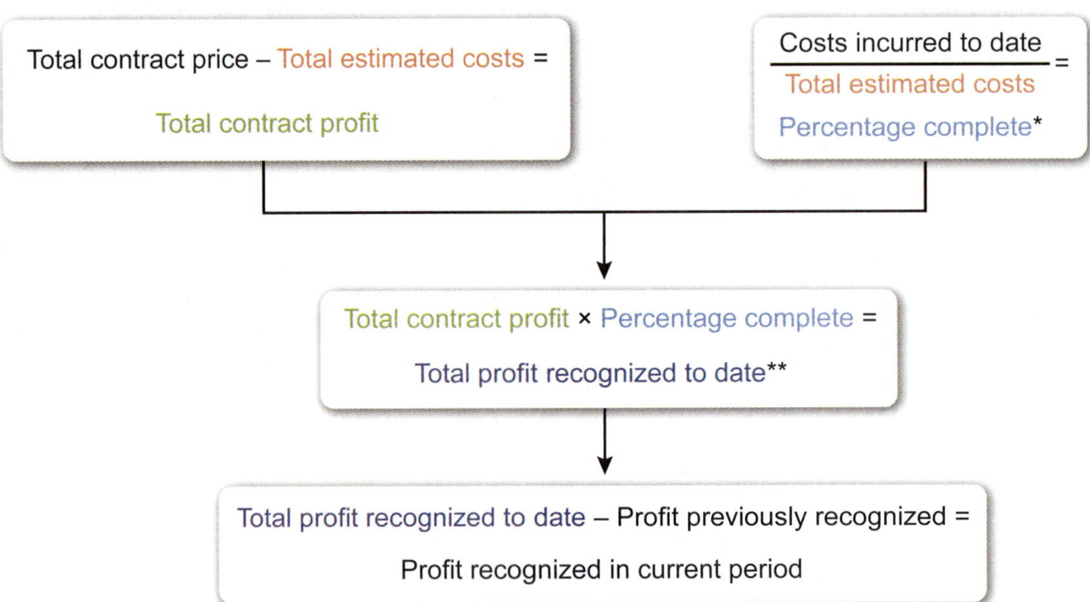

**Using an input method based on costs incurred to measure contract progress*

***Progress billings are not used in calculating income from construction contracts*

- At year end, billings and CIP are netted on the balance sheet to report either of the following:
  - *Current contract asset:* CIP in excess of billings
  - *Current contract liability:* Billings in excess of CIP
- The income statement will report the following:

Revenue earned to date = (Total contract price × % complete) − Revenue previously recognized

Cost of sales equal to costs (not profit) added to CIP during the current period

Roger Builders has agreed to construct a building for CPA Inc. at a total contract price of $4,000,000. The estimated construction costs at inception are $3,000,000, and the actual costs for both Years 1 and 2 are below. The construction was completed after Year 2.

Total contract price	$4,000,000
− Estimated costs	3,000,000
= Estimated profit	$1,000,000

	Cumulative	
	Year 1	**Year 2**
Costs incurred to date	700,000	1,650,000
Estimated costs to complete	2,800,000	1,650,000
Billings	850,000	1,800,000
Cash collections	800,000	1,500,000

Answers and journal entries are expressed in thousands.

		Year 1		**Year 2**	
Percentage complete	Costs incurred to date / Total estimated costs**	700 / 700 + 2,800	= 20%	1,650 / 1,650 + 1,650	= 50%
	Total contract price	4,000		4,000	
× Total profit*	− Total estimated costs	− 3,500	= 500	− 3,300	= 700
= Profit recognized to date			100		350
− Profit previously recognized			(0)		(100)
= Profit to recognize this year			100		250

** Total profit may change, so use new profit amount if applicable*

*** Total estimated costs = actual costs + estimated costs to complete*

Percentage-of-Completion Method

Year 1			
Costs incurred	CIP*	700	
	Cash		700
Billings	Construction receivable	850	
	Billings*		850
Collections	Cash	800	
	Construction receivable		800
Recognize gross profit ($100) in Year 1	CIP*	100	
	Construction expense (3,500 est. costs × 20% complete)	700	
	Construction revenue (4,000 revenue × 20% complete)		800

**Net billings (850) and CIP (800) on B/S at end of Year 1 = $50 contract liability (ie, billings in excess of CIP)*

For brevity, the first three journal entries (for costs incurred, billings, and collections) for Year 2 are not shown. These entries are the same as the first year's entries but for different amounts. The entry to recognize profit in Year 2 is shown below:

Year 2			
Recognize gross profit ($250) in Year 2	CIP	250	
	Construction expense [(3,300 × 50%) − 700 already recognized]	950	
	Construction revenue [(4,000 × 50%) − 800 already recognized]		1,200

At the end of the contract, the final journal entry will debit the billings account (the contra-asset account) for the full contract price. The entry will credit the CIP account (the asset account) because the project is complete. The CIP account balance is total cost plus total gross profit. At the end of the contract, total cost plus total gross profit equals the full contract price. Thus, the entry balances.

Completed-Contract Method

Under the completed-contract method, the previous example would be accounted for as follows:

Year 1			
Costs incurred	CIP	700	
	Cash		700
Billings	Construction receivable	850	
	Billings		850
Collections	Cash	800	
	Construction receivable		800

Under the completed-contract method, *no gross profit is recognized* until the end of the contract. When the contract is completed, the entry will be as follows:

Recognize revenue	Billings	Contract price	
	Construction revenue		Contract price
Recognize expense	Construction expenses	Costs incurred	
	CIP		Costs incurred

Losses on Contracts

There are two types of losses on long-term contracts:

- **Single-period loss:** When the total gross profit through the end of a given year is less than the gross profit recognized in previous years, a loss has occurred in the given year, although the contract still may be profitable. The completed contract method is unaffected by single-period losses
- **Overall losses:** When an overall loss on a contract is anticipated, the loss must be recognized in full for both methods. An overall loss occurs when the total estimated costs of the project exceed the contract price

A contractor begins construction of a building for a client.

- Contract price is $10,000
- Through Year 2:
  - Total revenue of $8,000 recognized
  - Total gross profit of $2,000 recognized
- The estimated remaining cost is updated at the end of each year

Data for three years follows:

	Year 1	Year 2	Year 3
Costs incurred	2,000	4,000	2,400
Estimated costs to complete	6,000	1,500	1,800

In Year 3, determine how the loss is recognized under the percentage-of-completion and completed-contract methods.

First, determine the amount of the loss on the contract.

$10,000 contract price − $10,200 total estimated cost* = **$200 loss**

**$2,000 + $4,000 + $2,400 + $1,800*

The loss is recognized in full for *both methods*. Any previous gross profit under percentage-of-completion is removed from the construction-in-progress account.

Percentage-of-completion adjusting entry		
Construction expenses (plug)	2,435	
CIP		2,200*
Construction revenue		235**

The loss recorded by this entry is $2,200, the difference between the revenue and expenses.

When an overall loss is anticipated, the amount recorded as construction expense is no longer the year's incurred cost.

**Reversal of $2,000 profit recorded during the first two years, plus the overall loss of $200*

***The amount of construction revenue to be recognized is calculated as follows:*

$$\text{Percentage of completion} = \frac{\text{Costs incurred to date}}{\text{Total estimated costs}} = \frac{\$2,000 + \$4,000 + \$2,400}{\$2,000 + \$4,000 + \$2,400 + \$1,800} = 0.8235$$

0.8235 × $10,000 revenue = $8,235

Previous revenue recognized	$ 8,000
Less: Updated revenue recognized	8,235
Equal: Construction revenue	$ 235

The construction-in-progress account balance is now total cost to date, less the overall loss. The same holds true for the completed-contract method.

Completed-contract entry *(No previous profit must be removed)*		
Loss on construction contract	200	
CIP		200

FAR 19 Accounting for Income Taxes

FAR 19: Accounting for Income Taxes

19.01 Accounting for Income Taxes

Overview

Financial statements (F/S) are governed by Generally Accepted Accounting Principles (GAAP), and income taxes are governed by the Internal Revenue Code (IRC). Because of differences in recognition and measurement under GAAP and the IRC, income tax expense as reported for the books is generally not the same as the amount of tax actually due for the period.

Consistent with the matching principle, under GAAP, income tax expense is recognized when it is incurred, regardless of when the payment is actually made to the Internal Revenue Service (IRS). Income tax expense is a derived (ie, plug) figure. Income tax expense for the period reflects the amount that will ultimately be payable for the year's transactions, even though the timing of the payment will differ from the timing of the expense recognition.

The asset and liability approach is used to determine income tax expense. That is, there are two objectives of accounting for income taxes: to recognize the current-year amount of taxes payable or refundable and to recognize the amount of deferred tax assets (DTAs) and deferred tax liabilities (DTLs) reported for future tax consequences.

The process of recognizing income tax expense and associated deferred tax accounts is called **interperiod tax allocation**. Interperiod tax allocation is the application of accrual accounting to the measurement of income tax effects on the financial statements.

Income Tax Expense (Benefit)

Representative Task (Application): Calculate the income tax expense and current taxes payable/receivable.

Representative Task (Application): Calculate deferred tax assets/liabilities resulting from book to tax basis differences (eg, allowance for credit losses, inventory costing methods, property, plant and equipment).

GAAP income tax expense comprises two components: a **current tax expense (benefit)** based on taxable income and a **deferred tax expense (benefit)** based on temporary differences:

Current income tax expense/benefit ± **Deferred income tax expense/benefit** = Total income tax expense/benefit

Current income tax expense/benefit	Deferred income tax expense/benefit
Taxable income	Ending net DTA or DTL
× Current income tax rate	± Beginning net DTA or DTL
Current tax expense/benefit	**Deferred tax expense/benefit**
Reported in Income Tax Payable B/S account	*Reported in DTA or DTL B/S accounts*

B/S = balance sheet; DTA = deferred tax asset; DTL = deferred tax liability

Remember that income tax expense (benefit) is a plug figure.

The current portion of tax expense is recorded on the balance sheet in the Income Tax Payable account. The initial recognition/changes in the DTAs and DTLs (ie, deferred tax expense) are recorded on the balance sheet in the DTA/DTL accounts.

The total of these two balance sheet items equals income tax expense (benefit) on the income statement.

To determine the current portion of tax expense, first pretax book income must be adjusted for permanent and temporary differences to arrive at **taxable income**:

Adjustments to Arrive at Taxable Income	
Permanent Differences	• An item that appears in the tax return or income statement but **not both** • Never reverse
Temporary Differences	• An item that is taxable or deductible on the tax return in a **different period** than that reported on the books • Reverse over time

Once taxable income is determined, the **current income tax expense** is calculated by **multiplying taxable income by the current enacted tax rate**.

The process of calculating current income tax expense is as follows:

Calculation of Taxable Income and Current Tax Expense

- Municipal interest
- Fines, penalties
- Life insurance proceeds and policy premiums (if beneficiary)

- Warranty expense
- Credit loss expense
- Rent received in advance
- Installment sales
- Depreciation expense

Pretax income per financial reporting	$XXX
± Permanent differences	XXX
± Temporary differences*	XXX
Taxable income	**$XXX**
× Current enacted tax rate	XX%
Current tax expense/liability	$XXX
− Tax prepayments	XXX
Net income tax payable	$XXX

**Taxed at future enacted tax rate*

Current tax expense, less any prepayments, is reported in the **Income Tax Payable** account on the balance sheet.

For the year ended December 31, Year 5, Parin Inc. reported pretax financial income of $450,000, including $50,000 of municipal bond interest income. Parin deducted $80,000 of additional depreciation on its tax return. Parin's current effective income tax rate is 30% and future enacted rate is 25%. The company made estimated payments of $75,000 during Year 5. Determine the amount of tax that Parin still owes for Year 5:

Pretax accounting income	$450,000	
+/− Permanent differences	−50,000	*Subtract the 50,000 municipal interest that was added for book purposes*
+/− Temporary differences	−80,000	*Subtract the 80,000 additional depreciation for tax purposes*
Taxable income	$320,000	
× Current tax rate	30%	
Current tax expense/payable	$ 96,000	
− Estimated payments	(75,000)	
Net taxes owed	$ 21,000	

Deferred income tax expense (benefit) is then calculated based on the change in the company's **DTAs and DTLs**. Initial recognition of DTAs and DTLs and the changes in the deferred balances are reported on the balance sheet in the **Deferred Tax Asset/Liability** accounts.

DTAs, DTLs, and calculation of deferred income tax expense (benefit) related to temporary differences are covered below.

Permanent Differences

A **permanent difference** is an item that will appear on either the F/S or the tax return, but not both (ie, the treatment of these items under the two reporting systems is **permanently** different). These items do not result in deferred tax differences since they will never reverse.

For each of the examples listed below, an amount is recognized in one system of reporting but not in the other:

Example	Taxable/deductible?	Included in pretax
Tax-free interest income	No	Yes
Life insurance expense (on key employee, firm is beneficiary)	No	Yes
Life insurance proceeds (on key employee)	No	Yes
Certain fines/penalties	No	Yes
Dividends received deduction	Portion of dividends received included	Entire amount of dividends received included

During Year 1, Wally Inc. recognized $170,000 of pretax book income. Included in this book income was $10,000 of life insurance premiums on a key employee (where Wally was the beneficiary) and $15,000 of nondeductible penalties. Determine the amount of permanent differences reported, and calculate the taxable income.

The firm would report permanent differences of $25,000 ($10,000 nondeductible premiums + $15,000 nondeductible penalties).

Taxable income is $195,000 ($170,000 book income + 10,000 nondeductible premiums deducted from book income + 15,000 nondeductible penalties deducted from book income).

Note: Some permanent differences lower taxable income; others increase taxable income. Permanent differences are netted together when calculating taxable income.

Permanent differences are not allocated; therefore, they **do not impact interperiod tax allocation**.

Temporary Differences

Temporary differences apply to revenues or expenses that will be recognized in **different amounts** in any given year for financial reporting and tax purposes. Over the total life of the item, however, these items will affect pretax accounting income and taxable income in the same total amount. The key difference is in their **timing**. Therefore, these differences will reverse over time.

Temporary differences are **used in both the calculation of current tax expense/benefit** (because they are used to determine taxable income) and the **calculation of deferred tax expense/benefit**.

Deferred Tax Assets and Liabilities

Temporary (ie, timing) differences often result in a future deductible amount (DTA) or future taxable amount (DTL):

Calculating Deferred Tax Asset (DTA) or Liability (DTL)

Temporary difference during the reporting period × *Future* enacted tax rate* = DTL or DTA

**Rate expected to be in effect when a temporary difference is reversed or realized.*

Deferred tax liabilities, or taxable temporary differences, arise when book expense is less than tax expense or when book revenue is greater than tax revenue. In both scenarios, the item increases book income for the period, relative to taxable income:

Deferred Tax Liabilities

	Book Income	Tax Return
Revenues or Gains	Revenue now	Taxable later
Expenses or Losses	Expense later	Deductible now

Because, in the current period, book income is greater than taxable income, in future periods, taxable income will be greater than book income (ie, the difference will reverse). The company is "saving" on taxes now (because taxable income now is lower), but the entity will have to pay more in taxes later, creating a future liability.

Examples of deferred tax liabilities include the following:

- **Depreciation for book versus tax:** Typically leads to lower taxable income because depreciation is accelerated
- **Investments accounted for under the equity method for book purposes:** Typically leads to higher book income
- **Use of the installment sales method for tax purposes:** Typically leads to lower taxable income because cash is not taxable until received
- **Prepaid expenses:** Typically leads to lower taxable income as expenses are deductible when initially paid
- **Goodwill:** Typically leads to lower taxable income because, for tax purposes, goodwill is amortized over 15 years but tested annually for impairment under GAAP.

During Year 1, a firm sells $6,000 worth of goods. For financial reporting purposes, the firm uses the point-of-sales method and recognizes the entire $6,000 as revenue in Year 1. For tax purposes, the firm uses the installment sales method, which postpones revenue recognition until cash is actually received. No cash is received in Year 1. Assume that the future tax rate is 30% and that, in Year 1, pretax book income (before accounting for the $6,000 sale) is $100,000. Determine the amount of DTL that the firm should record.

After recording the sale in Year 1, the amount of book income and taxable income is as follows:

- Book income: $106,000*
- Taxable income: $100,000**

The firm has a DTL of $1,800 ($6,000 × 30%). Because taxable income is less than book income, the company is paying less in taxes now. However, at some point in the future, the $6,000 sale will be recognized for tax purposes. At that point, the company's taxable income will be $6,000 higher, and the company will owe more in taxes.

**($100,000 + $6,000 revenue from sale)*

***Cash has not been received, so $6,000 is not yet recognized.*

Deferred tax assets, or deductible temporary differences, arise when book expense is more than tax expense or when book revenue is less than tax revenue. In both scenarios, the item decreases book income for the period, relative to taxable income:

Deferred Tax Assets

	Book Income	**Tax Return**
Revenues or Gains	Revenue later	Taxable now
Expenses or Losses	Expense now	Deductible later

Because, in the current period, book income is less than taxable income, in future periods, taxable income will be less than book income (ie, the difference will reverse). The company is paying more in taxes now (because taxable income now is higher), but the company will have to pay less in taxes later, creating a future benefit (ie, asset).

Examples of deferred tax assets include the following:

- **Warranty expense:** Typically leads to higher taxable income because the expense is not deductible until paid
- **Rent, royalty, and interest received in advance:** Typically leads to higher taxable income because the cash is taxable when initially received
- **Credit loss expense:** Typically leads to higher taxable income because the direct write-off method is used for tax purposes (ie, accounts are only written off when the customer actually fails to pay) and the allowance method is used for GAAP.

During Year 1, a firm recognizes estimated warranty expense of $8,000 for book purposes. Also, during Year 1, the firm spent $1,000 servicing warranty claims. Assume that the tax rate is 30%. Determine the amount of DTA resulting from the warranty transaction.

The firm will expense $8,000 on its books but can only deduct $1,000 for tax purposes (as warranty claims are not deductible until paid). At the end of Year 1, the company has a DTA of $2,100 ($7,000 × 30%). The firm expects to spend $7,000 ($8,000 estimated expense − $1,000 paid) servicing claims in the future. When the firm pays the future claims, the $7,000 will become deductible for tax purposes.

Because the claims cannot be deducted yet for tax purposes, taxable income is $7,000 higher now. Therefore, the company owes more in taxes now. However, when the remaining claims are paid, taxable income will decrease by $7,000 compared to book income. The company will owe less in taxes in the future.

Remember, DTAs and DTLs are created from temporary timing differences:

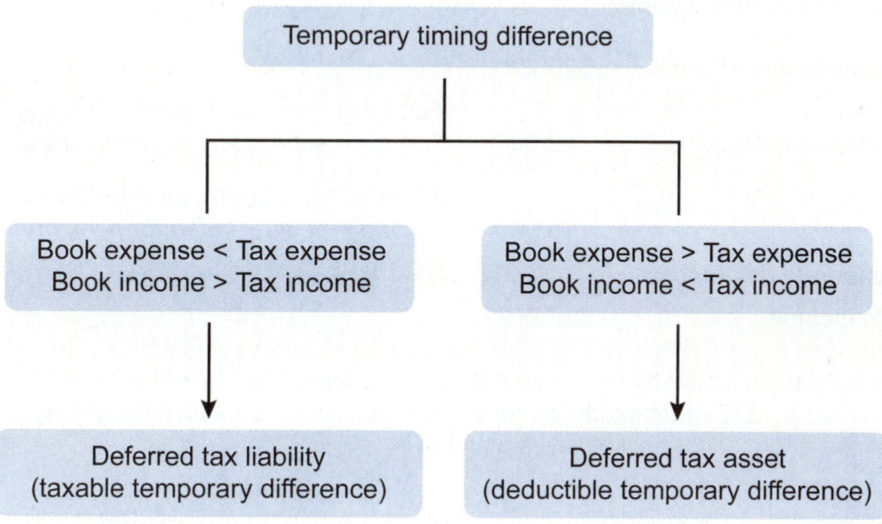

Presentation of the Tax Provision

Representative Task (Application): Prepare journal entries to record the tax provision.

Permanent Differences

If only permanent differences exist, no deferred tax asset or liability will be recognized. Only income tax expense and income tax payable will be recorded.

During Year 1, ABC Co. recognizes $20,000 of pretax accounting income. Included in this income is $2,000 of nondeductible fines and $5,000 of interest income on municipal bonds. Assume that the tax rate is 30%. Determine the entry that ABC will record to recognize income tax expense and liability.

Since no temporary differences exist, there is no deferred income tax. To find income tax payable, ABC first calculates current taxable income:

Pretax accounting income	$20,000	
+/− Permanent differences	+2,000	*Add back the $2,000 non-deductible fines that were subtracted for book purposes*
	−5,000	*Subtract the $5,000 municipal bond interest income that was added for book purposes*
+/− Temporary differences	0	
Taxable income	$17,000	

Taxable income is then multiplied by the current tax rate to determine current income tax expense (ie, income tax payable). $17,000 taxable income × 30% tax rate = $5,100. ABC's entry to record income tax expense and income tax liability is as follows:

Income tax expense	5,100	
Income tax payable		5,100

Temporary Differences: Deferred Tax Liabilities

If temporary differences exist, deferred tax assets and liabilities may be recognized.

When a DTL is recorded, the typical initial journal entry is as follows:

Income tax expense	Plug	
Deferred tax liability		Temporary difference × future tax rate
Income tax payable		Taxable income × current tax rate

Typically, a DTL decreases (ie, reverses) over time. In this case, each period, the journal entry is as follows:

Income tax expense	Plug	
Deferred tax liability	Change to ending balance required*	
Income tax payable		Taxable income × current tax rate

**The ending balance of a DTL is the remaining future temporary difference × the future tax rate. Each period, the DTL account is debited (ie, decreased) or credited (ie, increased). This adjustment is made so that the DTL reflects the correct remaining ending balance. If the DTL increased (eg, due to an increase in future tax rate) instead of decreased, the DTL account would be credited rather than debited.*

Rog Co. prepays a $50 expense at the start of Year 1. Assume that the current tax rate is 20% and the future rate is 30%. Determine how the recording of this expense differs for book and tax purposes.

For book purposes, the expense is recognized evenly across the next five years. On the books, each year Rog reports an expense of $10 ($50 / 5 years). However, for tax purposes, prepaid expenses are deductible when paid. As such, Rog deducts the entire $50 in Year 1.

	Book			Tax		
Year 1	Expense	10		Expense	50	
	Prepaid expense (Asset)	40		Cash		50
	Cash		50			
Year 2	Expense	10		Expense	0	
	Prepaid expense (Asset)		10	Cash		0

Assume that pretax income in Year 1 (before the $50 expense) was $150 and that pretax income in Year 2 was $200. Determine the book income, taxable income, and DTA or DTL to be recorded for Year 1 and Year 2.

Year 1

Book		Tax	
Pretax income	$150	Pretax income	$150
Expense	(10)	Expense	(50)
Net income	$140	Taxable income	$100

Taxable income of $100 × 20%* = **$20 income tax payable.**

Temporary difference of $40 results in a DTL (because taxable income is less than book income). $40 × 30%* = **$12 DTL.**

Year 2

Book		Tax	
Pretax income	$200	Pretax income	$200
Expense	(10)	Expense	(0)
Net income	$190	Taxable income	$200

Taxable income of $200 × 30%* = **$60 income tax payable.**

As more of the expense is recognized for book purposes, the difference starts to reverse out at $10 each year. At the end of Year 2, the remaining liability of $30 ($40 − $10) is calculated based on the future tax rate of 30%*. New ending **DTL balance is $9** ($30 × 30%**).

**The current tax rate is used to calculate income tax payable, and the future tax rate is used to calculate the deferred items.*

*** The cumulative difference is analyzed over time to determine the amount needed in the DTL account at year end.*

The corresponding journal entries are as follows:

Year 1			
Income tax expense	32		← (20 current/12 deferred)
Deferred tax liability		12	
Income tax payable		20	

Year 2			
Income tax expense	57		← (60 current/3 deferred)
Deferred tax liability	3		← (to get to ending balance of $9)
Income tax payable		60	

The total income tax expense is recorded as follows (assuming no prepayments):

Presentation on the Income Statement	**Year 1**	**Year 2**
Provision for income taxes		
Current	$(20)	$(60)
Deferred	$(12)	$ 3
Total provision for income taxes	$(32)	$(57)

Temporary Differences: Deferred Tax Assets

When a DTA is recorded, the typical initial journal entry is as follows:

Income tax expense	Plug	
Deferred tax asset	Temporary difference × future tax rate	
Income tax payable		Taxable income × current tax rate

Typically, a DTA decreases (ie, reverses) over time. The journal entry for the reversal of the DTA journal entry is as follows:

Income tax expense	Plug	
Deferred tax asset		Change to ending balance required*
Income tax payable		Taxable income × current tax rate

**The ending balance of a DTA is the remaining future temporary difference × the future tax rate. Each period, the DTA account is debited (ie, decreased) or credited (ie, increased). This adjustment is made so that the DTA reflects the correct remaining ending balance. If the DTA increased (eg, due to an increase in future tax rate) instead of decreased, the DTA account would be debited rather than credited.*

Rog Co. receives rental revenue in advance of $50 at the start of Year 1. Assume that the current tax rate is 20% and the future rate is 30%. Determine how the recording of this revenue differs for book and tax purposes.

For book purposes, the revenue is recognized evenly over the next five years. On the book, each year Rog records revenue of $10 ($50 / 5 years). However, for tax purposes, rental revenue is recorded when received. As such, Rog recognizes the entire $50 in Year 1.

	Book			**Tax**		
Year 1	Cash	50		Cash	50	
	Rent revenue		10	Rent revenue		50
	Unearned revenue		40			
Year 2	Unearned revenue	10		Unearned revenue	0	
	Rent revenue		10	Rent revenue		0

Assume that pretax income in Year 1 (before the $50 revenue) was $150 and that pretax income in Year 2 was $200. Determine the book income, taxable income, and DTA or DTL to be recorded for Year 1 and Year 2.

Year 1

Book		**Tax**	
Pretax income	$150	Pretax income	$150
Revenue	10	Revenue	50
Net income	$160	Taxable income	$200

Taxable income of $200 × 20%* = **$40 income tax payable**.

Temporary difference of $40 results in DTA (because taxable income is more than book income). $40 × 30%* = **$12 DTA**.

Year 2

Book		**Tax**	
Pretax income	$200	Pretax income	$200
Revenue	10	Revenue	0
Net income	$210	Taxable income	$200

Taxable income of $200 × 30%* = **$60 income tax payable**.

As more revenue is recognized for book purposes, the difference starts to reverse out at $10 each year. At the end of Year 2, the remaining asset of $30 ($40 − 10) is remeasured at the future tax rate of 30%*. New ending **DTA balance is $9** ($30 × 30%**).

**The current tax rate is used to calculate income tax payable, and the future tax rate is used to calculate the deferred items.*

***The cumulative difference is analyzed over time to determine the amount needed in the DTL account at year end.*

The corresponding journal entries are as follows:

Year 1			
Income tax expense	28		← (40 current/12 deferred)
Deferred tax asset	12		
Income tax payable		40	

Year 2			
Income tax expense	63		← (60 current/3 deferred)
Deferred tax asset		3	(to get to ending balance of $9)
Income tax payable		60	

The total income tax expense is recorded as follows (assuming no prepayments):

Presentation on the Income Statement	Year 1	Year 2
Provision for income taxes		
Current	$(40)	$(60)
Deferred	$ 12	$ (3)
Total provision for income taxes	$(28)	$(63)

Valuation Allowances

Representative Task (Remembering & Understanding): Recall the criteria for recognizing or adjusting a valuation allowance for a deferred tax asset.

A DTA, like any other asset, is an asset only if it has future benefit. A DTA will reduce income tax payments in the future, but only if there is taxable income in the future to reduce. When there is not a sufficient probability of realizing the deferred tax asset, a valuation allowance (contra-account) is recorded to reduce the DTA to the amount expected to be realized.

When a company has a DTA, it must determine if it is **more likely than not** (i.e., 50% or more likelihood) that **some or all of the asset will not be realized** (eg, due to insufficient future taxable income). If that is the case, a DTA valuation allowance is established for the portion that is not expected to be realized. This is a contra-asset to the DTA, thus reducing it.

Valuation Allowance Assessment

A valuation allowance may need to be recorded if any of the following are present:

- A history of unused net operating losses
- A history of operating losses
- Losses expected in future years
- Very unfavorable contingencies

The company should also consider evidence suggesting that a valuation allowance is not needed, such as the following:

- Existing contracts or sales backlog will produce more than enough taxable income to realize the deferred tax asset.
- An excess of appreciated asset value over the tax basis of the entity's net assets will produce more than enough taxable income to realize the deferred tax asset.
- A strong earnings history suggests that taxable income in the future will be enough to realize the deferred tax asset.

Both **positive and negative evidence** is used when making the decision about whether to recognize a valuation allowance.

A company had a deferred tax asset of $12 but only expected to use $8. Determine how this would be reflected on the company's books.

Based on these facts, it is more likely than not that $4 will not be realized. Therefore, a valuation allowance must be established for $4. By recording this allowance, income tax expense increases by $4 from $28 (if no valuation allowance was needed) to $32.

Income tax expense	32	
Deferred tax asset	12	
Income tax payable		40
DTA valuation allowance		4

Reporting a Valuation Allowance

The DTA and the valuation allowance accounts may be reported on the balance sheet as (1) two separate line items or (2) a net amount. If the net amount is reported, the footnotes should disclose the separate amounts.

The DTA and valuation allowance accounts are classified as noncurrent assets.

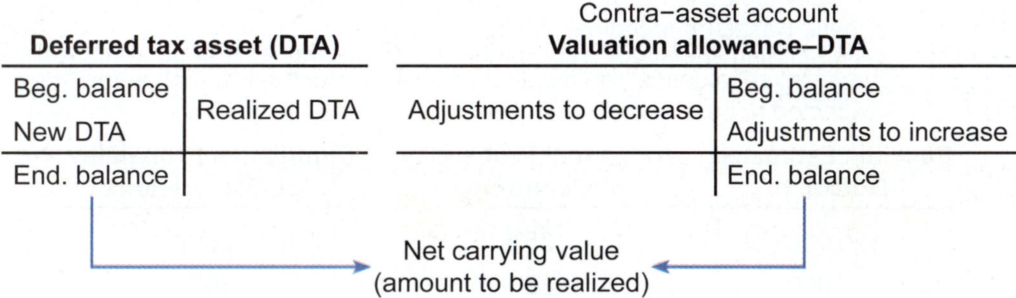

Uncertain Tax Positions

Representative Task (Remembering & Understanding): Recall the accounting treatment for uncertainty in income taxes.

The preparation of a firm's tax return is affected by many estimates and uncertainties. **Uncertain tax positions (UTPs)** are those that **may not be sustainable on audit by the IRS**. Examples include uncertain deductions, tax credits, and revenue exemptions.

The firm includes the uncertain position in its tax return, thus reducing its income tax liability, but there remains uncertainty about the actual benefit of that deduction. These UTPs must be reviewed to determine if potential accruals and disclosure are required in the F/S.

Income tax expense is reduced (benefit recognized) for an uncertain tax position only if it is **"more likely than not"** (ie, greater than 50%) that the position **will be sustained** upon audit by the IRS. A two-step approach is applied:

Recognizing Tax Benefits for Uncertain Tax Positions

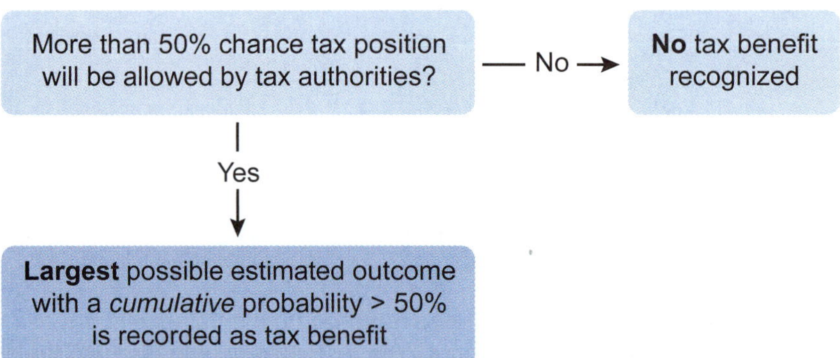

Assume that an entity took a tax position on its current-year tax return resulting in a $20,000 deferred tax benefit. Based on technical merits, it is determined that the position has a greater than 50% chance of being sustained. The amounts and possible outcomes of the position being allowed are as follows:

Possible Estimated Outcome	Individual Probability of Occurrence	Cumulative Probability of Occurrence
$20,000	25%	25%
15,000	35%	60%
10,000	30%	90%
5,000	10%	100%
	100%	

Since the entity has determined that the more-likely-than-not threshold has been met, the tax benefit qualifies for recognition. Determining the amount to be recorded requires an analysis of the cumulative probability of occurrence.

Three possible outcomes have a cumulative probability of occurring that is greater than 50% ($15,000, $10,000, and $5,000). The entity will record the outcome with the largest dollar amount (not percentage) as the tax benefit. Here, the entity will record $15,000. The $5,000 remaining portion of the deduction ($20,000 − $15,000) is recognized as a liability.

If taxable income is $100,000 and the tax rate is 30%, the company will record the following journal entry:

Income tax expense	31,500	
Income tax payable ($100,000 × 30%)		30,000
Liability for unrecognized tax benefit ($5,000 × 30%)		1,500

Income tax expense is reduced by $4,500 ($15,000 × 30%) as a result of recognition of the current tax benefit associated with the $15,000 amount.

Effective Tax Rate

The effective tax rate can be derived from the information reported in a company's financial statements. The effective tax rate (ETR) is used to determine the actual tax percentage a corporation pays on its pretax book income. The ETR is calculated as follows:

Effective Tax Rate

$$\frac{\text{Total income tax expense}}{\text{Pretax book income}}$$

Classification of Tax Items

All deferred tax assets and liabilities are classified as noncurrent amounts on the balance sheet.

The **net amount** of all deferred tax assets and liabilities, along with any related valuation allowance, is presented on the balance sheet as a single noncurrent amount:

Deferred tax asset	10
Deferred tax liability	(30)
Deferred tax asset − Valuation allowance	(5)

Net balance sheet presentation: Noncurrent deferred tax liability of 25

Conversely, income tax payable/receivable is classified as a current amount on the balance sheet.

Disclosures

Certain disclosures are required in relation to the items reported on the balance sheet. In general, they may be provided on the face of the F/S, in supplementary schedules, or in the notes to the F/S. These include the following:

- The components of the net DTA or DTL (including valuation allowances) reported on the balance sheet
- Income (or loss) from continuing operations before income tax expense, disaggregated between domestic and foreign
- The significant components of income tax expense arising from continuing operations, disaggregated by federal (national), state, and foreign
- A reconciliation between reported income tax expense from continuing operations and the amount computed by multiplying the income (or loss) from continuing operations before income taxes by the applicable statutory federal (national) income tax rate
- Quantitative and qualitative description of state, local, and foreign income taxes paid
- Adjustments to deferred tax assets or liabilities resulting from changes in tax laws, tax rates, or the entity's tax status
- Information about temporary differences, including the approximate tax effect and carryforward that affects DTAs and DTLs
- Adjustments to the valuation allowance due to changes in judgment about the realizability of DTAs
- Amounts of operating loss carryforwards and tax credit carryforwards, along with their expiration dates
- Quantitative and qualitative disclosures related to UTPs

FAR 20
Fair Value Measurements

FAR 20: Fair Value Measurements

20.01 Fair Value Measurements

Overview

Representative Task (Remembering & Understanding): Identify the valuation techniques used to measure fair value.

Representative Task (Remembering & Understanding): Recall assumptions (eg, highest and best use, market participant assumptions, unit of account) and approaches (cost, income, market) used to measure fair value.

Fair Value Definition

ASC 820 defines fair value (FV) as "the price that would be received to *sell an asset* or paid to *transfer a liability* in an *orderly transaction* between *market participants* at the measurement date."

Several components of this definition ("asset or liability," "orderly transaction," and "market participants") are further described below.

Asset or Liability

A FV measurement relates to a *specific* asset or liability. As such, a FV determination should consider the attributes (eg, condition, location, restriction on asset use or sale, etc.) of the specific asset or liability being measured. In addition, the **unit of account** must be established prior to FV determination. Unit of account refers to the aggregation (or disaggregation) of assets and liabilities. FV can be assessed for a single asset/liability (eg, a financial instrument) or a group of assets/liabilities (eg, a reporting unit or business).

Orderly Transaction

For a transaction to be orderly, it cannot be assumed to occur as part of a forced liquidation or distress sale. Instead, the hypothetical transaction is *assumed to take place at the measurement date under current market transactions* after a period of market exposure that is customary for that type of asset or liability.

Market Participants

Market participants are parties that are acting in their best economic interest. Market participants are assumed to be the following:

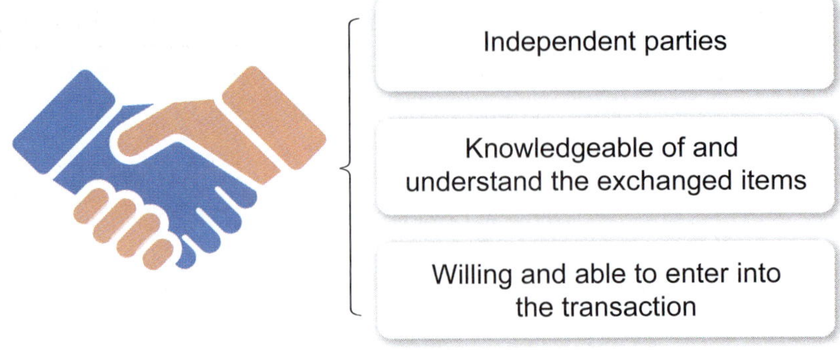

FV is based on the **exit price**, or the price that would be received to sell an asset or paid to transfer a liability under the conditions listed above. It is not based on the *entry price*, or transaction price, which is the price that was paid for the asset or that was received to assume the liability. The exit price and entry price are conceptually different.

The entry price can differ from the exit price for various reasons (eg, the transaction involves related parties, the market in which the transaction takes place is different from the principal market, the seller is under duress).

Items Required to Be Reported at FV

An entity is required to recognize various items at FV, including the following:

- Investments in **marketable debt securities** classified as either **trading** securities or **available-for-sale (AFS)** securities
- Investments in **equity securities**, except those accounted for under the equity method
- Investments required to be consolidated
- Investments for which the market value is not readily determinable (assuming the appropriate election has been made)
- With very few exceptions, **assets acquired and liabilities assumed in a business combination**
- **Impairment losses** (ie, reduces asset's carrying value to its FV in the period of impairment)
- All **derivatives**, except for interest rate swaps that are hedges when the alternative accounting approach available to nonpublic entities is elected

Principal Market

It is assumed that a transaction will occur in the **principal market** in which the asset or liability would most frequently be traded. When there is no principal market, values are based on the assumption that a transaction would occur in the **most advantageous market**.

Transaction and transportation costs are considered in determining the most advantageous market. However, **transaction costs** (ie, incremental direct costs to sell the asset or transfer the liability) *are not* considered in determining the asset or liability's FV. Conversely, costs incurred to **transport the asset or liability** to its principal or most advantageous market are considered in determining the asset or liability's FV.

Determine the FV of the financial asset for which there is no principal market. The asset is actively traded on two different exchanges: Market X and Market Y. The information on the two exchanges is as follows:

	Quoted Asset Price	Transaction Costs	Transportation Costs
Market X	$100	$10	$7
Market Y	105	5	20

The financial asset's FV is $93, calculated as follows:

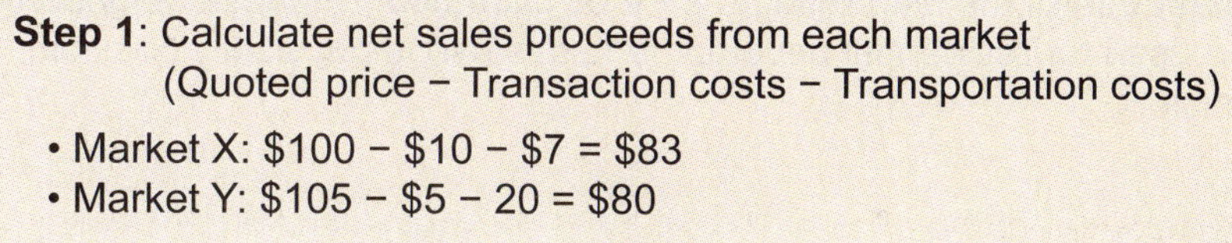

Step 1: Calculate net sales proceeds from each market
(Quoted price − Transaction costs − Transportation costs)

- Market X: $100 − $10 − $7 = $83
- Market Y: $105 − $5 − 20 = $80

↓

Step 2: Identify most advantageous market

- Market X: $83

↓

Step 3: Determine fair value
(Quoted price − Transportation costs)

- Market X: $100 − $7 = **$93**

Highest and Best Use

The **FV** of **nonfinancial assets** should reflect each asset's **highest and best use** because sellers will transact wherever they will receive the most consideration. That use must be physically possible, legally permissible, and financially feasible. If the highest and best use for an asset differs from its current use, the highest and best use is used to determine FV.

Some assets are more valuable **in exchange** and are measured at what would be received upon their sale. Other assets are more valuable **in use** and are measured at the value represented in the form of some combination of potential revenues earned and cost savings that result from their use.

Assume that a company owns land and a building that houses its manufacturing operations. When the company purchased the manufacturing facility, the purchase price allocated to the land account was $100,000.

The manufacturing facility is located in an area that was once the site of many factories. The owners of several of the neighboring factories have recently sold their facilities to residential real estate developers. The company's land is also suitable for residential development.

The estimated current value of the land as part of the manufacturing facility is $150,000. The estimated current value of the land as an undeveloped investment is $160,000, and the current value of the land as part of a residential development is $200,000.

The **highest and best use** of the land reflects a **FV of $200,000**. Because neighboring factories have sold their land to be used for residential development, this use is physically possible, legally permissible, and financially feasible.

When determining the FV of a liability, it is assumed that the liability is transferred to a market participant at the measurement date; it is not settled or canceled.

Valuation Approaches

There are three main approaches used in determining FV. Within each approach, there are more granular techniques that can be used to ascertain FV. The approaches and examples of techniques are summarized below:

Approach	Description	Techniques
Market	Information generated by market transactions for identical or similar items	• Quoted price from stock exchange • The use of multiples from recent transactions
Income	Estimated future amounts discounted to a single, current amount	• Discounted cash flow analysis • Capitalization of earnings
Cost	Amount currently required to replace the benefit derived from an asset	• Replacement cost • Reproduction cost

The most appropriate approach to measure FV will depend on the circumstances, including the availability and reliability of data. Sometimes, a single valuation technique will be appropriate (eg, using quoted prices in an active market for identical assets or liabilities). Other times, multiple valuation techniques will be appropriate (eg, when valuing an entire business).

Valuation techniques used to measure FV should be consistently applied. A change in valuation technique or its application is appropriate if the change will result in a more representative FV.

Three Levels of Input

Representative Task (Application): Use the fair value hierarchy to determine the classification of a fair value measurement.

FV approaches depend on various **inputs** (ie, data and assumptions used by market participants). Inputs used may be *observable* (ie, developed based on market data obtained from sources independent of the company) or *unobservable* (ie, developed based on the company's own assumptions using the best information possible).

Valuation approaches and techniques used to measure FV should *maximize the use of observable inputs* and minimize the use of unobservable inputs. Inputs are categorized based on their reliability, as follows:

- **Level 1**, the most reliable, involves the use of observable data from actual market transactions, occurring in an active market, for identical assets or liabilities
- **Level 2** also involves the use of observable data from actual market transactions but with *either* of the following conditions:
  - The transactions did not occur in an active market
  - The transactions relate to similar, but not identical, assets or liabilities
- **Level 3**, the least reliable, involves the use of unobservable data and is largely based on management's judgment
  - Management should take care that such judgments are reasonable and based on the best information available

Fair Value Hierarchy for Eligible Assets and Liabilities

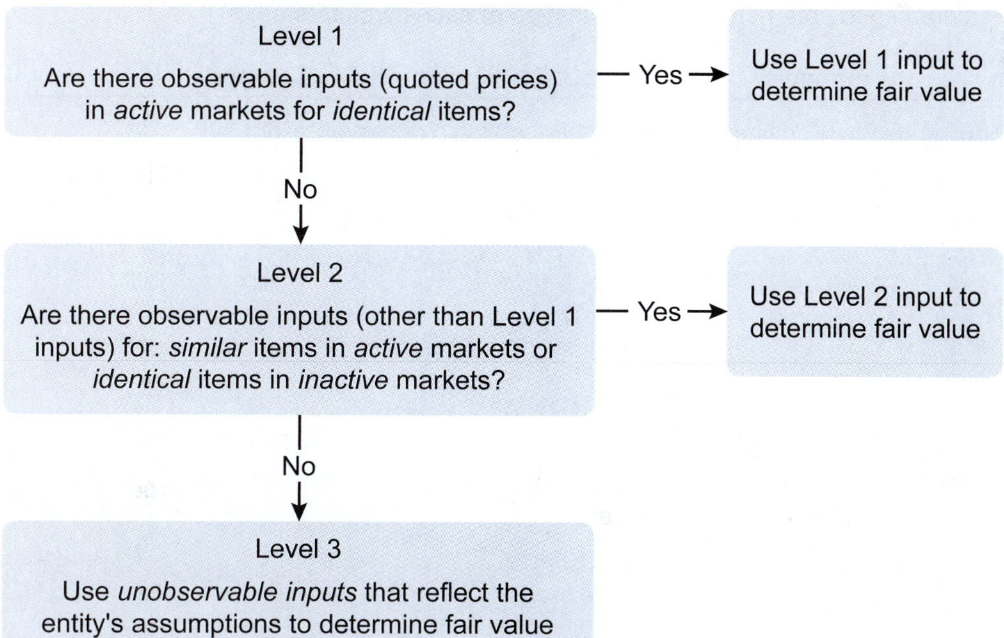

A company has an equity investment with a historical cost of $500,000 that is traded in an **active market**. On December 31, the quoted price for an identical investment was $400,000 and the quoted price for a *similar* investment was $430,000. Using the company's internal present value of cash flows model, the company arrived at a value of $410,000. What is the value of the investment on December 31?

The equity investment should be measured at **$400,000**, the price sold for an *identical* asset traded in an active market (ie, market approach). This price represents the asset's FV and uses a Level 1 (most reliable) input.

Practical Expedient for Certain Equity Interests

In some cases, an entity will have an equity interest in another entity that reports its net asset value (NAV) per share. As a *practical expedient*, such an investment may be reported at the published NAV per share.

Since the FV is not determined using a technique designated by standards for doing so, the FV measurement does not fit into the hierarchy. As a result, an entity applying the practical expedient is *not required to disclose* the level of inputs used to determine FV. Entities using the practical expedient are required to provide a reconciliation of the FV hierarchy disclosure to the balance sheet. They must disclose the FV of investments measured at NAV per share.

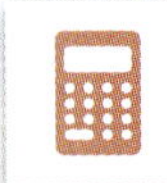

A company has the following investments:

- Equity ownership in a private company; discounted cash flow analysis is used to value investment
- 5,000 shares of stock, publicly traded
- Hedge fund, not traded on an exchange; NAV per share is reported to investors quarterly

Use the FV hierarchy to determine the classification of each investment.

Investment	Category
Equity ownership in a private company	Level 3: No observable inputs
5,000 shares of stock	Level 1: Based on active market with identical assets
Hedge fund	Practical expedient

Fair Value Option

In addition to those items that are required to be measured at FV, an entity can *elect* to report some or all of its **financial instruments** (ie, financial assets and liabilities) at their FV. A financial instrument is defined as *cash*, evidence of an *ownership interest* in an entity, or certain *contracts*. When the FV option is elected, unrealized gains and losses are reported in income.

If an entity decides to elect the FV option, it may apply it to any qualifying financial instrument, without being required to apply it to others, including those that are similar. An election may be made only when a financial asset or liability is acquired or, in other limited circumstances, referred to as "election dates." Likewise, once elected, the FV option is permanent and may only be discontinued on a subsequent election date.

Examples of financial assets and liabilities that would qualify for the FV option include the following:

- Most investments that do not already require FV measurement, such as investments accounted for under the equity method
- Firm commitments involving financial instruments, such as forward exchange contracts to purchase or sell a foreign currency

Certain items (eg, leases, share-based payments, stock options) have their own established accounting principles that must be followed. These items may involve measurements at FV, but they do not qualify for the FV option.

Fair Value Measurement Summary

FV measurement may be applied using the following approach:

1. Identify the asset or liability to be measured
2. Determine the principal or most advantageous market *(highest and best use)*
3. Determine the valuation premise *(in-use or in-exchange)*
4. Determine the appropriate valuation technique *(market, income, or cost approach)*
5. Obtain inputs for valuation *(Level 1, Level 2, or Level 3)*
    - **FV hierarchy** must be used to prioritize the inputs used in valuation techniques
6. Calculate the FV of the asset

FAR 21
Lessee Accounting

FAR 21: Lessee Accounting

21.01 Lessee Accounting

The AICPA Blueprint splits coverage of lease content between Financial Accounting and Reporting (FAR) and Business Analysis and Reporting (BAR). FAR focuses primarily on **lessee** activity, while BAR addresses **lessor** transactions.

Lease Basics and Classification

Representative Task (Remembering & Understanding): Identify the criteria for classifying a lease arrangement for a lessee.

Lease Definition

ASC 842 defines a lease as "a contract, or part of a contract, that conveys the **right to control** the use of identified property, plant, or equipment (an identified asset) for a period of time in exchange for consideration."

"Control" is further defined such that a business must be able to achieve "substantially all" of the economic benefits from the asset's use and direct its use throughout the contract period.

A lessee is the party that *pays rent* to the lessor for the right to use the lessor's property for a period of time. When a lease involves real property, the lessee is also called the *tenant*, and the lessor is called the *landlord*. A lessor owns the property and grants the lessee the right to use it for a period of time in exchange for rental payments.

Lease Classification

From the perspective of a lessee, long-term (ie, longer than 12 months) leases can be classified as finance or operating. Use the mnemonic "Special-PO-T-75-90" to remember the steps required to determine the classification of a lease.

These five steps are used to determine the proper classification of a lease and are performed at lease commencement (not when the lease is signed).

Finance Lease Criteria: Special-PO-T-75-90

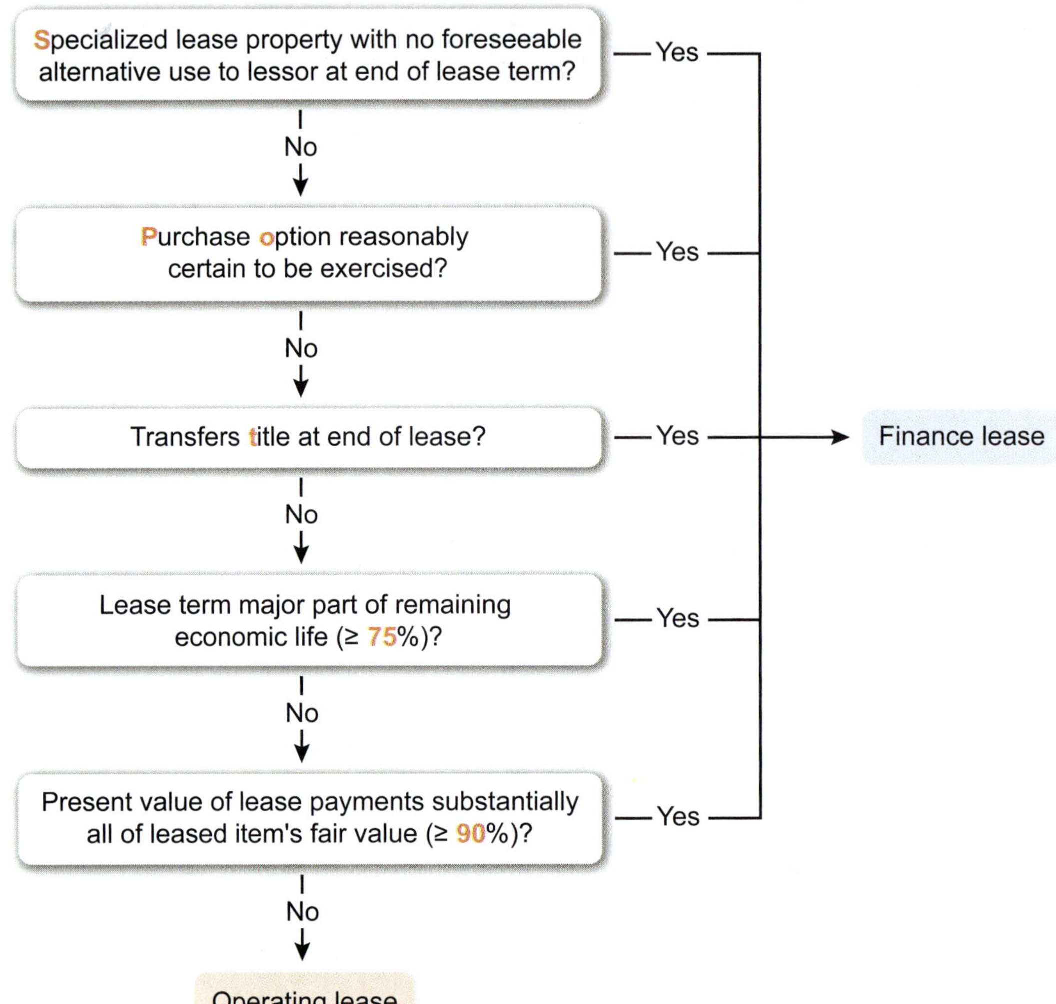

Colton, Inc., enters into a 20-year lease on an office building. The building is estimated to have a 30-year economic useful life. Title of the building does not transfer at the end of the lease, and Colton is not offered a purchase option. The PV of the lease payments is $450,000, and the fair value of the building is estimated to be $600,000.

Determine if Colton should classify the lease as operating or finance.

Colton will use the "Special-PO-T-75-90" criteria to determine how to classify the lease:

- The building is **not** a specialized property.
- There is **no** purchase option.
- There is **no** title transfer.
- The lease term constitutes **less than** 75% of the building's economic useful life (20-year lease / 30-year useful life = 67%).
- The PV of the lease payments constitutes **less than** 90% of the building's fair value ($450,000 / 600,000 = 75%).

Because the lease does not meet any of the "Special-PO-T-75-90" criteria, Colton should classify it as an operating lease.

At inception, lessee accounting for finance leases and operating leases is the same. However, finance leases have similar characteristics to those of an owned asset, while operating leases mimic a rental agreement. In a finance lease, the rights and risks of ownership are effectively transferred from a lessor to a lessee. As such, following initial recognition of the finance lease, the lessee records the lease as if they had purchased the asset. After initial recognition in an operating lease, the lessee records the lease in a different manner.

Lease Term

The lease term is the period of time during which the lessee can reasonably be expected to continue leasing the asset. It begins at the commencement date and is the sum of the following:

- Initial lease term: This is the original *noncancelable* term of the lease that does not include any renewal periods
- Periods for which a renewal option is likely to be exercised by the lessee
- Periods for which an option to terminate is unlikely to be exercised: This might be the case when a lease contains a provision that requires the lessee to pay a significant penalty to the lessor for not renewing the lease
- Periods for which a renewal option (or option not to terminate) is controlled by the lessor

Lessees are required to **recognize assets and liabilities** for any lease with a term **exceeding 12 months**.

If the lease does not exceed 12 months and does not include an option to purchase the underlying asset, it is considered to be a **short-term lease**. The lessee may choose to treat such leases the same as operating leases or simply recognize lease expense each period.

Lease Payments

Representative Task (Remembering & Understanding): Recall the appropriate accounting treatment for residual value guarantees, purchase options, and variable lease payments included in leasing arrangements for a lessee.

Lease payments represent the amount that the lessee is likely to pay for the use of the underlying asset under the terms of the lease during the lease term.

Lease Payments

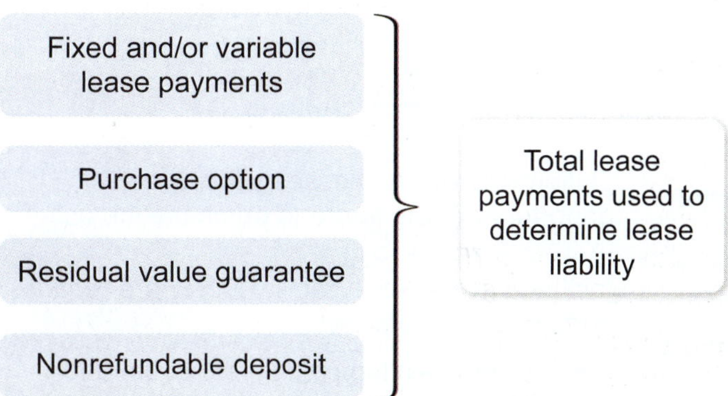

The lease liability is equal to the present value of the lease payments.

Lease payments (and, therefore, the lease liability) may include fixed and/or variable lease payments:

Fixed Lease Payments	
Definition	Amount the lessee is required to pay over the term of the lease, minus any lease incentives paid/payable to the lessee (eg, payments made to or on behalf of the lessee)
Treatment	Included in the lease liability

Variable Lease Payments	
Definition	Payments that may change over the course of the lease • Change in payment may be linked to an external market rate (eg, consumer price index), a performance measure (eg, percentage of sales), or a usage measure (eg, mileage)
Treatment	If the *lease specifies the amount that payment will change each year*, it is included in the lease liability • Here, variable lease payments are known throughout the lease and are, in substance, fixed payments If the change in payment each year is unknown, it is not included in the lease liability and is expensed in the period incurred

Fixed and/or variable lease payments may include recurring lease components (eg, rent), nonlease components (eg, maintenance), and noncomponents (eg, taxes, insurance).

For example, a company enters into a five-year lease. The lease payment is set to increase by $3,000 each year over the life of the lease. Because the lease specifies the increase each year, the lessee will include the present value of the payment increases ($3,000 per year) in the lease liability.

Lease payments (and, therefore, the lease liability) may include purchase options:

Purchase Options	
Definition	Option whereby the lessee will have an opportunity in the future to purchase the asset
Treatment	Included in the lease liability if they are *reasonably certain to be exercised* • Treated as a lump sum paid at the end of the noncancelable lease term

Note: If a lease contains a purchase option that the lessee is reasonably certain to exercise, the lease will be classified as a finance lease by the lessee.

For example, a company enters into a six-year lease. The company has the option to purchase the leased asset for $15,000 at the end of the lease term, when the asset's value is expected to be $45,000. Because the asset's value greatly exceeds what the company would pay for it, the company is likely to exercise the purchase option. The present value of the $15,000 lump sum will be included in the lease liability.

Lease payments (and, therefore, the lease liability) may include residual value guarantees:

Residual Value Guarantees (RVG)	
Definition	**Residual value:** Estimated value of a leased asset at the end of the lease term **Residual value guarantee:** The lessee guarantees that the leased asset's residual value will be at least equal to the lessor's expected value at the end of the lease term
Treatment	Lease liability includes the *probable amount* that the lessee will owe at the end of a lease for an RVG • Included because the lessee has an obligation to return the leased asset's expected value to the lessor • To determine probable amount, guaranteed value is compared with the lease asset's expected residual value at the end of the lease term: ○ If guaranteed value is greater than expected residual value, the difference is included in the total lease payments ○ If guaranteed value is less than expected residual value, the guarantee is excluded from total lease payments as the lessee will not have to pay any extra to the lessor related to the guarantee

For example, a company enters into a seven-year lease. The residual value of the leased asset at the end of the lease term is expected to be $3,000. The company guarantees a residual value of $4,000. The present value of the $1,000 difference ($4,000 − $3,000) will be included in the lease liability because the company is expected to owe this shortfall at the end of the lease term.

The lease liability and/or right-of-use (ROU) lease asset may include nonrefundable deposits and up-front fees:

	Nonrefundable Deposits	Up-Front Fees
Definition	Fee paid by the lessee to secure the use of the leased asset; once the lessor receives the fee, the asset's availability is no longer advertised • Lessor will not return the payment to the lessee at the end of the lease	Fees or costs incurred as a result of execution of the lease • Also called initial direct costs
Treatment	Included in *lease liability*	Included in *ROU lease asset*

For example, a company enters into an eight-year lease. The company incurs $500 in legal fees related to the lease execution. The $500 would be included in the initial measurement of the ROU lease asset. If the legal fees were not incurred because of the lease execution, they would be expensed in the period incurred.

Examples of other initial direct costs include document fees associated with preparing the lease documents, commissions paid to agents to secure the lease, and fees paid for third-party guaranteed residual values.

Operating Leases

Representative Task (Application): Calculate the carrying amount of lease-related assets and liabilities and prepare journal entries that a lessee should record.

Representative Task (Application): Calculate the lease costs that a lessee should recognize in the income statement.

As mentioned above, an **operating lease** is similar to a *rental* because it does not involve transferring ownership of a leased asset from a lessor (ie, owner) to a lessee (ie, tenant).

At the **inception** of an operating lease, the lessee recognizes a **ROU asset** and **lease liability** recorded at present value (PV) of the lease payments at the lease's interest rate.

Initial entry to record operating lease		
ROU asset	XX	
Lease liability		XX

The lease's interest rate is either the interest rate implicit in the lease, if known, or the lessee's incremental borrowing rate (ie, the rate of interest that the lessee would have to pay to borrow funds from a lender over a similar term to the lease term).

Each period, the lessee records straight-line lease expense, cash payment of the lease, reduction of the ROU asset, and reduction of the lease liability:

Lease expense	XX	
Lease liability	XX	
ROU asset		XX
Cash (lease payment)		XX

Lease Expense

Lease payments are expensed over the lease term, generally on a straight-line (S/L) basis:

$$\text{Lease expense} = \frac{\text{Total lease payments}}{\text{Lease term}}$$

Lease expense is composed of accreted interest expense and amortization of the ROU asset. Although these components can be calculated separately, they are reported as a single S/L lease expense each period on the income statement.

Component	Calculation
Accreted interest	Lease liability × Lease interest rate × Time period
ROU asset amortization	Accreted interest − Lease expense

Right-of-Use (ROU) Asset

The ROU asset initially includes the following:

ROU asset =
  Lease liability (present value of lease payments)
+ Initial direct costs
  (eg, commissions, certain legal fees)
+ Prepaid lease payments
− Lease incentives received
  (eg, lease-signing bonus)

For operating leases, the ROU asset is **amortized** (ie, reduced) over the term of the lease for the **difference between the lease expense and accreted interest for each period** (see ROU asset amortization calculation in the table above). At the end of the lease term, the ROU asset on the balance sheet will equal zero.

Lease Liability

The lease liability is initially recorded at PV of lease payments.

The "Lease Payments" section above covers items included in the lease liability.

Each period, the lease liability is reduced by the **difference between lease payment and accreted interest for each period**. At the end of the lease term, the lease liability on the balance sheet will equal zero.

Reduction in lease liability = Accreted interest − Lease payment

Components of an operating lease are accounted for as follows:

Operating Lease Components: Lessee Accounting	
Right-of-Use (ROU) Asset and Lease Liability	Recorded at present value of lease payments
Prepaid Rent	Prepaid asset until recognized as rent
Refundable Security Deposit	Long-term receivable
Leasehold Improvements	Capitalized and amortized over the shorter of remaining lease term or useful life
Lease (Rent) Expense	Expensed uniformly over lease term on straight-line basis

Examples

On January 1, a company enters into an operating lease for office space and receives control of the property to make leasehold improvements. The company begins alterations to the property on March 1, and the company's staff moves into the property on May 1. The monthly rental payments begin on July 1.

Determine when the recognition of rental expense for the new offices should begin.

Operating Lease: Recognize Lease Expense

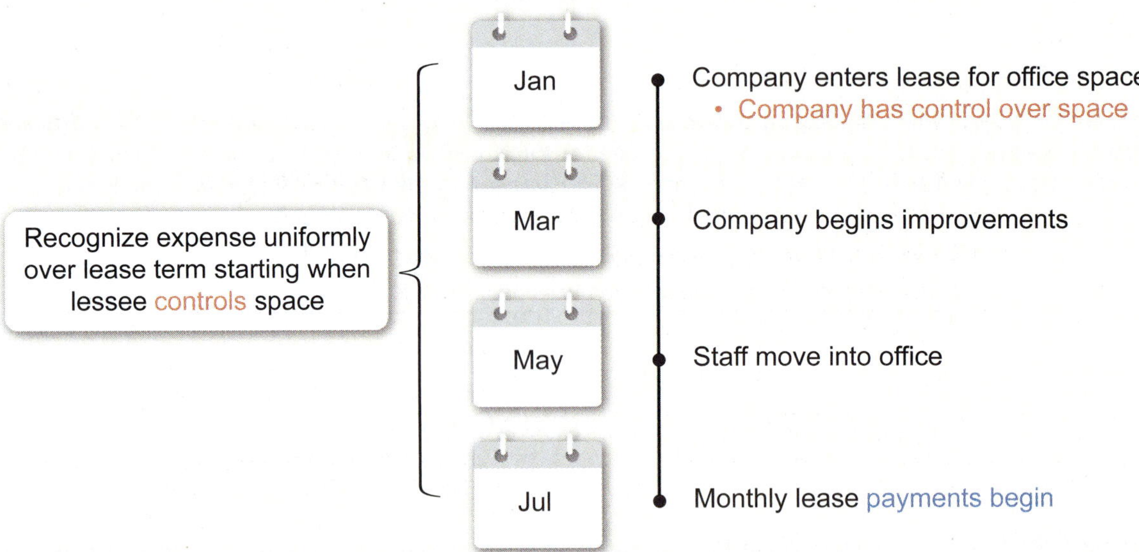

An operating lease takes effect when the lessee **takes control of the property** at the commencement of the lease. The date when the lessee makes leasehold improvements to the space (ie, March) or moves into the space (ie, May) does not determine control. Rent payments can begin at a later date, but rent expense begins when the lessee has control of the property.

Here, the lessee enters into the lease agreement in January. At that point, the lessee has control over the space, so the rent expense begins in January.

Mitten Co. signed a five-year rental contract (with no renewal option) for office equipment on January 1, Year 1.

- The economic useful life is estimated to be 10 years
- The client has an incremental borrowing rate of 6%, and the payments are $10,000 per year, due at the end of each year
- As an inducement to enter the agreement, the client has been offered the first six months free and a $1,000 signing bonus
- The lessee has incurred $1,000 in initial direct costs
- The PV factor for a lump sum at 6% for one year is 0.943, and the PV factor for an ordinary annuity at 6% for five years is 4.212
- The payment schedule will be as follows:

12/31/Y1	$ 5,000
12/31/Y2	10,000
12/31/Y3	10,000
12/31/Y4	10,000
12/31/Y5	10,000
Total	$45,000

The lease does not meet any of the "Special-PO-T-75-90" criteria. The property is not specialized, there is no purchase or renewal option, title does not transfer at the end of the lease, the lease term is only 50% of the asset's economic useful life, and the PV of the lease payments are not substantially equal to the asset's FV. Therefore, the lessee should account for this lease as an operating lease.

At January 1, Year 1, the initial entry is as follows:

ROU asset*	37,405	
Lease liability**		37,405

**The right-of-use asset is calculated as follows:*

Lease liability at PV of lease payments ($37,405; see calculation below)
+ Lease payments made at or before the commencement date ($0)
− Lease incentives (eg, lease-signing bonus) received (−$1,000)
+ Initial direct costs incurred (eg, commissions) (+$1,000)
Right-of-use asset ($37,405)

***The PV of the lease payments is calculated as follows:*

- *The lump sum of $5,000 at 6% in Year 1 ($5,000 × 0.943 = $4,715)*
- *The PV of an ordinary annuity of $10,000 at 6% over five years, minus the first-year lump-sum value of $10,000 at 6% [($10,000 × 4.212 = $42,120) − ($10,000 × 0.943 = $9,430)] = $32,690*

Lease liability: $4,715 + $32,690 = $37,405

Now, since the total of lease payments is $45,000, **lease expense will be recognized on an S/L basis at $9,000 each year (ie, $45,000 / 5 years)**. In an operating lease, the two components of lease expense (accrued interest expense and amortization expense) may be calculated separately, but they are reported as a single straight-line lease expense each period on the income statement.

Each period, the lease liability will be reduced by the difference between the accreted interest (lease liability × lease interest rate) and the lease payment. The following table shows how the lease liability will change over the life of the lease under the effective interest method.

Lease Liability	Interest Rate	=	Accreted Interest Expense	–	Lease Payment	=	Net Reduction in Lease Liability
37,405	6%	=	2,244	–	5,000[D]	=	2,756[B]
(2,756)							
34,649	6%	=	2,079	–	10,000[H]	=	7,921[F]
(7,921)							
26,728	6%	=	1,604	–	10,000	=	8,396
(8,396)							
18,332	6%	=	1,100	–	10,000	=	8,900
(8,900)							
9,432	6%	=	566	–	10,000	=	9,434
(9,434)							
0*							

**Note that there is a $2 difference due to rounding for simplicity purposes.*

Each period, the ROU asset is reduced by the difference between the lease expense and accreted interest. The following table shows how the ROU asset will change over the life of the lease under the effective interest method.

ROU Asset	Accreted Interest Expense	–	Lease expense	=	Net Reduction in ROU Asset
37,405	2,244	–	9,000[A]	=	6,756[C]
(6,756)					
30,649	2,079	–	9,000[E]	=	6,921[G]
(6,921)					
23,728	1,604	–	9,000	=	7,396
(7,396)					
16,332	1,100	–	9,000	=	7,900
(7,900)					
8,432	566	–	9,000	=	8,434
(8,434)					
0*					

**Note that there is a $2 difference due to rounding for simplicity purposes.*

At December 31, Year 1, the following is recorded:

Lease expense	9,000[A]	
Lease liability	2,756[B]	
ROU asset		6,756[C]
Cash		5,000[D]

At December 31, Year 2, the following is recorded:

Lease expense	9,000[E]	
Lease liability	7,921[F]	
ROU asset		6,921[G]
Cash		10,000[H]

Remember:

Reduction in lease liability = Accreted interest − Lease payment

Reduction in ROU asset = Accreted interest − Lease expense

In the above example, the amount paid in Year 1 is different from the amounts paid in subsequent years. Because of this, lease payment ($5,000 in Year 1 and $10,000 in subsequent years) does not equal lease expense ($9,000 in each year).

If the amount paid were the same in all years, lease payment would equal lease expense. For example, assume that a company enters into a three-year lease, with payment of $15,000 due at the end of each year. Here, **lease payment is $15,000** each period. S/L lease expense each period is calculated as [total payment / lease term] or ($15,000 × 3) / 3. **S/L lease expense is also $15,000**.

When the amount paid is the same in all periods, lease payment = lease expense, and, therefore, the reduction in the lease liability = the reduction in the ROU asset every period.

Main, a pharmaceutical company, signed an operating lease agreement to use office space for five years. Main took possession and began to use the building on July 1, Year 1. Rent was due the first day of each month. Monthly lease payments escalated over the five-year period of the lease as follows:

Period	Lease Payment per Month
July 1, Year 1–September 30, Year 1	$0 – rent abatement during move-in, construction
October 1, Year 1–June 30, Year 2	$17,500
July 1 Year 2–June 30, Year 3	$19,000
July 1, Year 3–June 30, Year 4	$20,500
July 1, Year 4–June 30, Year 5	$23,000
July 1 Year 5–June 30, Year 6	$24,500

Determine the amount that Main should report as lease expense in its income statement for the year ended June 30, Year 2.

In an operating lease, lease expense is expressed uniformly over the lease term on a straight-line basis. Monthly lease expense equals the total lease payments divided by the months in the lease term.

Here, Main has a 60-month operating lease with escalating lease payments each year. Although the payments are variable, the lease specifies the amount that payment will change each year. Therefore, the payments are, in substance, fixed, and all payments should be included in the lease liability.

Monthly lease expense is $20,025, as calculated below:

October 1, Year 1–June 30, Year 2 ($17,500 × 9 months)	$ 157,500
July 1, Year 2–June 30, Year 3 ($19,000 × 12 months)	228,000
July 1, Year 3–June 30, Year 4 ($20,500 × 12 months)	246,000
July 1, Year 4–June 30, Year 5 ($23,000 × 12 months)	276,000
July 1, Year 5–June 30, Year 6 ($24,500 × 12 months)	294,000
Total lease payments	$1,201,500
Monthly lease expense ($1,201,500 / 60 months*)	$ 20,025

**Although Main began payment on October 1, Year 1, the company took possession of the space on July 1, Year 1. The monthly lease expense should be calculated over the number of months that Main held possession of the space, rather than the number of months that Main actually paid in.*

Main took possession of the space on July 1, Year 1. Therefore, Main should report **$240,300 in lease expense** on its income statement for the year ended June 30, Year 2 ($20,025 × 12 months).

Finance Leases

Recall that if a lease meets any of the "Special-PO-T-75-90" criteria, it is classified as a finance lease. A **finance lease** is generally one in which the rights and risks of ownership have essentially transferred from the lessor to the lessee. In substance, it is a purchase, although in form it is considered a lease.

Just as with an operating lease, at **inception**, the lessee recognizes both **ROU asset** and a **lease liability** at the PV of the lease payments at the lease's interest rate.

Initial entry to record finance lease		
ROU asset	XX	
Lease liability		XX

The lease's interest rate is either the interest rate implicit in the lease, if known, or the lessee's incremental borrowing rate.

While an operating lease liability would generally not be considered debt for purposes of ratios and debt covenants, a finance lease liability is *considered part of the lessee's total debt* (eg, it is part of "debt" in the debt-to-equity ratio). Another key difference is that the ROU asset will normally be amortized on an S/L basis, not unevenly as with an operating lease. **Each period**, the lessee records cash payment of the lease, reduction of the ROU asset, reduction of the lease liability, and two expenses: interest expense and amortization expense:

Interest expense	XX	
Lease liability	XX	
Amortization expense	XX	
ROU asset		XX
Cash (lease payment)		XX

Right-of-Use (ROU) Asset and Amortization Expense

The ROU asset initially includes the following:

ROU asset = Lease liability (present value of lease payments)
+ Initial direct costs (eg, commissions, certain legal fees)
+ Prepaid lease payments
− Lease incentives received (eg, lease-signing bonus)

For finance leases, the ROU asset is **amortized** (ie, decreased) on a **straight-line (S/L) basis each period**. Finance leases effectively transfer the rights and risks of ownership from a lessor to a lessee. As such, the lessee records straight-line amortization expense on the lease assets, similar to how a company would record straight-line depreciation on PP&E. At the end of the lease term, the ROU asset on the balance sheet will equal zero.

The ROU asset is amortized over the **shorter of the leased asset's useful life or the lease term**. However, if there is a purchase option that is reasonably certain to be exercised or if the title transfers at the end of the lease, the asset is amortized over the useful life regardless of the lease term because the lessee will ultimately own the title:

Amortization of Right-of-Use Asset

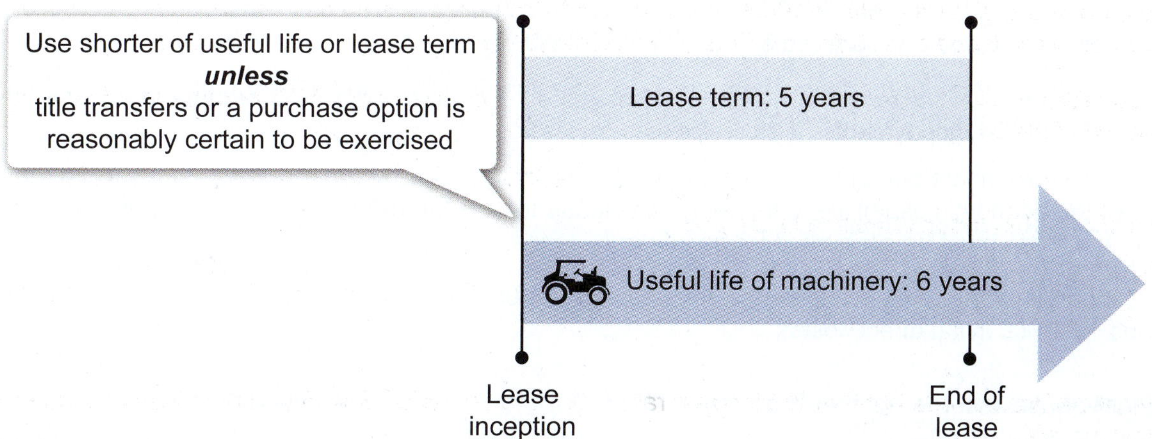

Each period, the ROU asset is amortized, and S/L amortization expense is recorded:

$$\text{Reduction in ROU asset} = \text{Amortization expense} = \frac{\text{ROU asset}}{\text{Useful life or lease term}}$$

Lease Liability and Interest Expense

The lease liability is initially recorded at PV of lease payments.

The "Lease Payments" section above covers items included in the lease liability.

Each period, interest expense is recorded, and the lease liability is reduced by the **difference between lease payment and interest expense for each period**. At the end of the lease term, the lease liability on the balance sheet will equal zero.

Interest expense = Lease liability × Lease interest rate × Time period

Reduction in lease liability = Interest expense − Lease payment

Remember, if the first payment in a finance lease is made at lease inception, no time has passed for interest to accrue. Therefore, the payment consists entirely of a reduction in the lease liability.

Examples

We will continue with the same fact pattern used in the Mitten Co. operating leases example. However, now, assume that the economic useful life of the equipment is five years rather than 10 years.

- Mitten has signed a five-year rental contract for office equipment on January 1, Year 1
- The client has an incremental borrowing rate of 6%, and the payments are $10,000 per year, due at the end of each year
- As an inducement to enter the agreement, the client has been offered the first six months free and a $1,000 signing bonus
- The lessee has incurred $1,000 in initial direct costs
- The PV factor for a lump sum at 6% for one year is 0.943, and the PV factor for an ordinary annuity at 6% for five years is 4.212

The lease now meets one of the "Special-PO-T-75-90" criteria. The lease term constitutes more than 75% of the economic useful life of the asset (the lease term is for 100% of the asset's useful life). As such, the lease must be accounted for as a finance lease.

On January 1, Year 1, the initial entry is the same ($37,405 PV of $45,000 in lease payments − $1,000 bonus + $1,000 initial direct costs):

Right-of-use asset	37,405	
Lease liability		37,405

However, after lease inception, the accounting for a finance lease differs from the accounting for an operating lease.

Each period, amortization expense (and the corresponding reduction in the ROU asset) will be calculated as ROU asset / useful life or lease term. Here, the useful life and lease term are the same (ie, five years). Therefore, **amortization expense is $7,481 per year (ie, $37,405 / 5 years)**.

Each period, interest expense (lease liability × lease interest rate) will be recorded. The lease liability will also be reduced by interest expense − the lease payment. The following table shows how the lease liability will change over the life of the lease under the effective interest method.

Lease Liability	Interest Rate	=	Interest Expense	−	Lease Payment	=	Net Reduction in Lease Liability
37,405	6%	=	2,244[I]	−	5,000	=	2,756[J]
(2,756)							
34,649	6%	=	2,079[K]	−	10,000	=	7,921[L]
(7,921)							
26,728	6%	=	1,604	−	10,000	=	8,396
(8,396)							
18,332	6%	=	1,100	−	10,000	=	8,900
(8,900)							
9,432	6%	=	566	−	10,000	=	9,434
(9,434)							
0*							

**Note that there is a $2 difference due to rounding for simplicity purposes.*

At December 31, Year 1, the following is recorded:

Account	Debit	Credit
Amortization expense	7,481	
Right-of-use asset		7,481
Interest expense	2,244[I]	
Lease liability	2,756[J]	
Cash		5,000

At December 31, Year 2, the following is recorded:

Account	Debit	Credit
Amortization expense	7,481	
Right-of-use asset		7,481
Interest expense	2,079[K]	
Lease liability	7,921[L]	
Cash		10,000

On January 1, Year 1, Scarf Co. has signed an eight-year equipment lease with payments of $75,000 per year, due at the beginning of the year. The estimated economic life of the equipment is 10 years. The depreciation method is straight-line, and there is no residual value. Title to the equipment passes at the end of the lease. The lessee's incremental borrowing rate is 12%, but the lessor has made it known to the lessee that the rate implicit in the lease is 11%.

The lease meets multiple "Special-PO-T-75-90" criteria. Title transfers at the end of the lease, and the lease constitutes over 75% of the equipment's economic useful life (8-year lease / 10-year useful life = 80%). Therefore, it is accounted for as a finance lease.

The rate implicit in the lease, if known, should be used to calculate the PV of lease payments. The first payment of $75,000 is due on day 1 (ie, annuity due). The PV factor for an annuity due with eight payments at 11% is 5.7122. The PV of lease payments is $428,415 ($75,000 × 5.7122).

Note: there are no initial direct costs or lease incentives to be added to or subtracted from the ROU asset.

Scarf will record the following journal entry at lease inception (January 1, Year 1):

Right-of-use asset	428,415	
Lease liability		428,415

Scarf will also record the first payment made on January 1, Year 1:

Lease liability	75,000	
Cash		75,000

Each subsequent period, amortization expense (and the corresponding reduction in the ROU asset) will be calculated as ROU asset / useful life or lease term. Here, title transfers at the end of the lease, so useful life should be used. Therefore, **amortization expense is $42,842 (ie, $428,415 / 10 years)**.

Each subsequent period, interest expense (lease liability × lease interest rate) will be recorded. The lease liability will also be reduced by interest expense − the lease payment. The following table shows how the lease liability will change over the life of the lease under the effective interest method.

Lease Liability	Interest Rate	=	Interest Expense	−	Lease Payment	=	Reduction in Lease Liability
428,415					75,000	=	75,000
(75,000)							
353,415	11%	=	38,876[M]	−	75,000	=	36,124[N]
(36,124)							
317,291	11%	=	34,902	−	75,000	=	40,098
(40,098)							
277,193	11%	=	30,491	−	75,000	=	44,509
(44,509)							
232,684	11%	=	25,595	−	75,000	=	49,405
(49,405)							
183,279	11%	=	20,161	−	75,000	=	54,839
(54,839)							
128,440	11%	=	14,128	−	75,000	=	60,872
(60,872)							
67,568	11%	=	7,432	−	75,000	=	67,568
(67,568)							
0							

At December 31, Year 1, amortization is recorded:

Amortization expense	42,842	
ROU asset		42,842

Because payment won't be made until January 1, Year 2, the company will also report interest expense and accrued interest at December 31, Year 1:

Interest expense	38,876[M]	
Interest payable		38,876

At January 1, Year 2, when the second lease payment is made, the interest payable is reversed, and the reduction in the lease liability is recorded:

Lease liability	36,124[N]	
Interest payable	38,876	
Cash		75,000

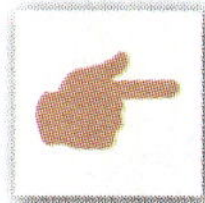

Remember, the ROU asset can include items (eg, initial direct costs incurred, lease incentives provided) that the lease liability does not. If those items are incurred, the ROU asset will not equal the lease liability. The difference in the ROU asset and lease liability will be debited or credited to cash.

For example, if the PV of lease payments was $561,800 and an initial direct cost of $5,000 was incurred, the following journal entry would be recorded at inception of the lease:

ROU asset ($561,800 + $5,000)	566,800	
Lease liability		561,800
Cash ($5,000 paid for initial direct costs)		5,000

Accounting for Leases: Lessee Summary

Lessee Accounting for Leases

		Operating Lease	**Finance Lease**
Lease Inception	**ROU Asset**	PV of payments + Initial direct costs + Prepaid lease payments − Lease incentives received	Same
	Lease Liability	PV of payments	Same
Income Statement Expense Each Period		One straight-line lease expense (total lease payments / lease term)	Two expenses: • Amortization expense (straight-line) • Interest expense (lease liability × interest rate)
Reduction of ROU Asset Each Period		Accreted interest (lease liability × interest rate) − Lease expense	Straight-line (ROU asset / Useful life or lease term)
Reduction of Lease Liability Each Period		Accreted interest − Lease payment	Interest expense − Lease payment

Disclosure Requirements

Required disclosures for leases by the lessee are very comprehensive. Generally, the requirement is to show disclosures that enable users of financial information to assess the amount, timing, and uncertainty of cash flows from leases. Disclosure requirements are both qualitative and quantitative.

Qualitative disclosures for lessees include a general description of the following: lease arrangement, variable lease payments, options, nonlease payments, and residual values.

Quantitative disclosures for lessees include the following:

- Interest and amortization costs for finance leases
- Lease costs disclosed separately for operating and short-term leases
- Any variable lease costs
- Weighted average lease term
- Discount rate used in calculation of PV
- Reconciliation of beginning and ending balances of right-of-use asset
- Contractual obligations and options that the lessee is expected to exercise for each of the next five years and a total for the remaining years in the aggregate
- Future lease payments by type of lease for each of the next five years and a total for all remaining years, undiscounted
- Lease transactions with related parties

FAR 22
Subsequent Events

FAR 22: Subsequent Events

22.01 Subsequent Events

Overview

Representative Task (Remembering & Understanding): Identify a subsequent event and recall its appropriate accounting treatment.

Representative Task (Application): Calculate required adjustments to financial statements and/or note disclosures based on identified subsequent events.

Subsequent events are events or transactions that have a **material effect** on the financial statements (F/S). Subsequent events occur **after** the date of the F/S but **before** the statements are issued or are available to be issued.

Although the F/S date is the "closing date" for reporting, users of F/S typically read the disclosures as if they are current as of the date of issue. Furthermore, the full disclosure principle mandates that all relevant information be disclosed.

Examples of subsequent events include lawsuits, changes in corporate structure, issuances of debt and equity securities, major acquisitions, and significant gains and losses.

There are two categories of subsequent events, each requiring different accounting treatment:

- **Type I:** The condition leading to the subsequent event existed at the balance sheet date
- **Type II:** The condition leading to the subsequent event did not exist at the balance sheet date but, rather, arose after the balance sheet date

Subsequent Events

Financial statements (F/S) | Subsequent event

Year end 12/31/Y1 — F/S issue date* X/XX/Y2

Does event provide additional evidence that **condition** existed at year end?

- Yes → **Type 1**
  - Recognized (may require adjustment)
  - Additional disclosure may be required
- No → **Type 2**
  - Not recognized
  - Disclose if material

**Issue date applicable to public entities only; for all other entities, the available to be issued date is used.*

Type I (Recognized) Subsequent Events

When a Type I subsequent event occurs, a company should **accrue for and disclose (ie, recognize)** the event in its F/S.

Example 1: A major customer's financial situation has been deteriorating during the reporting year (Year 4), with bankruptcy being declared early in Year 5. As a result, a receivable from that customer is deemed worthless after the Year 4 balance sheet date but before the issuance of the financial statements.

The loss from the write-off of the receivable should be recognized in Year 4 income, and the Year 4 balance sheet should reflect the write-off because the condition leading to the bankruptcy existed at the balance sheet date.

Example 2: Information is discovered early in Year 5 indicating that the total useful life of certain plant assets will be significantly less than originally estimated due to obsolescence. This condition developed gradually during Year 4. The useful lives of the affected assets should be re-estimated, and depreciation expense for Year 4 should reflect those revised estimates.

Example 3: Verona Co. had $500,000 in short-term liabilities at the end of the current year. Verona issued $400,000 of common stock subsequent to the end of the year but before the F/S were issued. The proceeds from the stock issue were intended to pay the short-term debt. Determine the amount Verona should report as a short-term liability on its balance sheet at the end of the current year.

If an entity can demonstrate the intent and ability to refinance a short-term obligation, the obligation is *reclassified* out of current liabilities. Verona Co. demonstrated the intent and ability to refinance and pay $400,000 of the $500,000 current liabilities by issuing equity securities.

Since the securities were issued **after** the F/S date but **before** the F/S were issued, the transaction qualifies as a **Type 1 subsequent event** and requires a F/S adjustment. Consequently, $400,000 of the short-term obligations is *reclassified to equity*, and the remaining **$100,000 is reported as a current liability**.

Type II (Non-recognized) Subsequent Events

This category of subsequent event **requires only footnote disclosure** of events that have *material effects* on the F/S. The footnote disclosures include a description of the nature of the event and an estimate of the financial effect or a statement that an estimate cannot be made. Recognition is inappropriate because the condition existed after the balance sheet date.

Example 1: A major customer declared bankruptcy as a result of a casualty in early 20X5. As a result, a receivable from that customer is deemed worthless after the 20X4 balance sheet date but before the issuance of the financial statements. The loss from the worthless receivable is disclosed in the footnotes, but recognition is postponed until the 20X5 statements because the casualty occurred after 20X4.

Example 2: A firm completes a large issuance of bonds early in 20X5, before the issuance of the 20X4 statements. The footnotes to the 20X4 statements should disclose the relevant information about the issuance, but recognition is postponed until the 20X5 statements.

Example 3: On March 15, Year 2, a calendar-year company issued its Year 1 financial statements. On March 1, Year 2, a fire destroyed the company's only manufacturing plant. Determine the correct treatment of the loss in the December 31, Year 1, financial statements.

In this scenario, the fire is a *subsequent event* because it occurred after the F/S date but prior to the issuance of the F/S. As of 12/31/Y1, it would have been impossible to predict losses from a fire that had not yet occurred. Because it was not related to any condition existing at the F/S date, the fire is a **Type 2** (non-recognized) event. No accrual or balance sheet adjustment is recorded for a Type 2 event. However, the fire is still important information that should be **disclosed** on the company's F/S notes.

Period of Evaluation for Subsequent Events

The recognition and disclosure requirements for subsequent events apply to both annual and interim financial statements but do not apply to subsequent events or transactions that are governed by other applicable GAAP.

The period during which subsequent events are evaluated is the period between the balance sheet date and either of the following:

- The date the F/S are issued (ie, when they are widely distributed for general use)
- The date the F/S are available to be issued (ie, when they are complete, comply with GAAP, and have all the approvals necessary for issuance)

Public entities or any entities that widely distribute their F/S use the *issued* date.

All other entities use the *available to be issued* date. These entities are not required to evaluate subsequent events after the point of availability. However, a non-SEC filer must also disclose the date through which the subsequent events were evaluated and whether that date is the date the F/S are issued or available to be issued.

Impact on Financial Statements

Representative Task (Analysis): Derive the impact to the financial statements and required note disclosures due to identified subsequent events.

Analysis-level tasks are typically tested in a task-based simulation (TBS). Below is an example of a TBS involving subsequent events that might appear on the CPA exam.

Edge Co., a toy manufacturer, is in the process of preparing its financial statements for the year ended December 31, Year 3. Edge plans to issue its Year 3 financial statements on March 1, Year 4.

Required:

Items 1 through 4 represent various information that has not been reflected in the financial statements. For each item, the following two responses are required:

A. Determine if an adjustment is required and select the appropriate amount, if any, from the list below
B. Determine (Yes/No) if additional disclosure is required, either on the face of the financial statements or in the notes to the financial statements

Item	Scenario	Amount	Additional Disclosure?
1	On January 5, Year 4, a warehouse containing a substantial portion of Edge's inventory was destroyed by a fire. Edge expects to recover the entire loss, except for a $250,000 deductible, from insurance.	**$0**	**Yes**

Since the warehouse fire did not occur until January 5, Year 4, after the balance sheet date, accrual would not be appropriate. The loss, however, represents a subsequent event that affects the amount reported on the balance sheet, requiring disclosure.

Item	Scenario	Amount	Additional Disclosure?
2	On January 24, Year 4, inventory purchased FOB shipping point from a foreign country was detained at that country's border because of political unrest. The shipment is valued at $150,000. Edge's attorneys have stated that it is probable that Edge will be able to obtain the shipment.	**$0**	**No**

Detaining the inventory shipment on January 24, Year 4, is a subsequent event relating to a condition that did not exist at the balance sheet date. As a result, accrual would not be appropriate. In addition, since it is likely that Edge will obtain the shipment, it is not likely that a loss will be incurred, and disclosure would not be required.

Item	Scenario	Amount	Additional Disclosure?
3	On January 30, Year 4, Edge issued $10,000,000 bonds at a premium of $500,000.	**$0**	**Yes**

Issuance of debt after the balance sheet date is a subsequent event relating to a condition that did not exist at the balance sheet date. As a result, accrual would not be appropriate. The issuance of debt after the balance sheet date but prior to the issuance of the financial statements would require disclosure.

Item	Scenario	Amount	Additional Disclosure?
4	On February 4, Year 4, the IRS assessed Edge an additional $400,000 for the Year 2 tax year. Edge's tax attorneys and tax accountants have stated that it is likely that the IRS will agree to a $100,000 settlement.	**$100,000**	**Yes**

Although the IRS assessment occurred after the balance sheet date, it is a subsequent event that relates to a condition that did exist as of the balance sheet date, since it relates to a previous tax period. It is a contingency loss that is probable and can be reasonably estimated at $100,000. As a result, it will be accrued and disclosed.

Contingencies and commitments often go hand in hand with subsequent events. The table below summarizes the key disclosure issues related to commitments and contingencies. For additional information, refer to the FAR chapter on this content.

Accounting for Contingent Events

	Disclose	**Accrue**
Remote (gain or loss)	No	No
Reasonably possible (gain or loss)	Yes	No
Probable and not estimable (gain or loss)	Yes	No
Probable and estimable gain	Yes	No
Probable and estimable loss	Yes	Yes